Mac® OS X System Administration

GUY **HART-DAVIS**

New York   Chicago   San Francisco
Lisbon   London   Madrid   Mexico City   Milan
New Delhi   San Juan   Seoul   Singapore   Sydney   Toronto

The McGraw·Hill Companies

Cataloging-in-Publication Data is on file with the Library of Congress

McGraw-Hill books are available at special quantity discounts to use as premiums and sales promotions, or for use in corporate training programs. To contact a representative, please e-mail us at bulksales@mcgraw-hill.com.

Mac® OS X System Administration

1234567890   WFR WFR   109876543210

ISBN   978-0-07-166897-2
MHID   0-07-166897-7

Sponsoring Editor Jane K. Brownlow	**Copy Editor** Julie Smith	**Illustration** Glyph International
Editorial Supervisor Jody McKenzie	**Proofreader** Carol Shields	**Art Director, Cover** Jeff Weeks
Project Manager Vasundhara Sawhney, Glyph International	**Indexer** Robert Swanson	**Cover Designer** Jeff Weeks
Acquisitions Coordinator Joya Anthony	**Production Supervisor** Jim Kussow	
Technical Editor Dwight Spivey	**Composition** Glyph International	

This book is dedicated to Rhonda and Teddy.

About the Author

Guy Hart-Davis is the author of more than 50 computer books, covering Mac OS X, iPods and iPhones, Windows, and other topics. His recent books include *AppleScript: A Beginner's Guide* and *Mac OS X Leopard QuickSteps*.

About the Technical Editor

Dwight Spivey has authored several books pertaining to the Mac, iPod touch, and iPhone. He resides on the Gulf Coast of Alabama with his beautiful wife and three fantastic kids (with number four very much on the way).

At a Glance

Contents

Part I

Plan and Create the Network

PART II

Provide Services and Applications

PART III

Secure and Maintain Your Network

Acknowledgments

My thanks go to the following people for making this book happen:

- Jane Brownlow, for getting the book approved and signing me to write it
- Joya Anthony, for handling the administration, schedule, and finances
- Dwight Spivey, for performing the technical review and providing helpful suggestions and encouragement
- Vasundhara Sawhney, for coordinating the project
- Julie Smith, for editing the text with care and a light touch
- Glyph International, for laying out the pages
- Carol Shields, for proofreading the book
- Robert Swanson, for creating the index

Introduction

Introduction

Most everybody who uses computers knows the client version of Mac OS X, Apple's sleek and user-friendly operating system for Macs.

As yet, relatively few people know its bigger brother, Mac OS X Server—but this is changing rapidly, because of the features, ease of use, and affordable cost of the latest version, Mac OS X Server 10.6. Snow Leopard Server, as it's often called, lets you swiftly create powerful, effective networks using a single server or many servers, with client computers in the dozens or in the thousands.

Is This Book for Me?

Yes.

If you need to build a network based on Mac OS X Server, this book is for you. From starting off with nothing more than a working knowledge of Mac OS X and Macs, this book shows you how to plan, set up, and maintain a complete network.

You'd probably like some specifics. Read on…

What Will I Learn in This Book?

Here's what you will learn from this book:

- Chapter 1 shows you how to assess what you need for your Mac network, decide how to connect the computers and devices in the network, choose network hardware, and gather the Internet connection information you will need.

- Chapter 2 explains how to set up the hardware for your network. Because there are many ways of setting up a wired network, this chapter provides only general advice on this topic, and gives more detail on setting up a wireless network based on the type of wireless access point you're most likely to use.

- Chapter 3 covers installing Mac OS X Server on your server or servers. You learn both how to install from scratch and how to upgrade an installation of the client version of Mac OS X to Mac OS X Server.

- Chapter 4 walks you through a half-dozen essential steps you must perform to secure your server. These steps start with updating the server with the latest fixes, continue through securing the server's hardware and changing its root password, and culminate in installing an SSL certificate to allow clients to authenticate the server and connect to it securely.

- Chapter 5 teaches you how to set up Open Directory, the directory service you use to administer your Mac network and keep it running smoothly. You learn how to set up either a single-server network or a multi-server network. I also show you how to install the Server Administration Software on a client Mac so that you can administer your servers remotely from it.

- Chapter 6 shows you how to set up client systems and connect them to your network. You can install the software on your client Macs manually, but you'll probably prefer to automate the process by creating a custom disk image containing the software your Macs need.

- Chapter 7 explains how to create users and groups for your network. You'll meet Mac OS X Server's tools for configuring and managing your network, learn about the different types of administrator accounts, and then roll up your sleeves and get down to work.

- Chapter 8 covers adding the iPhone or iPod touch to your Mac OS X Server network. As with your network's Macs, you can set up these shiny toys—I mean, vital communications devices—manually with a little effort, but you'll probably prefer to download Apple's free iPhone Configuration Utility and set it up to do as much of the grunt work as possible for you.

- Chapter 9 tells you how to configure the Web service and control users' Internet access. While you *can* simply point your network's users at the Internet and let them go hog wild, you'll normally want to use proxy servers to cache content that's frequently needed and filter out some of the grosser content and temptations the Internet offers.

- Chapter 10 walks you through setting up Mac OS X Server's Mail service to provide your network's users with effective and reliable e-mail. The chapter makes sure you know how e-mail works from the administrator's point of view, and then shows you the moves you need to make to get Internet e-mail up and running on your network.

- Chapter 11 shows you how to configure and manage file services for your network's clients. You first sort out the network protocols used for file services, create share points for sharing files and volumes, and then set up home folders for the users. You can also set up external accounts and mobile accounts for users who need them—starting with yourself.

- Chapter 12 covers installing and managing applications on your network's Macs. What you'll usually want to do is install an initial set of applications onto the Mac during setup, as that's the easiest time. You may then need to choose which applications the user may run and may not run. And you'll almost certainly need to install further applications and updates on your network's Macs in due course.

- Chapter 13 explains how to run Windows applications on your Macs. You learn to decide between using Mac OS X's Boot Camp feature to install Windows as a separate operating system alongside Mac OS X and using a virtual-machine application to run Windows within Mac OS X. You also learn about an alternative way of making Windows applications available to Macs that need them only once in a while.

- Chapter 14 takes you through installing printers on your Mac network and making them available to your client Macs. After physically attaching the printers to the network, you configure the print service on your server so that you can manage printing centrally, create printer pools as needed, and then decide which users are allow to print to which printers. Once you've set up the Macs to use the printers, you can retreat to your aerie and manage your print queues to the strains of improv jazz or classic metal.

- Chapter 15 explains how to provide remote access to your network via a virtual private network (VPN). You learn how to set up the server to accept VPN connections, decide who's allowed to use them, and then connect the client Macs to the VPN. You also connect any iPhones or iPod touches that need remote access to the network.

- Chapter 16 shows you what you need to do to secure your Macs and your network. Starting with an overview of the threats your Macs and your network will typically face, you'll then learn concrete measures you can take to improve matters.

- Chapter 17 walks you through using Software Update to keep your network's Macs up to date. To save your Internet connection from punishment, you'll probably want your client Macs to get their updates from a server on your network—which means you need to set up that server to haul down the updates, and then tell the clients where to grab the updates.

- Chapter 18 covers backing up data to keep it safe and restoring it from backup after something disastrous has happened to it. Mac OS X's built-in means of backup is Time Machine, which you use both for backing up the client Macs to the server and for backing up the server itself to an external hard disk.

- Chapter 19 introduces you to the AppleScript scripting language that comes built into both the Server and client versions of Mac OS X. You learn how to get started with AppleScript and the AppleScript Editor, how to use essential programming structures, and how to find the AppleScript items that you want to manipulate.

- Chapter 20 explains how to set up peer-to-peer networks using the client version of Mac OS X. You'll learn how to share folders, printers, and an Internet connection on Macs, and how to connect other Macs to the shared items.

Conventions Used in This Book

To make its meaning clear and concise, this book uses a number of conventions, four of which are worth mentioning here:

- The pipe character, or vertical bar, denotes choosing an item from the menu bar. For example, "choose Server | Connect" means that you should click the Server menu on the menu bar, and then click the Connect item on the menu that opens.

- Note, Tip, and Caution paragraphs highlight information that's worth extra attention.

- Sidebars provide extra information on important topics.

- The ⌘ symbol represents the Mac COMMAND key.

PART I | Plan and Create the Network

CHAPTER 1 | Plan Your Mac Network

The first thing is to plan your network so that you can set it up the right way. In this chapter, you'll assess what you need for the network, decide how to connect the computers and devices in the network, choose the hardware, and gather Internet connection information. Chapter 2 then shows you how to put your network hardware together, and Chapter 3 walks you through installing Mac OS X Server.

NOTE   This chapter—and most of this book—assumes that you're creating a server-based network for your Macs. If you need to network only a handful of Macs—for example, at a branch office or at home—you may want to consider a peer-to-peer network instead, in which the client Macs share files and provide services to each other without using a server. See Chapter 20 for a discussion of how to set up a peer-to-peer network using Mac OS X.

Establishing the Numbers of Clients and Servers

Establishing the number of clients for your network should be straightforward enough: All you need do is count each of the site's existing computers that you intend to connect together, add other devices that you will connect to the network (for example, printers), and allow for any others that you plan to add within the next couple of years.

Deciding how many servers you will need is much more tricky. A small network—for example, a small company or branch office with 20–30 computers—will usually be fine with only a single server running all the services the clients need. But as soon as you get into the 50–100 client range, you may need to add extra servers to share the load.

NOTE   Most of the examples in this book show a single server, as this is the configuration that readers are likely to use.

Choosing How to Connect Your Network

For connecting your network, you have three main choices:

- **Wired network**   Each computer connects to the network hardware via a network cable.

- **Wireless network**   Each computer connects to the network hardware via radio waves.

- **Combination network**   Some computers use wired connections; others use wireless connections.

The following sections discuss the pros and cons of these three network types and help you choose the right one for your needs.

Understanding the Advantages of Wired Networks

Wired networks have several advantages over wireless networks:

- **Speed**   Despite impressive increases in the speed of wireless networks, wired networks remain much faster. Gigabit Ethernet, the leading standard at this writing, can transfer one gigabit per second (1Gbps), or around 125MB of data per second. The fastest wireless networks, which use the 802.11n standard, top out at 270–600 megabits per second (Mbps)—and that's in perfect conditions you'll seldom encounter in the messy real world.

- **Security**   Unless someone hacks in via the Internet connection or taps into one of the cables, a wired network is reasonably secure. You'll want to take sensible safely measures, as explained later in this book, but you don't normally have to worry about the network extending invisibly beyond your company's physical premises the way you do with a wireless network.

- **Cost**   Wired networks used to be much less expensive than wireless networks. Nowadays, the difference is much smaller, as the cost of wireless access points keeps dropping, and almost all Macs include built-in wireless network adapters. (The exception is the Mac Pro, for which a wireless network adapter is a build option.)

- **Reliability**   Wired networks are usually more reliable than wireless networks because they suffer from less interference.

Figure 1-1 shows a diagram of a wired network. To show the layout clearly, the diagram shows only two client Macs connecting to the network. In practice, you will normally connect many more Macs, but the principle will remain the same.

Understanding the Advantages of Wireless Networks

To compensate for the advantages that wired networks have (as discussed in the previous section), wireless networks have several advantages over wired networks. These are the main ones:

- **Easy to install**   Without the need to run cables to each workstation, you can get a wireless network up and running within an hour.

TIP   Wireless networks are great for temporary networks, such as those you may need to set up at trade shows or in stopgap premises.

- **Flexible**   As long as the wireless network covers the whole of the area the wireless clients will be in, you have greater flexibility in positioning the wireless access point. You can also easily add clients to the network up to the capacity of the wireless access point, and extend the network quickly and easily by deploying another wireless access point.

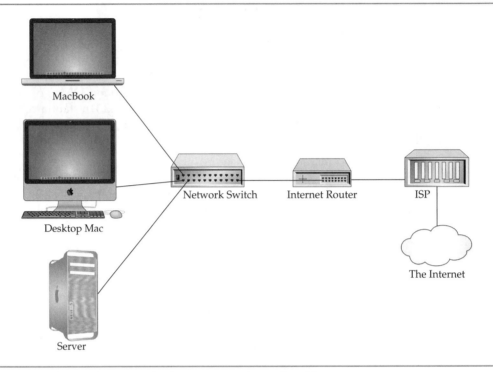

Figure 1-1. A wired network with a server and two client Macs

■ **Clients can roam** Instead of being tethered by a network cable, wireless network users can take their Macs to anywhere within the area covered by the wireless network. For example, Alice can take her MacBook to a meeting, Bill can move his iMac into a conference room to give a demo, or Charlie can check e-mail on his iPhone from the coffee shop across the street.

■ **Required for iPhones and iPod touch to connect** If users need to connect iPhones or iPod touches to the network or the Internet, you'll need a wireless network.

■ **Visitors can easily connect—if you let them** Any visitors to your company or organization can connect to the wireless network if you allow them to. Being able to add computers to the network can be handy if you have temps or consultants working on the premises. But you need to make sure that uninvited visitors can't connect from off your premises—more on this later in the book.

Figure 1-2 shows a diagram of a wireless network built around AirPort Extreme wireless access point. As in the previous figure, the diagram shows only a handful of

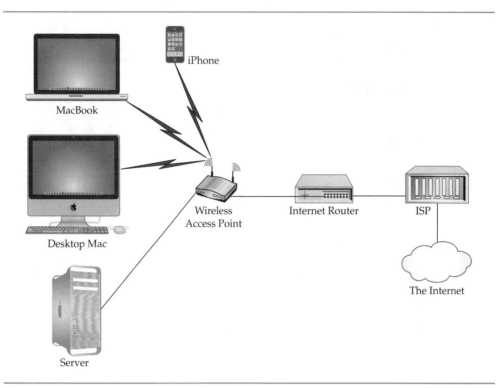

Figure 1-2. A wireless network with a server and a small number of Mac clients. The server is connected to the wireless access point via a cable for greater speed and reliability.

clients connecting to the network so that you can see clearly what's what. In practice, you will normally connect many more Macs to the network.

Understanding the Pros and Cons of Combination Networks

For most networks these days, the best choice is a network that combines wired and wireless. Use the wired part of the network for the computers and devices that remain in place; use the wireless part of the network for any computer or device that needs to be able to move.

The main disadvantages of a combination network compared with a wired-only network or a wireless-only network are that you have to buy more hardware, configure it, and support it. Murphy's Law guarantees that the more gear you have that can go wrong, the more will go wrong.

Figure 1-3 shows a diagram of a combination wired and wireless network. As before, the number of clients is limited for clarity.

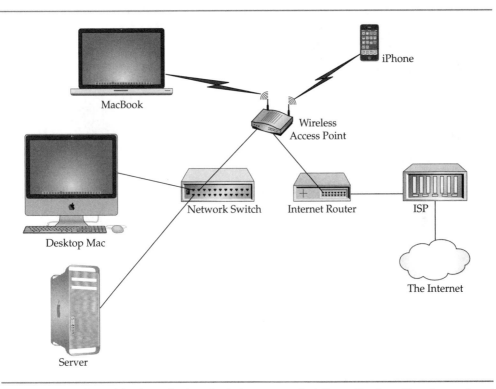

Figure 1-3. A combination wired and wireless network delivers the benefits of speed and reliability to the wired clients and of flexibility and roaming to the wireless clients.

Choosing the Right Network Type for Your Needs

With your needs and the pros and cons of each network type in mind, you're all set to choose the right type of network. This can be a tough choice, but in many cases you'll find factors such as the following pushing you toward a particular network type:

- **Existing cabling** If your building is already wired with Ethernet cables to each workstation, you'll probably choose either a wired network or a combination network.

- **Lack of cabling** If your building doesn't have cables and you can't afford the time or money to install them, a wireless network is an easy way out. The same goes if you're in temporary premises or ones where drilling through the walls, floors, and ceilings will send the landlord through the roof.

- **Mobile clients** If your colleagues need to roam with their MacBooks, or if they have iPhones or iPod touches for business purposes, you'll need a wireless network or a combination network to enable them to connect.

Choosing Network Hardware

Once you've chosen the type of network you will create, it's time to choose hardware for it. The following sections discuss what you'll need first for a wired network and then for a wireless network. For a combination wired and wireless network, you'll need both.

Choosing Network Switches and Cables for a Wired Network

For a wired network, you'll need to get network switches and cables to create the physical infrastructure of the network. First, decide on the Ethernet network standard you'll use, then select network switches and a type of cable to match.

Choosing an Ethernet Network Standard

At this writing, the main standards for network switches and cables are Fast Ethernet and Gigabit Ethernet:

- **Fast Ethernet**   This long-established standard gives 100 megabits per second, or 100Mbps.

- **Gigabit Ethernet**   This more recent standard gives one gigabit per second, 1Gbps (1000Mbps).

If you're buying network switches and cables, the only standard that makes sense is Gigabit Ethernet; prices of Gigabit Ethernet equipment have fallen nearly to the same level as Fast Ethernet equipment, and all current Macs (as well as most recent Macs) come with Gigabit Ethernet ports built in. The one exception is the port-challenged MacBook Air, which offers only Fast Ethernet through its single USB port.

NOTE   If you already have Fast Ethernet switches, you may find that a Fast Ethernet network is adequate for the time being. But given that network traffic continues to increase in any typical network, with network users needing to transfer ever more files of larger and large file sizes, Gigabit Ethernet is a much better choice in the long run. And 10 Gigabit Ethernet will bring 10Gbps speeds before too long. 10 Gigabit Ethernet is variously abbreviated as 10GE, 10GbE, or 10 GigE.

Choosing Network Switches

From each Mac or device on the network, the network cable runs to the network switch, which is the connecting box that connects the cables together and routes data along the right cables.

You can find a wide variety of different models of network switches. Narrow down the selection first by the network standard you've chosen (for example, Gigabit Ethernet) and then by the number of ports you want on the switch. Switches typically come with 8, 16, or 24 ports, and you can link switches together to give the total number of ports you need.

Depending on the layout of your premises, you may do better to position the network switches in separate areas rather than placing them all in one location. For example, in a network with 20 clients and devices split between two distinct areas of a building, it may be more convenient to place one 16-port switch in each area rather than a single 24-port switch centrally.

 NOTE   Most switches have auto-sensing ports that can change their speed automatically to suit 10Mbps, 100Mbps, and 1Gbps devices. Even so, you'll want as many devices as possible to use the highest speed the switch supports to get high performance from your network.

Choosing a Cabling Standard

To connect your Gigabit Ethernet network switches, use Category 5 Enhanced (Cat 5e) or Category 6 (Cat 6) network cables. Cat 6 has better protection against interference than Cat 5e, which in turn has better protection than Category 5 (Cat 5). Cat 5 cable does work with Gigabit Ethernet equipment, but Cat 5e or Cat 6 is a better choice unless you already have the Cat 5.

 NOTE   Category 7 (Cat 7) cable has better protection against system noise and crosstalk than Cat 6 cable, but it's not yet widely used. Cat 6 cable is more than adequate for Gigabit Ethernet networks.

Choosing a Wireless Access Point

When choosing a wireless access point for a network, it's a good idea to understand the prevalent standards for wireless networks and the features you should look for in an access point. However, you may simply want to get one of the access points that Apple makes, as these work well with Macs.

Understanding Wireless Network Standards

As of this writing, four standards for wireless networking are in general use. Table 1-1 explains these four standards, starting with the fastest.

 NOTE   Most wireless access points support more than one standard. For example, many access points support Wireless-N, Wireless-G, and good old WiFi. Apple's AirPort Extreme and Time Capsule access points support Wireless-N, Wireless-G, 802.11a, and WiFi. Make sure the access point you buy supports all the standards your clients need.

Knowing Which Features to Look For

Many hardware manufacturers make wireless access points, and it can be tough to choose among them. Apart from the wireless standard, consider the following factors:

■ **Number of wireless clients**   Some access points support more wireless clients than others. Bear in mind that the more clients that connect to an access point, the lower the data rate for each client will drop. Usually, it's better to have multiple access points running well below capacity rather than have a single access point groaning under the weight of users and giving each a wafer-thin slice of bandwidth.

Standard Number	Name	Maximum Speed	Explanation
802.11n	Wireless-N	600Mbps	802.11n equipment has a theoretical maximum speed of 600Mbps, with most equipment claiming speeds in the 270–300Mbps range.
802.11g	Wireless-G	54Mbps	802.11g equipment is widely used and can communicate with 802.11b equipment at 802.11b speeds.
802.11a	802.11a	54Mbps	802.11a is a long-established standard that is not widely used, largely because it is incompatible with the widely used 802.11b.
802.11b	WiFi	11Mbps	802.11b is a formerly very widely used standard, but it has largely been taken over by 802.11g. 802.11b wireless cards can connect to 802.11g access points, though only at 802.11b speeds.

Table 1-1. Wireless Network Standards and Speeds

- **Ethernet ports** Apart from connecting the wireless access point to the wired portion of your network and to your Internet connection, you may need to connect other computers to the wireless access point via cables. Make sure the wireless access point has enough Ethernet ports for your needs, or plan to connect it to a switch to provide extra Ethernet ports.

- **USB connections** Many wireless access points let you share a printer or a USB hard drive by connecting it via USB. If you will find this capability useful, make sure the access point has it.

- **Internet access** Many wireless access points come with a DSL or cable router built in—or the routers come with a wireless access point built in, if you prefer to look at it that way. These combined devices are great for home use, but they work well for small offices too.

- **Power over Ethernet** Some wireless access points include the Power over Ethernet (PoE) feature, which enables them to draw power along an Ethernet cable rather than requiring a separate power supply. PoE lets you place a wireless access point anywhere you can run an Ethernet cable rather than being limited to within striking distance of a power socket.

Deciding Whether to Choose an Apple Wireless Access Point

If you're setting up a Mac-based network, the natural place to start looking is the three types of wireless access points that Apple makes. Not only are these wireless access points guaranteed to work well with Macs, but you configure them using Apple's AirPort Utility application rather than having to mess about with a third-party application or browser-based configuration screens.

 NOTE   Apple also makes a version of AirPort Utility for Windows, so you can use a Windows PC to configure an AirPort or Time Capsule.

These are the three types of wireless access points that Apple sells:

- **AirPort Extreme**   This is the candidate for use in corporations and larger organizations. The AirPort Extreme has 802.11n wireless networking plus standard 802.11g, 802.11b, and 802.11a networking. You can connect three computers to its wired ports and up to 50 wireless clients at once.

- **Time Capsule**   Time Capsule is essentially an AirPort Extreme with a built-in hard drive for storage and for making automatic backups. Like the AirPort Extreme, Time Capsule has four types of wireless network: 802.11n, 802.11g, 802.11b, and 802.11a networking. Time Capsule has three Ethernet ports for connecting computers with wires, and you can connect up to 50 wireless clients at once.

- **AirPort Express**   AirPort Express has features for home use, such as a combined analog-and-digital audio port that lets you connect speakers and play music through the AirPort Express from iTunes on any Mac or PC connected to the network. AirPort Express works in business settings as well, and its compact size means you can position it anywhere there's a power socket. AirPort Express plugs directly into a power socket rather than using an extension lead, and supports up to 10 wireless clients at once.

Choosing a Server

Next, you'll need to choose the server (or servers) on which to run Mac OS X Server. Here are the minimum requirements for Mac OS X Server 10.6:

- **A Mac with an Intel processor**   Mac OS X Server 10.6 won't run on a G5 processor, no matter how powerful it is.

 NOTE   Apple recommends running Mac OS X Server only on desktop Macs or servers, but you can install and run Mac OS X Server on a MacBook that meets the processor, RAM, and hard disk requirements. Unless you travel with your server, though, installing Mac OS X Server on a MacBook isn't usually a good idea.

■ **10GB of free hard disk space**   This is the absolute minimum for installing and running Mac OS X Server, and usually you'll want to have far more space on your server's hard disk for storing files and making backups.

 ___TIP___ If your server is short of hard disk space, consider adding a high-capacity external drive connected via FireWire 800.

■ **2GB of RAM**   As usual with RAM, much more is much better.

■ **A network connection to your network**   You'll need this when setting up directory services.

Because Mac OS X Server will run on any Mac that has an Intel processor, you can run your server on a regular Mac that you don't need as a workstation. For example, a Mac mini can make a great server for a small office network or a home network, especially if you go for Apple's server model that comes with two hard disks, and a Mac Pro can handle a substantially larger network.

For a heavier-duty role, you'll probably want to get one of Apple's Xserve servers. Xserves come with up to 24GB of RAM and up to 3TB of internal storage. You can buy Xserves from the Apple Store (http://store.apple.com; if your budget is tight, it's worth looking at the Refurbished Mac section for reconditioned Xserves) or from Apple resellers.

Getting a Copy of Mac OS X Server

If you've decided to buy one or more Xserves, you're all set on this front, as each Xserve comes with the Unlimited Client Edition of Mac OS X Server already installed. Similarly, you can buy the Mac mini with Mac OS X Server already installed.

If you're planning to install Mac OS X Server on a Mac you've bought separately, buy the Unlimited Client Edition of Mac OS X Server for $499. This is a big improvement on Leopard Server, in which $499 bought you only the 10-Client License version, and the Unlimited Client Edition set you back $999.

Choosing Which Version of TCP/IP to Use

For communicating, your network will use the Transmission Control Protocol/Internet Protocol, or TCP/IP for short. There are two main versions of TCP/IP:

■ **IPv4**   Internet Protocol version 4 is the current version of the Internet Protocol and is used by most networks and the overwhelming majority of the computers on the Internet. IPv4 still works fine, but because its address space was set up before the Internet became massive, it's running out of different addresses. This is one reason why most networks connect to the Internet through a router or other device that has a single IP address on the Internet rather than each computer on the network having its own Internet address.

■   **IPv6**   Internet Protocol version 6 is the new and improved version of the Internet Protocol and has an address space large enough to allow for almost unimaginable amounts of growth. But so far IPv6 is used in relatively few networks, mainly because the cost of transitioning from IPv4 to IPv6 is high and few companies and organizations yet feel a compelling need to make the move.

Mac OS X works seamlessly with both IPv4 and IPv6, but unless you and your ISP are on the cutting edge, you'll almost certainly want to stick with IPv4 for the time being.

Getting the Information for Setting Up Your Internet Connection

The last item you'll need on the planning front is the information needed to connect your network to the Internet. (If yours will be one of the few networks that remain offline, you can skip this item.)

If you will use an existing Internet connection to connect your network to the Internet, you will need to set up your server or router to use that connection.

If you will use a new Internet connection to connect your network to the Internet, set up the account from another computer, and make sure you have the details to hand: the account name and password, the public IP address your network will have, the addresses of the ISP's DNS servers, and any other connection information.

If you want Internet users to be able to access your network, you will need to register an Internet domain through a domain name registrar or your Internet service provider. At this writing, leading domain name registrars include these three:

■   Network Solutions (www.networksolutions.com) was the first domain registration site and remains the largest.

■   eNom (www.enom.com) is a large domain registrar that specializes in business services and reselling domain registrations.

■   Register.com (www.register.com) is another large registration site with a good reputation.

When you've secured your domain and know the IP address your server will have, get the registrar to set the domain to point to that address. Once this setting is in place, Internet requests for your domain will come to your server.

CHAPTER 2 | Set Up the Network Hardware

A fter you plan your network, as discussed in the previous chapter, you'll need to set up the network hardware. This chapter discusses the main considerations for doing so.

What you have to do to set up the hardware for a wired network will depend greatly on the size of network you're creating and the types of hardware you've chosen. You'll need to choose where to locate the hardware, and set up the server physically for installation—but beyond that, the specifics vary wildly. Consequently, this chapter offers only general advice on setting up the hardware for a wired network.

But if you're creating a wireless network or a wired-and-wireless network, you'll need to set up one or more wireless access points. So this chapter provides specifics for setting up an AirPort Extreme wireless access point, as this is the type of wireless access point you're most likely to use if you create a small or medium-size network running Mac OS X Server.

Installing a Wired Network

To create a wired network, set up your network hardware by following these general steps:

1. **Ensure that each computer has a suitable network interface.** If you're using Macs built since the turn of the millennium, you'll have no problems on this front, as every Mac will include either a Fast Ethernet network interface or (more likely) a Gigabit Ethernet network interface. If your network includes PCs that currently lack network interfaces, install Gigabit Ethernet network cards.

2. **Position the switches in secure but convenient locations.** Depending on the layout of the building or area you're networking, you may need to place all the switches together, or position the switches separately where they can better serve groups of computers. Locate the switches securely, and protect their power supplies against accidental (or deliberate) switching off.

3. **Configure any managed switches.** If your network uses managed switches, use the software that comes with them, or web-based configuration utilities, to configure the switches. If your network uses unmanaged switches (as is common in smaller networks), you will not need to configure them.

4. **Run cables to the workstations.** Normally, you'll run cables from the switches to wall plates in offices or cubicles, or to connection boxes built into modular furniture, and then use a patch cable to connect the client computer to the wall plate or connection box. But in some cases, such as with smaller networks or temporary networks, it may be simpler to run a cable that ends in an Ethernet jack (an RJ-45 connector, like a phone connector on steroids), which can go straight into the client.

Cabling Your Network

If the place where you plan to create your network already include network cables, you're all set. Otherwise, you will need to get your landlord to install cables, pay professional cable contractors to install them, or install the cables yourself.

Cabling a network tends to be slow and arduous work, so unless you're building only a small network, using professionals usually saves time and gives a better result.

If you choose to install the cables yourself, here are some points of guidance:

- **Choose where to locate the switches** For some networks, you may need to have all the switches in a central location. For other networks, positioning the switches at the end of cable runs will enable you to connect the switches to an area's computers more easily.

- **Treat the cable gently** With each new layer of shielding, cables get tougher, but it's still easy enough to damage them when pulling them around obstacles or through conduits. Kinked or damaged cables can slow down data transmission, so pull the cable in stages rather than around several obstacles at once. Use cable lubricants if necessary to grease the cable's passage.

- **Pull plenty of cable** It's always better to have extra cable that you can coil and hide than to end up a couple of inches or a couple of feet short.

5. **Position and connect the servers and desktop computers.** Typically, you'll have the servers in a server room or another separate room that you can secure against the depredations of users and cleaners.

6. **Connect a DHCP server to provide IP addresses and other network configuration information to the computers on the network.** Depending on your network setup, the DHCP server may run on your Internet router, on your Mac OS X server (or one of your other servers), or (if your network includes wireless connectivity) on a wireless access point such as an AirPort Extreme.

Installing a Wireless Network

If you've decided to create a wireless network or a combination wired and wireless network, you'll need to install each wireless access point the network requires.

Macs will work with any standards-compliant wireless access point, but if you're buying a wireless access point for a Mac-based network, the obvious choice is Apple's AirPort series—they're easy to use, guaranteed to work well with Macs' AirPort cards, and you can manage them using Mac OS X's AirPort Utility rather than a third-party utility or a browser-based configuration tool.

This section walks you through setting up a network based on an AirPort Extreme access point, which is the top-end model in the AirPort series. The setup process for the other models, the home-oriented AirPort Express and the Time Capsule model (which is essentially an AirPort Extreme with built-in hard drives for storage and backup), is almost the same.

NOTE You can set up the AirPort Extreme using either a client Mac or a server—whichever is more convenient. This example uses a client Mac.

Setting up an AirPort Extreme involves four main steps:

1. Choosing where to locate the AirPort Extreme logically and physically.

2. Setting up the AirPort Extreme physically.

3. Getting the latest version of AirPort Utility.

4. Running AirPort Utility and configuring the AirPort Extreme.

As usual, the devil is in the details, which we'll look at in the following sections.

Choosing Where to Locate the AirPort Extreme

First, decide where to locate the AirPort Extreme. There are two aspects to this:

- **Logical location** Decide among the different roles the AirPort Extreme can play in the network.

- **Physical location** Choose the physical location for the AirPort Extreme.

Choosing the Logical Location for the AirPort Extreme

Your key decision is among the different roles the AirPort Extreme can play in a network:

- **Wireless access point only** In this role, the AirPort Extreme connects the wireless clients to the wired part of the network. Either your server or your router provides DHCP to the AirPort Extreme and the computers on the network. You typically run the AirPort Extreme as a bridge, simply passing along the network traffic to and from the wireless clients. Figure 2-1 illustrates this setup.

- **Wireless access point and router** In this role, the AirPort Extreme not only connects the wireless clients to the network, but also provides DHCP services. Figure 2-2 illustrates this setup. In the example, the server is connected to the AirPort Extreme via a cable, but it could also be connected wirelessly if lower transfer speeds are acceptable.

- **Wireless access point, router, and firewall** In this role, the AirPort Extreme connects the wireless clients, provides DHCP services to the wireless and wired portions of the network, and also runs a firewall to protect the network from threats. Figure 2-3 shows this setup.

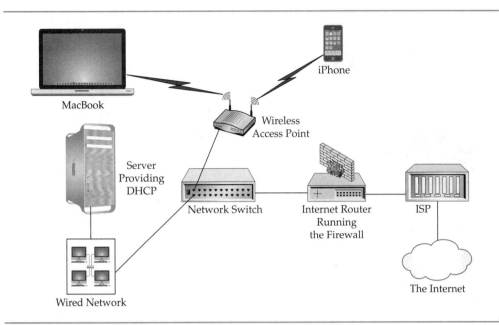

Figure 2-1. Acting as only a wireless access point, the AirPort Extreme simply links the wireless clients to the wired part of the network.

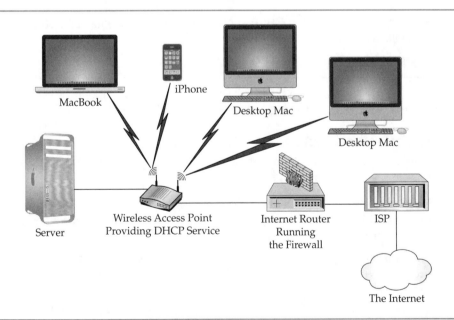

Figure 2-2. Acting as the central point of the network, the AirPort Extreme provides DHCP service to the network.

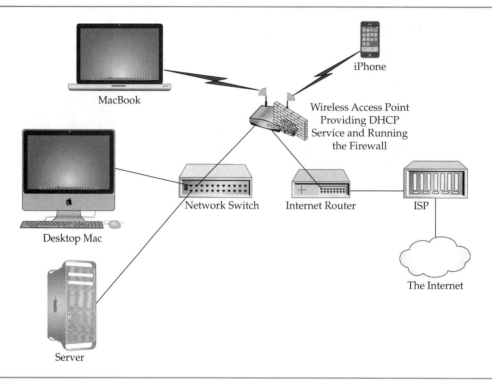

iPhone

Wireless Access Point
Providing DHCP
Service and Running
the Firewall

MacBook

Network Switch   Internet Router   ISP

Desktop Mac

The Internet

Server

Figure 2-3. Apart from providing DHCP services, the AirPort Extreme can also run firewall protection for the network.

NOTE In any of these roles, the AirPort Extreme can share one USB device using its USB port. For example, you can connect a printer or an external hard drive.

Choosing the Physical Location for the AirPort Extreme

Now choose the physical location for the AirPort Extreme. Finding a suitable location will depend on several factors:

- **Physical connections** Depending on the logical location you have chosen for the AirPort Extreme, you will need to connect it to your Internet router, network switch, server, or all three.

- **Wireless coverage** You will need to position the AirPort Extreme so that it provides wireless coverage to the whole area that the wireless clients will need to access.

- **Power supply** The AirPort Extreme will need a power socket within striking distance. The AirPort Extreme does not support Power Over Ethernet (PoE), so you cannot power it with just a network cable.

Connecting the AirPort Extreme's Hardware

Now connect the AirPort Extreme's hardware:

1. Plug the AirPort Extreme's power supply into a socket, and then connect it to the AirPort Extreme.

2. Use an Ethernet cable to connect the AirPort Extreme's WAN port (marked with a circle of dots) to your Internet router, network switch, or switch, depending on the choice you made in the previous section.

3. If you will use the AirPort Extreme to share a USB device, such as a USB hard drive or printer, plug that device into the AirPort Extreme's USB port and make sure the device has power.

Getting the Latest Version of AirPort Utility

Next, make sure you have the latest version of AirPort Utility. Choose Apple | Software Update to launch Software Update. Software Update automatically checks for new versions of all your system software and Apple applications.

 NOTE   Your AirPort Extreme should include a CD containing AirPort Utility, and you can use this version to install the AirPort Extreme in a pinch. But usually you'll do better to download the latest version from Apple's website (http://support.apple.com/downloads/#airport). If you already have an older version, you can get the latest version from Software Update.

If Software Update gives the message *New software is available for your computer*, click the Show Details button to see what's on offer (see Figure 2-4).

If a version of AirPort Utility is available, select its check box in the Install column, decide which other updates to install, and then click the Install button. (The button shows the number of items—Install 1 Item, Install 2 Items, or however many items are available).

Authenticate yourself when Software Update prompts you to do so, and then let Software Update download the updates (if it hasn't downloaded them already) and install them. If Software Update prompts you to restart your Mac, do so. Otherwise, click the OK button when Software Update tells you the updates were successfully installed, and then click the Quit button to quit Software Update.

Configuring the AirPort Extreme

Now connect your Mac to the AirPort Extreme, either wirelessly or via an Ethernet cable. If your Mac has an AirPort card, connecting wirelessly is usually the easier option.

Connecting to the Airport Extreme via Wireless

To connect to the AirPort Extreme via a Mac's AirPort card, follow these steps:

1. Click the Desktop to activate the Finder, and then choose Go | Utilities to display the contents of the /Applications/Utilities folder.

2. Double-click AirPort Utility to launch the utility.

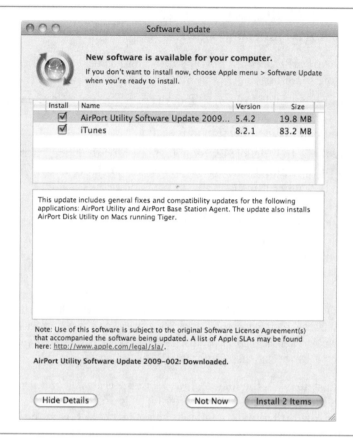

Figure 2-4. Use Software Update to make sure you have the latest version of AirPort Utility before installing the AirPort Extreme.

3. Click the OK button in the information dialog box that opens:

4. Click the OK button in the AirPort Software Update dialog box that opens:

5. AirPort Utility now scans for AirPorts and then display a screen showing those it has found (see Figure 2-5).

Connecting to the AirPort Extreme via an Ethernet Cable

If you don't have a Mac with an AirPort card that you can use to set up the access point, you can use an Ethernet cable instead. Follow these steps:

1. Connect one end of an Ethernet cable to one of the Ethernet ports on the back of the AirPort Extreme.

2. Connect the other end of the Ethernet cable to your Mac's Ethernet port.

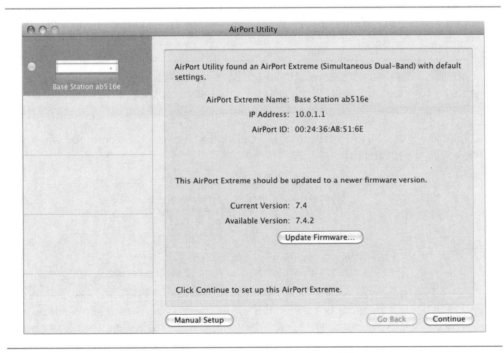

Figure 2-5. AirPort Utility locates any AirPort access points within range.

3. Click the Desktop to activate the Finder, and then choose Go | Utilities to display the contents of the /Applications/Utilities folder.

4. Double-click AirPort Utility to launch the utility.

5. Click the OK button in the information dialog box and in the AirPort Software Update dialog box, if these dialog boxes appear.

6. AirPort Utility now scans for AirPorts and then displays a screen showing those it has found.

7. If AirPort Utility finds more than one AirPort device, click the AirPort Extreme you want to configure.

NOTE   If AirPort Utility cannot locate an AirPort Extreme connected to your Mac via an Ethernet cable, choose Apple | System Preferences, and then click the Network icon. Click the Ethernet item in the left list box; open the Configure IPv4 pop-up menu and choose Using DHCP; and then click the Apply button. In AirPort Utility, click the Rescan button. This time, AirPort Utility should find the AirPort Extreme.

Updating the AirPort's Firmware

If the Update Firmware button on the initial screen in AirPort Utility is available, it's a good idea to apply the update before setting up the AirPort Extreme. If the Update Firmware button isn't available, click the Continue button, and move along to the next section.

NOTE   AirPort Utility will discover firmware updates only if the Mac you're using has an active Internet connection. But you can apply firmware updates afterward once you've established an Internet connection.

Click the Update Firmware button; then, click the Continue button in the warning dialog box that appears:

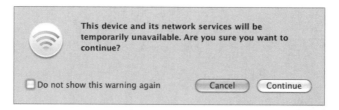

This device and its network services will be temporarily unavailable. Are you sure you want to continue?

☐ Do not show this warning again   (Cancel)   (Continue)

NOTE   When you're setting up the AirPort Extreme for the first time, you shouldn't need to worry about disconnecting users during the update, because there won't be any. But when you apply firmware updates in the future, either warn users that they'll lose the wireless network for a while, or perform the updates outside business hours.

AirPort Utility downloads the firmware update from the Apple Internet site, and then uploads the firmware update to the AirPort Extreme. When that's done, it restarts the AirPort Extreme, reconnects to it, and then automatically displays the next screen.

Setting the Base Station's Name and Password

The next screen that appears is the Base Station screen, shown in Figure 2-6 with settings chosen.

In the AirPort Extreme Name text box, type the name you want to give the AirPort. This is the name that you will see when managing the AirPort, so if you're using multiple wireless access points, make clear which one is which. For example, you may want to give the access point a name that indicates the area of the building it covers or the department in which it is located.

In the AirPort Extreme Password text box and the Verify Password text box, enter a password for keeping the AirPort locked down to prevent unauthorized changes.

CAUTION   Wireless access points are an easy target for crackers and freeloaders, so secure the access point with a strong password—at least eight characters, including uppercase and lowercase, at least one number, and at least one symbol. If you're having trouble devising a tough-to-crack password, click the key icon to use Password Assistant. See Chapter 3 for details on using Password Assistant.

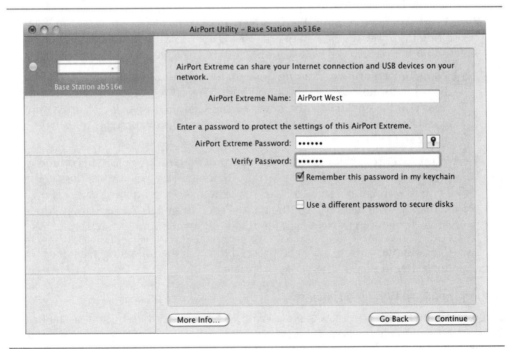

Figure 2-6.   Name your AirPort Extreme and give it a tough password.

Select the Remember This Password In My Keychain check box if you want to store the password so that you don't need to type it in the future.

Select the Use A Different Password To Secure Disks check box if you will connect disks to the AirPort and want to use a different password than the AirPort's own password to secure them. Type the password in the disk Password text box and Verify Password text box that appear (as shown here). Select the Remember This Password In My Keychain check box below these text boxes if you want to store this password too.

NOTE   Using a different password for disks you attach to the AirPort lets you protect the disks even from people you permit to manage the AirPort.

Click the Continue button. AirPort Utility displays the first Network Setup screen.

Choosing the Type of Network Setup

On the first Network Setup screen (see Figure 2-7), select the appropriate option button:

- **I Want To Create A New Wireless Network**   Select this option button if you're setting up a new wireless network. This is the most likely scenario, so we'll deal with it first, in the next section, "Setting Up a New Wireless Network."

- **I Want To Replace An Existing Base Station Or Wireless Router With AirPort Extreme**   Select this option button if you're upgrading your current access point to an AirPort Extreme. See the section "Replacing Your Existing Access Point with an AirPort Extreme," later in this chapter, for the steps you'll need to take next.

- **I Want AirPort Extreme To Join My Current Network**   Select this option button when you're adding an AirPort Extreme to an existing wireless network or you're setting up a string of AirPort Extremes and you've already set up the first. See the section "Adding an AirPort Extreme to Your Existing Wireless Network," later in this chapter, for details on what happens next.

Click the Continue button, and then proceed through the following section or one of the sections later in this chapter, as appropriate.

Setting Up a New Wireless Network

If you select the I Want To Create A New Wireless Network option button on the first Network Setup screen, the next screen you see is the Network Setup screen shown in Figure 2-8.

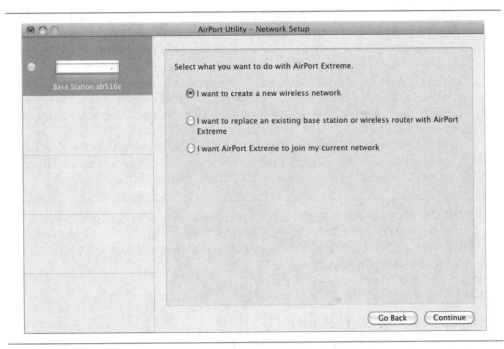

Figure 2-7. On this Network Setup screen, choose the type of network you're creating.

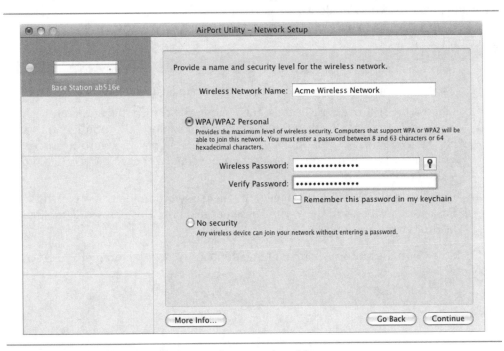

Figure 2-8. Set the network name and password on this screen.

In the Wireless Network Name text box, type the name you want to give the network as a whole. This is the name that users will see when connecting to the network, so make it easy to identify—you don't want users mistakenly connecting to the coffee shop across the street because they don't recognize your network's name.

Select the WPA/WPA2 Personal option button—it should be selected already—and then type a password in both the Wireless Password text box and the Verify Password text box. The password must be at least 8 characters long and can be up to 63 characters.

As before, you can click the key button to launch the Password Assistant for help in picking a password, and you can select the Remember This Password In My Keychain check box if want to store the password in your Mac OS X keychain so that you don't have to type it in future when configuring this AirPort from this Mac.

 CAUTION   Never use the No Security option button unless you're setting up a public network that anybody can connect to. Normally, you will not want to do this; instead, set up a guest network that allows anybody to connect to the Internet but not to your network. See the following section for instructions on creating a guest network.

Click the Continue button. The Guest Network Setup screen appears.

Setting Up a Guest Wireless Network

If your premises will entertain guests who will need to connect to the Internet, you can set up a guest network that also runs through the AirPort Extreme, but which is kept separate from your wireless network. Guests can connect to the Internet, but they can't see your private network, let alone connect to it.

To set up a guest network, follow these steps on the Guest Network Setup screen (see Figure 2-9):

1. Select the Enable Guest Network check box.

2. Type the name for the guest network in the Enable Guest Network text box.

3. Choose the security type in the Guest Network Security pop-up menu. Your choices are WPA/WPA2 Personal or None. Normally, you'll want to choose WPA/WPA2 Personal so that you can assign a password to share with guests; choosing None leaves your guest network wide open to anyone within range.

4. If you chose WPA/WPA Personal, type the password in the Guest Network Password text box and the Verify Password text box. This password, too, must be 8–63 characters long.

Click the Continue button when you're ready to move on. The Internet Setup screen appears.

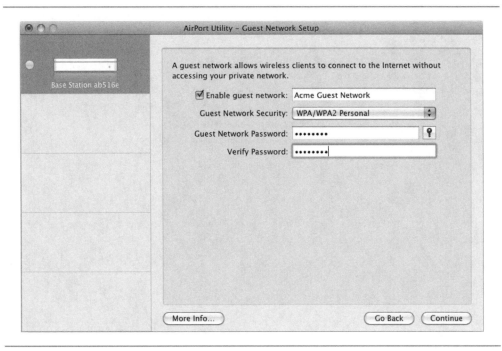

Figure 2-9.   You can also set up a second wireless network on the AirPort Extreme to allow guests to connect to the Internet.

At this point, if you haven't connected your Internet router or your network switch to the AirPort Extreme, AirPort Utility prompts you to connect it, as shown here. Plug the cable in, and then click the OK button.

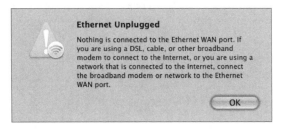

Choosing the Internet Setup

On the Internet Setup screen (see Figure 2-10), choose how your AirPort Extreme connects to the Internet:

- ■ **I Use A DSL Or Cable Modem With A Static IP Address Or DHCP**   Select this option button if your network uses a DSL router or cable router that has either a static IP address or gets an address via DHCP.

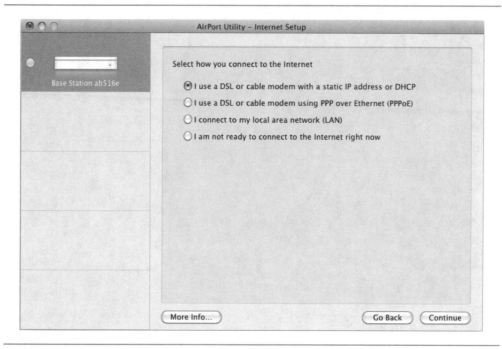

Figure 2-10.   Tell AirPort Utility how your AirPort Extreme connects to the Internet.

- **I Use A DSL or Cable Modem Using PPP Over Ethernet (PPPoE)**   Select this option button if your DSL router or cable router uses PPPoE to establish its Internet connection.

- **I Connect To My Local Area Network**   Select this option button if you're using the AirPort Extreme to connect wireless clients to the wired portion of your LAN.

- **I Am Not Ready To Connect To The Internet Right Now**   Select this option button if you haven't finalized your network details yet. You can then set the details later by running the Wizard again or using the Manual Setup option.

Click the Continue button, and then move on to the appropriate one of the following three sections:

- If you chose the I Use A DSL Or Cable Modem With A Static IP Address Or DHCP option button or the I Connect to My Local Area Network option button, go to the next section.

- If you chose the I Use A DSL or Cable Modem Using PPP Over Ethernet (PPPoE) option button, go to the section titled "Entering Your PPPoE Information."

- If you chose the I Am Not Ready To Connect To The Internet Right Now option button, skip ahead to the section titled "Checking and Applying Your Settings."

Entering Your TCP/IP Information

If you chose the I Use A DSL Or Cable Modem With A Static IP Address Or DHCP option button or the I Connect to My Local Area Network option button, the next screen you see is the Internet Setup screen shown in Figure 2-11.

In the Configure IPv4 pop-up menu, choose Using DHCP or Manually, as appropriate, and then fill in the available fields below the pop-up menu.

If you choose Using DHCP, the AirPort Extreme takes care of the IP address, subnet mask, and router address automatically; it can also fill in the DNS server address or addresses if your DHCP server provides them. You can fill in the DNS server address or addresses manually, as you can the domain name and the DHCP client ID.

If you choose Manually, type in the IP address, subnet mask, router address, DNS server address or addresses, and domain name. (The DHCP Client ID text box doesn't appear, because you're not using DHCP.)

Click the Continue button when you've chosen the settings, and you'll see the Summary screen. Move ahead to the section titled "Checking and Applying Your Settings."

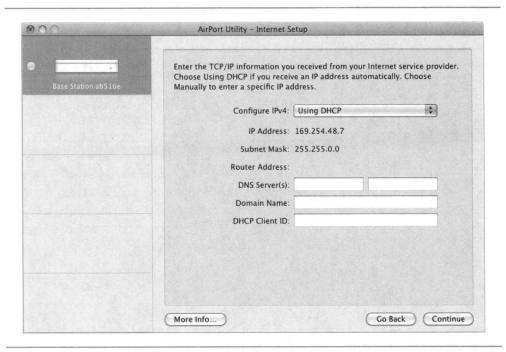

Figure 2-11.   On this Internet Setup screen, choose between using DHCP and providing the IP address and TCP/IP configuration information manually.

Entering Your PPPoE Information

If you chose the I Use A DSL Or Cable Modem Using PPP Over Ethernet (PPPoE) option button, the next screen you see is the Internet Setup screen shown in Figure 2-12.

1. Type your account name in the Account Name text box, and then type your password in both the Password text box and the Verify Password text box.

2. In the Service text box, type the descriptive name you want to give the service.

3. In the Connection pop-up menu, choose how you want to run the Internet connection:

   ■ **Always On**   Choose this setting if you want to keep the Internet connection open all the time.

   ■ **Automatic**   Choose this setting if you want the AirPort Extreme to establish the connection when it's required and tear it down after a period of inactivity.

   ■ **Manual**   Choose this setting if you need to establish the Internet connection manually.

Click the Continue button when you've finished entering settings. You'll see the Summary screen, which is discussed next.

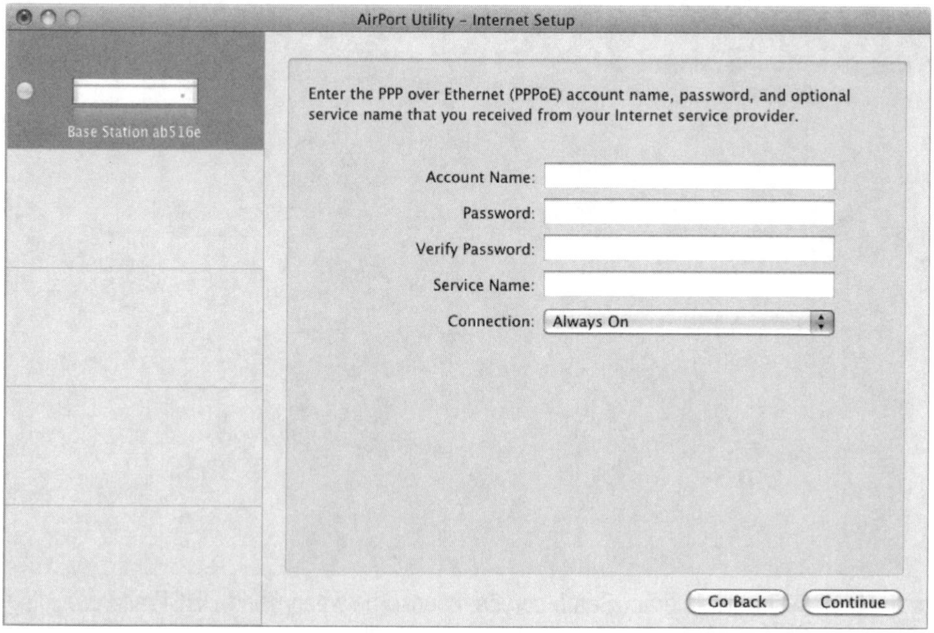

Figure 2-12.   If your Internet connection uses PPPoE, fill in your account details on this screen.

Checking and Applying Your Settings

On the Summary screen (see Figure 2-13), verify the settings you've chosen. If you need to change any of the settings, click the Go Back button as many times as is needed to reach the relevant screen. When you've fixed the problem, click the Continue button to move forward again until you get to the Summary screen.

When you're satisfied with the settings, click the Update button. AirPort Utility displays a warning that the device will be temporarily unavailable. Click the Continue button. Unless there are any problems (as discussed next), you'll see the Setup Complete screen (see Figure 2-14), on which you can simply click the Quit button to quit AirPort Utility.

Dealing with Configuration Problems

If AirPort Utility runs into any problems when trying to apply the settings you've chosen, it will show you a screen explaining the first problem and giving suggestions for fixing it. Figure 2-15 shows one of the most common problems you'll run into: The settings you've chosen call for the AirPort Extreme to provide network address translation (NAT) services, but there is already a NAT server on the network. The solution is to change the AirPort Extreme to Bridge mode, allowing it to link the wireless clients

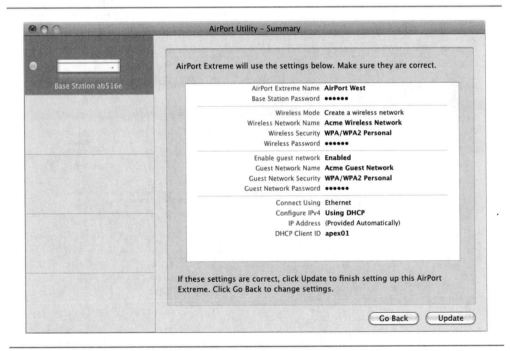

Figure 2-13.   On the Summary screen, check that all the settings are correct, and then click the Update button.

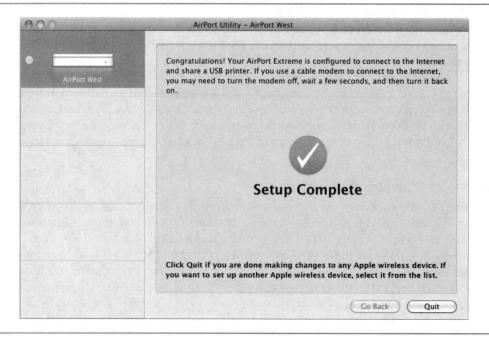

Figure 2-14. Your AirPort Extreme is set up and ready for use.

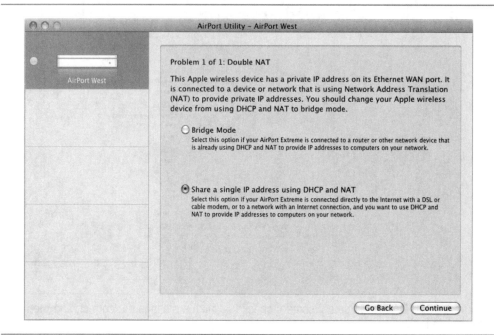

Figure 2-15. If AirPort Utility runs into a problem with the settings you've chosen, it displays suggestions for fixing them.

to the network without providing NAT; the clients then pick up IP addresses and NAT from the existing NAT server.

Replacing Your Existing Access Point with an AirPort Extreme

If you already have a wireless network, but you want to replace your existing access point with an AirPort Extreme, follow these steps:

1. On the first Network Setup screen (shown in Figure 2-7, earlier in this chapter), select the I Want To Replace An Existing Base Station Or Wireless Router With AirPort Extreme option button.

2. Click the Continue button. AirPort Utility displays the Network Setup screen shown in Figure 2-16.

3. Click the Continue button. AirPort Utility displays the Summary screen (see Figure 2-17).

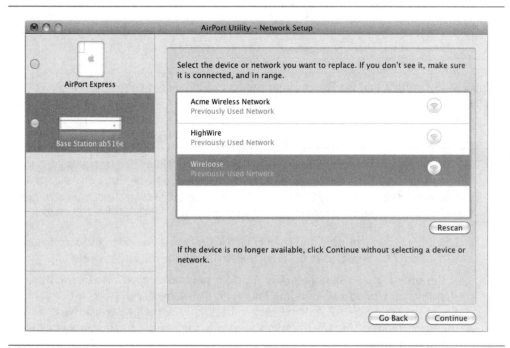

Figure 2-16.   Choose the existing access point from which you want the AirPort Extreme to take over.

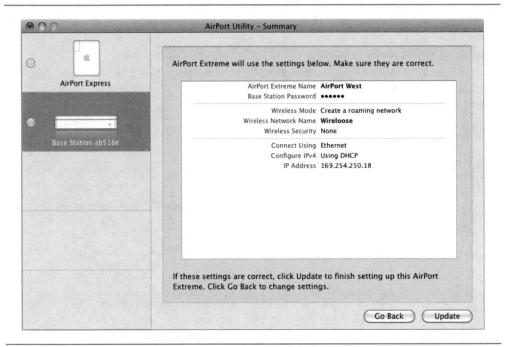

Figure 2-17. Check that the Summary screen has all the details correct, and then click the Update button.

NOTE If the access point you're replacing uses WEP security, AirPort Utility suggests using no security for the AirPort Extreme you're installing. This is because the AirPort Extreme doesn't support WEP, because it's a weaker and thoroughly compromised security standard. After updating the AirPort Extreme, AirPort Utility encourages you to apply WPA/WPA2 Personal security to it.

4. Click the Update button, and then click the Continue button in the confirmation dialog box. AirPort Utility updates the AirPort Extreme and restarts it.

5. If the previous access point used WEP (or was unsecured), AirPort Utility displays an Unsecured Wireless Network problem screen (see Figure 2-18). Select the WPA/WPA2 Personal option button, type the password twice, decide whether to have Mac OS X remember it in your keychain, and then click the Continue button.

Setup next continues with the Guest Network Setup screen. Turn back to the section "Setting Up a Guest Wireless Network," earlier in this chapter, for details.

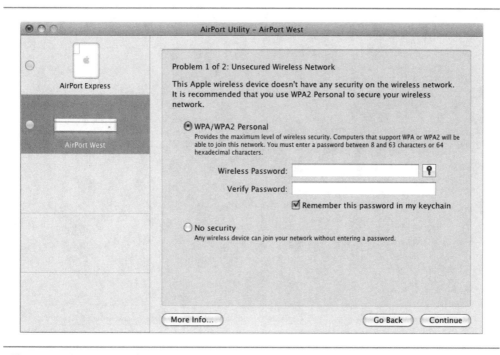

Figure 2-18.   Apply WPA/WPA2 Personal security to the AirPort Extreme if the previous network used WEP or was unsecured.

Adding an AirPort Extreme to Your Existing Wireless Network

If you already have a wireless network and are adding an AirPort Extreme as a new access point to it, or if you've just set up the first of a series of AirPort Extremes, follow these steps to add an AirPort Extreme to the network.

1. On the first Network Setup screen (shown in Figure 2-7, earlier in this chapter), select the I Want AirPort Extreme To Join My Current Network option button.

2. Click the Continue button. The Network Setup screen shown in Figure 2-19 will now appear.

3. Select the appropriate option button:

   ■ **I Want AirPort Extreme To Wirelessly Join My Current Network**   Select this option button if you want to connect the AirPort Extreme to your existing network via wireless. This option provides additional wireless capacity to the network, but does not extend its range as far as using Ethernet (see the next example).

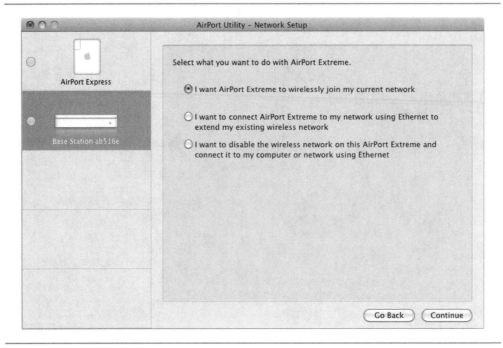

Figure 2-19. Choose how you want to make the AirPort Extreme join your current network.

■ **I Want To Connect AirPort Extreme To My Network Using Ethernet To Extend My Existing Wireless Network** Select this option button if you want to connect this AirPort Extreme to your network via an Ethernet cable, and then position it to extend your wireless network. This is the option you'll use when setting up a series of AirPort Extremes to cover different areas of a building or site.

■ **I Want To Disable The Wireless Network On This AirPort Extreme And Connect It To My Computer Or Network Using Ethernet** Select this option button if you want to use the AirPort Extreme only as a router and firewall, not as a wireless access point. This chapter does not discuss this option further.

4. Click the Continue button, and then follow through the appropriate one of the following two sections.

Joining the AirPort Extreme to Your Existing Wireless Network Wirelessly   If you selected the I Want AirPort Extreme To Wirelessly Join My Current Network option button, the next screen you see is the Network Setup screen shown in Figure 2-20. Open the Wireless Network Name pop-up menu and choose the network, choose the security type in the Wireless Security pop-up menu, and then type the password in the Wireless Password text box and the Verify Password text box.

   Click the Continue button, and the Summary screen appears. Review your settings, and then click the Update button.

Joining the AirPort Extreme to Your Existing Wireless Network via Ethernet   If you selected the I Want To Connect AirPort Extreme To My Network Using Ethernet To Extend My Existing Wireless Network option button, the next screen you see is the Network Setup screen shown in Figure 2-21.

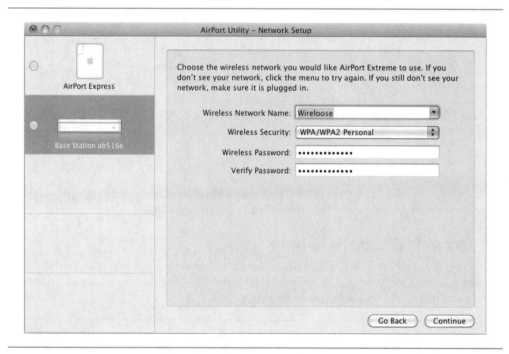

Figure 2-20.   Choose the existing wireless network to which you're connecting the AirPort Extreme wirelessly.

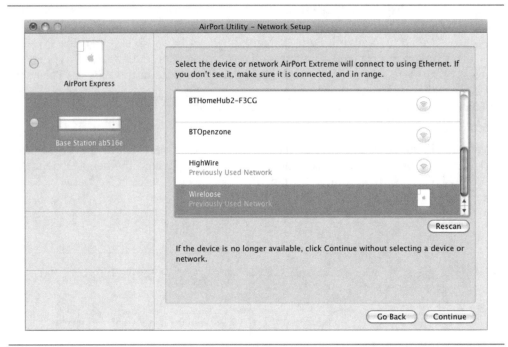

Figure 2-21. Select the wireless network to which you're connecting the AirPort Extreme via an Ethernet cable.

Click the network, and then click the Continue button. Check your settings on the Summary screen that appears, and then click the Update button.

Closing Your AirPort Extreme Network

When you use AirPort Utility to set up an AirPort Extreme as described earlier in this chapter, AirPort Utility creates an *open* wireless network—one that broadcasts its network name so that any wireless-equipped computer can see it.

 NOTE The network name of a wireless network is also called its service set identifier (SSID).

Broadcasting the network name is often useful, as it enables people to see that the network is there. But if you will set up each wireless client that is authorized to access the network, you may prefer to make the network *closed*, preventing it from broadcasting its network name. To close the network, follow these steps:

1. On the first AirPort Utility screen, click the AirPort Extreme, and then click the Manual Setup button. The screens for manual configuration appear (see Figure 2-22).

2. Click the Wireless tab at the top of the configuration screens to display the Wireless settings (see Figure 2-23).

3. Click the Wireless Options button to display the Wireless Options dialog box.

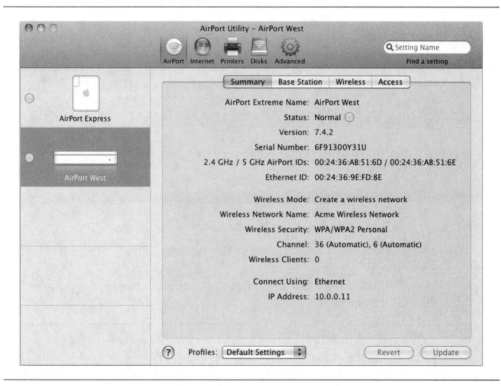

Figure 2-22.   You can also configure an AirPort Extreme manually.

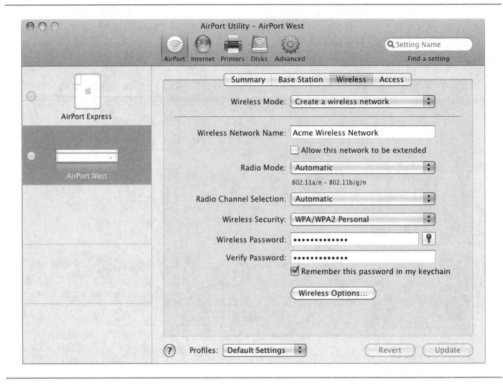

Figure 2-23.   Click the Wireless Options button on the Wireless tab.

4. Select the Create A Closed Network check box.

5. Click the Done button to close the Wireless Options dialog box and return to the Wireless tab.

6. Click the Update button, and then click the Continue button in the confirmation dialog box that appears.

NOTE   Closing your network by hiding its SSID provides only a veneer of security. It's worth doing, because casual freeloaders will not be able to see the network and so will not try to access it. But anyone who aims a wireless sniffer at the area will see the network's packets and be able to detect its name. At this point, the next layer of protection—the network password—comes into play.

CHAPTER 3 | Set Up Your Mac OS X Server

In this chapter I discuss how to install Mac OS X Server on your server. I assume that you're using a Mac—for example, a Mac mini or a Mac Pro—as your server rather than an Xserve. If you've bought an Xserve, it will have Mac OS X Server already installed on it, so you can skip this chapter; the same goes if you've bought a Mac mini with Mac OS X Server already installed.

This chapter covers the two main methods of installation: Installing from scratch, and upgrading an installation of the client version of Mac OS X to Mac OS X Server.

Installing Mac OS X Server from Scratch

To install Mac OS X Server from scratch, insert the Mac OS X Server DVD, and then restart the Mac. When you hear the startup sound, hold down c until you hear the Mac start reading the DVD.

When you see the Mac OS X Server screen shown in Figure 3-1, click your language, and then click the arrow button.

Choosing Which Disk to Install Mac OS X Server On

The next screen you see is titled Install Mac OS X Server (see Figure 3-2). If your installation will simply take over the whole of the Mac's hard disk, or the whole of an existing volume, click the Continue button. But if you need to partition the Mac's hard

Figure 3-1. Start the installation process by choosing the language you want to use.

Figure 3-2.   The Install Mac OS X Server screen has minimalist controls, but you can open the Utilities menu if you need to prepare the server's disk for the installation.

disk before installing Mac OS X Server, choose Utilities | Disk Utility from the menu bar, and then use Disk Utility (see Figure 3-3) to rearrange the partitions. When you've finished, quit Disk Utility to return to Installer, and then click the Continue button.

The next screen is the software license agreement. Click the Agree button once you've waded through the small print. You then reach the Install Mac OS X Server screen that lets you select which disk to use (see Figure 3-4).

Customizing the Installation

If you want to install Mac OS X Server with its default options, just click the drive you want on the Install Mac OS X Server screen, and then click the Install button.

But if you want to save some space on your server by stripping out items that you will not need, click the Customize button on the Install Mac OS X Server screen to display the Customize panel shown in Figure 3-5.

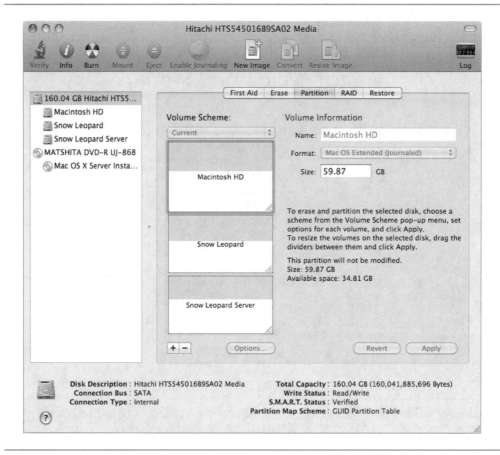

Figure 3-3. Use Disk Utility if you need to rearrange the partitions on your server.

There are four items you can remove:

- **Language Translations** These are the files required for displaying the Mac OS X interface in other languages—for example, French, German, or Japanese. If you will never need to use these languages, you can safely remove the Language Translations.

- **Printer Support** These are printer drivers—and there are more than 2GB of them. Installer breaks them up into three categories: Printers Used By This Mac, Nearby And Popular Printers, and All Available Printers.

NOTE It's usually a good idea to select the Nearby And Popular Printers check box, as this gives you enough printer drivers for many needs without installing the full set. You can install drivers for other, unpopular printers manually if you need to. But if you're desperate for disk space, you can save the best part of 1.5GB by installing only Printers Used By This Mac.

Figure 3-4.   Choose the disk on which you want to install Mac OS X Server.

- ■ **X11**   X11 is the window server used for running UNIX programs on Mac OS X. At its relatively modest size—around 160MB—X11 is usually a helpful addition to your Mac OS X server.

- ■ **Rosetta**   Rosetta is the Mac OS X application for running PowerPC-based applications on Intel-based Macs. At a mere handful of megabytes, this is usually worth including too, even if you don't yet know of any PowerPC applications you want to run on your server.

NOTE   If you get confused about which check boxes were initially selected, click the Restore Defaults button to restore the default settings. Then clear the check boxes for any items you don't want to include.

Click the OK button when you've finished customizing the installation. Installer returns you to the Install Mac OS X Server screen.

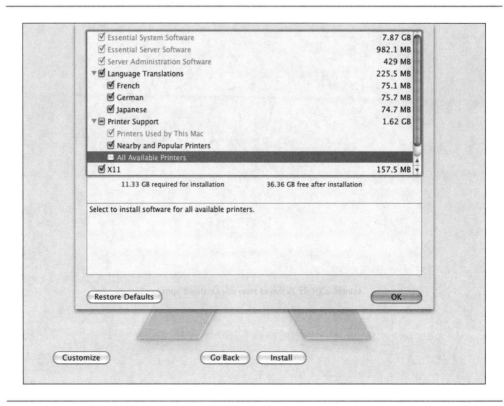

Figure 3-5. You can customize the Mac OS X Server installation by removing items you don't need, such as language translations.

Click the Install button to go ahead with the installation. Installer runs the main part of the installation, which takes a while, and then displays the Welcome screen. The next section discusses how to proceed from here.

Performing the Initial Configuration

From the Welcome screen (see Figure 3-6), you're ready to perform the initial configuration of your server.

If your country or region appears on the short list, click it; otherwise, select the Show All check box, and then click the country or region. Then click the Continue button. Installer displays the Keyboard screen.

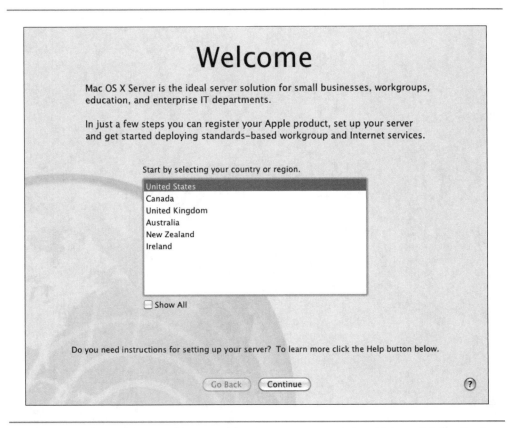

Welcome

Mac OS X Server is the ideal server solution for small businesses, workgroups, education, and enterprise IT departments.

In just a few steps you can register your Apple product, set up your server and get started deploying standards–based workgroup and Internet services.

Start by selecting your country or region.

United States
Canada
United Kingdom
Australia
New Zealand
Ireland

☐ Show All

Do you need instructions for setting up your server? To learn more click the Help button below.

Go Back   Continue   ⑦

Figure 3-6.   On the Welcome screen, pick your country or region, and then click the Continue button.

Choosing the Keyboard Layout

At first, the Keyboard list shows just a short list of keyboard layouts for the country or region you choose. If the keyboard layout you want appears, click it—for example, click U.S. for a standard U.S. keyboard layout. If you want a keyboard layout that doesn't appear, such as one of the Dvorak layouts, select the Show All check box to display the full list of keyboards layouts (as shown in Figure 3-7), and then click the right layout.

Entering the Serial Number

Click the Continue button. Installer displays the Serial Number screen. Enter the serial number and your registration information—type your name and organization name character for character, because the check is case sensitive—and then click the Continue button.

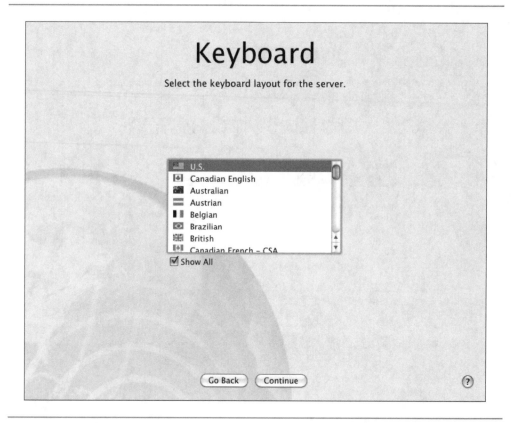

Figure 3-7. On the Keyboard screen, choose the layout for the keyboard you want to use. Select the Show All check box, as shown here, to reach alternative keyboard layouts such as Dvorak.

Choosing Whether to Transfer an Existing Server

Next, Installer displays the Transfer An Existing Server? screen (see Figure 3-8).

Assuming you're setting up a network from scratch, select the Set Up A New Server option button, and then click the Continue button. Installer displays the Registration screen.

If you want to register Mac OS X Server, fill in the information, and select the Stay In Touch! check box if you want Apple to e-mail you with software updates, news, and product information. Registration is optional, so don't feel compelled to fill in the fields—you can just leave them blank and click the Continue button. Registration doesn't affect your warranty.

Installer then displays the A Few More Questions screen, which lets you tell Apple where you'll use the server, what type of clients you use, and which services the server

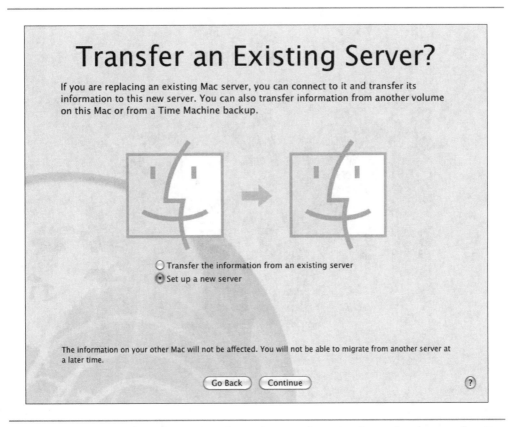

Figure 3-8. The Transfer An Existing Server? screen lets you choose between setting up a new server and pulling across information from a Mac server that's already on your network.

will run. This information is also optional; it's useful for Apple, but you may not want to provide it. Click the Continue button when you're ready to move on.

Choosing the Time Zone

Next, Installer displays the Time Zone screen (see Figure 3-9). Aim the mouse pointer at your location on the map and click, and then choose the nearest city from the Closest City pop-up menu.

The Network Time Server readout then shows the time server Mac OS X will use— for example, Apple Americas/U.S. (time.apple.com) if you choose a U.S. city. If you prefer to use a different time server, click the Edit button to open the dialog box shown in Figure 3-10, and then identify the server you want. You can pick one of the servers from the Use Network Time Server pop-up menu, type the IP address or DNS name

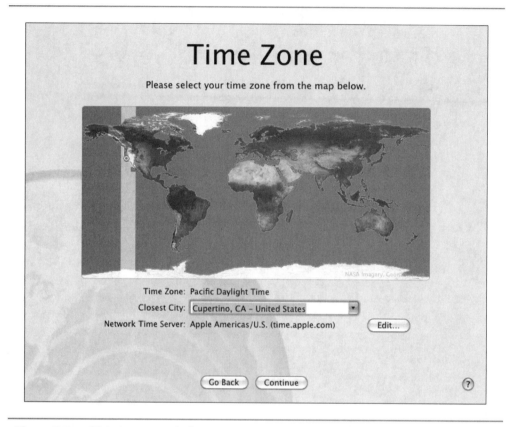

Figure 3-9. Click the map to indicate your general time zone, and then pick the nearest city from the Closest City pop-up menu.

of your own time server, or even turn off the use of network time by clearing the Use Network Time Server check box. Click the OK button when you've finished.

 NOTE Turning off the use of network time isn't usually a good idea, but it's sometimes necessary—for example, because your network doesn't have an Internet connection.

Click the Continue button when you're satisfied with your time server choices.

Setting Up the Administrator Account

On the next screen Installer displays, the Administrator Account screen (see Figure 3-11), you'll set up the account you will use to administer this server. This account is local to the server—in other words, it is stored on it.

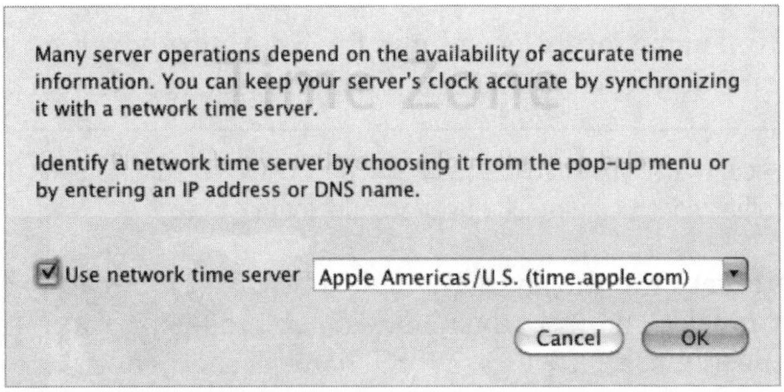

Many server operations depend on the availability of accurate time information. You can keep your server's clock accurate by synchronizing it with a network time server.

Identify a network time server by choosing it from the pop-up menu or by entering an IP address or DNS name.

☑ Use network time server   Apple Americas/U.S. (time.apple.com) ▾

Cancel   OK

Figure 3-10.   You can choose a different time server; specify one of your own by typing an IP address or DNS name, or by stopping Mac OS X Server from using network time.

Administrator Account

Create a local account that will be used to administer this server. After setup, use Server Preferences to create users and administrators for use with your services.

Name:

Short Name:
This will be used as the name for the administrator's home folder and cannot be changed.

Password:

Verify:

Password Hint:
(Recommended)

☑ Enable administrators to log in remotely using SSH

☑ Enable administrators to manage this server remotely

Go Back   Continue   ?

Figure 3-11.   On the Administrator Account screen, you must make several critical choices for the first administrator account—starting with the short name.

To set up the administrator account, follow these steps:

1. Type the full name for the account in the Name text box. For example, you may want to type your own name, or a role name, such as Network Admin.

NOTE For security, use your administrator account only when administering the server. If you use the server for other work, use a regular user account for that work.

2. Press TAB to move to the Short Name text box. Mac OS X automatically suggests a short name derived from the name you entered—for example, it could be the same name, but in all lowercase if the name is short enough.

NOTE The short name is the fixed name for the account—you can't change it after you create it (unlike the name, which you can change anytime you care to). You can use uppercase and lowercase letters, numbers, underscores, hyphens, and periods, but no spaces or symbols. The name doesn't actually have to be short—it can be up to 255 characters long—but names of 8 characters or fewer are recommended, as they're easier to type.

3. Type a password in the Password text box, and then type it again in the Verify text box so that Mac OS X can check that you've gotten it right. The password appears in these two text boxes as security-conscious dots rather than the letters, which is why it's possible to make a mistake. If you're not confident about creating strong passwords, click the key icon to the right of the Password text box and use the Password Assistant to create a hard-to-crack password, as discussed in the sidebar entitled "Using the Password Assistant to Create Hard-to-Crack Passwords."

4. If you want, type a password hint in the Password Hint text box. Apple puts "Recommended" next to this box, because forgetting a password can create a major problem.

NOTE Even though Apple recommends creating a password hint, for security, it's far better *not* to create one. This is because any effective hint will help others to crack your password, while any ineffective hint will be useless to you.

5. Select the Enable Administrators To Log In Remotely Using SSH check box if you want to use the Secure Shell (SSH) protocol to connect to this Mac server from other servers.
6. Select the Enable Administrators To Manage This Server Remotely check box if you want to enable remote management. This lets you connect via Screen Sharing or Remote Desktop.

NOTE Normally, you will want to select the Enable Administrators To Log In Remotely Using SSH check box and the Enable Administrators To Manage This Server Remotely check box so that you can check on the server and perform emergency fixes—or regular maintenance, if you wish—on the server from wherever you happen to be. But if you know you (and other administrators) will always be physically present when you administer the server, clear these check boxes for security.

Click the Continue button when you've made your choices.

Using the Password Assistant to Create Hard-to-Crack Passwords

If you're finding it hard to come up with a hard-to-crack password off the top of your head, click the Password Assistant button—the button with the key icon—to the right of the Password text box to bring the Password Assistant to your help.

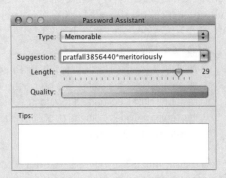

Open the Type pop-up menu at the top of the window and choose the type of password you want to create:

- **Manual**   You type the password yourself. Use this setting if you want to use Password Assistant to see how strong your password is.

- **Memorable**   Password Assistant creates a password that's (relatively) easy to remember—for example, **tent148!leer** or **priest916aura**. This is often the best choice for general use, especially if you increase the Length slider setting to a suitable length.

- **Letters & Numbers**   Password Assistant creates a password that consists of uppercase and lowercase numbers but no symbols.

- **Numbers Only**   Password Assistant creates a password that consists only of numbers.

- **Random**   Password Assistant pulls a random password out of its hat.

- **FIPS-181 Compliant**   Password Assistant creates a password that meets Federal Information Processing Standard 181 (FIPS-181), which covers automatic password generators. The FIPS-181 passwords that Password Assistant produces consist of only lowercase letters.

Drag the Length slider untill it shows the number of characters you want the password to have. The Quality meter shows how tough the password is to break—red for easy, yellow for moderate, green for hard.

The Suggestion box shows the current suggestion, but you can open the pop-up menu and choose another suggestion from it. If none of the suggestions appears, click the More Suggestions item at the bottom of the pop-up menu to make Password Assistant try again.

The Tips box at the bottom of the Password Assistant window shows tips when you're creating a password manually—for example, "Mix upper and lower case, punctuation, and numbers."

Choosing Network Settings for Your Server

Next, you'll see the Network screen (see Figure 3-12). Depending on what the Mac on which you're installing Mac OS X Server is connected to, you may not have to do anything here, or you may have to do a fair amount of setup.

NOTE   Dynamic Host Configuration Protocol (DHCP) is a means of allocating IP addresses automatically to the computers on a network. On joining the network, a computer configured to use Dynamic Host Configuration Protocol (DHCP) applies to the DHCP server for an IP address, which the server provides from the pool of available addresses. After the computer leaves the network, the server reclaims the address.

If your Mac is connected to a network with a DHCP server in place, Mac OS X Server automatically acquires an IP address from the server. This is what you see in Figure 3-12, where the server has an Ethernet connection to the network and has picked

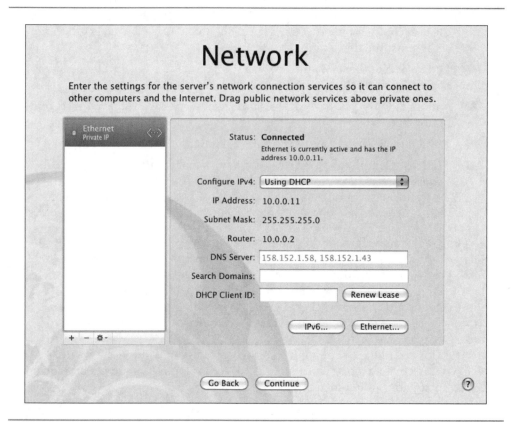

Figure 3-12.   On the Network screen, you can configure each of your server's network interfaces.

up the IP address, the subnet mask, the router address, and the DNS servers from the DHCP server.

Configuring a network interface has plenty of options, but this is normally how you'll want to approach it:

1. If your server has multiple network interfaces, click the interface you want to configure. In a typical server, this will be the Ethernet interface, or (if your server has two or more Ethernet interfaces) the first Ethernet interface.

2. Open the Configure IPv4 pop-up menu, choose the basic means of configuration, and enter the necessary information:

   ■ **Using DHCP** Select this item to have the network pick up the network settings from an existing DHCP server on the network. The IP address, subnet mask, router address, and DNS server addresses are all set for you; you just need to set the search domains and the DHCP client ID if necessary. If you've set up your network router to provide DHCP service, this will get your server on the network immediately.

   ■ **Using DHCP With Manual Address** Select this item when you need to set the IP address for the server manually, but pick up the subnet mask, router address, and DNS server addresses from the DHCP server. Again, you can set the search domains and the DHCP client ID if your server needs them. This option lets you set a static IP address for your server rather than have it grab an address from the pool each time you start it or restart it.

   ■ **Using BootP** This item is primarily for Macs that boot from a NetBoot image—pulling a disk image across the network from a server rather than booting from the hard drive. NetBoot is normally used for client Macs rather than for servers.

   ■ **Manually** Select this item when you want to specify all the network settings manually.

   ■ **Off** Select this item if you need to turn IPv4 off.

   ■ **Create PPPoE Service** Select this item if you need to create a network interface using Point-to-Point Protocol over Ethernet (PPPoE). PPPoE is a service for establishing a connection between two points in an Ethernet network; it is mostly used for DSL connections. Type the name you want to give the PPPoE service in the dialog box that appears (see Figure 3-13) and click the Done button. The PPPoE connection then appears in the list of network interfaces. Click it, and then type the account name and password into the boxes provided.

NOTE When entering multiple items in the same text box, such as entries in the DNS Server text box, separate them with commas—for example, **206.216.4.52, 206.216.4.43**.

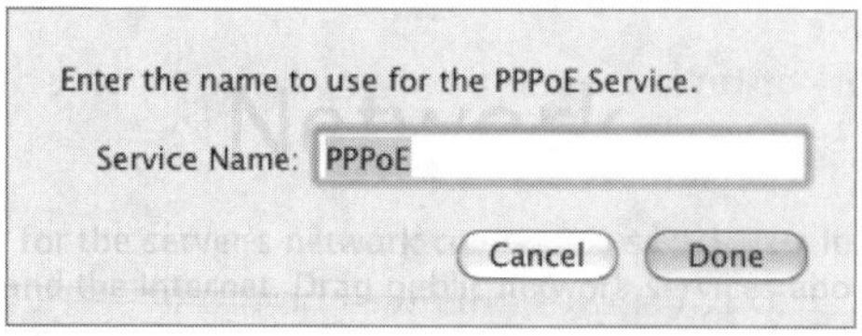

Enter the name to use for the PPPoE Service.

Service Name: PPPoE

Cancel   Done

Figure 3-13.   Name your PPPoE service in this dialog box.

3. If the network interface will use IPv6 with manual settings, set it up like this:

   a. Click the IPv6 button to display the dialog box shown in Figure 3-14.

   b. Open the Configure IPv6 pop-up menu and choose Manually. The dialog box expands to show a Router text box, an Address text box, and a Prefix Length text box (see Figure 3-15).

   c. Enter the router address, IP address, and prefix length.

   d. Click the OK button.

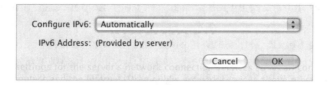

Configure IPv6: Automatically

IPv6 Address: (Provided by server)

Cancel   OK

Figure 3-14.   Mac OS X expects to configure IPv6 automatically (if you use it at all).

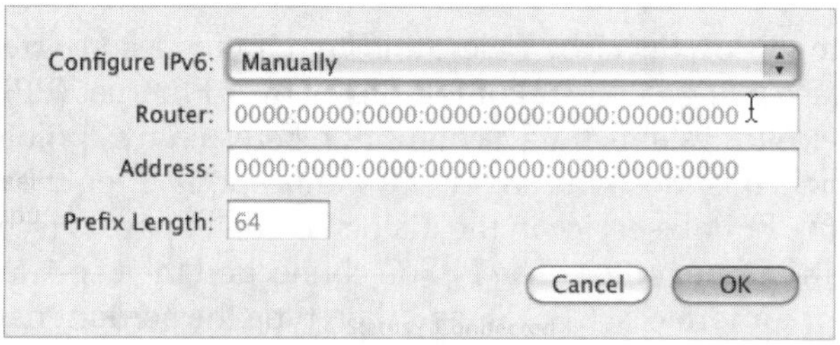

Configure IPv6: Manually

Router: 0000:0000:0000:0000:0000:0000:0000:0000

Address: 0000:0000:0000:0000:0000:0000:0000:0000

Prefix Length: 64

Cancel   OK

Figure 3-15.   You can also configure IPv6 manually by providing the router address, IP address, and prefix length.

Ethernet ID: 00:0c:29:85:7e:c6
Configure:
Automatically
Cancel
OK

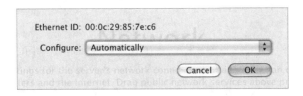

Figure 3-16. For some networks, you may need to choose Ethernet settings for the network adapter. Open the Configure pop-up menu and choose Manually from it.

4. If you need to configure Ethernet for the network interface manually, do so like this:
   a. Click the Ethernet button to display the dialog box shown in Figure 3-16.
   b. Open the Configure pop-up menu and choose Manually. The dialog box expands to show the Speed pop-up menu, Duplex pop-up menu, and MTU pop-up menu (see Figure 3-17).
   c. Open the Speed pop-up menu and choose the speed. For example, choose 1000baseT for a Gigabit Ethernet network.
   d. Open the Duplex pop-up menu and choose the means of duplexing—for example, Full-Duplex, Flow-Control.
   e. Open the MTU pop-up menu and choose the size of the maximum transmission unit—the size (in bytes) of the largest data packet the interface can shift. Your choices are Standard (1500), Jumbo (9000), or Custom.
   f. Click the OK button when you've finished configuring Ethernet settings.

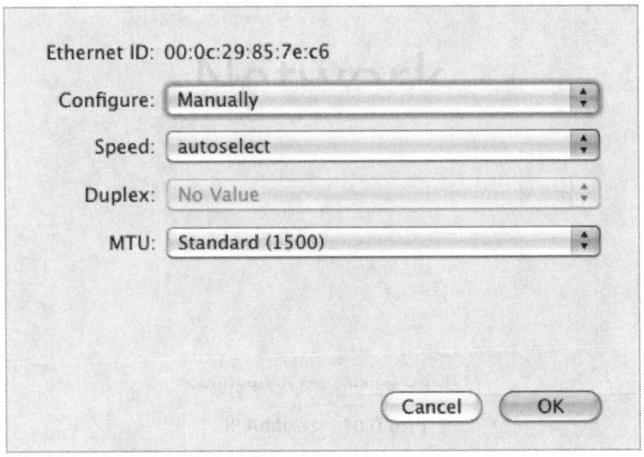

Ethernet ID: 00:0c:29:85:7e:c6
Configure:
Manually
Speed:
autoselect
Duplex:
No Value
MTU:
Standard (1500)
Cancel
OK

Figure 3-17. You may need to configure an Ethernet connection manually by providing the speed, duplex, and MTU information.

5. Select the next network interface on the list, and then configure it as described in steps 2–4.

6. If you create multiple network connections, drag them up and down the list box on the left of the Network screen into the order in which you want the server to use them. Put the primary network service at the top of the list.

When you've finished configuring your server's network interfaces, click the Continue button.

Assigning Network Names to Your Server

The next screen is the Network Names screen (see Figure 3-18), where you assign a primary DNS name and a computer name to your server.

The primary DNS name is the name of the server that provides the Domain Name Service (DNS) for your network—a name such as dnssvr.acmevirtualindustries.com.

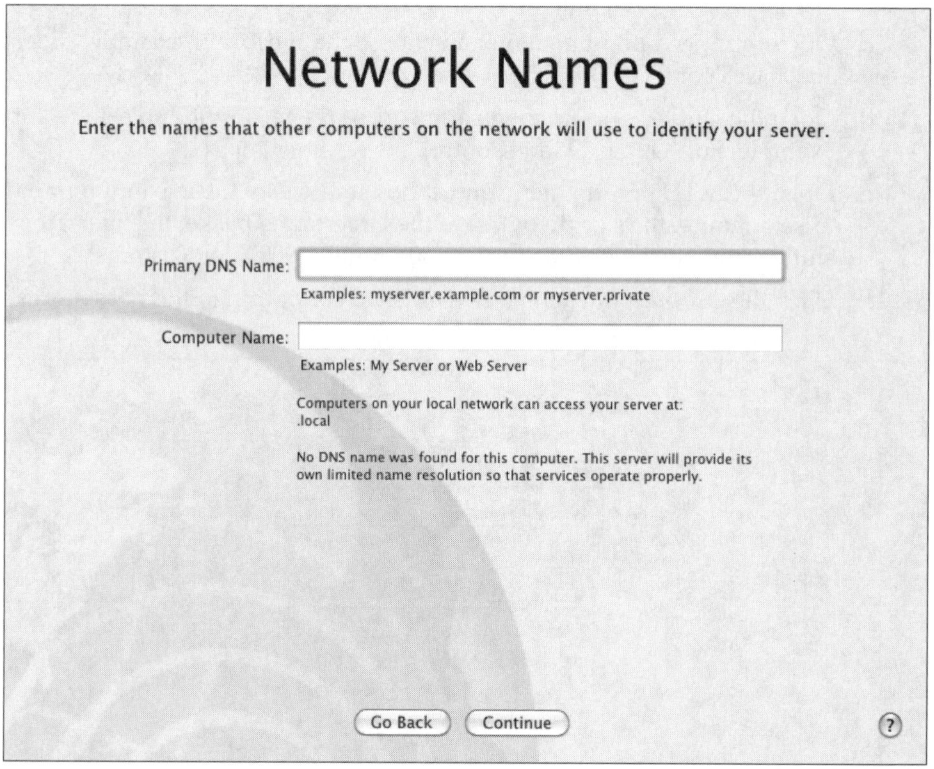

Figure 3-18. On the Network Names screen, give your server a DNS name and a computer name so that other computers on your network can access it.

If your network has a DNS server that supplies this information, Mac OS X Server picks it up from there. Otherwise, type the name in yourself.

The computer name is the "friendly" name by which your server appears on the network—for example, Server or Network Server. This is the name that users will see when they're browsing the network by names rather than IP addresses, so make the name one that's easy to grasp. You can use up to 63 characters, including spaces or underscores, but many fewer than that is usually better—if you can't give the server a helpful and descriptive name in 20 characters or fewer, it's probably time to rethink your naming conventions with brevity and clarity in mind.

When you've chosen the network names for your server, click the Continue button to move along.

Setting Up Users and Groups

The next screen you see is the Users And Groups screen (see Figure 3-19).

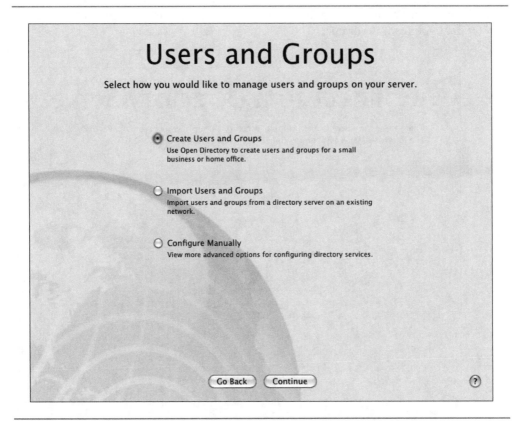

Figure 3-19. On the Users And Groups screen, choose whether to set up users and groups manually, import them from a directory server or network, or configure directory services manually.

Select the option button for the approach you want to take in creating the users and groups for your network:

■ **Create Users And Groups**   Select this option button if you want to set up this server for managing users and groups. If your company or organization doesn't have an existing directory server, this is the way to go. When you click the Continue button, Installer takes you to the Services screen. After finishing the installation, you can then set up users and groups as discussed in Chapter 4.

■ **Import Users And Groups**   If your company or organization already has a directory server that contains the users and groups that this server will use, select this option button. When you click the Continue button, Installer displays the Connect To A Directory Server screen (see Figure 3-20), on which you enter the address of the server that contains the users and groups you want to import.

■ **Configure Manually**   Select this option button if you're experienced with directory services and you want to connect to a directory server manually. When you click the Continue button, Installer displays the Connect To A Directory Server screen, where you can enter the address of the directory server that you want to connect to.

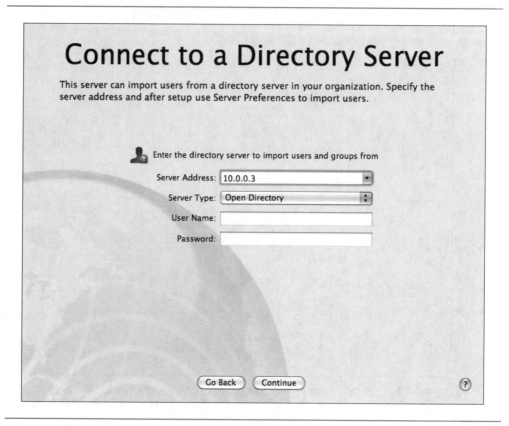

Figure 3-20.   You can import users and groups from an existing server if you have one.

Choosing Which Services to Run on Your Server

After you've chosen how to create the users and groups for your network, you'll see the Services screen (see Figure 3-21), which lets you decide which standard services you want to run on your server. Select the check box for each service you want to set running; clear the check boxes for those you don't want.

> **NOTE**   You can easily change the services your server runs at any point.

If the Store Service Data On pop-up menu appears, select the hard disk where you want to store the data for the services you choose to run. If your server has only one hard disk, this pop-up menu doesn't appear.

Table 3-1 gives an overview of the services.

Click the Continue button when you're ready to proceed.

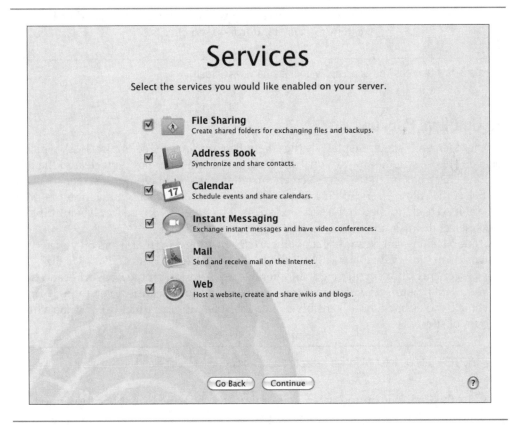

Figure 3-21.   Choose which services you want to run on your server.

Service	Explanation
File Sharing	Sharing files among the various computers on the network. Macs, Windows PCs, and PCs running Unix or Linux can share the files.
Address Book	Sharing addresses using Address Book on Macs or CardDAV-compliant applications on other computers.
Calendar	Sharing calendars using iCal, the iPhone and iPod touch Calendar application, and CalDAV-compliant applications on PCs.
Instant Messaging	Communicating via iChat, Google Talk, or Jabber clients. (Jabber uses the XMPP protocol.)
Mail	Sending e-mail via Apple Mail, Mail on the iPhone or iPod touch, or standards-based e-mail clients on any computer.
Web	Creating and accessing websites, blogs, wikis, and web calendars via standards-based clients.

Table 3-1.   Services You Can Enable from the Services Screen

Setting Up Client Backup

The next screen Installer displays is the Client Backup screen (see Figure 3-22), which lets you choose whether to turn on Time Machine for this server. If you cleared the File Sharing check box on the Services screen, Installer skips displaying this screen.

Select the Allow Users To Back Up To This Server check box if you want users' Macs to be able to back up files to the server via Time Machine. If your server has multiple disks, select the disk on which you want to store the backups.

Time Machine can be a great convenience for making sure that users on your network don't lose valuable files. But don't select the Allow Users To Back Up To This Server check box if you've got another backup solution on the network—and do make sure that your server has enough free disk space for backups. Even though Time Machine handles backups as sensibly as possible, backups can quickly consume a huge amount of space.

 NOTE   See Chapter 18 for an in-depth discussion of Time Machine and how to use it effectively.

Click the Continue button when you've finished choosing Client Backup options.

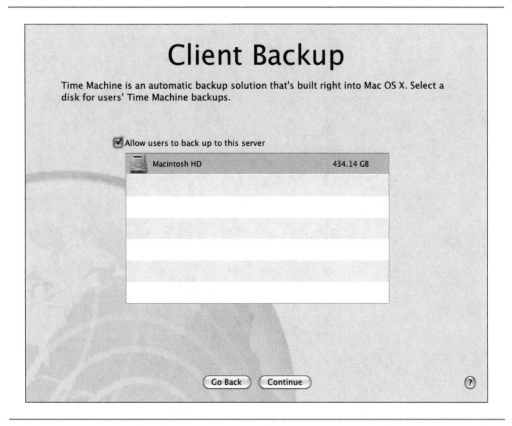

Figure 3-22. On the Client Backup screen, choose whether to let Time Machine back up client Macs' files to the server.

Choosing Mail Options

Next, you'll see the Mail Options screen (see Figure 3-23) if you selected the Mail check box on the Services screen. (If not, Installer skips this screen.)

If your network sends e-mail through a relay server rather than directly, select the Relay Outgoing Mail Through check box and type the server's DNS name in the text box. If the SMTP server used for sending mail requires authentication, select the Enable SMTP Relay Authentication check box and type the user name and password in the text boxes below it.

 CAUTION Many mail setups don't use relaying, so turn it on only if you're certain you need it. Using a relay server unnecessarily may make your network appear to be sending spam.

The other setting on the Mail Options screen lets you send a welcome message to new users of your network. Select the Send A Welcome Message To New Users check box and type the message in the Custom Introduction text box.

Click the Continue button when you've finished choosing mail options.

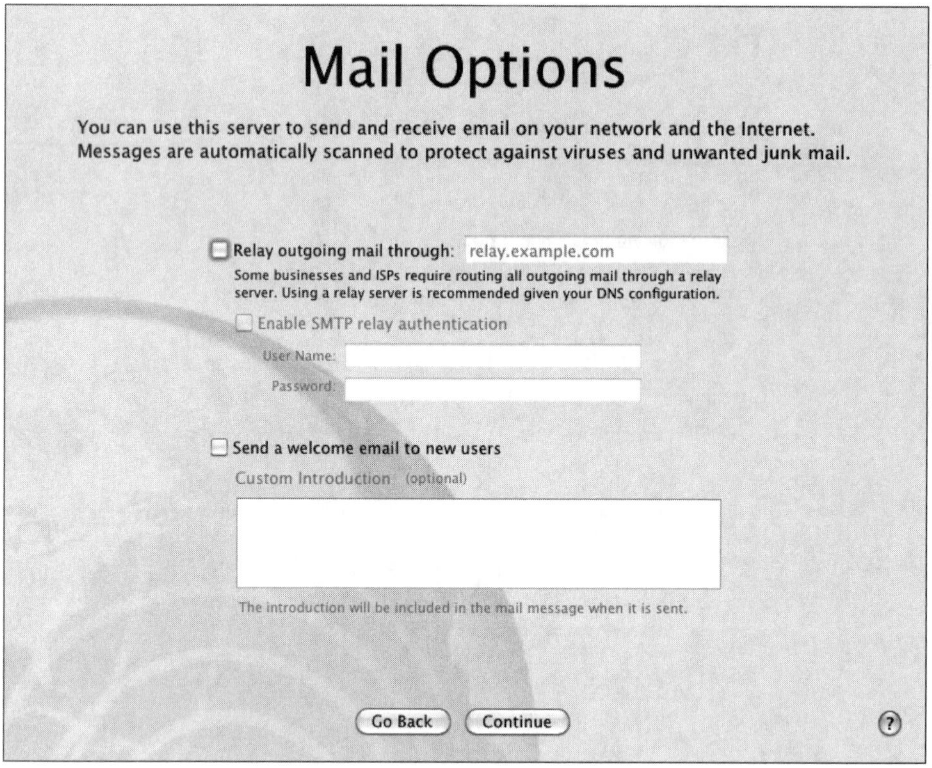

Mail Options

You can use this server to send and receive email on your network and the Internet. Messages are automatically scanned to protect against viruses and unwanted junk mail.

☐ Relay outgoing mail through: relay.example.com

Some businesses and ISPs require routing all outgoing mail through a relay server. Using a relay server is recommended given your DNS configuration.

☐ Enable SMTP relay authentication

User Name:

Password:

☐ Send a welcome email to new users

Custom Introduction (optional)

The introduction will be included in the mail message when it is sent.

(Go Back) (Continue)   ⑦

Figure 3-23.   On the Mail Options screen, you can set up relaying for outgoing mail and specify a welcome message to send to new e-mail users.

Reviewing the Options You've Chosen

When you click the Continue button from the Mail Options screen, Installer displays the Review screen (see Figure 3-24). Scan the list of icons and make sure that none of the services were ones you meant to turn off—and that none of the services you chose are missing.

If there's a problem, click the Go Back button and retrace your steps until you reach the screen where you can fix it. Then make your way forward again using the Continue button.

To see the details of the setup options you've chosen, click the Details button on the Review screen. Installer displays a screen (see Figure 3-25) with a breakdown of the options.

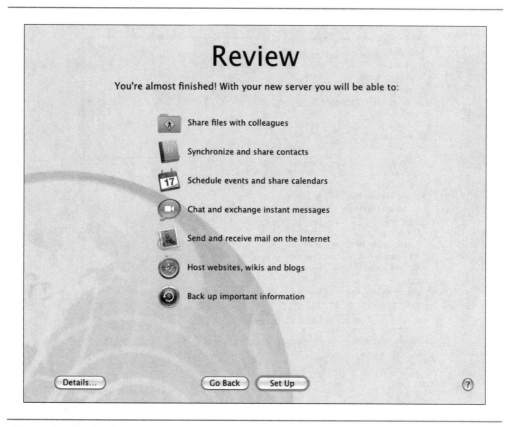

Figure 3-24. On the Review screen, make sure that the options shown are the ones you want for your server. Click the Details button to drill down to the settings.

Saving a Profile of the Server's Setup

From the Details screen, you can save your server's details as a profile that you can apply automatically to another server you set up. To save a setup profile, follow these steps:

1. Click the Save Setup Profile button. Installer displays the Auto Server Setup dialog box.

2. Select the appropriate option button for your needs:

   ■ **Apply This Profile To Any Server** Select this option button if you want to be able to use this profile to set up any server automatically. This is the default choice.

   ■ **Apply This Profile Only If Any Of The Following Conditions Are Met** Select this option button if you want to be able to restrict the profile to work only on certain servers. Use the first row of controls to set up the first condition—for example, open the first pop-up menu and choose Serial Number, open the second pop-up menu and choose Begins With, and then type the

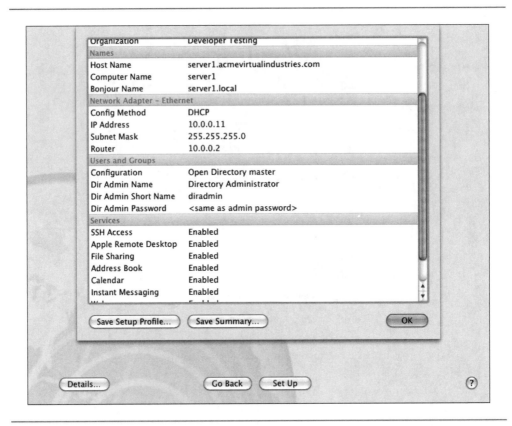

Figure 3-25. The Details screen lets you see exactly which settings you've chosen—and save a setup profile or a summary if you want.

number in the text box. Click the + button at the right end of the first row if you want to add another condition. For example, you might want to tie the profile to a range of IP addresses and to various DNS names, so that the profile would run if either condition were true.

3. In the Encryption pop-up menu, choose the type of encryption you want to apply to the profile. These are your choices:

    ■ **None**   Avoid using this setting, because the administrator passwords for the server are stored in clear text. This means any intruder can read them without breaking a sweat.

    ■ **Passphrase Encrypted**   Select this item, and then type the passphrase—preferably a strong one of eight characters or more, using letters, numbers, and symbols—in the Passphrase text box that appears.

4. Click the Save button. In the Save As dialog box that appears, choose where to save the file, and then click the Save button.

NOTE   To use the setup profile you've created, place it in a folder named Auto Server Setup at the root of the volume on the Mac you're setting up as a server. This makes Installer apply the setup profile automatically. If you're setting up the server for the first time, place the Auto Server Setup folder on a FireWire hard drive connected to the server.

Saving a Summary of the Server's Settings

If you want to save a summary of the server's settings, which is often a good idea for your records, click the Save Summary button. In the Save As dialog box that appears, choose where to save the file, change the name from ConfigurationSummary.txt if you want (for example, add the name of the server), and then click the Save button.

Applying Your Settings

When you've finished reviewing the settings and are satisfied with them, click the Set Up button. You'll see the Setting Up screen (see Figure 3-26) as Installer applies the settings you chose to the server. When the screen displays a green circle bearing a check mark, click the Go button to fire up your server.

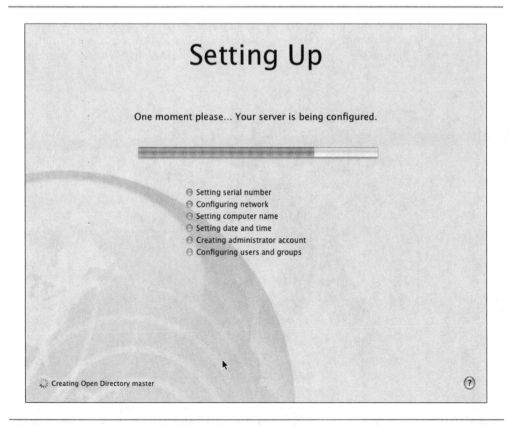

Figure 3-26.   The Setting Up screen shows you Installer's progress in finalizing your server's setup.

Upgrading Mac OS X Client to Mac OS X Server

If your Mac already has the client version of Mac OS X 10.6 installed on it, you can upgrade it to Mac OS X Server.

 NOTE   The upgrade process works only from Mac OS X 10.6, not from earlier versions of Mac OS X.

If Mac OS X is running, wait for the Finder to open the Mac OS X Server Install Disc window (see Figure 3-27), and then double-click the Install Mac OS X Server icon. When the Install Mac OS X Server screen appears, click the Install button to start the installation.

On the Welcome To The Mac OS X Server Installer screen, click the Continue button. Click the Continue button on the Software License screen and then the Agree button on the dialog box that then appears.

The next screen is the Standard Install screen (see Figure 3-28), whose name includes the name you've given to the hard disk volume on which you're installing Mac OS X Server (in the figure, the disk is named "Snow Leopard Server").

The installation routine assumes you want to upgrade the current installation of Mac OS X to Mac OS X Server. If you want to upgrade Mac OS X Server on a different volume, click the Change Install Location button to reach the Select A Destination screen shown in Figure 3-29, click the volume you want, and then click the Continue

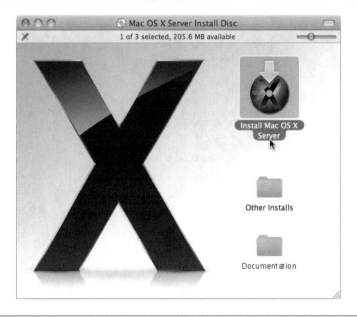

Figure 3-27.   From Mac OS X, double-click the Install Mac OS X Server icon to start the installation.

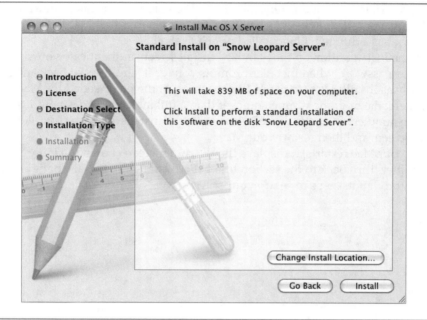

Figure 3-28. Click the Change Install Location button on the Standard Install screen if you want to change the disk on which you're installing Mac OS X Server.

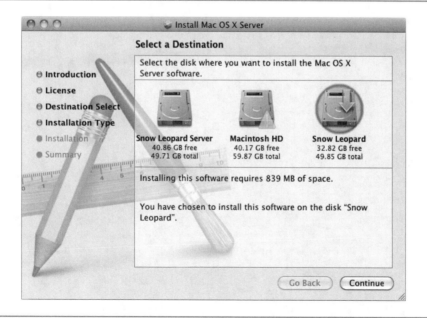

Figure 3-29. If necessary, use the Select A Destination screen to change the copy of Mac OS X you're upgrading to Mac OS X Server.

button to return to the Standard Install screen. The volume you choose must also have Mac OS X 10.6 installed on it—you can't use this screen to install Mac OS X Server on a volume that has a different OS installed or no OS at all.

Click the Install button on the Standard Install screen, authenticate yourself by providing your password when Installer prompts you for it, and then sit back and smile contentedly as Installer gets to work. Because most of the files needed for Mac OS X are already there, the upgrade is much quicker than a full installation. Usually, it's finished within five minutes. Click the Close button on to the Installation Was Completed Successfully screen, and then restart your Mac.

When your Mac restarts, it displays the Welcome screen shown in Figure 3-6, earlier in this chapter. Turn back to the section titled "Performing the Initial Configuration" and work through its steps to set up your server.

CHAPTER 4 | Secure Your Server

A fter running through setup as described in Chapter 3, you now have a server set up with your customized version of a regular configuration.

So far, so good—but you will probably want to make some changes to your server immediately to increase its security and enhance your serenity. These changes include:

- Updating the server with the latest fixes
- Securing the server's hardware
- Changing the password on the server's root account
- Enabling the Mac OS X firewall if your server is not yet protected by a firewall
- Choosing which services to expose through the Mac firewall (if you turn the firewall on)
- Installing an SSL certificate to allow clients to authenticate the server and connect to it securely

You'll learn how to do all this in this chapter. You will also need to set up Open Directory on your server, but we'll get to that in Chapter 5.

Updating Your Server with the Latest Fixes

Pretty much the first thing you should do after installing Mac OS X Server is to install any updates that Apple has released since the version on your installation disc. The easiest way to do this is to run Software Update—and to set it to check for updates when you want it to.

Let's look first at how to run Software Update manually, as you'll want to do if you've just installed Mac OS X Server. After that, I'll show you how to set Software Update to behave the way you want it to.

Running Software Update Manually

To run Software Update manually, follow these steps:

1. Choose Apple | Software Update to launch Software Update. The application automatically checks for updates to all the Apple software you're running.

2. If Software Update displays a dialog box saying that software updates are available for your computer, as shown in Figure 4-1, click the Show Details button to see a list of what's available (see Figure 4-2).

3. Clear the check box for any update you don't want to install. For example, if you won't play music or watch QuickTime movies on the server, you probably don't need to download the hulking updates for iTunes.

Figure 4-1.   Click the Show Details button in the first Software Update dialog box.

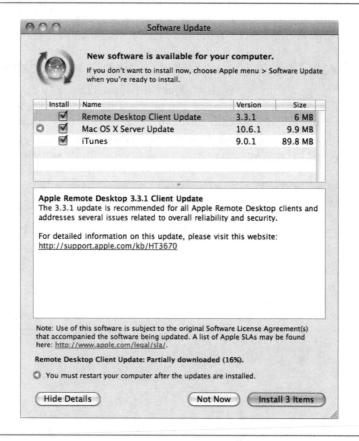

Figure 4-2.   When you see the list of updates, clear the check box for any update you don't want to install.

TIP   Scan the list of updates for the reversed Play symbol that appears alongside the Mac OS X Server Update in Figure 4-2. This symbol means you'll need to restart the server after installing the update—so if you see this symbol when the server is in use on the network, you may want to delay installing the updates until after hours.

4. Click the Install button, whose name shows the number of items—Install 1 Item, Install 2 Items, or however many you've left selected.

5. Accept any license agreements that Mac OS X throws at you.

6. When Software Update prompts you to authenticate yourself, type your password, and then click the OK button.

7. Software Update downloads the updates (unless it has already downloaded them for you) and installs them.

8. If Software Update prompts you to restart the server (see Figure 4-3), click the Restart button if now is an okay time. Otherwise, click the Not Now button, and then restart the server manually as soon as is convenient.

Configuring Software Update to Check Automatically for Updates

Running Software Update manually, as you just did, works fine, as does running Server Updates manually, as you'll learn to do in a moment. But normally it's more convenient to have Software Update automatically check for updates however frequently you want it to. Software Update can then either prompt you to install the updates or just wait until you decide to consult it. Software Update can also download the updates automatically for you, which can save you precious time when you're ready to install them.

Here's how to tell Software Update whether and how frequently you want it to check for updates:

1. Choose Apple | System Preferences to open the System Preferences window.

2. In the System category, click the Software Update icon to open the Software Update pane.

3. If the Scheduled Check tab isn't selected, click it now to bring the Scheduled Check pane to the front (see Figure 4-4).

Figure 4-3.   You may need to restart the server to finish installing the updates.

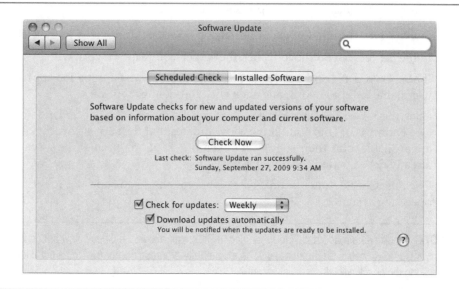

Figure 4-4.   In the Scheduled Check pane of Software Update, choose how to check for updates and whether to download them automatically.

4. To check regularly (often a good idea), select the Check For Updates check box, and then choose the frequency in the pop-up menu: Daily, Weekly, or Monthly. Daily gives you the best protection, but you may prefer to choose Weekly to reduce the number of times the server pesters you for attention. Monthly is too seldom for most servers—you risk leaving the server unprotected against the latest threats for long enough to give an attacker time to move in on it.

5. Assuming you select the Check For Updates check box, you can select the Download Updates Automatically check box if you want the server to haul down the necessary files for you. For many servers, this is a good idea, as it increases the chance that the updates will be ready to install when you're ready to install them. But if bandwidth is limited and you need to download updates only outside work hours, clear the Download Updates Automatically check box.

6. When you've made your choices, press ⌘-Q or choose System Preferences | Quit System Preferences to quit System Preferences.

Updating a Server via Server Updates

The second main way of updating a server running Mac OS X Server is to use the Server Updates feature in Server Admin. The advantage of this method is that it works both for a server you're sitting at and for remote servers you're manipulating via Server Admin. By contrast, to run Software Update on a remote server, you must establish a Screen Sharing connection rather than a Server Admin connection. Screen Sharing tends to be much slower and more awkward, so Server Admin is the way to go when you have the choice.

To update a server using Server Updates, follow these steps:

1. Open Server Admin. For example, click the Server Admin icon in the Dock.

2. In the Servers list on the left, click the server you want to work with.

3. If Mac OS X Server prompts you to authenticate yourself, type the appropriate user name and password, and then click the Connect button.

4. Click the Server Updates tab on the toolbar to display the Server Updates pane (see Figure 4-5). This pane shows any updates that the server already knows are available, plus their status—for example, *Ready To Install* if the server has already downloaded the updates for you.

5. Click the Check Now button. Server Updates checks for updates to the server's operating system.

 NOTE   You'll see a readout saying "Scanning In Progress" above the Check Now button while Server Updates checks for the updates. There's no hefty progress bar to give you a good idea of how long the check will take, so just be patient.

6. Clear the check box for each update you don't want to install.

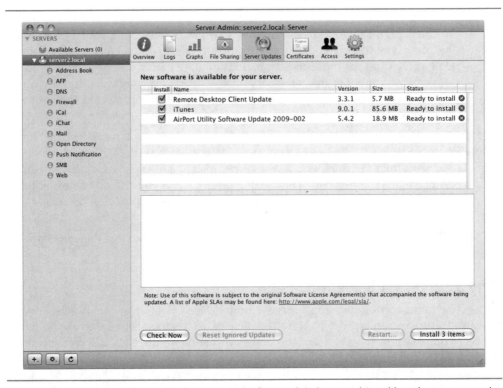

Figure 4-5.   Use the Server Updates pane in Server Admin to update either the server you're sitting at or a remote server.

Are you sure you want to remove the
update "iTunes" from the list?

You will no longer be notified of new versions of this
update. To see this update again, click the Reset
Ignored Updates button.

Cancel   OK

Figure 4-6.   If you don't want to see an update ever again, tell Server Updates to remove it.

7. If you want to remove an update from the list, click the X button in the right-most column on its line. Server Updates displays a confirmation dialog box like the one shown in Figure 4-6, warning you that you'll need to reset the ignored updates before it will tell you about this update again. Click the OK button, and the update will disappear from the list.

8. Click the Install button (again, its name includes the number of items that you selected—Install 13 Items, or whatever). Server Updates downloads any files it hasn't already downloaded, and then installs them.

9. If you need to restart the server, click the Restart button, and then click the Restart button in the confirmation dialog box that opens.

Understanding Other Ways of Getting Updates

For your main server, getting the updates via Software Update or the Server Updates pane in Server Admin is usually easiest. But Mac OS X also gives you two other ways to get software updates:

■ **Get the updates from a server on your network**   What you'll normally want is to have your server pull down the updates from Apple across your Internet connection, and then have the client Macs on your network get the updates from the server. There's no point in having the client Macs beat your Internet connection into submission when they can get the same updates much more quickly across your network connection. Chapter 17 shows you how to persuade your server to provide software updates to the clients. If you have multiple servers, you can have them pluck the updates off the update server as well.

Resetting Ignored Updates

Once you've told Server Updates to ignore a particular update, Server Updates suppresses it from appearing in the New Software Is Available For Your Server list box. If you realize you need one of those ignored updates after all, just click the Reset Ignored Updates button at the bottom of the Server Updates pane. Server Updates fetches the list of all the updates you've shunned and adds them to the list, where you can use them as you could have done before.

■   **Download the updates as disk images**   You can also download the updates
as disk images from Apple's Downloads site (www.apple.com/support/
downloads/). You can then either apply the updates from the files or put them
on an optical disc or a USB drive and take them with you. Having the updates
to hand is great when you need to apply the updates to servers that do not have
fast or reliable Internet connections—especially if you need to apply the same
updates to many servers.

Securing Your Server's Hardware

In most cases, the first step toward keeping your server safe is to secure its hardware.
When push comes to shove, all the firewalls and encryption in the world won't do you
much good if someone can waltz into your building, slide the server under their trench
coat, and then vamoose to parts unknown.

Locating Your Server Safely

First, locate your server somewhere safe. Chances are, you've done this already—but if
not, better now than later.

In most cases, the best location for a server is a dedicated computer room protected
by decent locks (and, if you have them to hand, some of the more ingenious booby traps
from the Temple of Doom). Failing that, a locked office will do—or a locked closet. Don't
leave the server right out in the middle of the action, no matter how deeply you trust
and adore your colleagues. Bad things will happen to it.

Make sure that your server room—or closet, or whatever—has its own power
supply that won't get turned off accidentally. You've probably heard stories about
grizzled network administrators lurking in wait to solve apparently intractable
power problems, only to see the office cleaner briskly unplug the server to provide a
handy socket for the vacuum. There's painful truth behind such stories, and this is an
experience you can certainly do without.

Protecting Your Server Against Power Outages

Within your server's stockade, use an uninterruptible power supply, or UPS, to protect
the machine against power outages and surges.

Uninterruptible power supplies come in wildly differing capabilities, ranging from
the cost of a family dinner somewhere mildly tasty to the cost of a decent car. Chances
are that you'll need something in the middle for your server.

Use a template such as the one at the American Power Conversion website (www.apc
.com/tools/ups_selector/) to calculate the amount of power it'll take to keep your
server running until you can either shut it down gracefully or switch it to an alternative
source of power. Make sure that the UPS has enough power sockets and juice to run
all the hardware you need, not just the server—you don't want to find that the ancient
CRT that you've burdened the server with leaves you high and dry by scarfing down
vital minutes of battery life.

Also make sure that the UPS provides surge protection for as much equipment as you need to shield. Many UPS models include both surge-protected sockets that run on battery power and surge-protected sockets that do not; the latter are for equipment that needs surge protection, but that you do not need to run when the power goes out.

Securing Your Server's Software

As well as protecting your server against hardware problems, you need to secure its software. This section discusses five main steps toward this goal:

- Enabling the Mac OS X firewall if your network needs it
- Changing the default password on the root account
- Setting up other administrator accounts as needed…
- … and keeping the administrator accounts secure
- Getting and installing an SSL certificate on your server

Let's dive in with the firewall.

Enabling the Mac OS X Firewall and Choosing Which Services to Expose

If you have connected your server directly to the Internet rather than connecting it through a firewall (for example, the firewall on your router), you need to turn on the Mac OS X firewall to protect the server from Internet threats. Once on, the firewall prevents any services from reaching the server except for services that you allow to come through the firewall. Allowing a service through the firewall is called *exposing* a service.

NOTE If you have protected your server with an external firewall, you do not need to enable the Mac OS X firewall.

To enable the firewall and choose which services to expose, follow these steps:

1. In the main pane of Server Preferences, click the Security icon to open the Security pane (see Figure 4-7).
2. Slide the master switch from the Off position to the On position. The Security pane displays controls for specifying which services to expose through the firewall (see Figure 4-8).
3. Check the list of services that the server is currently exposing.

NOTE If you chose to enable remote login during installation, the Remote Login (SSH) service appears in the Expose These Services On My Firewall list box. Otherwise, a fresh installation of Mac OS X Server exposes no services.

Figure 4-7.   In the Security pane in Server Preferences, slide the master switch to On to turn on the firewall.

4. To remove an exposed service, click it, and then click the – button.

5. To add a service, follow these steps:

    a. Click the + button below the Expose These Services On My Firewall list box to open the Add Service dialog box.

    b. Click the pop-up menu, and then choose the service from the list shown in Figure 4-9.

Figure 4-8.   With the firewall turned on, you can choose which services to allow through it.

Figure 4-9. You can quickly add one of the most widely exposed services from the pop-up menu in the Add Service dialog box.

    c. If the service doesn't appear in the pop-up menu, click Other to display an additional line of controls in the dialog box (see Figure 4-10). Fill in the service name and the port it uses.

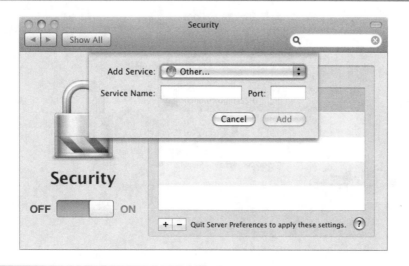

Figure 4-10. Use the Other option to add a service by name and port.

    d. Click the Add button. The dialog box closes, and the service appears in the Expose These Services On My Firewall list box.

6. To apply the changes you've made, press ⌘-Q or choose Server Preferences | Quit Server Preferences. Server Preferences quits, and Mac OS X Server turns on the firewall and exposes only the services you chose.

Changing the Password on the Root Account

During setup, you applied a password to the Administrator account that you set up. When you did this, Mac OS X automatically applied this password to the System Administrator account—the root account—to give it a password for protection.

To keep your server secure, give the root account a different password than the Administrator password. To change the root password, follow these steps:

1. Choose Apple | System Preferences to open the System Preferences window.

2. In the System area, click the Accounts icon to display the Accounts screen.

3. Click the Login Options button to display the Login Options pane (see Figure 4-11).

Figure 4-11.   Click the Join button in the Login Options pane in Accounts preferences. If there's no Join button, click the Edit button.

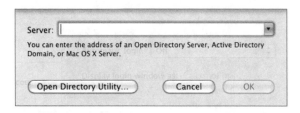

Figure 4-12. Click the Open Directory Utility button in this dialog box.

4. Click the Join button to display the dialog box shown in Figure 4-12. If the Edit button appears instead of the Join button, click it instead.

5. Click the Open Directory Utility button to launch Directory Utility (see Figure 4-13).

6. If the lock icon in the lower-left corner of the Directory Utility window is closed, click the icon to display the authentication dialog box (see Figure 4-14). Make sure the user name is correct, type the right password, and then click the OK button to spring the lock open.

7. Choose Edit | Change Root Password to display the dialog box shown in Figure 4-15.

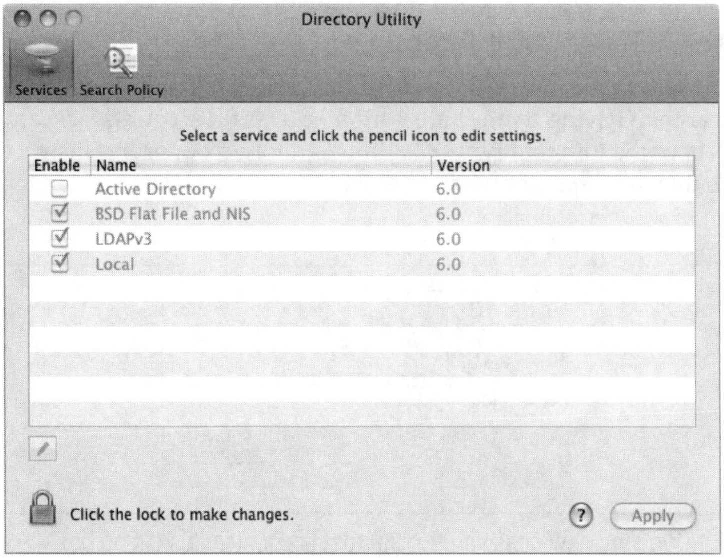

Figure 4-13. From Directory Utility, you can change the root password.

Figure 4-14. You'll need to authenticate yourself before you can change the password on the root account.

8. Type the new password in both the Password text box and the Verify text box.

9. Click the OK button. The dialog box closes, and Directory Utility applies the password with no comment.

10. Click the open lock icon to close the lock again and prevent further changes.

11. Press ⌘-Q or choose Directory Utility | Quit Directory Utility to quit Directory Utility.

12. Press ⌘-Q or choose System Preferences | Quit System Preferences to quit System Preferences.

Setting Up Other Administrator Accounts

If other people will need to administer the server, set up suitable administrator accounts for them rather than having them share your all-powerful accounts. See Chapter 7 for information about the different types of administrator accounts and instructions on how to create both them and regular user accounts.

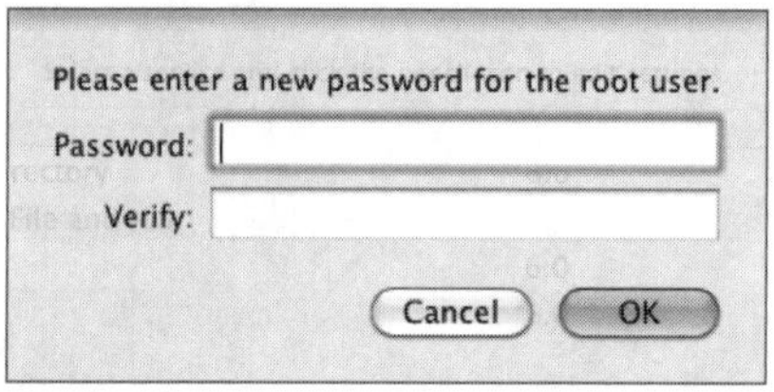

Figure 4-15. Type the new password for the root account in this dialog box.

Keeping the Administrator Accounts Secure

To keep your server's Administrator accounts secure, make sure that nobody unauthorized can log on to your server. Follow these measures:

- **Keep your account names and passwords secret** Avoid using standard names such as Administrator for your accounts, and never share the account names with others, no matter how trustworthy they may seem. Never tell anyone a password other than the password for their own account. (And don't write the passwords on sticky notes and tape them to the server's monitor either.)

- **Use a standard user account for normal work** If you work on the server rather than a workstation, log on using a standard user account. When you need to administer the server, either log out from the standard account and log back in using an Administrator account, or simply provide your Administrator account name and password when Mac OS X Server displays the Authenticate dialog box.

- **Turn off automatic login** Mac OS X's automatic login feature (in the Login Options pane in System Preferences) is dangerous even on standalone Macs in home settings. Never use automatic login on servers, even with a standard account rather than an Administrator account: Instead, make sure the server displays the login screen so that each user must log in.

- **Log out when you are not using the server** Staying logged in to the server when you are not physically present to defend the keyboard and mouse is asking for trouble, even if you just march into the next office for a minute to quell a colleague. Ideally, you'd log out manually each time you step away from the server, but it's sensible to have Mac OS X help you on this by making the screen saver activate as soon as possible and requiring a password to turn it off. Follow these steps:

  1. CTRL-click or right-click the Desktop and choose Change Desktop Background to open the Desktop & Screen Saver pane in the System Preferences window.

  2. Click the Screen Saver tab to display its contents (see Figure 4-16).

  3. Choose the screen saver you want to use.

  4. Drag the Start Screen Saver slider all the way to the left—to 3 Minutes or a similar setting.

  5. Click the Show All button to display all the System Preferences.

  6. In the Personal category at the top, click the Security icon to open the Security preferences pane (see Figure 4-17).

  7. Select the Require Password After Sleep Or Screen Saver Begins check box.

  8. Open the pop-up menu and choose either Immediately (the best choice) or a short time (such as 5 Seconds or 1 Minutes).

  9. Press ⌘-Q or choose System Preferences | Quit System Preferences to quit System Preferences.

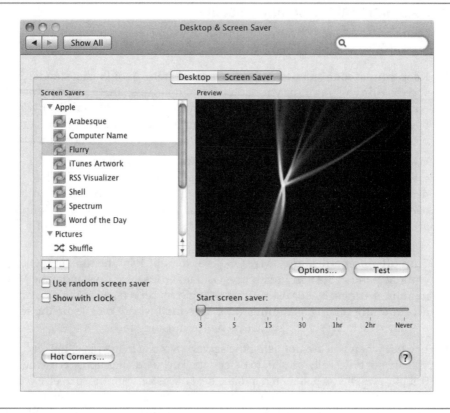

Figure 4-16.   Set the screen saver to start as soon as possible when you leave your server idle.

Getting and Installing an SSL Certificate

Next, you may need to install a digital certificate on your server so that clients can connect to it securely and authenticate it. The type of digital certificate you need is a Secure Sockets Layer (SSL) certificate, which gives three main benefits:

- **Secure connection**   The certificate provides a secure connection across a network that's not secure—for example, the Internet—by encrypting the information passed between the computers.

- **Authentication**   The certificate enables another computer to authenticate your server, establishing its identity beyond doubt.

- **Identity and trust**   As the old joke goes, on the Internet, nobody knows you're a dog. But because the SSL certificate is tied to its holder's real-world identity, a client that connects to your server can check exactly what kind of dog your company is. (Well, your server, anyway.)

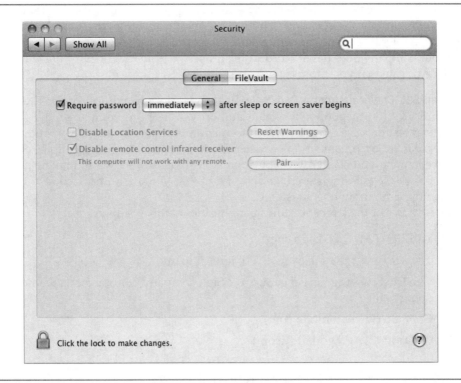

Figure 4-17.   Select the Require Password After Sleep Or Screen Saver Begins check box on the General tab of the Security pane, and then choose Immediately or a short time in the pop-up menu.

SSL certificates come from certificate authorities, abbreviated to CAs. You can also create an SSL certificate of your own using a tool that Mac OS X Server provides.

Getting an SSL Certificate

The first step is to get an SSL certificate that you can use. You can do this in three main ways:

- **Get a certificate from your company**   This is the best option—but only if your company runs its own certificate authority.
- **Buy a digital certificate from a certificate authority**   This is the normal approach.
- **Create a digital certificate yourself**   A certificate you create this way is not trustworthy but can act as a stopgap until you get a commercial SSL certificate. You also use a self-signed certificate to create the certificate signing request (CSR) file that you send to a CA when applying for a commercial certificate.

Getting an SSL Certificate from Your Company   Your company may run a certificate authority of its own to supply the certificates it needs; as you'd imagine, this is something that larger companies tend to do more than small companies.

If your company does have a certificate authority, apply to whoever runs the CA for an SSL certificate that you can use with your server.

Getting an SSL Certificate from a Certificate Authority   The normal approach is to get an SSL certificate from a public certificate authority. These are companies that provide SSL certificates for a fee. You provide information that enables the CA to authenticate your company's or organization's existence and credentials—for example, checking that the company you claim owns your domain actually does own it; making sure that the company is legally registered; and verifying that you are authorized to act for the company rather than pulling a fast one.

Here are five of the largest certificate authorities at this writing:

- **VeriSign** (www.verisign.com)
- **Thawte** (www.thawte.com; a VeriSign company)
- **GeoTrust** (www.geotrust.com; a VeriSign company; you can see a theme developing here)
- **Comodo** (www.comodo.com)
- **GoDaddy** (www.godaddy.com)

NOTE   Most certificate authorities offer a free trial of SSL certificates. For example, Thawte offers a 21-day free trial, while Comodo offers a 90-day free trial.

To get your commercial SSL certificate, you'll need to create a self-signed certificate that you can use to generate the CSR file the CA needs. We'll look at this process next.

Creating an SSL Certificate Yourself   The third way of getting an SSL certificate is to create it yourself by using a tool that Mac OS X Server provides.

An SSL certificate you create yourself inspires as much trust as a three-dollar bill, so it's not something you'll want to use for authentication for long. But you can use it for two purposes:

- As a temporary certificate to identify your server
- To create the CSR file required for a CA to authenticate you and your company so that the CA can provide a commercial-grade certificate

To create an SSL certificate you can use like this, follow these steps:

1. Open Server Preferences. For example, click the Server Preferences icon on the Dock.
2. Click the Information icon to display the Information pane (see Figure 4-18).

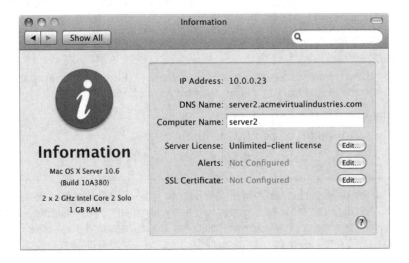

Figure 4-18.   Click the Edit button on the SSL Certificate line to start creating an SSL certificate.

3. Click the Edit button on the SSL Certificate line to display the Use An SSL Certificate dialog box (see Figure 4-19).

4. Select the Use SSL Certificate check box.

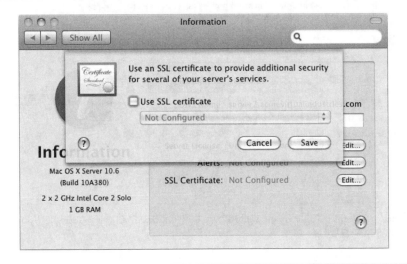

Figure 4-19.   Use this dialog box to tell Mac OS X Server which SSL certificate to use.

5. Click the pop-up menu and choose Certificate Import | Create Self-Signed Certificate (see Figure 4-20).

6. Server Preferences launches Certificate Assistant, which displays an Introduction screen and then the Create Your Certificate screen (see Figure 4-21).

7. Type the name for the certificate in the Name text box—for example, your company name, department title, or your own moniker.

8. In the Identity Type pop-up menu, choose Self Signed Root.

9. In the Certificate Type pop-up menu, choose SSL Server.

10. Make sure the Let Me Override Defaults check box is cleared.

NOTE   If you select the Let Me Override Defaults check box, Certificate Assistant walks you through a half-dozen screens that let you specify everything from the serial number and validity period of the certificate to the type of encryption used and the uses for the certificate. If you're creating an SSL certificate to practice using certificates, the default settings should be fine.

11. Click the Continue button. Certificate Assistant displays the You Are About To Create a Self-Signed Certificate dialog box (see Figure 4-22), warning you that the certificate has no security guarantee.

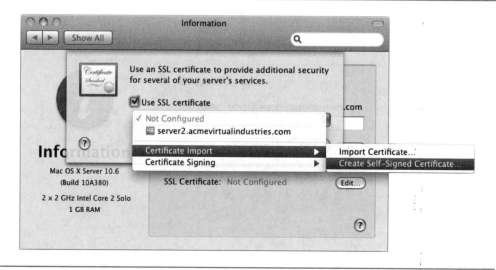

Figure 4-20.   You can create a self-signed SSL certificate to bridge the gap until you get a proper SSL certificate from a CA.

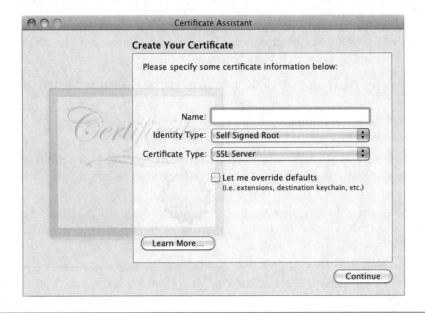

Figure 4-21. Type a name for your SSL certificate on the Create Your Certificate screen of Certificate Assistant.

12. This is fine, so click the Continue button. Certificate Assistant then creates the certificate and installs it.

13. Click the Save button to close the Use An SSL Certificate dialog box. The certificate's name appears on the SSL Certificate readout in the Information pane.

14. Leave Server Preferences open for the moment so that you can create your CSR file.

Figure 4-22. Certificate Assistant makes sure you know the shortcomings of the certificate you're issuing yourself.

Creating a Certificate Signing Request File from Your Self-Signed Certificate

Now that you have created a self-signed certificate, use it to create a certificate signing request (CSR) file that you can submit to a CA with your application for an SSL certificate. Follow these steps to create the CSR file:

1. In Server Preferences, click the Information icon to display the Information pane.

2. Click the Edit button on the SSL Certificate line to open the Use An SSL Certificate dialog box.

3. Click the pop-up menu and choose Certificate Signing | Generate Certificate Signing Request. Mac OS X displays a dialog box containing the CSR file (see Figure 4-23).

4. To save the CSR file, click the Save button, use the resulting dialog box to choose the folder in which you want to save the file and enter the file name, and then click the Save button.

NOTE If the CA requires you to paste the text of the CSR into a field in a web form, click in the text of the CSR, and then press ⌘-A to select all the text. You can then copy the text by pressing ⌘-C or Control+clicking or right-clicking and choosing Copy from the shortcut menu.

5. Click the Close button to close the dialog box.

6. Click the Save button to close the Use An SSL Certificate dialog box.

7. Press ⌘-Q or choose Server Preferences | Quit Server Preferences to quit Server Preferences.

Figure 4-23. From this dialog box, you can copy the text of the CSR file or save it to a text document that you can use later.

Installing an SSL Certificate

After you get a commercial SSL certificate, install it like this:

1. Open Server Preferences. For example, click the Server Preferences icon on the Dock.

2. Click the Information icon to display the Information pane.

3. Click the Edit button on the SSL Certificate line to open the Use An SSL Certificate dialog box.

4. Click the pop-up menu and choose Certificate Signing | Replace With Signed Or Renewed Certificate. Mac OS X displays the dialog box shown in Figure 4-24.

5. Drag in your replacement certificate from a Finder window or from the desktop, and drop it in this dialog box.

6. Click the Replace Certificate button.

7. Click the Save button to close the Use An SSL Certificate dialog box.

8. Press ⌘-Q or choose Server Preferences | Quit Server Preferences to quit Server Preferences.

Right, it's time to get to grips with Open Directory. Take a deep breath, and then turn the page.

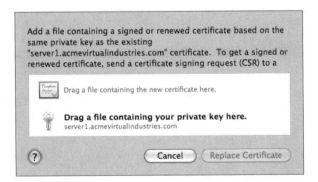

Figure 4-24.   Drag your signed certificate to this window to replace the self-signed certificate.

CHAPTER 5 | Set Up Open Directory

To keep your network organized and running smoothly and to keep you sane and smiling, Mac OS X Server provides a directory service called Open Directory. This chapter starts by running through what Open Directory is, how it works, and how it benefits you and your network. You'll then learn how to set up the three Open Directory configurations you're most likely to need:

- **Single-server network**   For a single-server network, you set up that server as an Open Directory master server. This server handles all the Open Directory data and requests for the entire network.

- **Multi-server network**   If your network will have large numbers of users, or will have users in several different locations that are not connected by high-speed network links, you set up one server as the Open Directory master server and other servers as Open Directory replica servers. The replica servers either provide directory services for different parts of the network (such as remote offices) or simply do some of the grunt work for the master server.

- **Standalone server**   For very small networks, you may need to set up the server so that it handles Open Directory only for itself rather than for other computers on the network. This setup is relatively unusual—but you may be, too.

At the end of the chapter, you'll learn how to install the Server Administration Software on a client Mac so that you can administer your servers remotely from it. You can also administer one server remotely from another as needed.

Right, let's get started.

Understanding Directory Services and Their Advantages

Mac OS X Server uses a directory called Open Directory to store network information. The directory is a central storage location that makes it easier to administer, maintain, and use the network. These are all advantages well worth having, as the only downside to having a directory is that you must do a little planning ahead of time and then set it up the right way.

By consolidating the network's data in a central location, directory services give you (and each other user of the network) a single user account on the directory that stores details of the Macs and resources you're permitted to use. This is much better than requiring a separate user account on each Mac you log on to, with separate permissions for each account controlling the printers, file servers, and other items you need to access.

If you need to work efficiently using different Macs on the network at different times, you can store your home folder on a network file server rather than on a particular Mac. When you log in to the network, the directory makes the items in your home folder available for you to use, no matter which physical Mac you are actually using. You don't waste precious minutes and brain cells tracking, copying, and synchronizing your files and folders manually.

That's great for you as the user—but who else benefits? First, the applications on the network benefit too, as the directory gives them a single standard way to access the information stored in the directory. Instead of needing to consult a variety of configuration files stored in different folders, an application need only consult the directory to find the information it needs.

If you're the one administering the network, as we're assuming here, you benefit too. You need enter or change information only in a single central location in the directory to change it throughout the network. This saves a huge amount of time and effort over making the changes on multiple servers separately, let alone having to make the changes on every computer on the network.

Similarly, because the directory logs most of the actions that occur on the network, you (or another administrator) can easily follow and audit what is going on. For example, you can review the logs to see when users log in and out, or to determine which files, disks, and printers are used the most. If someone goofs up and obliterates a vital file, you can identify the perpetrator and revoke his permissions to wreak havoc—after which you can restore the file from backup.

Understanding Local and Shared Directory Domains

Inside a directory, the information is organized into areas called *domains*. A directory domain can be either local or shared, as explained in the following sections.

Local Directory Domain

The *local directory domain* is stored on the Mac OS X client computer or server itself. The information in the local directory domain is accessible only to applications or system processes running on that Mac or server, not to those running on other computers on the network.

When you try to log in to your Mac, Open Directory first searches the Mac's local directory for your record to see whether you have permission to log in and (assuming you do), whether your password matches the stored password. If all is well, login continues, and you can then use the Mac. If you then try to access a server on the network, Open Directory checks your record on the server to see whether you have permission to access what you're attempting to reach and whether you're provided the required password. Figure 5-1 shows how this two-stage process typically works, using a shared directory domain on the server.

Shared Directory Domains

Local directory domains work fine when you're using a single Mac or a network built around a single server, but when your network is bigger, shared directory domains come into play. Mac OS X normally stores shared directory domains on servers rather than on workstations.

After you set a Mac up to use a shared domain, the applications and system processes on the Mac can access the data in the shared domain. This enables Open Directory to search the shared directory domains for the user's record.

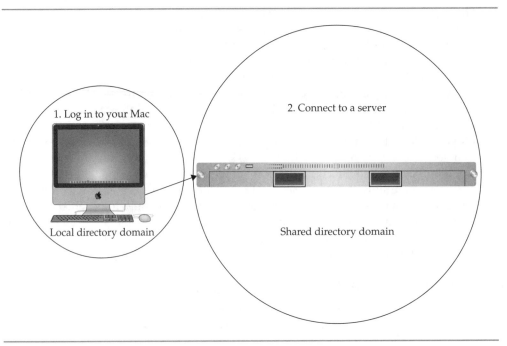

Figure 5-1. You log on to your Mac using its local directory domain. When you connect to a server, you use the shared directory domain.

So when you try to log in to a networked Mac on which you do not have an account, Open Directory first searches the local directory domain for a user record. When that search comes up drier than a good martini, Open Directory searches the shared directory domains accessible to the Mac, so it finds your user account in the network directory and can determine whether you may log in to the Mac.

NOTE Even when a Mac is a member of a domain, it always searches the local directory domain before the shared directory domains. So if the Mac is disconnected from the network (for example, because it's a MacBook that you've taken on the road), you can still log in.

Understanding How Open Directory Works with Windows Computers

If your network includes PCs running Windows, you can configure Open Directory to play nice with them.

You can set up your Open Directory master server running Mac OS X Server to act as a primary domain controller (PDC) for Windows PCs. This enables PC users to log in to domain accounts just as if they were logging in to a Windows Server network. What's even smarter is that Mac OS X Server makes the user account available to both

Windows and Mac OS X. So you can log in on a PC one day, on a Mac the next, and have the same network-based home folder and mail accounts on either platform.

NOTE Mac OS X Server works with Windows 7, Windows Vista, Windows XP, Windows 2000 Professional, and even Windows NT 4 Workstation. You can also connect Linux and UNIX clients to your Mac OS X Server network.

In case your PDC takes a break or a tumble, you can set up another Mac OS X server to act as a backup domain controller (BDC). First, you make that server an Open Directory replica by using Server Admin, and then you tell it to play the BDC role.

The BDC automatically copies the directory data from the PDC and keeps it synchronized so that it can handle directory requests when the PDC is not available.

Figure 5-2 shows a Mac OS X Server network that uses both a PDC and a BDC to look after its Windows clients. The Mac clients log straight into Open Directory on the master server as usual, or on the replica server if the master server is fully entertained.

NOTE Your network can have only one PDC. If you try to set up two PDCs, they joust for directory supremacy.

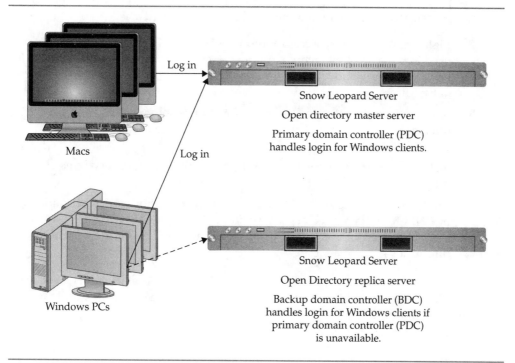

Log in

Macs

Log in

Snow Leopard Server

Open directory master server

Primary domain controller (PDC)
handles login for Windows clients.

Windows PCs

Snow Leopard Server

Open Directory replica server

Backup domain controller (BDC)
handles login for Windows clients if
primary domain controller (PDC)
is unavailable.

Figure 5-2. By setting up your master server as a primary domain controller and another server as a backup domain controller, you can enable Windows PCs to log into the network easily.

Understanding Authentication and Authorization

When you log in to the network, Open Directory *authenticates* you: It verifies that the password you provide matches the user name. Assuming it does, Open Directory considers that it has established your identity satisfactorily.

NOTE   Open Directory doesn't really establish your identity, as you could have shared your user name and password with anyone under the sun. Open Directory's authentication is more like an ATM checking that the PIN you provide matches the bank card you slide in than the Highway Patrol checking that your face matches the photo on your driver's license. But let's leave this nicety aside. One day, networks will establish our identity up to the eyeballs—perhaps by using them.

After authenticating you, Open Directory checks what you are authorized to do: for example, access this server, but not that one; reserve a projector, but not a conference room; or add comments to one wiki, but not scribble insults on another.

Directory Domains That Open Directory Can Access

There are various different standards for directory services on networks. Open Directory can access the following five widely used standards:

■ **Lightweight Directory Access Protocol (LDAP)**   LDAP is an open standard used in networks that include different operating systems (such as Mac OS X, Windows, and UNIX computers). Mac OS X Server uses LDAP as its native directory service for shared directories.

■ **Active Directory**   Active Directory (sometimes abbreviated to AD, but often not to avoid confusion) is the directory service used by Microsoft's Windows Server networks.

■ **Network Information System (NIS)**   NIS is the directory service used by most varieties of UNIX.

■ **BSD flat files**   These files are used by the Berkeley Software Distribution of UNIX to contain directory information. ("Flat" means that the files are more like spreadsheets than the relational database tables used by other directories.)

Open Directory also accesses directory domains in the Local Directory Domain format. This is the format that Mac OS X and Mac OS X Server use for storing local directory information.

Understanding the Tools for Working with Open Directory Services

Mac OS X Server provides three main tools for working with Open Directory:

- **Server Admin**   Server Admin is the set of tools you use for setting Mac OS X Server to be an Open Directory master, replica, server connected to a directory system, or a standalone directory service. You also use Server Admin to configure the services running on the server, and much more. You'll use Server Admin extensively in this chapter, not to mention the rest of the book.

 NOTE   Server Admin and Workgroup Manager appear on the Dock in a default installation of Mac OS X Server. You can also find them in the /Applications/Server/ folder together with most of the other administration tools.

- **Directory Utility**   Directory Utility is the tool you use to configure how a Mac uses directory services and searches for authentication and contacts. You also use Directory Utility to connect to other servers and configure them remotely. Directory Utility is included in a standard Mac OS X installation on both client Macs and servers, but where earlier versions put Directory Utility in the /Applications/Utilities/ folder, Mac OS X 10.6 hides Directory Utility in the /System/Library/CoreServices/ folder and encourages you to run it only from Accounts Preferences. You'll start using Directory Utility in the next few chapters.

- **Workgroup Manager**   Workgroup Manager is the tool you use to create and manage user accounts, group accounts, and computer groups; manage share points for home folders and file services; and set up the folders and computers users see in the Network category in the Finder. You can also open a directory entry in the Inspector to view its details. You'll start using Workgroup Manager in the next several chapters.

 NOTE   Mac OS X Server also includes command-line tools for administering servers. See Chapter 19 for a brief discussion of some of these tools and how you can automate them.

Planning Your Network's Directory

If your network will be small, medium-size, or even moderately large, you need only one shared directory domain to handle all the directory information. In fact, Apple reckons just one shared directory domain can handle several thousand users, computers, and all the other items that need management—share points for home directories, documents, and applications; printer queues; and other shared resources. This makes everything pretty straightforward, as you don't need to worry about which domain to put any piece of information in—it all goes in your one and only shared directory domain.

NOTE   To keep the examples easy, this book assumes you will use a single shared directory domain for your network.

Creating a Single-Server Network

If your network is small or medium size, as most networks are, you can run it off a single server. You set up the server as the network's Open Directory master server, so it handles all the Open Directory data and requests for the entire network.

Creating a Multi-Server Network

If your network does have several thousand users and objects, you still need only one shared directory domain—but it's replicated across multiple servers to spread the load. Otherwise, the network may experience serious slowdowns at rush hour, such as when everyone's trying to log in and haul their home folder and settings across the network so that they can appear productive when their manager marches into the office.

To spread the load across different servers, you create an Open Directory master server with replica servers. The master server is responsible for maintaining the master copy of the directory. Each replica server picks up a copy of the directory from the master server, keeps it synchronized with the latest information, and handles login and authentication requests as needed to reduce the load on the master server.

NOTE   In a huge network that requires many replica servers, you can *cascade* the replica servers in several levels to reduce the load on the master server. In a cascading arrangement, the replica servers linked to the master server pick up their replicas of the directory from it. The second level of replica servers grab their replicas from the first level, and so on down the line.

For a large network on a single site, you locate the replica servers on the site to provide additional capacity. Or if your network has remote offices, you can position a replica server in each office so that the Macs can suck down the data through the LAN at full speed rather than drag it slowly through a WAN link from the master server. Figure 5-3 shows a simple example of this arrangement.

You can update the replica servers either every time the master directory changes or on a schedule:

■   Immediate updating is great when the replica servers have a high-speed connection to the master server.

■   Scheduled updating is best when the replica servers have only a slow connection to the master server—for example, when the replica servers are in remote offices—and you need to conserve bandwidth for important activities, such as senior management checking their 401(K)s online.

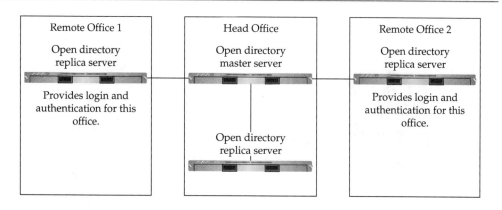

Figure 5-3. To reduce the load on your master server, add replica servers. You can also position a replica server in each remote office to take the pressure off lower-bandwidth connections.

NOTE An Open Directory server can provide up to 1,000 client connections at any given time. LDAP directory connections typically take less than two minutes, and Open Directory Password Server connections usually take less than a minute. This means that the Open Directory server can normally handle far more than 1,000 computers on the network—and the LDAP directory domain database can easily handle 200,000 records at once. So an Open Directory server can handle multiple thousand Macs on the network—but you will get better performance if you do not push the limits.

Creating a Standalone Server for a Very Small Network

If you have only a very small network, you can get away without setting up a shared directory domain by simply running on a local directory domain.

Here's how this works:

1. On each Mac, create an account for each person who will use that Mac—just as you would do if you were using a standalone Mac. Open Directory stores these accounts in the local directory domain on the Mac on which you create them, so when a user tries to log in, the data required for authentication is right there.

2. On your server, create an account for each person who will need to access files on the server, collect mail, or use other services that require authentication. (In a typical network, this means creating an account for everybody who uses the network.) Open Directory stores these accounts in the server's local directory domain, so when a user tries to access the server or another service, the authentication comes from the server's local directory domain rather than from the workstation's local directory domain.

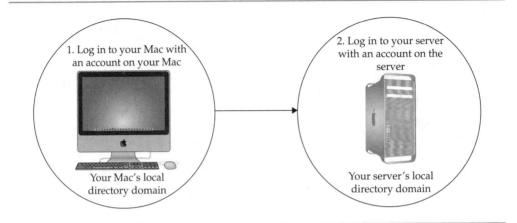

Figure 5-4. In a very small network, you can use separate accounts on each client Mac and on the server, each of which runs its own local directory domain.

If you're tempted to use this arrangement, which Figure 5-4 illustrates, it's important to understand its limitations:

■ First, the user is using two user accounts rather than one—one account for logging on to the workstation Mac, and another for logging on to the server. The user can store their password for the server in their keychain, however, so they need not supply the server password each time they tap into it for files, mail, or another service that requires authentication.

■ Second, and more seriously, the directory information is not shared among the Macs. This means you need to administer the user accounts on each workstation Mac *and* the user accounts on the server. This is practicable for a truly small network, but once your network has more than a couple handfuls of users, admin chores multiply and grow old at terminal velocity.

Setting Up Open Directory on Your Servers

Enough preliminaries—it's time to set up Open Directory on your servers. This section shows you how to do so.

Your first move is to turn on the Open Directory service if it's not already running. You can then set up your Open Directory master server and any replica servers you need. If your network includes Windows PCs, you can set up a primary domain controller to keep them happy, plus a backup domain controller if you have a replica server that's looking for extra action.

Turning On the Open Directory Service

Start by turning on the Open Directory service like this:

1. Click the Server Admin icon on the Dock (or run Server Admin from the /Applications/Server folder) to open Server Admin.

2. Expand the Servers list in the sidebar if it is collapsed, so that you see the list of servers—or a single server if that is all your network has so far.

3. Double-click the server on which you will turn on the Open Directory service.

4. If Mac OS X Server displays the login dialog box shown in Figure 5-5, follow these steps:

    a. Type your password.

    b. Select the Remember This Password In My Keychain check box if you want to store the password.

    c. Click the Connect button. The details for the server appear.

5. Click the Settings button on the toolbar to display the Settings pane.

6. Click the Services tab to display the services (see Figure 5-6).

7. Select the Open Directory check box.

8. Click the Save button to save the change.

9. Leave Server Admin open for the moment, because you can now set up your Open Directory master server.

Setting Up an Open Directory Master Server

Next, you'll need to make your server the Open Directory master so that it runs Open Directory for your network. To do so, follow these steps:

1. In Server Admin, double-click the server in the sidebar, and then authenticate yourself for it if Mac OS X Server challenges you.

2. Expand the server by clicking the disclosure triangle to its left.

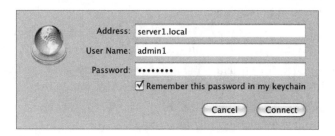

Figure 5-5. You may need to log in to the server to start the Open Directory service. Select the Remember This Password In My Keychain check box if you want to store your password for future use.

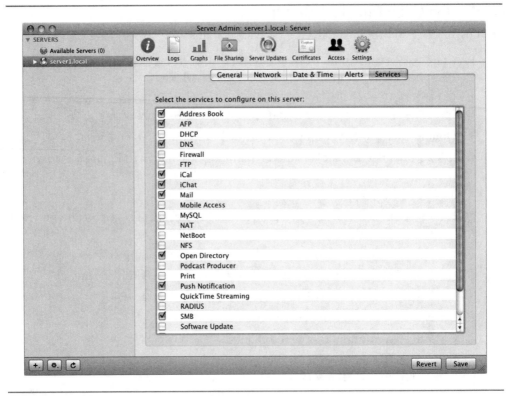

Figure 5-6. Turn on the Open Directory service on the Services tab of the Settings pane in Server Admin.

3. In the list of services under the server, click the Open Directory item.

4. Click the Settings button to display the Settings pane.

5. Click the General tab to display its contents (see Figure 5-7) if the General tab is not already displayed.

6. Look at the Role readout to double-check what the server is currently doing. You'll see one of these roles:

   ■ **Standalone Directory**   The server is hosting only its own directory and is not providing directory information to other computers on the network.

   ■ **Open Directory Master**   The server is already an Open Directory master, which is what you want. You don't need to change the server's role.

   ■ **Connected To Another Directory**   The server is connected to the directory on another server to get its information.

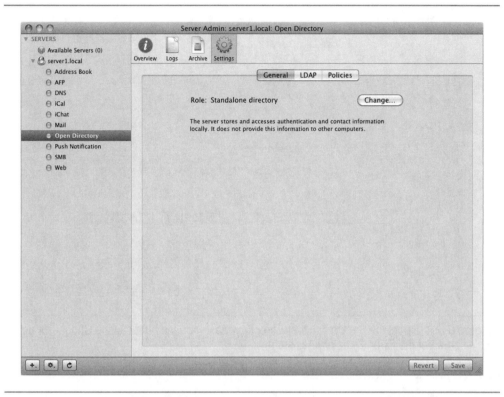

Figure 5-7.   Click the Change button on the General tab of the Settings pane for Open Directory in Server Admin to change your server's role.

■ **Open Directory Replica**   The server is acting as a replica server for an Open Directory master server. The list box on the General tab of the Settings pane shows the replica server's status and the replica tree (click the Replica Tree button) that connects it to the master server.

7. If the server is anything but a master, click the Change button to launch the Open Directory Assistant. The Assistant displays the Choose Directory Role screen (see Figure 5-8).

8. Select the Set Up An Open Directory Master option button.

9. Click the Continue button. The Open Directory Assistant displays the Directory Administrator screen (see Figure 5-9).

10. If necessary, change the account name in the name box. You may wish to leave the account named Directory Administrator for clarity.

11. Similarly, change the account's short name if you want. Again, you may find it easier to leave the account with the default name of diradmin.

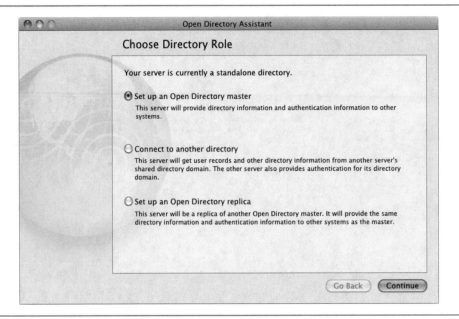

Figure 5-8. Select the Set Up An Open Directory Master option button in the Choose Directory Role screen of the Open Directory Assistant.

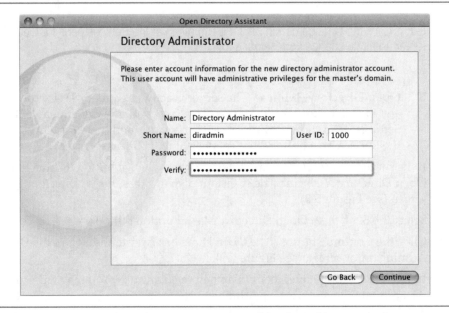

Figure 5-9. On the Directory Administrator screen of the Open Directory Assistant, name your directory administrator account and set a tough-to-break password.

12. Whether you change the names or not, type a strong password in the Password text box and the Verify text box.

13. Click the Continue button. The Open Directory Assistant displays the Domain screen (see Figure 5-10).

14. Verify that the Kerberos Realm text box shows the correct realm for the domain. If not, type in the correct realm.

15. Make sure that the LDAP Search Base text box shows the right search base. Again, correct it if it's wrong.

16. Click the Continue button. The Open Directory Assistant displays the Confirm Settings screen (see Figure 5-11).

17. Click the Continue button. The Open Directory Assistant creates the Open Directory master, and then displays the Summary screen.

18. Click the Done button to close the Open Directory Assistant.

Leave Server Admin open unless you've finished configuring your server.

Setting Up an Open Directory Replica Server

If your network will need Open Directory replica servers, first set up the Open Directory master server as described in the previous section.

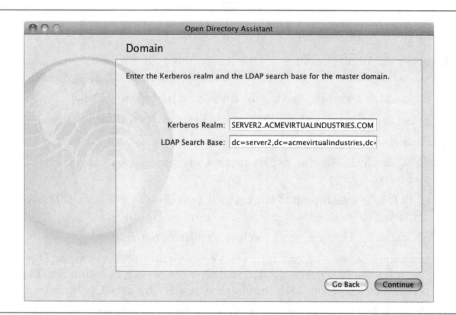

Figure 5-10. On the Domain screen of the Open Directory Assistant, check or change the Kerberos realm and the LDAP search base for the domain.

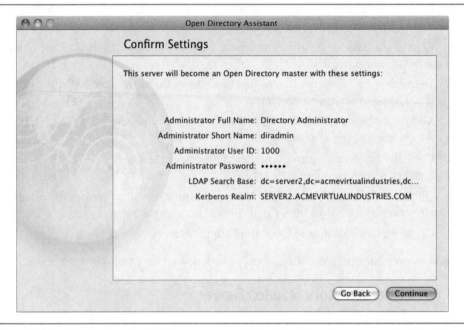

Figure 5-11. On the Confirm Settings screen, double check the changes you're about to make to the Open Directory master server.

You can then set up each replica server like this:

1. In Server Admin, double-click the server in the sidebar, and then authenticate yourself for it.

2. Expand the server by clicking the disclosure triangle to its left.

3. In the list of services under the server, click the Open Directory item.

4. Click the Settings button to display the Settings pane.

5. Click the General tab to display its contents if the General tab is not already displayed.

6. Click the Change button to launch the Open Directory Assistant. The Assistant displays the Choose Directory Role screen (see Figure 5-12).

7. Select the Set Up An Open Directory Replica option button.

8. Click the Continue button. If this server was a master server, Open Directory Assistant displays the confirmation dialog box shown in Figure 5-13 to make certain you know you're destroying the master. Click the Continue button.

9. Open Directory Assistant displays the Replica screen (see Figure 5-14).

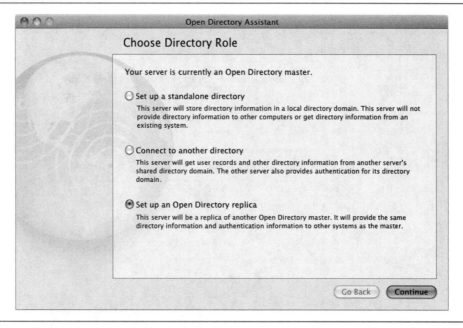

Figure 5-12. Select the Set Up An Open Directory Replica option button on the Choose Directory Role screen of the Open Directory Assistant.

10. Type the details of the Open Directory master server you want to replicate:

- **IP Address Or DNS Name Of Master**   Type the IP address (often easier) or the DNS name of the master server.

- **Root Password On Master**   Type the master server's root password—the password for the **system administrator** user.

- **Domain administrator's short name**   Type the name of the domain administrator's account you're using to authenticate yourself.

- **Domain administrator's password**   Type the password for the account you're using.

Figure 5-13. If you're destroying a master server to create a replica server, you'll need to confirm the action.

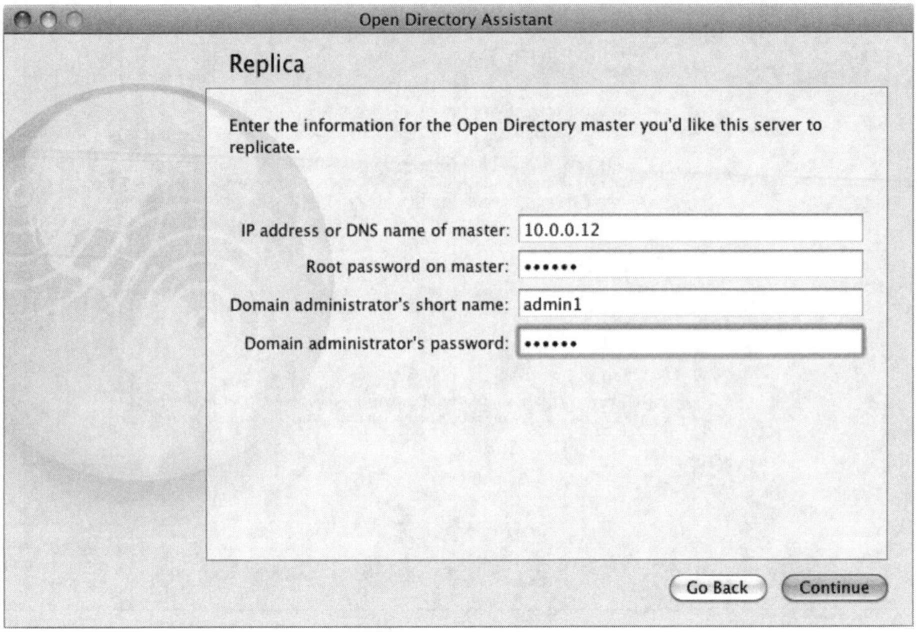

Figure 5-14. On the Replica screen, tell Open Directory Assistant which Open Directory master server you're replicating.

11. Click the Continue button. Open Directory Assistant verifies the information, and then displays the Confirm Settings screen (see Figure 5-15).

12. Check through the information—getting something wrong here can have painful results—and then click the Continue button when all is in apple-pie order.

13. The Open Directory Assistant creates the Open Directory replica on the server. Depending on how big your directory is, this can take quite a while, so you might want to plan some entertainment or sustenance while it runs.

14. When the replica is complete, the Open Directory Assistant displays the Summary screen.

15. Click the Done button to close the Open Directory Assistant.

The details of the replica then appear on the General tab of the Settings pane for Open Directory (see Figure 5-16).

Set Up Primary and Backup Domain Controllers for Windows Boxes

If your Mac OS X Server network includes Windows boxes, you will probably want to set up your master Open Directory server as a primary domain controller (PDC) so that the Windows users can log in to the network with a single name and password. You may

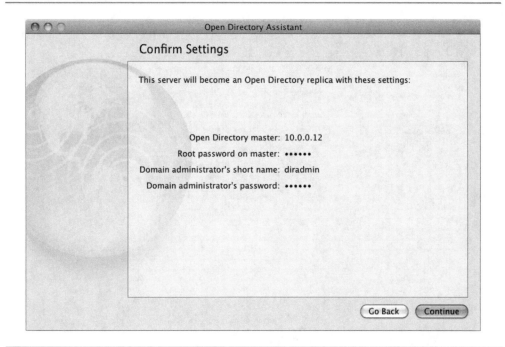

Figure 5-15.   Verify the information on the Confirm Settings screen of the Open Directory Assistant.

also want to set up an Open Directory replica server as a backup domain controller (BDC) to provide login and authentication services for Windows users when the PDC is on strike.

NOTE   If your network uses a single server, you'll be able to create only a PDC. This will do the job fine unless and until you expand the network.

Set Up a Primary Domain Controller

To make your Mac OS X Open Directory master server into the PDC for Windows PCs on the network, follow these steps:

1. In Server Admin, double-click the server in the sidebar, and then authenticate yourself for it.

NOTE   You must authenticate yourself using a directory administrator account rather than a local administrator account for the server.

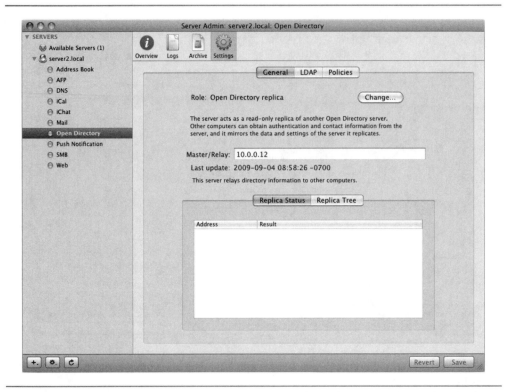

Figure 5-16. The General tab of the Settings pane for Open Directory in Server Admin shows the details of the replica.

2. Click the Settings button to display the Settings pane.

3. Click the Services tab to display its contents (see Figure 5-17).

4. If the SMB check box is not selected, select it, and then click the Save button. (If the SMB check box is already selected, you needn't take either action.) Mac OS X Server saves the changes and makes the Save button unavailable again.

5. If the server is collapsed, expand the server by clicking the disclosure triangle to its left.

6. Click the SMB service in the left pane to display the SMB settings (see Figure 5-18).

7. Open the Role pop-up menu and choose Primary Domain Controller (PDC) from it.

8. Type the description for the PDC in the Description text box—for example, **Acme Primary Domain Controller** or **Acme Windows Login Server**.

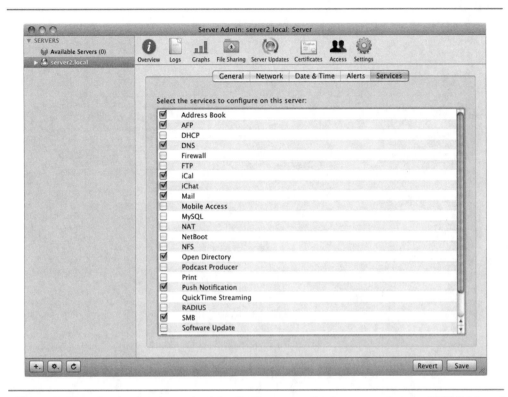

Figure 5-17. On the Services tab of the Settings pane for the server, turn on SMB if it is not already on.

9. If necessary, edit the server's name in the Computer Name text box. This is a NetBIOS name, so keep it to 15 characters or fewer, with letters and numbers only and no punctuation.

10. Also if necessary, edit or change the domain name in the Domain text box. This also has a 15-character limit.

11. Click the Save button to save the changes you've made.

12. If Mac OS X Server displays the Authentication Is Required To Save Role, Name, Or Domain Changes dialog box (see Figure 5-19), type the domain administrator's login name and password, and then click the OK button.

13. Leave Server Admin open if you need to perform further configuration. Otherwise, press ⌘-Q to quit Server Admin.

Set Up a Backup Domain Controller

If your network is large or complex, or if it simply needs redundancy, set up one or more backup domain controllers (BDCs) to help out the PDC. Each BDC must be an

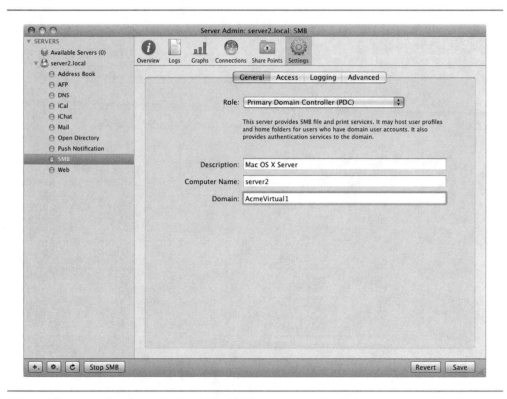

Figure 5-18. In the General tab of the SMB pane, open the Role pop-up menu and choose Primary Domain Controller.

Figure 5-19. You may need to authenticate yourself as a domain administrator when you are turning an Open Directory master server into a primary domain controller.

Open Directory replica server, so make sure you've set up your replica servers, as discussed earlier in this chapter, before you try to set up a BDC.

To set up a BDC, follow these steps:

1. In Server Admin, double-click the server in the sidebar, and then authenticate yourself for it. As when creating the PDC, you must authenticate yourself using a directory administrator account rather than a local administrator account.

2. Click the Settings button to display the Settings pane.

3. Click the Services tab to display its contents.

4. If the SMB check box is not selected, select it, and then click the Save button. (If the SMB check box is already selected, you needn't take either action.) Mac OS X Server saves the changes and makes the Save button unavailable again.

5. If the server is collapsed, expand the server by clicking the disclosure triangle to its left.

6. Click the SMB service in the left pane to display the SMB settings.

7. Open the Role pop-up menu and choose Backup Domain Controller (BDC) from it.

8. Type the description for the BDC in the Description text box—for example, **Acme Backup Domain Controller**.

9. Type the server's name in the Computer Name text box. As before, this is a NetBIOS name, so you're limited to 15 characters or fewer, and you can't use punctuation or spaces, just letters and numbers.

10. Type or edit the domain name in the Domain text box. Again, 15 characters is your max, but you know the drill by now.

11. Click the Save button to save the changes you've made.

12. If Mac OS X Server displays the Authentication Is Required To Save Role, Name, Or Domain Changes dialog box, type the domain administrator's login name and password, and then click the OK button.

Setting Up a Standalone Directory

If you're creating a small network that will not use a shared directory domain, set the server up like this:

1. In Server Admin, double-click the server in the sidebar, and then authenticate yourself for it.

2. Expand the server by clicking the disclosure triangle to its left.

3. In the list of services under the server, click the Open Directory item.

4. Click the Settings button to display the Settings pane.

5. Click the General tab to display its contents if the General tab is not already displayed.

6. Click the Change button to launch the Open Directory Assistant. The Assistant displays the Choose Directory Role screen.

7. Select the Set Up A Standalone Directory option button.

8. Click the Continue button. If this server was a master server, Open Directory Assistant displays a dialog box to confirm that you want to destroy the master and get rid of the account information. Click the Continue button.

9. Open Directory Assistant displays the Confirm Settings screen.

10. Click the Continue button. The Open Directory Assistant sets up the server as a standalone directory, and then displays the summary screen confirming the setup.

11. Click the Done button to close the Open Directory Assistant.

12. Quit Server Admin if you have finished working in it.

Managing Your Servers Remotely

If your servers are located somewhere inaccessible or inhospitable, you can administer them either from another server located somewhere more pleasant or from a client Mac instead—for example, from your MacBook.

To administer your servers from a client Mac, you must first install the Server Administration Software on that Mac, as discussed next. You can then connect to your servers from anywhere that has an Internet connection, as explained in the section after that.

 NOTE   The Server Administration Software consists of Server Admin, Server Monitor, Server Preferences, Workgroup Manager, System Image Utility, Xgrid Admin, iCal Server Utility, and Podcast Composer.

Installing the Server Administration Software on a Client Mac

To install the Server Administration Software on a Mac running Snow Leopard, follow these steps:

1. Insert the Mac OS X Server installation disc in the optical drive.

2. In the Finder window that opens showing the contents of the disc, double-click the Other Installs folder to open it.

Figure 5-20.   You can install the Server Administration Software on any client Mac from which you want to manage your servers.

    NOTE   If Mac OS X doesn't open a Finder window showing the contents of the disc, click the Finder button on the Dock to open a Finder window; then click the DVD's icon in the sidebar.

3. Double-click the ServerAdministrationSoftware.mpkg icon.

4. Installer opens and displays the Install Server Administration Software screen (see Figure 5-20).

5. Click the Continue button, and then follow through the process of installing the software. You'll need to accept the license agreement and authenticate yourself, but beyond that there are no complications.

Running the Server Administration Software Applications on a Client Mac

Once you've installed the Server Administration Software, you can run any of the applications just like any other application on your Mac. You'll find the Server Administration applications in the same place on the client Mac as on your servers— in the /Applications/Server/ folder.

You can run the applications from here, but you may prefer to give yourself an easier way to run them. For example, drag Server Admin itself to the part of the Dock to the left of the Dock's divider line to keep it there, or drag the whole Server folder to the right side of the Dock to create a stack that gives you instant access to each of the applications.

Connecting to a Remote Server Using Server Admin

To connect to one of your servers using Server Admin on a client Mac, follow these steps:

1. Launch Server Admin from the /Applications/Server/ folder or from whichever Dock icon or alias you've created. Server Admin opens and displays the login dialog box shown in Figure 5-21.

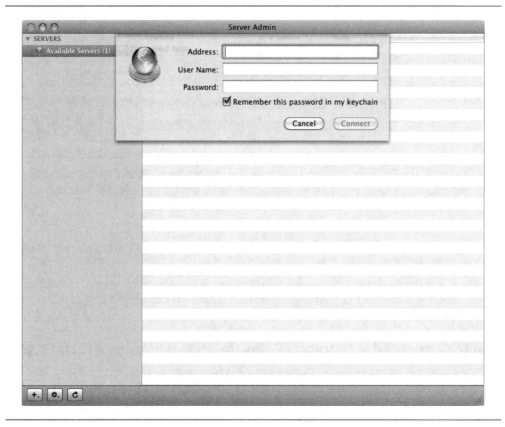

Figure 5-21.   Specify the address of the server to which you want to connect.

2. If you know the hostname or IP address of the server to which you need to connect, you can simply type it in, together with your user name and password, and click the Connect button. But what you'll often need to do is click the Cancel button to dismiss the login dialog box so that you can choose a server from the Available Servers list (see Figure 5-22).

NOTE If you're connecting from outside your company's premises, you'll probably want to connect via VPN for security. See Chapter 15 for instructions on setting up a VPN and using it to connect to your network.

3. Double-click the server in the Available Servers list, and up pops the login dialog box with the server's address and your user name already populating the text boxes.

4. In the User Name text box, change the user name if you use a different one for the server you're accessing than for the Mac you're using.

5. Type your server password in the Password text box.

6. Select the Remember This Password In My Keychain check box if you want to store the server password in this Mac's keychain for future use. Storing the password is convenient, but reduces your network's security—for example, someone might lift your MacBook while you're still logged in, which would let them take advantage of your keychain.

7. Click the Connect button. Server Admin connects to the server and displays its details (see Figure 5-23). You can then manage the server just as if you were sitting at it—short of administering perfectly judged slaps upside its case to cure hardware niggles, anyway.

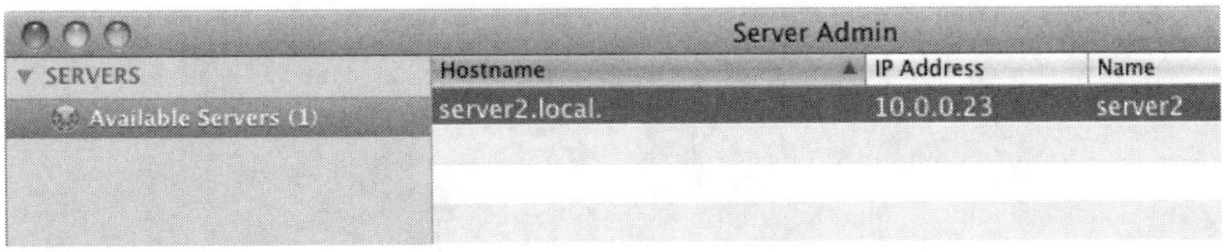

SERVERS	Hostname	IP Address	Name
Available Servers (1)	server2.local.	10.0.0.23	server2

Figure 5-22. Double-click a server in the Available Servers list to enter its address and your current user name automatically in the login dialog box.

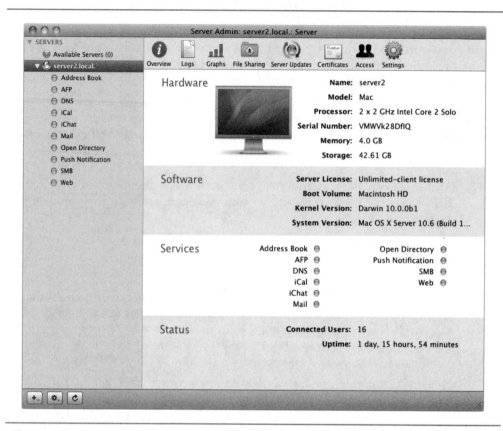

Figure 5-23. Once you've connected to the server, you can manage it as usual from the remote Mac.

CHAPTER 6 | Set Up Client Systems

B y this point, your server should be cruising along on autopilot, chatting to the flight attendants, yawning between languid sips at a cup of high-octane coffee—and wondering when a client will connect to it.

That means it's time to sort out your network's clients.

This chapter starts by discussing your options for setting up client systems—doing it the hard way, automating the process, or booting the Macs from the network. You'll then learn how to create a custom disk image containing the software and settings you need for your Macs, set Mac OS X Server to serve it up, and tell your client Macs to boot from it.

Understanding the Options for Setting Up Client Systems

Generally speaking, you have four options for getting a client system set up the way you need it:

- **Set up the Mac yourself manually** You can install the software that's needed on the Mac, remove any items the user doesn't need, and customize the settings.

- **Have someone else set the Mac up for you** If you buy your Macs customized the way your network needs them, you can roll them straight out. You'll save time, but most likely spend more money.

- **Set up the Mac with a disk image** You can create a custom disk image that contains the software and settings you need, and then use the disk image to install Mac OS X, the applications, and the settings on the Macs. This feature is called NetInstall, and it's one of the main topics of this chapter.

- **Boot the Macs off the network** You can set a Mac to boot off the network by pulling a disk image from a server and then loading it. This feature is called NetBoot; we'll look at it briefly in this chapter so that you can decide whether to use it.

Setting Up a Client Mac Manually

The most straightforward way to set up a client Mac is to do so manually: Set up the Mac either at the workstation it will inhabit or in your lab, boot it, install the software the user needs, and set the Mac's configuration manually.

This procedure scores high on the straightforwardness scale, but loses points to being time and labor intensive. It works fine when you need to roll out only a small number of Macs at a time, or when each Mac needs a different customized setup—for example, a different set of applications peculiar to the user's needs.

If your network's users don't have such exacting needs, and if your workplace isn't run along the lines of the Tsarist bureaucracy, you'll almost certainly want to automate the setup process when wheeling out larger numbers of Macs. You can automate it either fully or partially using the tools discussed from here on.

Booting a Mac Client from the Network

Mac OS X Server's NetBoot service lets you boot your network's Macs from the server across the network instead of booting from their own hard drives.

When Should You Use NetBoot?

Use NetBoot when you need to ensure that the Mac starts up with the same software configuration each time. NetBoot puts the user in a virtual straitjacket, preventing them from customizing the Mac's software with their own settings. This is great for public computers in a lab or library, but it'll drive your average user up the wall—so if you choose to use NetBoot, pick your battles (or at least your victims) carefully.

NetBoot also enables you to roll out software updates and configuration changes easily. All you need to do is update the NetBoot image and reboot the Mac to make it haul the latest files and configuration across the network.

Can Your Network Handle NetBoot?

When a Mac starts up using NetBoot, it hauls an entire disk image across the network. The size of the disk image varies depending on what you've stuffed in it, but between 6GB and 12GB is pretty typical for Mac OS X 10.6.

If you have many Macs trying to do this at the same time, it'll put a strain on your network. For NetBoot to work smoothly, you'll want to have a wired network rather than a wireless network, and Gigabit Ethernet rather than Fast Ethernet.

You can improve NetBoot performance in three ways:

- **Stagger the Macs' boot times** For example, if all your Macs turn on at the second chime of 8:30 AM every morning and start booting, the network and the server will take a thrashing, and booting will take forever and a day. But if a few of the Macs start at a time, the network and the server will have a much easier time, and the Macs will boot faster. How quickly you can boot the Macs will depend on your network, but experiment with starting a few Macs every five minutes, and see how you go.

- **Use multiple servers** If your network is handling NetBoot comfortably, but the server isn't, add one or more servers to provide the disk images.

- **Reduce the number of times the Macs boot** Depending on the Macs involved and what they're doing, you may be able to keep them running for several days—most of the week, perhaps—rather than turning them off every night. This makes NetBoot much more viable, especially if you're using, say, power-sipping Mac minis that you can leave running at night without running up an Enron-size power bill.

(continued)

Understanding How NetBoot Works

When you turn on a Mac configured to use NetBoot, the Mac contacts your DHCP server, which allocates it an IP address. Armed with this essential information, the Mac sends out a request for a server running Bootstrap Service Discovery Protocol, or BSDP.

When the server responds, the Mac tells the server which operating system it needs, and the server begins shunting across the files needed for the Mac to start up. Once the Mac has enough files to start running, it uses Trivial File Transfer Protocol (TFTP) to transfer the files. NetBoot uses a boot image folder with the file extension .nbi. This folder is a bootable network volume and contains a disk image file (in the .dmg format).

After pulling the disk image across the network, NetBoot stores it on the Mac's hard disk as a shadow file. From here, it can instantly grab the files it needs without having to trouble the server, so performance is at full speed—and it doesn't use the network either.

If you update the server with new boot images, NetBoot pulls the appropriate one of the new boot images down to the Mac the next time you restart the Mac. You don't have to restart it immediately unless there's a good reason for doing so, such as a vital security update or missing file that you've put in the new boot image.

Creating Images with System Image Utility

To create the disk images you use for NetBoot, NetInstall, or NetRestore, you use System Image Utility. This section walks you through using System Image Utility. The best way to learn to use it is to see it in action, so this section shows you how to build an example NetInstall image, as this is the image type you're arguably most likely to need. When you're creating your own image, change the specifics to suit your needs rather than blindly following along.

Starting to Create a Disk Image

Follow these steps to start creating a disk image:

1. Insert the Mac OS X Install DVD that you will use to create the image.

TIP   You can also use a disk image file of the Mac OS X Install DVD.

2. Launch System Image Utility (see Figure 6-1). The easiest way to do this is to click the System Image Utility icon on the Dock. If you've removed this icon from the Dock, open your server's Applications folder, open the Server folder inside it, and then double-click the System Image Utility icon.

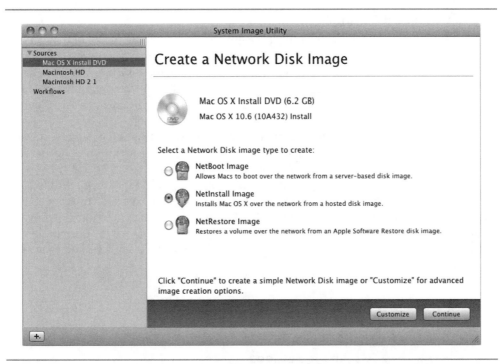

Figure 6-1.   On the opening screen of System Image Utility, choose whether to create a NetBoot image, a NetInstall image, or a NetRestore image.

3. In the Sources list on the left, make sure that System Image Utility has selected your Mac OS X Install DVD. If not, click it.

 NOTE   If you don't install the DVD before launching System Image Utility, the NetInstall Image option button is unavailable.

4. Select the option button for the type of network disk image you want to create: NetBoot Image, NetInstall Image, or NetRestore Image. This example uses NetInstall Image, as it's the type of image you're most likely to need.

 NOTE   A NetBoot image is essentially the same thing as a NetInstall image, except that in a NetBoot image, the disk image is wrapped up in a folder. The folder contains files that enable the Mac to boot enough to load the disk image.

From here, you can either create an image of the Mac OS X Install DVD as it is, or you can customize the installation. Let's look at each option in turn.

Creating a Vanilla Disk Image

The simpler option is to create a vanilla disk image—one that contains only the contents of the install DVD, with no extra software and no customized settings. This is occasionally useful, but normally you'll want to customize the disk image to save time.

To create a vanilla disk image, click the Continue button in the System Image Utility window. System Image Utility then displays the Image Settings screen shown in Figure 6-2.

Change the text in the Network Disk text box as needed. This is the name you'll see for the disk image on the server. Similarly, change the default description as needed to help you identify the disk image easily and beyond doubt.

If you will put this disk image on two or more servers, select the Image Will Be Served From More Than One Server check box. This setting makes System Image Utility add an index ID to the disk image that the servers can use for load balancing.

Click the Create button. Up comes a Save As dialog box that lets you specify the name for the disk image and choose where to save it. Make your choices, and then click the Save button.

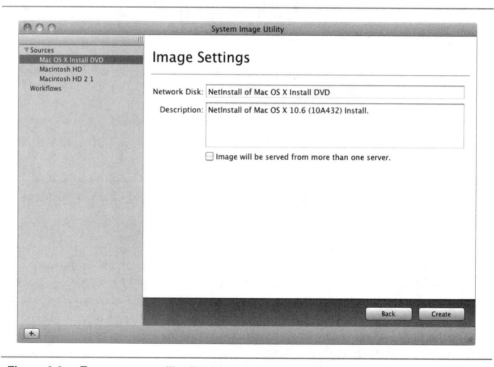

Figure 6-2.   To create a vanilla disk image, edit the name and description on the Image Settings screen as needed, and then click the Create button.

NOTE To use the disk image with NetBoot, you must put it in the /Library/NetBoot/NetBootSP0/ folder on your server's hard disk. You can either put the disk image there when you create it or move it there later.

System Image Utility then creates the disk image, keeping you updated on its progress as it does so (see Figure 6-3). As you'd imagine, this takes a while, so be prepared to entertain yourself while it does so.

When System Image Utility displays the Done button, click it. System Image Utility then displays its first screen, from which you can either choose to create another disk image or simply quit System Image Utility (press ⌘-Q as usual).

Creating a Customized Disk Image

When you're creating a disk image, you'll normally want to customize it so that it contains exactly the software your Macs need. For example, you will likely want to add application software to the Macs and apply network settings to them. You may also want to strip out some items included in the default Mac OS X install that you don't want the Macs to have.

To create a customized disk image, pick your disk image type on the opening screen of System Image Utility, and then click the Customize button. System Image Utility

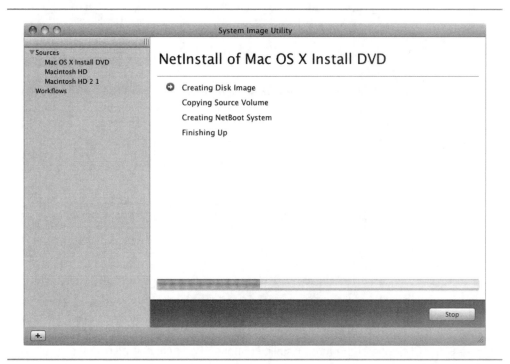

Figure 6-3. System Image Utility creates the disk image. Don't hold your breath.

displays the Automator Library window (which you'll meet in a moment) and adds the two default actions to the System Image Utility window, as shown in Figure 6-4.

If you've used the Mac OS X Automator, you'll be in hog heaven when the Automator Library window opens. If not, you may worry you've slipped down the rabbit hole into Wonderland. Don't worry—it'll all make sense shortly.

Here's what's happening in the System Image Utility window:

■ The whole thing is called a *workflow*. A workflow consists of a series of actions—different steps, if you like. You build the workflow by adding the actions you want, setting options for them, and shuffling them into the right order.

■ Two actions appear in the System Image Utility window: The Define Image Source action at the top, and the Create Image action below it.

■ Each action is a self-contained unit. You can click the disclosure triangle to the left of the action's name to collapse or expand it.

■ Each action has various settings. For example, the Define Image Source action has the Source pop-up menu, in which you choose the source image for the

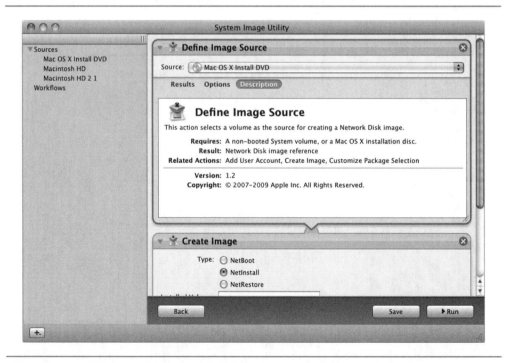

Figure 6-4. Click one of the three visibility buttons in an action to display the results, options, or description (shown here).

image file you're creating. (If you've done this already, as I suggested, you don't need to do it again.)

■   Each action has three visibility buttons at the bottom—Results, Options, and Description—that you can click to show the action's results, options, and description, respectively, in an area below the buttons. For example, if you click the Options button in the Define Image Source action, you see the options shown in Figure 6-5. Click the same button again (Options, in this case) to hide the area again.

■   To remove an action, click the X button to the right of it.

■   To rearrange the order in which actions occur, you can drag an action up or down the right pane of System Image Utility by grabbing its toolbar. Rearranging is easier if you collapse all the actions first.

The Automator Library window (see Figure 6-6) shows a list of actions and variables you can add to the workflow to make it do what you want—in this case, create a custom installation of Mac OS X. The Automator Library window shows either actions or variables; you can switch between the two by clicking the Actions visibility button or the Variables visibility button.

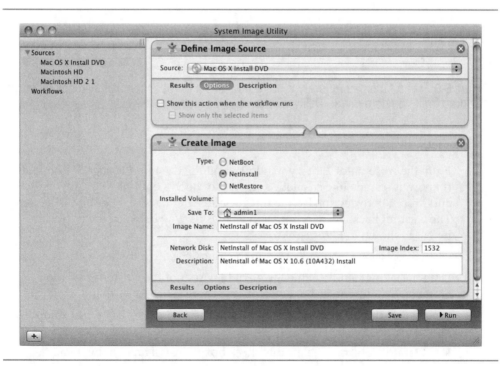

Figure 6-5.   Build the list of actions in the System Image Utility window.

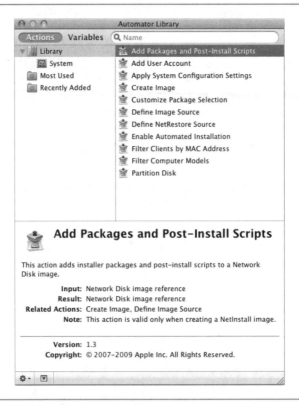

Figure 6-6. The Automator Library window provides a list of actions and variables that you can drag to the System Image Utility window.

Okay, let's dig in:

1. From the Automator Library window, drag the Custom Package Selection item (I know, it sounds like cosmetic surgery) to the System Image Utility window and drop it between the Define Image Source item and the Create Image item. The Custom Package Selection item elbows its way between the two other items, as shown in Figure 6-7.

2. Click the disclosure triangle next to the Mac OS X item to display its contents.

3. Drag the sizing handle at the lower-right corner of the Customize Package Selection box downward to give yourself more space to work in.

4. Choose which packages to include and which to remove, as in the example in Figure 6-8:

   ■ **Default column**   Select this check box to install an item by default.

   ■ **Visible column**   Select this check box to make an item available to whoever sets the Mac up.

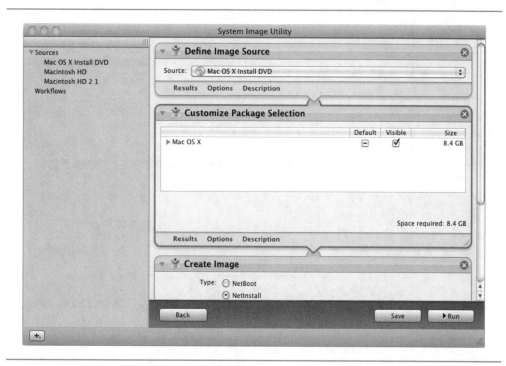

Figure 6-7. Add the Custom Package Selection item to the workflow so that you can choose which Mac OS X packages to install.

5. Click the disclosure triangle to the left of Customize Package Selection to collapse the box and give yourself more space.

6. From the Automator Library window, drag the Add Packages And Post-Install Scripts item to the System Image Utility window and drop it between the Customize Package Selection item and the Create Image item. The Add Packages And Post-Install Scripts item appears in the System Image Utility window as shown in Figure 6-9.

7. Click the + button near the lower-right corner of the Add Packages And Post-Install Scripts box to open a dialog box for adding packages. Select the package or script you want, and then click the Open button. The package or script appears in the Add Packages And Post-Install Scripts box (see Figure 6-10).

TIP You can add a folder full of packages or scripts if necessary. See the section "Creating Your Own Package Files," later in this chapter, for instructions on creating custom package files for your network's needs.

8. Repeat step 7 to add other packages or scripts as needed.

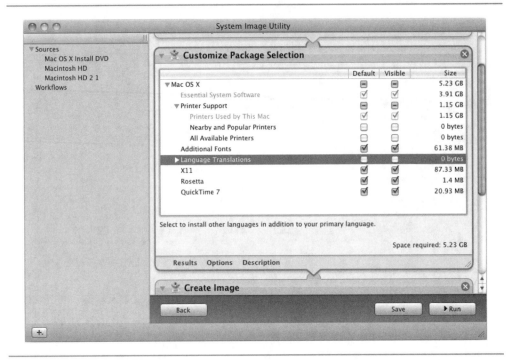

Figure 6-8. Clear the Default check boxes for items you do not want to install. Clear the Visible check boxes for icons you do not want to be visible.

 NOTE You can use the Add User Account action only when creating a NetBoot image, not when creating a NetInstall image. Normally, you use this action to create an administrator account for the Mac you're booting.

9. If you want to perform automated installations on your client Macs, drag the Enable Automated Installation action to the System Image Utility window and drop it after the Add Packages And Post-Install Scripts action. Figure 6-11 shows the Enable Automated Installation action in place.

10. On the On Volume line, select the Selected By User option button if you want the user to be able to choose the drive on which to install Mac OS X. Otherwise, select the Named option button and type the name of the volume to use—for example, **Macintosh HD**.

 TIP You can use the Partition Disk action before the Enable Automated Installation action to partition the disk and name the volumes. You can create a single volume when partitioning the disk.

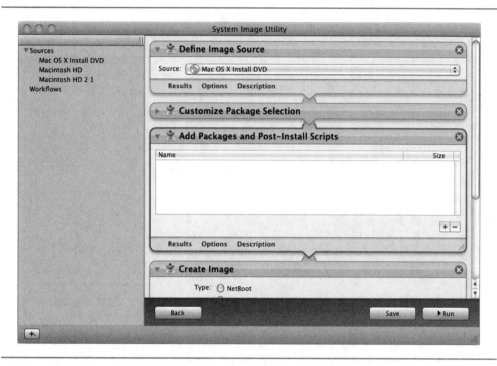

Figure 6-9.   Drag in the Add Packages And Post-Install Scripts item to enable yourself to add further software packages to the disk image you're creating.

11. Select the Erase Before Installing check box if you want to erase the disk before installing Mac OS X. Erasing is usually a good idea.

12. In the Main Language pop-up menu, select the language to set as the main language for the installation—for example, English or Spanish.

13. If you want to automatically configure the system, drag the Apply System Configuration Settings action from the Automator Library window to the System Image Utility window and drop it after the Enable Automated Installation action. Figure 6-12 shows the Apply System Configuration Settings action added to the workflow.

14. If you want to automatically bind each client to a directory server, follow these steps:

    a. Select the Connect Computers To Directory Servers check box.

    b. Click the + button at the lower-right corner of the list box to add a line of controls to the list box.

    c. Open the Server pop-up menu and choose the directory server.

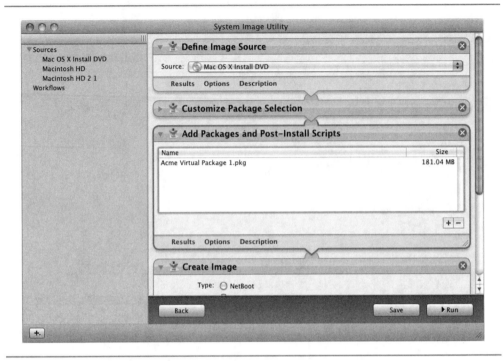

Figure 6-10.   Add the software packages to the Add Packages And Post-Install Scripts box.

    d. If you want to apply these settings to a particular Mac, click in the Ethernet box and type the MAC address of the Mac's network card—for example, **00:26:4a:02:e6:9e**. Leave the Ethernet box at its default setting, Any Computer, if you want the settings to apply to any Mac.

    e. Click in the User Name box and type the administrator's account name for the directory server. This is optional, but if you don't enter it here, you'll need to enter it on the client.

    f. Click in the Password box and type the administrator's password for the directory server. Again, this is optional, but you'll need to enter it later if you don't enter it here.

15. If you want the client to pick up a computer name and hostname from a file, select the Apply Computer Name And Local Hostname Settings From A File check box. Click the Select File button, use the resulting dialog box to select the file, and then click the Open button.

16. If you will use this image to set up multiple Macs, select the Generate Unique Computer Names Starting With check box, and then type the base name in the text box.

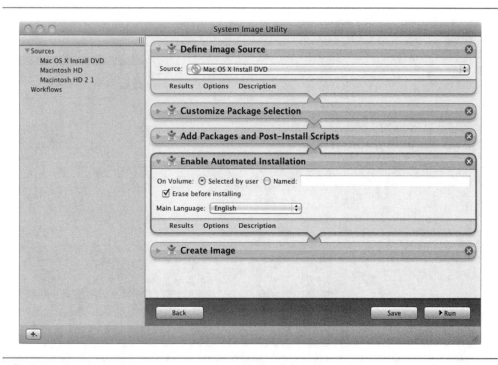

Figure 6-11. The Enable Automated Installation action lets you create NetInstall and NetRestore images that install automatically on client Macs.

17. If you want the Mac you're setting up to acquire the preferences of the Mac that you're building the image from, select the Change ByHost Preferences To Match Client After Install check box.

18. Nearly done… now make sure that the Create Image action appears at the end of your workflow, and then click the Save button. System Image Utility displays a Save As dialog box for saving the workflow you have created.

19. Type a name for the workflow in the Save As text box.

20. Choose the folder in which to save the workflow.

21. Click the Save button. The Save As dialog box closes, and System Image Utility adds the workflow to the Workflows list on the left side of the window.

22. Now click the Run button to start running the workflow. Type your password when System Image Utility prompts you to authenticate yourself.

After the workflow finishes running, your disk image is ready for use. If you need to create another disk image, press ⌘-N or choose File | New, and then start over. If you've already imaged yourself to the hilt, press ⌘-Q or choose System Image Utility | Quit System Image Utility to quit System Image Utility.

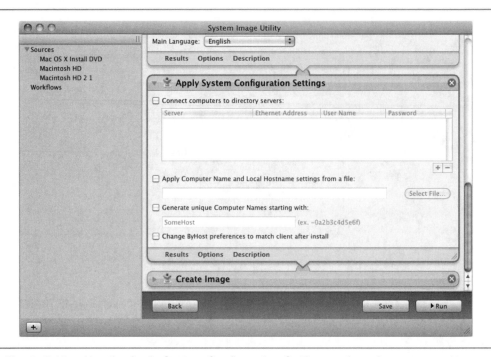

Figure 6-12. Use the Apply System Configuration Settings action when you need to configure the client Mac automatically.

Creating Your Own Package Files

To add software to a disk image, you use the PackageMaker tool. You'll find Package-Maker in the Utilities folder on the Mac OS X Administration Tools CD. You can run it from the CD by double-clicking its icon, but if you're planning to use it frequently, drag it to somewhere handier (for example, the /Applications/Server/folder) and then run it from that folder.

When you open PackageMaker, you'll see an Untitled window. In front of this window, PackageMaker automatically displays the Install Properties dialog box (see Figure 6-13).

Type your organization's name in the Organization text box. You need to create the name in the form com.example—for example, com.acmevirtualindustries or org.soporificadults—so that Mac OS X can generate suitable package identifiers for the components in the package.

Then open the Minimum Target pop-up menu and choose the lowest version of Mac OS X your clients will run—for example, Mac OS X v10.5 Leopard.

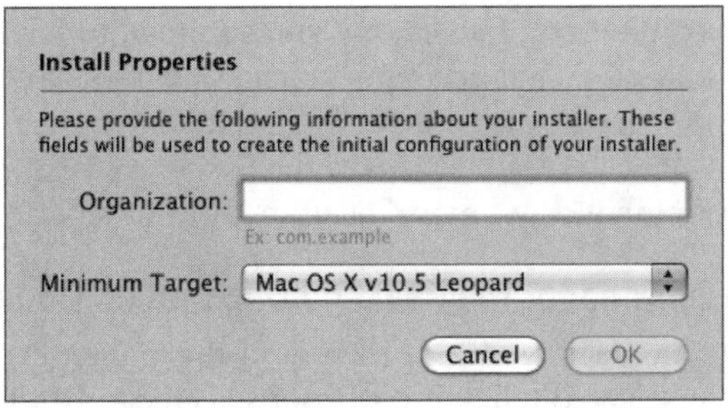

Install Properties

Please provide the following information about your installer. These fields will be used to create the initial configuration of your installer.

Organization: [   ]
Ex: com.example

Minimum Target: [Mac OS X v10.5 Leopard ▲▼]

(Cancel) (OK)

Figure 6-13. In the Install Properties dialog box, type your organization name and choose the minimum version of Mac OS X your clients will run.

Click the OK button to close the Install Properties dialog box. You can then see the PackageMaker window in all its glory (see Figure 6-14).

Saving Your Package Description Document

In PackageMaker, you create a package description document in the .pmdoc format that specifies the contents of the package. This document is tiny—just a few kilobytes—because

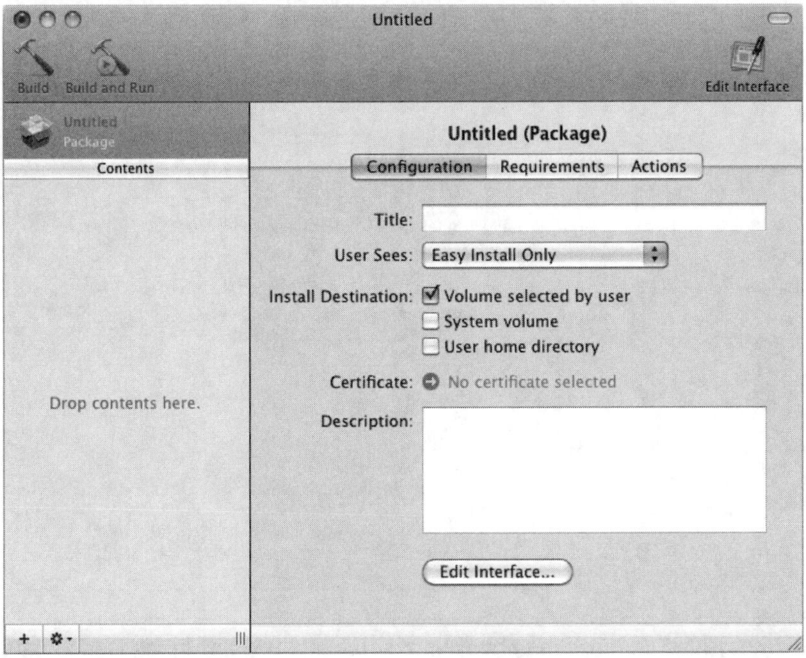

● ● ●   Untitled

Build   Build and Run   Edit Interface

Untitled
Package   **Untitled (Package)**

Contents   [Configuration Requirements Actions]

                        Title: [   ]

                   User Sees: [Easy Install Only ▲▼]

          Install Destination: ☑ Volume selected by user
                              ☐ System volume
                              ☐ User home directory

                 Certificate: ● No certificate selected

Drop contents here.   Description: [   ]

                        (Edit Interface...)

+ ✿▾ |||

Figure 6-14. PackageMaker is the tool for creating custom packages to include in your automated installations of Mac OS X.

all it contains is details of what you want. When the description is finished, you build the package to create the file in the .pkg format that you add to your installation workflow. This file contains all the files, so it's much bigger—roughly the size of all the files plus some packaging, depending how much the contents have settled in transit.

Press ⌘-S (or choose File | Save) to display the Save As dialog box, and then save the description document in a convenient location and under a descriptive name.

Setting the Title and Options for the Package Description Document

After you save the file, the package file at the top of the Contents pane is still called Untitled. With this item selected (click it if it's not selected), click the Configuration tab (see Figure 6-15) and type a title in the Title box.

The package title is the only required item, but you can also do the following in the Configuration pane:

■ **Choose which installation types are available to the user**   Open the User Sees pop-up menu, and then choose Easy And Custom Install, Custom Install Only, or Easy Install Only (often the best choice).

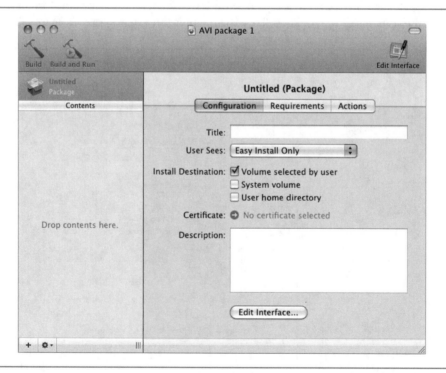

Figure 6-15.   Name your package by typing in the Title text box in the Configuration pane.

- **Choose where the user can install the package** In the Install Destination area, select the appropriate check boxes: Volume Selected By User, System Volume, or User Home Directory.

- **Choose which certificate to use to sign the package** Click the arrow button, pick the certificate in the Choose A Certificate To Be Used For Signing The Package dialog box, and click the Choose button.

- **Add a description to the package** Type the description in the Description text box. The package's contents will be blindingly obvious to you when you're creating the package, but will probably recede quickly into the mists of oblivion.

 NOTE You can also edit the Installer interface for the package by clicking the Edit Interface button. For example, you can add a readme file to the Installer.

If you need to set any hardware or software requirements for the package, click the Requirements tab and work in the Requirements pane (shown in Figure 6-16 with a requirement added).

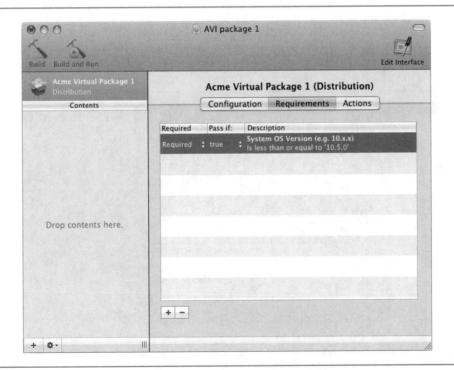

Figure 6-16. In the Requirements pane, set any hardware or software requirements for the package.

To add a requirement, follow these steps:

1. Click the + button to display the dialog box shown in Figure 6-17.

2. In the upper area, put together the condition.

   a. Open the If pop-up menu and choose the item—for example, System OS Version.

   b. Open the Is pop-up menu and choose the comparison—for example, <= (is less than or equal to).

   c. In the text box, type the value—for example, **10.5.0** for Mac OS X version 10.5 (Leopard).

3. In the Failure message area, type a message title and message text to display if the system fails the requirement.

4. Click the OK button. PackageMaker closes the dialog box and adds the requirement to the list.

5. If necessary, click the Required pop-up menu in the Required column and choose Optional instead.

6. Also if necessary, click the True item in the Pass If column and choose False instead.

As well as hardware and software requirements, you can add actions to your package. You can create actions that run before the installation, after the installation, or both.

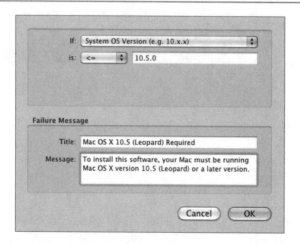

Figure 6-17. Use this dialog box to create a requirement for a software package.

To add actions, click the Actions button and work in the Actions pane (shown in Figure 6-18 with an action added). There's a Preinstall Actions list box for actions to run before the installation, a Postinstall Actions list box for actions to run after installation, and a pair of Edit buttons, one for setting up each list of actions.

To edit one of the lists of actions, click its Edit button, and then work in the dialog box that PackageMaker displays (see Figure 6-19). As you'll notice at once, this is an Automator workflow, so you drag the actions you want from the left pane to the workflow, choose options in them, and arrange them into the order in which you want them to occur. Click the Save button when you're done, and the list appears in the Actions pane in PackageMaker.

Adding Files to the Package Description Document

Now that you've named your package description document and chosen options for it, you're ready to add files to the package.

The easiest way to add files is to open a Finder window to the folder that contains the files, and then drag them to the Contents pane on the left side of the PackageMaker

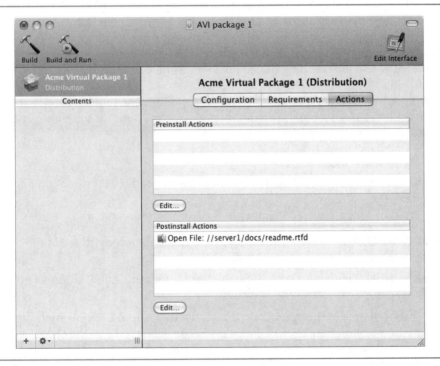

Figure 6-18.   Use the Actions pane to set up preinstall actions or postinstall actions for the package.

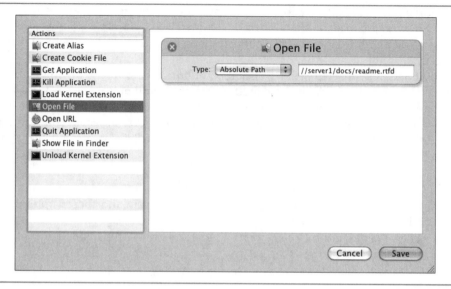

Figure 6-19.   Set up the list of preinstall actions or post-install actions in this dialog box.

window. Alternatively, you can click the + button in the lower-left corner of the Package-Maker window, use the resulting dialog box to pick the file, and then click the Choose button to add it.

When you've added one or more files to the package, each file appears as a collaps-ible choice in the contents pane. You can then set options both for the choice and for the package.

Setting Options for the Choice

To set options for the choice, click the choice and work in the Configuration pane (see Figure 6-20).

You can make the following changes in the Configuration pane:

- **Choice Name**   In this text box, type the name the user will see in the Customization pane of the Installer.

- **Identifier**   In this text box, type the text that identifies the choice inside the package.

- **Initial State**   In this area, choose how the item should appear in the Customization pane. Select the Selected check box to have the choice's check box appear already selected; select the Enabled check box if you want the user to be able to select or clear the check box; and select the Hidden check box if you want to hide the choice from the user.

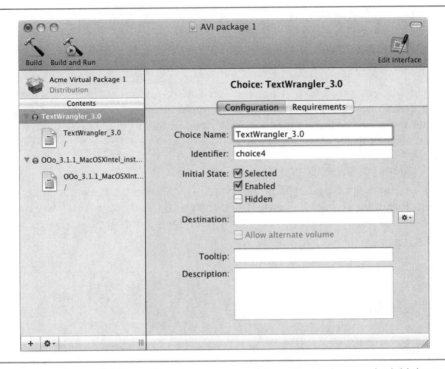

Figure 6-20. In the Configuration pane, you can name the choice, set its initial state and destination, and add a tooltip and description.

■ **Destination** Choose the folder in which to install the components of the choice. Click the Action button to the right of the text box, click Choose on the pop-up menu, select the folder in the resulting dialog box, and then click the Choose button. Click the Action button again, and then choose Absolute or Relative To Project on the pop-up menu, putting a check mark next to the item you want. Absolute means you're setting an absolute path in the file system; Relative To Project means you're setting a path that's relative to where the project files go.

NOTE After setting the destination, select the Allow Alternate Volume check box if you want to let the user install the choice on a different volume.

- **Tooltip** Type a short message—up to a dozen words or so—for the Installer to display in a tooltip when the user puts the mouse pointer over the choice.

- **Description** Type a longer description for display in the Customization pane in the Installer when the user selects the choice.

If necessary, you can set hardware and software requirements for the choice. Click the Requirements tab, and then work in the Requirements pane. Use the same techniques to set up the requirements as described in the previous section for setting requirements for the package as a whole.

Setting Options for the Package

To set options for the package, expand the choice in the Contents pane of the System Image Utility window (if the choice is collapsed), and then click the package. You'll see a screen with four tabs, as shown in Figure 6-21, in which the Configuration pane takes center stage.

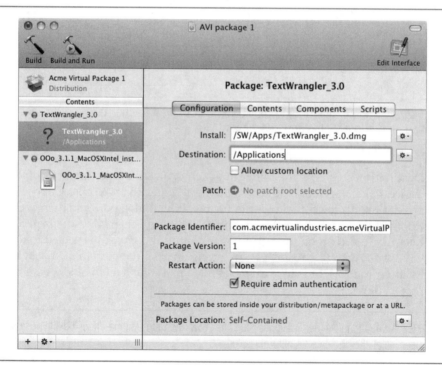

Figure 6-21. The Configuration pane includes options for choosing where to install the component package and whether to restart the Mac.

In this pane, you can set the following options for the component package you've selected:

- **Install**   This text box shows the path to the component package. Change the path as needed, either by typing or by clicking the Action button to the right of the text box, clicking Choose on the pop-up menu, using the resulting dialog box to select the file, and then clicking the Choose button. From the Action pop-up menu, you can also choose Absolute or Relative To Project on the pop-up menu if necessary. (Chances are you'll normally install from an absolute path.)

- **Destination**   Enter the folder to which you want to install the component package. For example, if this is an application, you may want to choose the Applications folder. Again, you can type in the path or click the Action button and then click Choose; again, the Action button also offers the choice of an absolute path or a relative path. You can select the Allow Custom Location check box if you want the user to be able to override the location you chose.

NOTE   If the application will patch an earlier version of the application, click the arrow next to Patch. In the Configure Patch Package dialog box that opens, specify the older version of the application by clicking the Action button, clicking Choose, and then using the Open dialog box to pick the application. Click the Save button to close the Configure Patch Package dialog box.

- **Package Identifier**   This is a Uniform Type Identifier (UTI) that uniquely identifies the package—for example, com.megaco.apps1.megacoapp.pkg.

- **Package Version**   A positive integer that identifies the version of the package. Start with 1 unless you enjoy delusions of grandeur.

- **Restart Action**   In this pop-up menu, choose whether the user needs to log out, restart, or shut down after installation. Your choices are None, Require Logout, Require Restart, and Require Shutdown.

- **Require Admin Authentication**   Select this check box if you want to force the user to authenticate as an administrator for the Mac before running the installation.

- **Package Location**   Normally, the readout says Self-Contained, because the package you added contains the files. You can also click the Action button and choose another option: Same Level, Custom Path, HTTP URL, or Removable Media. For the last three, you enter the path to the package in a text box.

After that little lot, click the Contents tab to display the Contents pane (see Figure 6-22). Here, depending on the files you're installing, you can choose to omit certain files, either by clearing their check boxes in the list box or by clicking the File Filters button and using the resulting dialog box to specify a list of filters to apply.

Click the Components tab to display the Components pane (see Figure 6-23). Here, you can make two decisions for any component listed:

- **Whether the user may relocate it**   Select the check box in the Allow Relocation column if the user may relocate the component.

- **Whether the component can be replaced with an earlier version during an install**   Select the check box in the Allow Downgrade column.

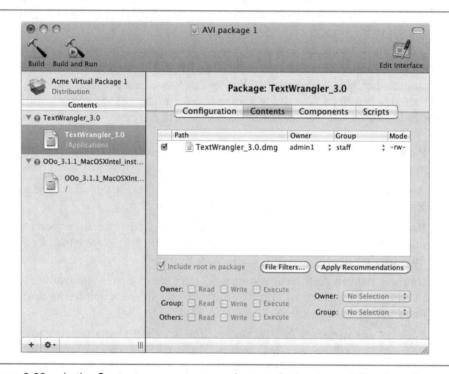

Figure 6-22.   In the Contents pane, you can choose whether to omit files from the component package.

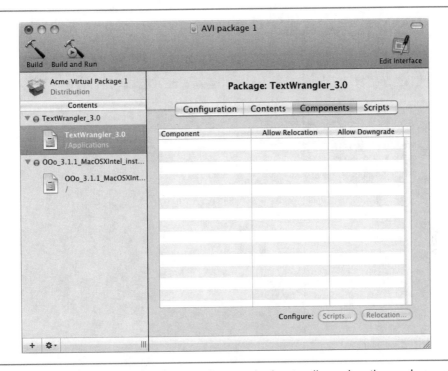

Figure 6-23.   In the Components pane, choose whether to allow relocation or downgrading for components of the package.

Finally, click the Scripts tab to display the Scripts pane (see Figure 6-24). Here, you can designate the scripts directory and choose scripts to run before and after install, as needed.

Right, that's the first component package set up. Lather, rinse, and repeat for each of the other component packages you're including in your package.

Building the Package File

You're now ready to build the package file—to have PackageMaker put the package file together using the components and settings you've specified. Press ⌘-s to save the changes you've made to the package description document, and then click the Build button on the toolbar.

PackageMaker displays a Save As dialog box. Choose the folder in which you want to save the package file, and then click the Save button to start the building

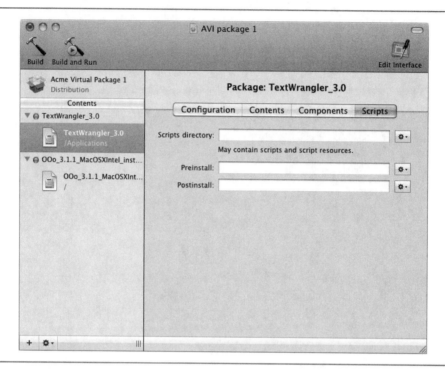

Figure 6-24.   Specify the scripts directory and set up any preinstall or postinstall script needed in the Scripts pane.

process. PackageMaker shows you its progress as it works, and then displays the Build Succeeded! screen (see Figure 6-25).

From here you have three choices:

- Click the Open In Installer button to open the package in Installer. This is a good way of finding out if the package works the way you intended.

- Click the View In Finder button to open the package in the Finder—for example, so that you can copy it to another disk.

- Click the Return To Editing button to return to editing the package in PackageMaker.

Figure 6-25.   From the Build Succeeded! screen, you can open the package in Installer, view it in the Finder, or return to editing in PackageMaker.

Creating an Image from a Mac You've Set Up

If you're not familiar with Automator, you may prefer to create a disk image the easier way: by setting up a Mac the way you want it, and then cloning the Mac's disk.

This is a great way to proceed, but there is one major constraint: You can't perform the cloning operation while the Mac is booted from the disk you want to clone. This is no big surprise, but it means that you need to proceed in one of these ways:

- Set up the Mac with two partitions (or more, if you need different configurations or are feeling frisky). Put Mac OS X on each partition. Set the first partition up the way you want your disk image. Then boot from the second partition and use Disk Utility to create a disk image from the first partition. Now run System Image Utility and specify the disk image as the source for the installation.

- Connect the Mac you will clone to the cloning computer via a FireWire cable (FireWire 800 for choice), and then boot the Mac in Target Disk mode so that it shows up as a drive on the cloning computer. Run Disk Utility on the cloning computer and do the deed. After making the image, eject the drive that represents the target Mac, and then turn its power off before disconnecting it.

NOTE The easiest way to boot a Mac in Target Disk mode is to press ⊤ during startup. You can also go into Startup Disk Preferences and click the Target Disk Mode button.

Once you've booted from the other partition, or you've connected the Mac in Target Disk mode, create an image in Disk Utility like this:

1. Open Disk Utility. For example, click the Desktop, choose Go | Utilities, and then double-click the Disk Utility icon.

2. Select the disk you want to clone. For example, in Figure 6-26, the Mac to be cloned is connected in Target Disk mode, so it shows up as a FireWire drive called AAPL FireWire Target Media.

3. Choose File | New | Disk Image From (the command shows the name of the disk). Disk Utility displays the Save As dialog box (see Figure 6-27).

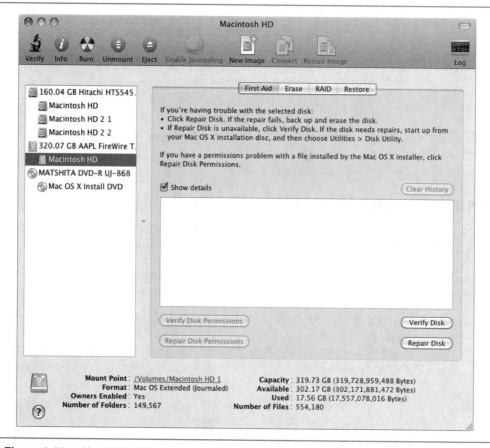

Figure 6-26. Use Disk Utility to create a disk image from a Mac that's already configured the way you want it. The selected AAPL FireWire Target Media disk is a Mac in Target Disk mode.

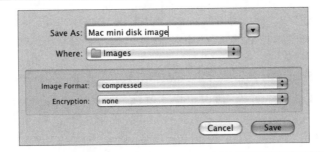

Figure 6-27.   Choose to save the disk image in compressed format with no encryption.

4. Type a name for the disk image, and choose the folder in which to save it. As before, the disk image needs to end up in the /Library/NetBoot/NetBootSP0/ folder on your server's hard disk, but you don't necessarily have to put it there when you're creating it—you can move it there later.

5. In the Image Format pop-up menu, choose Compressed.

6. In the Encryption pop-up menu, choose None.

7. Click the Save button, and then give Disk Utility some breathing space to create the disk image. Depending on how much stuff you've loaded on the Mac, it may take a while.

8. When Disk Utility has finished creating the disk image, press ⌘-Q or choose Disk Utility | Quit Disk Utility to quit the application.

Now switch to System Image Utility, select the disk image you've created, and follow through the procedure described earlier in this chapter to create a NetInstall disk.

Turning On and Setting Up the NetBoot Service

Your next step is to set up the NetBoot service to make your NetInstall images available on the network. You need to do this before the client Macs can find them.

Follow these steps to turn NetBoot on and make it do your bidding:

1. Open Server Admin. For example, click the Server Admin icon on the Dock.

2. In the Servers list, double-click the server.

3. Check or enter your credentials in the login dialog box, and then click the Connect button.

4. Click the Settings tab to display its contents.

5. Click the Settings button to display the list of services.

6. Select the NetBoot check box.

7. Click the Save button. Mac OS X Server turns on the NetBoot service and adds it to the list of services running under the server.

8. Click the NetBoot item under the server in the Servers pane to display the NetBoot screens.

9. Click the Settings button on the toolbar to display the Settings screen.

10. Click the General tab to display the General pane (see Figure 6-28).

11. In the Enable NetBoot On At Least One Port list box, select the Enable check box for the port on which to enable NetBoot—for example, the Ethernet port.

12. In the Select Where To Put Images And Client Data list box, select the appropriate check box in the Images column to indicate the disk on which you've stored the images.

13. Also in the Select Where To Put Images And Client Data list box, select the appropriate check box in the Client Data column to indicate where to store shadow files. The *shadow files* are used only by diskless clients, so if you're using NetInstall rather than NetBoot, your server won't have to store any.

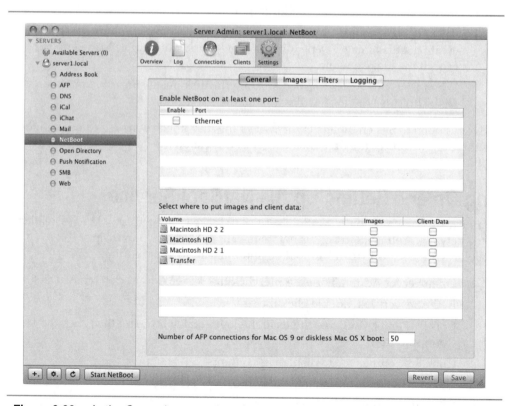

Figure 6-28. In the General pane, select the port on which to enable NetBoot.

14. Click the Images tab to display the Images pane (see Figure 6-29). The main list box shows a list of the images Server Admin has found in the /Library/ NetBoot/NetBootSP0/ folder on your server's hard disk.

15. In the Default column, select the option button for the image you want to use as the default.

16. In the Enable column, select the check box for each disk image you want to enable. You don't need to tell you that you must enable the disk image you've tagged as the default.

17. In the Diskless column, select the check box if you're using the image for NetBoot to launch diskless workstations. If you're using NetInstall, make sure this check box is cleared.

18. If your disk image contains both Intel and PowerPC code, you can open the pop-up menu in the Architecture column and choose which to use. If your disk image is Snow Leopard, only Intel will be available, so the pop-up menu is grayed out.

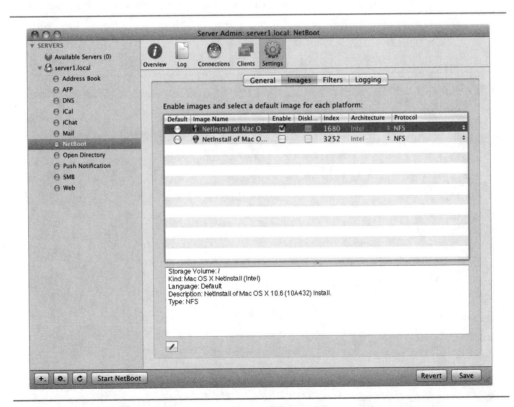

Figure 6-29.   In the Images pane, enable the NetInstall images you want to use.

19. In the Protocol column, open the pop-up menu and choose the network protocol you want to use for delivering the disk image to the workstation. Normally, you'll want to use NFS; the alternative is HTTP.

20. If you need to protect your disk images against unauthorized Macs using them, click the Filters tab to display the Filters pane (see Figure 6-30). Here, you can select the Enable NetBoot/DHCP Filtering check box, choose between the Allow Only Clients Listed Below (Deny Others) option button and the Deny Only Clients Listed Below (Allow Others) option button, and then build a list of the good guys or the bad guys, depending on the choice you made. You identify the Macs by the hardware (MAC) address of their network cards, which provides fairly good authentication.

21. Click the Logging tab to display the Logging pane, open the Log Level pop-up menu, and choose the level of logging you want for NetBoot:

   ■ **High (All Events)**   Use this level when you are getting started with Net-Boot and will find it helpful to be able to track everything that happens.

   ■ **Medium (Errors And Warnings)**   Use this level when you're getting more confident with NetBoot, but you still want to see every alert that crops up.

   ■ **Low (Errors Only)**   Use this level when NetBoot is configured to your satisfaction and working well.

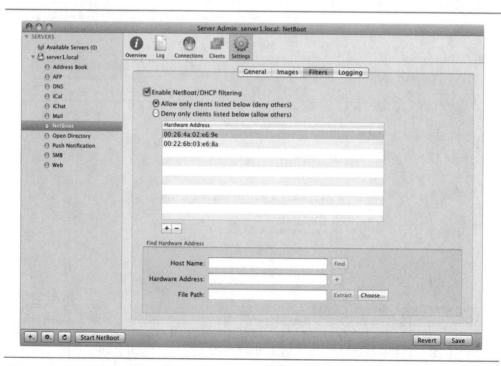

Figure 6-30.   The Filters pane enables you to set up a list of Macs that are allowed—or are not permitted—to use your NetBoot images.

22. Click the Save button to save the changes you've made to NetBoot.

23. Click the Start NetBoot button at the bottom of whichever pane you happen to be contemplating. The NetBoot light on the left glows green, and you can quit Server Admin if you're ready to.

Setting a Mac Client to Install from a NetInstall Image

Now that you've created your NetInstall images and set the NetBoot service to make them available, you just need to tell your Mac clients to boot from the network. To do so, follow these steps:

1. On the Mac client, open System Preferences. For example, click the System Preferences icon on the Dock, or choose Apple | System Preferences.

2. Click the Startup Disk icon in the System area to display the Startup Disk preferences pane (see Figure 6-31).

3. Select the Network Startup icon.

4. Click the Restart button. Mac OS X displays a confirmation dialog box.

5. Click the Restart button, and wait for the magic to start.

6. Follow any prompts required to complete the setup.

Figure 6-31. Choose Network Startup in the Startup Disk preferences pane.

CHAPTER 7 | Create and Control Users and Groups

Right, it's time to get users onto your network. To enable a user to join the network, you need to create a user account for that person. Unless you run the network on your own, you will also need to create an account for each other administrator. You can also create accounts for computers, and then marshal both users and computers into groups.

Understanding the Tools for Working with Accounts

Mac OS X Server provides several different tools for working with accounts. Having these different tools brings power and flexibility—at the risk of some accompanying confusion at first. Here's a quick summary before you dive into the details:

- **Server Preferences**   Server Preferences is the tool you'll normally want to use when you're getting started with user accounts. The Users pane in Server Preferences lets you quickly create and delete user accounts with mostly standardized settings. This is where you'll start.

- **Workgroup Manager**   Workgroup Manager is a powerful and complex tool that enables you to dig into the details of an account. You can use Workgroup Manager to create new user accounts or to edit an account you've created using Server Preferences—for example, by changing settings in Workgroup Manager that Server Preferences does not let you change. You'll learn more about Workgroup Manager after looking at Server Preferences.

- **Command-line tools**   As well as Server Preferences and Workgroup Manager, Mac OS X Server includes command-line tools for configuring user accounts. These tools are useful when you're performing tasks automatically, as discussed in Chapter 19.

Before you create any accounts, we'll run through the different account types that Mac OS X Server offers to make sure you understand what you're working with.

Understanding the Essentials of Accounts

To enable a user to access the server and use the services it's providing, you need to create a user account for that user. The user account is Mac OS X Server's mechanism for authenticating the user. For example, if you set up a user account named Ann Smith and assign a password to it, the server allows a user who claims to be Ann Smith to access it and use its services by supplying that password.

A user account typically contains the following:

- The user's e-mail address
- The user's instant messaging address for iChat

- The user's calendar for iCal
- The user's wiki portal, which is called My Page
- Details of the groups the user belongs to
- Details of the services the user has permission to access

Understanding the Three Ways of Creating User Accounts

You can create user accounts in three different ways. Mac OS X Server treats these accounts differently from each other:

- **Create accounts using Server Preferences or Workgroup Manager**   The straightforward way to create a user account is to use Server Preferences on the server. When you do this, the server stores them in its own directory. You can also create user accounts in Workgroup Manager, discussed later in this chapter.

- **Import user accounts from a directory server**   If your company or organization already has user accounts stored on a directory server, you can import the accounts into your server. When you do this, the original accounts stay on the directory server, which has the master copy, as it were. On your server, you can then add extra information to the imported accounts. For example, you can add or change a user's contact information or make the user a member of a group. Mac OS X Server stores this information on your server and uses it together with the information from the directory server to control what the user can do.

- **Create local user accounts using System Preferences**   If you've used a stand-alone Mac, you'll know that each Mac's administrator can create user accounts for other users via System Preferences. These accounts are local to the Mac on which they're created—they're not part of the network—and only enable the users to log on to the Mac and access their home folders on that Mac, not to access the server, its services, or the network. Generally you'll want to avoid creating local user accounts on your networked Macs, as your aim should be to retain centralized control through the directory.

For a small- or medium-size network, the best approach is usually to create accounts using Server Preferences on your directory server. That way, you work directly with the user accounts and can see exactly which permissions they have, which groups they belong to, and so on. You can then tweak the accounts as needed by using Workgroup Manager.

By contrast, when working with imported user accounts on one of the servers, you're essentially creating an extra set of users with partial information—only the information you've added on that server. This extra layer of accounts can be useful, especially in larger organizations broken up into departments whose administrators enjoy a thick slice of autonomy. But if you're trying to manage the network yourself, handling users and groups through the directory server will save you time, effort, and hair.

Understanding the Different Administrator Accounts

The administrator administers the network, obviously enough—but Mac OS X Server gives you four types of administrator accounts:

- Primary administrator
- Directory administrator
- Local administrator
- Server administrator

The following sections explain what you need to know about these administrator accounts.

Primary Administrator Account

The *primary administrator account* is the account you created when setting up the server. This account has the account name and password you assigned during setup. Each server has its own primary administrator account, which it stores on the server itself rather than storing it in the directory.

You can use the primary administrator account to manage the server either directly when logged in on the server itself or to manage the server remotely from another Mac on the network.

NOTE If you upgraded your server from Mac OS Server 10.5 to Mac OS Server 10.6, your server has a primary administrator account stored in your server's directory. This account has the name and password you chose when setting up Leopard Server and also serves as a directory administrator account. The server also has a local administrator account with the name Local Administrator and the short name localadmin; this account is stored on the server.

Directory Administrator Account

The directory administrator account is a special account that a server has if it hosts users and groups in its own directory—for example, your Open Directory Master server. This account has the standard name diradmin and the password you created for the primary administrator account during setup.

You can use the directory administrator account to manage accounts either directly when logged in on the server itself or remotely across the network.

Local Administrator Account

A *local administrator account* is an administrator account stored on a server that you have upgraded from Leopard Server to Mac OS X Server.

Server Administrator Account

Beyond the primary administrator account, directory administrator account, and local administrator account (if you upgraded your server), you can create further server administrator accounts as needed. A *server administrator* can install software on the server, create user accounts and groups, and use Server Preferences to configure the server.

Understanding the Three Categories of User Accounts and Where Mac OS X Server Stores Them

Mac OS X Server uses three different categories of user accounts: Server accounts, Imported accounts, and Local accounts. You need to understand the differences between them before you start creating or working with user accounts.

Server Accounts

A server account is an account that an administrator—probably you—creates on your Mac OS X server by using the Server Preferences application or the Workgroup Manager application. Mac OS X Server stores the account in your server's directory rather than in the network directory.

A server account is the type of account you use to create a new user for the network. The server account contains the user's contact information and details of the groups to which the user belongs. The account enables the user to log in to the network and use services on it.

Imported Accounts

An imported account is an account that you import to your Mac OS X server from your organization's directory server. The account is originally created by the administrator of the directory server (which may also be you, if you administer the whole network).

After importing the account, you can add further information and permissions to it by using Server Preferences. Mac OS X Server stores this extra information in your server's directory rather than in the directory server.

Local Accounts

The third category of accounts is local accounts. A local account is an account on an individual Mac rather than on a server (but see the nearby Note). The local account is not part of a Mac OS X Server network; rather, it's an account on the Mac itself rather than on the server or in the directory, and Mac OS X stores the account on the Mac on which you created it.

A local account is the type of account that you can create on a standalone Mac that does not connect to a Mac OS X Server on the network—for example, a Mac used in a home or dorm setting. To create a local account, you use an administrator account for the Mac and the System Preferences application rather than the Server Preferences application.

NOTE   A server can also have local accounts that you create through System Preferences. Generally, however, it's better not to create local accounts on a server—use Server Preferences or Workgroup Manager to create server accounts instead.

Understanding Groups and What You Can Do with Them

You can work with user accounts individually or manipulate multiple user accounts at the same time by making them part of a group. Groups are a way of saving time by treating multiple users in the same way. For example, you can put all the users who need access to the same shared folders or the same wikis into the same group.

Creating a User in Server Preferences

Now that you know the background, let's look at how to create a user account using Server Preferences.

First, open Server Preferences (see Figure 7-1). As usual, the easiest way is to click the Server Preferences icon on the Dock, unless you've removed it—in which case, open the /Applications/Server/ folder and double-click the Server Preferences icon.

 NOTE   You can run Server Preferences either on your directory server or on another Mac on the network. If the Mac you're working at is not the directory server but another server, be sure to log into the right server so that your user accounts don't wind up in the wrong place.

In the Server Preferences window, click the Users icon in the Accounts area to open the Users preferences. If you haven't added users yet, you'll see a blank slate, as in Figure 7-2.

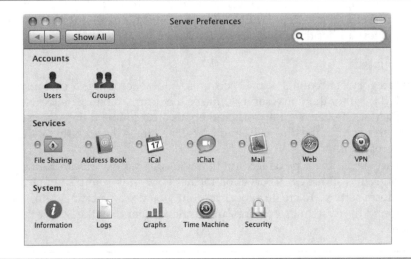

Figure 7-1.   Click the Users icon in the Accounts area of Server Preferences to get started creating accounts.

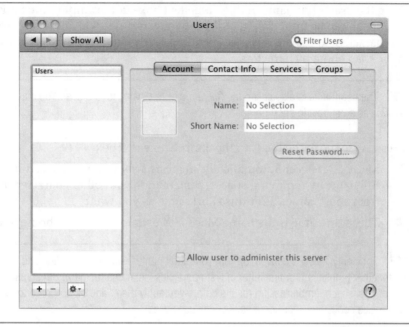

Figure 7-2. The Users preferences pane is where you create user accounts.

To get started adding a user, follow these steps:

1. Click the + button. Server Preferences displays the dialog box shown in Figure 7-3.

 NOTE If you're working on a server other than your directory server, you'll see a pop-up menu when you click the + button. Click the Create New User item to start creating a new user.

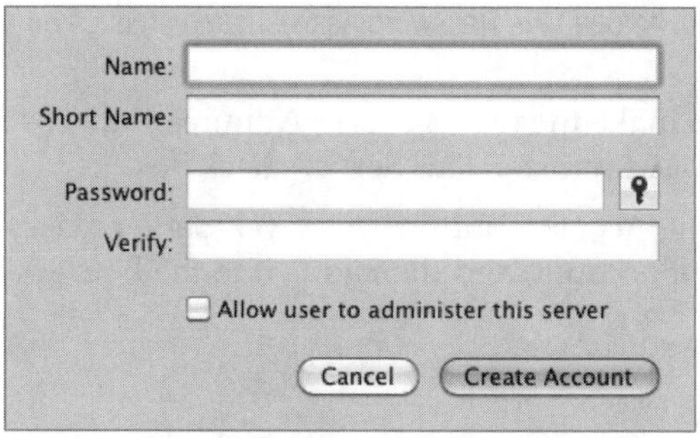

Figure 7-3. Create a new user account in this dialog box. Select the Allow User To Administer This Server check box if you want to make the user a Server Administrator.

2. Type the user's full name in the Name text box—for example, Ann Smith. The name can be up to 255 bytes long, which translates to anywhere from 63 characters to 255 characters depending on the character set—in any case, more than enough characters.

 NOTE The user name is also called the *full name* or *real name* for the user. You may also hear *long name* as a contrast to short name.

3. Press TAB to move the focus to the Short Name text box.

- Mac OS X Server automatically suggests a short name derived from the full name by removing spaces, punctuation, and other characters banned from short names. Edit this short name as you want.

- The short name is the name Mac OS X uses for the user's home folder.

 NOTE For clarity, follow a convention with your short names—for example, first and last name fused together (annsmith), or first letter of first name plus last name (asmith). But scrutinize each name for offensive or embarrassing results before you apply them, and be prepared to fall back on an alternative convention—or horse sense—in such cases.

- Each user account can have up to 16 short names. Start with one short name. Add others only as needed—for example, if you need to create aliases for e-mail accounts.

 TIP To avoid confusion, make each short name unique, even if doing so means distorting your naming convention. If you're not sure whether you've already used a short name, search for that name in Workgroup Manager (discussed later in this chapter).

4. Type the initial password in the Password text box and in the Verify text box.

 NOTE As when setting up Mac OS X Server in Chapter 3, you can click the key icon to the right of the Password text box to open the Password Assistant and produce an automated password.

5. If you want to make the user a Server Administrator for this server, select the Allow User To Administer This Server check box.

6. Click the Create Account button. Mac OS X Server closes the dialog box, creates the user account, and then adds it to the Users pane on the left of Users preferences.

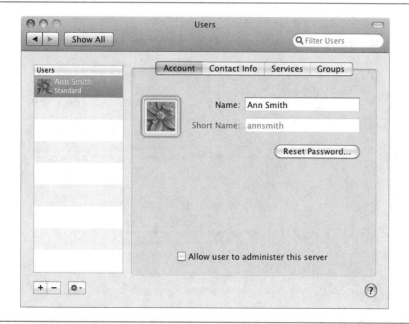

Figure 7-4.   After adding a user, you can apply a picture to their account or (usually later) reset their password.

With the user selected in the Users pane, as in Figure 7-4, you can apply a picture to the user account by clicking the picture panel. I've added one of Mac OS X's arty flowers here to make the panel more noticeable, but you'll probably want to apply the mug shot HR took after fingerprinting your colleague, as having the picture is useful both for security and for remembering who's who. You can also click the Reset Password button to display a dialog box for changing the user's password after he or she has forgotten it. Or you can change the other settings for the user account as described in the next sections.

Changing the User's Contact Information

To change the contact information for the user, click the user in the Users pane on the left of Users preferences, and then click the Contact Info tab. In the Contact Info pane (see Figure 7-5), you can change the user's name and address; chat, e-mail addresses, and phone numbers; and website and blog addresses.

Most of this is straightforward, but there are a couple of things to note:

- **Add a chat address, e-mail address, or phone number**   Click the + button with the drop-down arrow below the Contact box, and then choose the type of contact information you want to add. Mac OS X Server adds the appropriate field to the Contact list. You can then type in the address or phone number.

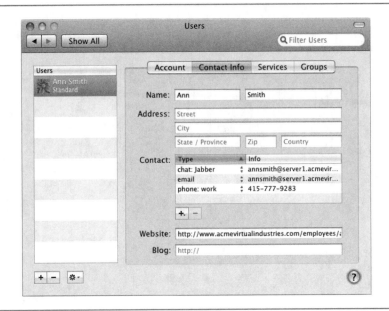

Figure 7-5.   Add the user's address, e-mail, website and more in the Contact Info pane.

- ■   **Change the type of phone number or chat address**   Click the button in the Type column of the Contact list to display a pop-up menu of phone number types or chat types. You can then choose a different type—for example, phone: fax instead of phone: work or chat: Jabber instead of chat: AIM.

Changing the Services Available to the User

Next, click the Services tab to display the Services pane (see Figure 7-6). With the appropriate user selected in the Users pane on the left, clear the check box for any service you do not want the user to be able to use, leaving selected only the check boxes for those services the user may use.

Assigning the User to Groups

To assign the user to the groups to which they belong, click the Groups tab and work in the Groups pane (see Figure 7-7).

When you first open the Groups pane, you'll probably see only the group named Workgroup. This is a default group that contains all members—so don't try to remove a user from it, as you can't.

Apart from Workgroup, you have full control over the groups to which you assign a user. The check boxes next to the list of groups are unavailable until you click the Edit Membership button. This is a toggle button, so when you click the button, it changes to reverse video—white text on a gray background. Select or clear check boxes in the list box as needed, and then click the Edit Membership button again to turn off editing.

Figure 7-6. In the Services pane, clear the check box for any service the user is barred from using.

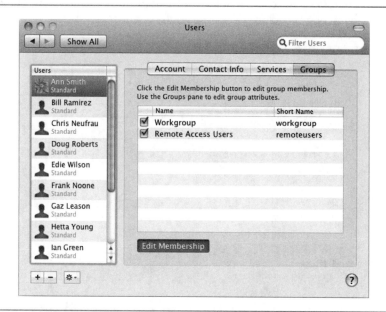

Figure 7-7. In the Groups pane, make the user a member of the appropriate groups.

NOTE   See the section "Working with Groups," later in this chapter, for instructions on setting up groups the way you need them.

Choosing E-mail Message Settings

When each new user logs on to the server for the first time, Mac OS X Server automatically sends a message to them telling them the server's DNS name and the services it provides (so that they know whether they have calendaring, wikis, or whatever). You get to choose what else goes in that message. For example, you may want to let the user know which folders they'll find reference documents in, whom to contact for help, or which of the local food shacks to avoid at all costs. You'll probably also want to include your name and e-mail address so that they know whom to hold responsible when the network goes south.

To set up this message, click the Action button (the button with the cog wheel) in the lower-left corner of the Users preferences and choose Email Message Settings from the pop-up menu. Mac OS X Server displays the Email Message Settings dialog box (see Figure 7-8).

Type your name the way you want it to appear in the Administrator Full Name text box, then type your e-mail address in the Administrator Email text box. (I'm assuming you're the administrator here.)

In the Custom Email Introduction area, you can add a message to the Welcome text box to make the automated message more human. You can also add text to the Invitation text box to customize the invitation message that goes out to users of the server.

When you've made your choices, click the Save button to save them. The Email Message Settings dialog box closes.

Email Message Settings (required)

Administrator Full Name: |

Administrator Email: john@example.com

Custom Email Introduction (optional)

Welcome: Not customized

Invitation: Not customized

(?)   (Cancel)   (Save)

Figure 7-8.   In the Email Message Settings dialog box, type a welcome message and invitation for your server to send to each new user who joins the network.

NOTE   You can also send an invitation manually at other times if you need to. Just select the user or group in the Users preferences pane, click the Action button, and then choose Send Invitation from the pop-up menu.

Importing User Accounts from Another Server

If your network already has a server running Open Directory, you can connect your new server to the Open Directory server and import user accounts from that server. You can also do this during the setup process, as discussed in Chapter 3, but in some cases it's more convenient to do it later—for example, if the directory server isn't available when you're setting up the next server.

Here's how to connect your new server to a directory server:

1. Click the System Preferences icon on the Dock to open the System Preferences window.

2. Click the Accounts icon to display the Accounts preferences pane.

3. Click the Login Options button to display the Login Options pane (see Figure 7-9).

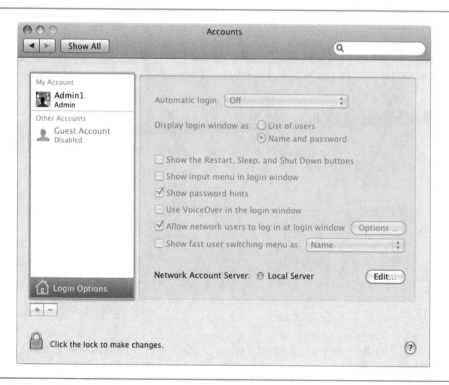

Figure 7-9.   Click the Edit button in the Login Options pane to display the dialog box for connecting to a directory server.

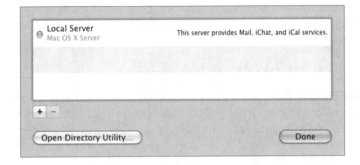

Figure 7-10. Click the Add button in this dialog box to connect your new server to an existing directory server.

4. Click the Edit button to open the dialog box for connecting to a directory server (see Figure 7-10).

5. Click the Add button (the + button) to open the dialog box for choosing the server (see Figure 7-11).

6. Open the Server pop-up menu and see if the server appears:

   ■ If the server appears, click its name to select it.

   ■ If the server does not appear, type the server's name or address in the Server text box.

7. Click the OK button. The dialog box closes, and Mac OS X Server tries to connect to the directory server.

8. If Mac OS X Server prompts you to authenticate yourself, type your password and click the OK button.

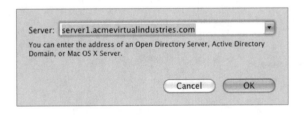

Figure 7-11. Enter the directory server's name or address in this dialog box, and then click the OK button.

9. Click the Done button. Mac OS X Server returns you to the Login Options pane.

10. Press ⌘-Q or choose System Preferences | Quit System Preferences to quit System Preferences.

After connecting to the server, you can import accounts from it like this:

1. Click the Add button below the Users pane and choose Import User From Directory from the pop-up menu.

2. Type the user's name (or part of it) in the search field.

3. Select the user's name.

4. Select the Send Imported Users An Email Invitation check box if you want Mac OS X Server to send the users an invitation.

5. Click the Import button.

6. Click the Done button when you have finished importing users.

Deleting a User Account

When someone leaves your company or organization, you will probably need to delete their user account from the server or from the directory. When you delete the account, the user can no longer log on with it, access group services or wikis, or view the address books or calendars—as you'd expect. As you'd probably also expect, any of the user's data stored in Time Machine backup is unaffected.

CAUTION   When you delete the account, Mac OS X Server also deletes all of the user's mail that's left on the server. If the user has left the company under unusual circumstances, it may be a good idea to double check with management that it's okay to get rid of the mail before you off the user account.

To delete an account, click it in the Users pane in Users preferences, and then click the – button. Mac OS X Server confirms the deletion, as shown in Figure 7-12; click the Delete User button if you're sure you want the account to sleep with the fishes.

Permanently delete user "Gaz Leason"?

This action is permanent and cannot be undone. The user account will be removed, its group memberships will be canceled, and it will no longer be an automatic iChat buddy.

Cancel   Delete User

Figure 7-12.   When you ask to delete an account, Mac OS X Server suggests there might be mitigating circumstances.

Working with Groups in Server Preferences

To set up your groups, open Server Preferences, and then click the Groups icon in the Accounts area. You'll see the Groups preferences pane (see Figure 7-13); click the Group tab if the Group pane isn't already displayed.

Mac OS X Server starts you off with a default group named Workgroup, and adds each user account you create to it. You can't remove anybody from Workgroup, so you need to use different groups to differentiate the users and their needs.

Creating a New Group and Adding Members

To create a new group, click the + button below the Groups pane. Mac OS X Server displays the dialog box shown in Figure 7-14, in which you type the group's descriptive name and short name.

 CAUTION You can't change a group's short name after you create it, so take a moment to make sure you choose a suitable name first time around.

When you click the Create Group button, Mac OS X Server closes the dialog box and adds the group to the Groups list in the Groups pane.

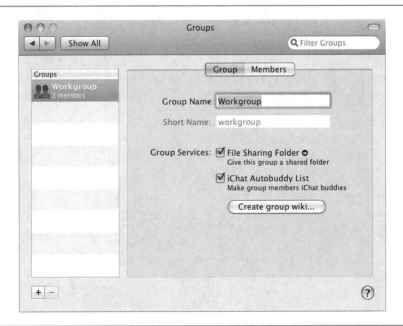

Figure 7-13. When you first open the Group pane in Groups preferences, it will likely contain only the default group, Workgroup.

Figure 7-14. Type the group's descriptive name and short name in this dialog box, and then click the Create Group button.

You can then set up the group like this:

1. Click the group in the Groups pane (if it's not already selected). In the Group Services area (see Figure 7-15), you'll see that Mac OS X Server has automatically selected the two check boxes in the Group Services area.

2. Clear the File Sharing Folder check box if you don't want the group to have a shared folder for exchanging files. Mac OS X Server creates this folder automatically for you in the /Groups/ folder on the server's startup disk. Click the arrow button to the right of File Sharing Folder to pop open a Finder window showing the shared folder.

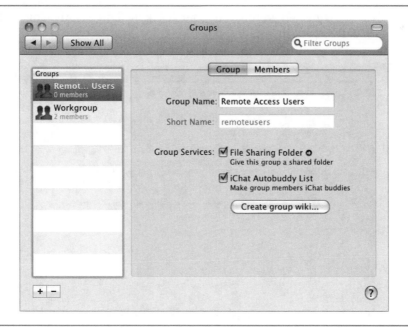

Figure 7-15. A new group added and ready for configuration.

NOTE Whether to have a shared folder for a group depends on the group's purpose and members. For example, if the group is a team who work on a project, odds are a shared folder will come in handy. But if the group consists of individuals who don't share a goal—for example, remote access users—a shared folder may be next to useless.

3. Clear the iChat Autobuddy List check box if you don't want Mac OS X to automatically add the IM screen names of the group members to each member's Jabber list.

4. If you want to create a wiki (a collaborative website) for the group, click the Create Group Wiki button. Your default web browser (for example, Safari) opens and launches the Create A New Wiki Assistant (see Figure 7-16). Follow through the screens of the Assistant to create the wiki.

5. To add members to the group, click the Members tab.

6. In the Members pane (see Figure 7-17), click the group you want to affect in the Groups pane on the left, then click the Edit Membership button. As when working with group membership in Users preferences, this is a toggle button that changes to reverse video (white letters on a dark gray button) when you click it.

7. With the Edit Membership button turned on, select the check box for each user you want to add to the group (see Figure 7-18).

8. When you've finished editing the group, click the Edit Membership button again to turn off editing mode.

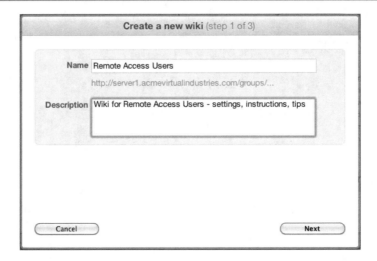

Figure 7-16. The Create A New Wiki Assistant walks you through the steps of creating a new wiki for a group of users.

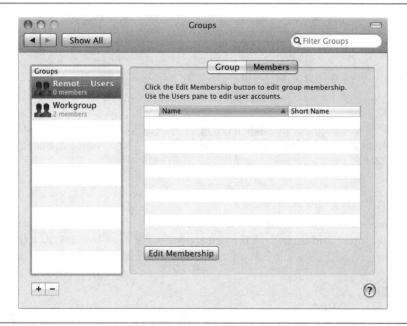

Figure 7-17. Click the group you want to affect, and then click the Edit Membership button.

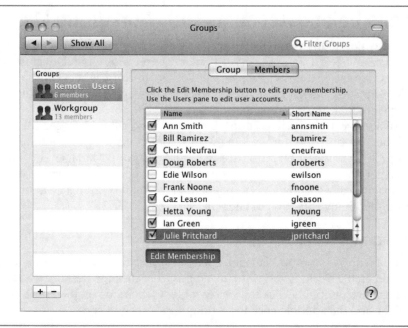

Figure 7-18. Select the check box of each member you want to assign to the group.

Figure 7-19. When you ask to delete a group, Mac OS X Server warns you that you won't be able to put Humpty Dumpty back together again. Click the Delete Group button if you're ready to make an omelet.

Removing Members from a Group

To remove members from a group, click the group in the Groups pane, click the Edit Membership button, and then clear the check box for each user you want to remove. When you've finished, click the Edit Membership button again to turn off editing mode.

Deleting a Group

To delete a group, click it in the Groups pane, and then click the – button below the Groups pane. When Mac OS X Server displays the confirmation dialog box shown in Figure 7-19, click the Delete Group button.

Creating and Editing Accounts with Workgroup Manager

As you saw earlier in this chapter, the quick and easy way to create user accounts is to use Server Preferences. If you use Server Preferences on your Open Directory Master server, the accounts go straight into your network's directory, which is usually easiest for small- or mid-size networks; if you use Server Preferences on another server, the accounts go into that server's directory.

You can also create and edit accounts by using Workgroup Manager, Mac OS X Server's heavier-duty tool for working with accounts, groups, computers, and computer groups. This section introduces you to Workgroup Manager and shows you how to get started with it. Workgroup Manager is a powerful weapon with wide-ranging capabilities; we'll cover various essential capabilities in this chapter but leave others for in-depth investigation in later chapters.

Opening Workgroup Manager

To get started with Workgroup Manager, open the application by clicking the Workgroup Manager icon on the Dock. If you've removed this icon, click the desktop, choose Go | Applications, click or double-click the Server folder (depending on the Finder view you're using), and then double-click the Workgroup Manager icon.

In the Workgroup Manager Connect dialog box (see Figure 7-20), type the address of the server that you want to connect to if it's different from the one the Address box

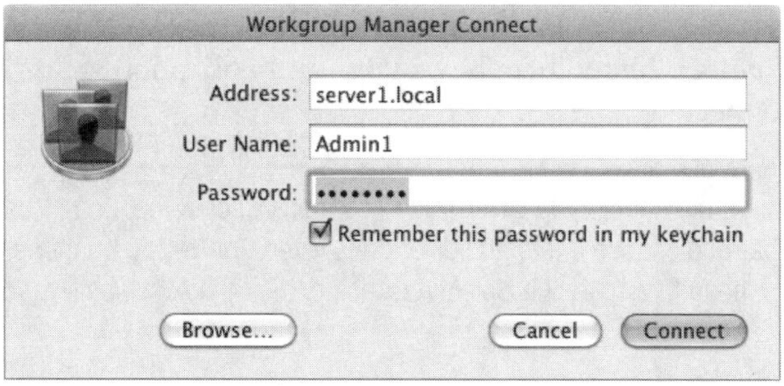

Figure 7-20. In the Workgroup Manager Connect check box, choose the server you want to work on.

is suggesting. (The Address box shows the server you most recently used.) Similarly, make sure the user name and password are correct, and then click the Connect button.

Workgroup Manager then opens in read-only mode because you haven't yet authenticated yourself. In read-only mode (see Figure 7-21), you can browse the

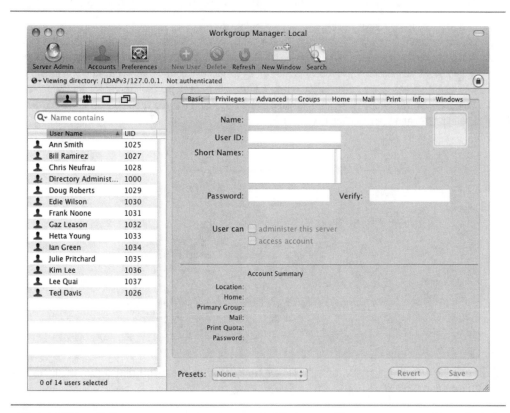

Figure 7-21. Before you can make changes in Workgroup Manager, you need to unlock the application and authenticate yourself.

information but not change it, so key controls such as the New User button on the toolbar are not available. The authentication bar across the top of the Workgroup Manager window below the toolbar shows your authentication status and the directory to which you're connected.

NOTE To change the directory to which you're connected, click the globe icon on the left of the authentication bar and choose one of the directories listed on the pop-up menu. Choose Other from the pop-up menu to display the Select A Directory dialog box, which lets you browse available directories.

Click the lock icon on the right side of the authentication bar to display the Authenticate To Directory dialog box (see Figure 7-22).

Type the directory administrator's user name in the User Name text box and password in the Password text box, select the Remember This Password In My Keychain check box if you want to store the password, and then click the Authenticate button.

Once you've authenticated yourself, the previously unavailable controls become available, and you can start creating new users—or groups, or computers, or groups of computers—or start editing them. On the basis that you've probably created users already using Server Preferences, this section focuses on editing an existing user.

NOTE To add a new user from Workgroup Manager, click the New User button on the toolbar. The first time you do this, Mac OS X Server displays a dialog box warning you that new users may not have access to servers: If your server is using service access controls, you may need to grant the new users access to the services you need. You use the Access pane of Server Admin to do this. Select the Do Not Show This Warning Again check box if you want to suppress the warning dialog box in future, and then click the OK button.

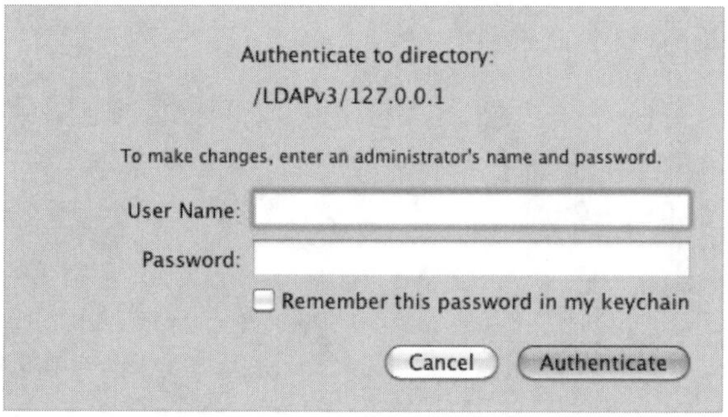

Authenticate to directory:
/LDAPv3/127.0.0.1

To make changes, enter an administrator's name and password.

User Name:
Password:
☐ Remember this password in my keychain

Cancel   Authenticate

Figure 7-22. Authenticate yourself to the directory by entering the directory administrator's user name and password.

Finding the Users You Need to Edit

If you've got a short list of users, finding the user name is as easy as shooting catfish in a barrel. But if you've got a telephone directory of users, use the Search field above the list of users to find your victim.

You can simply type in a string of text and get the default search item, Name Contains, or you can click the pop-up triangle next to the search icon and choose the type of search you want from the list, as shown here.

Click the last item, Advanced Search, when you need to dig deeper. The resulting dialog box, shown here, enables you to set up a search with multiple criteria. Use the first line of controls to specify the first criterion, and then click the + button at the right end if you need to add another line of controls.

After setting up a search, you can use the Search Presets pop-up menu to save the search as a preset that you can reuse later as needed. You can also select the Perform A Batch Edit On The Search Results check box if you want to apply the same change to each of the records you find. When you select this check box, you can also select the Preview And Edit Search Results Before Applying Changes check box if you want to look through the search results before having the change made, or select the Display Postview Of Changes And Errors check box if you want to see the result of making the changes. (Both checks are usually a good idea.)

Editing a User

In this section, we'll look at most of the settings you'll want to set for a user, but we'll leave some of the settings for other chapters. For example, we'll leave the Mail pane settings to Chapter 10 (which focuses on e-mail) and the Print pane settings to Chapter 14 (three guesses).

To start editing a user, follow these steps:

1. Click the Users button in the left pane if it's not already selected.
2. Click the user in the left pane. The current settings for the user appear in the right pane.

Choosing Basic Settings for a User

After you've selected the user you want to affect, click the Basic tab if the Basic pane isn't already displayed. In this pane (see Figure 7-23), you find essential information about the user, from their full name and user ID to whether they're allowed to administer the server (not usually) or access their user account (usually). You can change anything except the user's short name (or multiple short names, as the case may be).

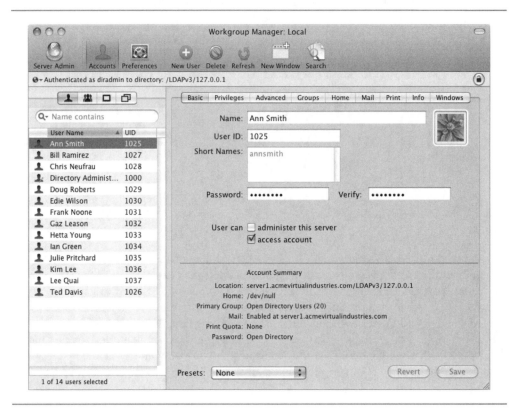

Figure 7-23. Information in the Basic pane includes the user's name, user ID, short name, and access level.

The Account Summary area toward the bottom of the Basic pane provides a summary of the user's location, home folder, primary group, mail status, print quota, and password type. More on most of these items shortly.

TIP To save time when setting up users, set up one user with settings that various other users need. Then open the Presets pop-up menu, choose Save Preset, type a name for the preset in the dialog box that opens, and then click the OK button. You can then choose the preset from the Presets pop-up menu to apply those settings to another user. The Presets pop-up menu also contains menu items for deleting and renaming presets,

If you make changes in the Basic pane, or any of the other panes in Workgroup Manager, click the Save button to save the changes.

TIP To get users' settings straight, you may need to look at two users' entries at the same time. You can do so by clicking the New Window button on the toolbar to open a new Workgroup Manager window to the same directory you're viewing. You can also view another server at the same time by choosing Server | Connect, entering the details in the Workgroup Manager Connect dialog box, and then clicking the Connect button.

Conferring Administrative Privileges on a User

The Privileges pane lets you spell out which administrative privileges the user has. For most users, only the Administration Capabilities pop-up menu appears in the pane, and it is set to None—the user can't do any administration.

The other choices in the Administration Capabilities pop-up menu are Limited and Full. When you choose Full, you give the user full administrative rein over Workgroup Manager; they can make all the changes you can.

What you're more likely to want to do is give the user some of the keys to the shop but not the full bunch. To do this, morphing the user into a limited administrator, follow these steps:

1. Choose Limited in the Administrative Capabilities pop-up menu. The Privileges pane displays controls for choosing what the user can administer.

2. Click the + button to the right of the User Can Administer list box to display the sidebar (see Figure 7-24).

3. To specify who or what the user can administer, drag users (from the Users tab of the sidebar) or groups (from the Groups tab of the sidebar) to the User Can Administer list box. If you add an item you don't want, select it and click the – button to remove it.

4. In the list box, select the item for which you want to set the limited administrator's administrative privileges. For example, click a group.

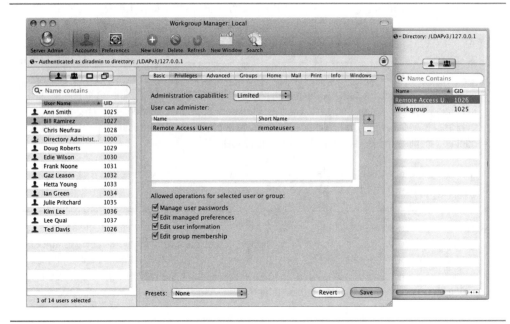

Figure 7-24. Drag users or groups to the User Can Administer list box to tell Mac OS X Server what to let the limited administrator administer.

5. In the Allowed Operations For Selected User area, clear the check box for any privilege you do not want to grant the limited administrator:

- **Manage User Passwords** Enables the limited administrator to change passwords for users or groups.

NOTE Rest easy—the limited administrator can't change the locks on you. Mac OS X Server sensibly prevents a limited administrator from changing a full administrator's password.

- **Edit Managed Preferences** Enables the limited administrator to change the managed preferences for users.

- **Edit User Information** Enables the limited administrator to change the user's information—for example, updating their address.

- **Edit Group Membership** Enables the limited administrator to change the members of a group.

6. Click the Save button to save the changes.

Choosing Advanced Settings for a User

The Advanced pane in Workgroup Manager (see Figure 7-25) lets you set up calendaring, control whether the user can log in on two or more managed computers at the same time, change their password type, and add comments and keywords.

To enable the user's calendar, select the Enable Calendaring check box, and then pick the appropriate server in the pop-up menu.

If you want the user to be able to log in using two or more computers at the same time, select the Allow Simultaneous Login On Managed Computers check box. Normally, you'll want to keep this feature for administrators; usually, when a user wants to move to another Mac, they should log out of the Mac they've been using.

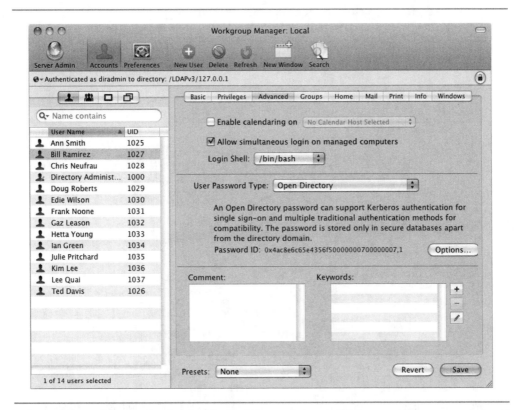

Figure 7-25.   Among other settings in the Advanced pane in Workgroup Manager, you can add comments and keywords to a user account.

To control which shell the user sees when they open a Terminal window, select the appropriate shell in the Login Shell pop-up menu. The menu offers standard shells from bash and csh through tcsh and zsh, but you can also click Custom and use the resulting dialog box to specify a custom shell if you have one.

To choose which type of password a user has, select the appropriate type in the User Password Type pop-up menu. You have three choices:

■ **Open Directory**   Use this password type for user accounts stored in Open Directory. Ideally, that should be most of them.

■ **Crypt Password**   Use this password type for connecting to older versions of Mac OS X Server.

■ **Shadow Password**   Use this password type for user accounts stored in the local domain directory rather than in Open Directory.

Usually you'll want to use Open Directory passwords for most of your users. You can then click the Options button and set options for the user in the resulting dialog box (see Figure 7-26).

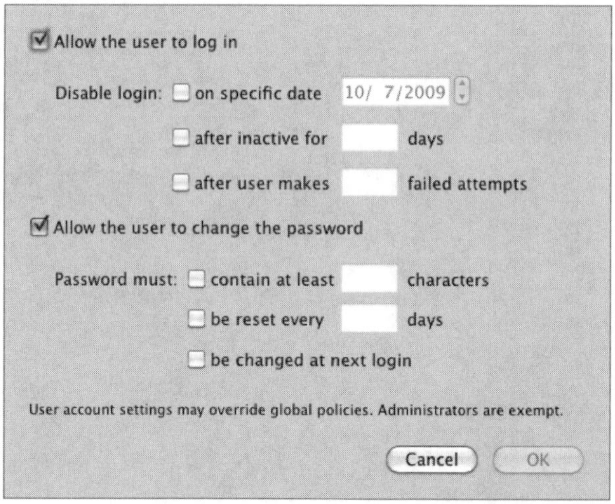

Figure 7-26.   Use this dialog box to disable login, to set a minimum length for the password, or to force password changes.

Most of the options are pretty straightforward.

- You can choose whether to allow the user to log in at all—which you'll normally want to do—but choose to disable login on a specific date, if the account remains inactive for too long, or if the user makes too many failed attempts to log in (which may indicate an attack—or arthritis).

- You can decide whether the user may change the password. If so, you can set a minimum password length, force the user to create a new password after a certain number of days, or change the password at next login.

 TIP   Setting a minimum password length is a good idea; eight characters is usually a safe minimum. Forcing the user to create a new password every so often is largely pointless, as the only attackers it takes out are ones who have learned a password and are using it to snoop delicately. If you suspect any password may have been compromised, use the Be Changed At Next Login check box to force a change sooner.

Click the OK button when you've finished setting password options. You can then add any comments needed to the Comment text box or add keywords to the Keywords list box. Click the + button to the right of the Keywords list box to open the Select The Keywords To Add dialog box, or click the Edit button (the button with the pencil icon) to display the Manage Available Keywords dialog box, where you can build your list of keywords.

Changing a User's Group Membership

To change the groups to which a user belongs, click the Groups tab and work in the Groups pane (see Figure 7-27). Here are the main moves you can make here:

- **Change the user's primary group**   The primary group is the group Mac OS X Server uses to determine the user's permissions when the user tries to access a file that belongs to someone else. At first, Open Directory assigns all your users to the Open Directory Users group, which has the short name staff. You can change the group by typing the new group's ID number in the Primary Group ID text box. Logically enough, the primary group doesn't appear in the Other Groups list box.

- **Add or remove groups**   To add the user to another group, click the + button, and then drag the group from the sidebar to the Other Groups list box. To remove a group, click it in the Other Groups list box, and then click the – button.

- **View the parent groups of groups**   Click the Show Inherited Groups button to display the parent groups in the Other Groups list box.

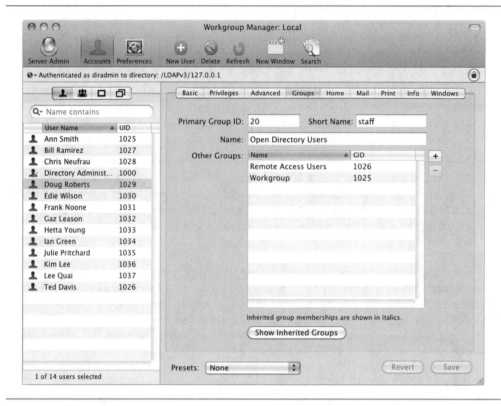

Figure 7-27. In the Groups pane in Workgroup Manager, you can change the user's group membership or primary group.

Choosing Home, Mail, and Print Settings for the User

We're going to skip over the next three panes in Workgroup Manager here, as they're covered in depth in later chapters:

- **Home pane** This pane lets you choose where to locate the user's Home folder and how it should behave. Chapter 11 explains how to set up home folders.

- **Mail pane** In this pane, you set up the user's access to e-mail. Chapter 10 shows you how to set up e-mail.

- **Print pane** In this pane, you can apply a print quota to the user. Chapter 14 discusses how to set up printing.

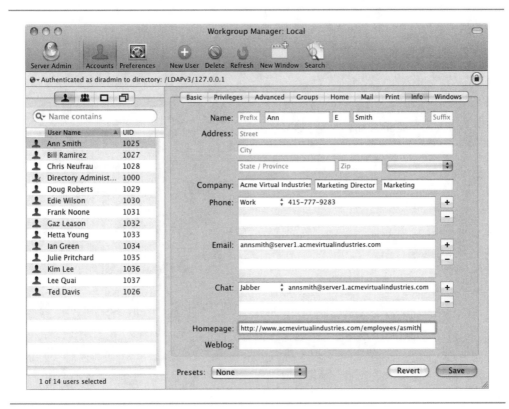

Figure 7-28. You can enter chapter and verse about the user in the Info pane in Work-group Manager.

Setting Information for the User

In the Info pane in Workgroup Manager, you can set everything from the user's real-world names (first, middle initial, last) and address to their homepage and blog addresses. As you can see in Figure 7-28, the fields are straightforward to use.

Choosing Settings for Windows Users

If your network includes Windows PCs, click the Windows tab to display the Windows pane (see Figure 7-29), and then enter the user profile path, login script, and path for the user. In the Hard Drive pop-up menu, select the drive letter that you'd like the home folder to appear on; the default drive is H:.

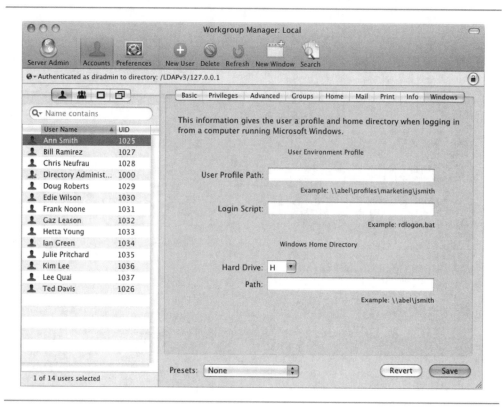

Figure 7-29. The Windows pane in Workgroup Manager contains settings for making Windows PCs comfortable on your network.

Creating and Editing Groups in Workgroup Manager

Workgroup Manager also enables you to create and edit groups. As discussed earlier in this chapter, you'll normally want to create your groups by using Server Preferences and then use Workgroup Manager to adjust those settings that Server Preferences can't reach. But you can also create a new group in Workgroup Manager by choosing Server | New Group.

To work with groups in Workgroup Manager, click the Groups button at the top of the left pane. Then click the group in the pane—search for it if you've got a plethora of groups—to display its contents. There are three panes—Basic, Members, and Group Folder. I'll unimaginatively start with the first one.

Choosing Basic Settings for a Group

The Basic pane for a group in Workgroup Manager (see Figure 7-30) lets you control the following:

- **Name** Enter or edit the group's long name here. You can use up to 255 bytes, which is enough for anywhere from 63–255 characters, depending on the character set you're using. So you can use long names, but you get bonus points for concision.

- **Short name** Enter or edit the group's short name. Short names are typically eight characters or fewer, but you can use up to 255 characters at the risk of losing your bonus points. You're limited to A through Z (uppercase or lower), 0 through 9, underscores, hyphens, and periods.

- **Group ID** This is a string of ASCII digits that identifies the group uniquely within your directory. If you've created a group using Server Preferences, there's little reason to change its group ID. If you do change it, you can use strings up to 2,147,483,647 (2^31 with a starting value of 0).

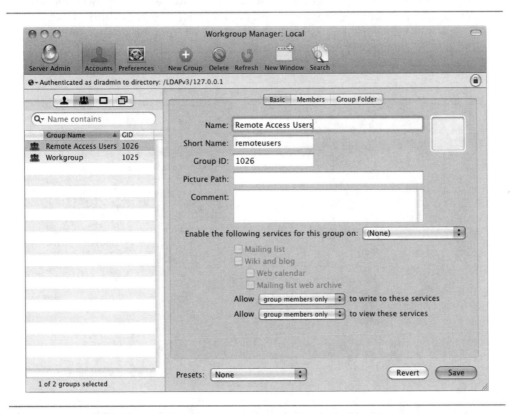

Figure 7-30. In the Basic pane, you can choose settings including the group's name, picture path, and services.

- ■ **Picture Path**   Enter or edit the path to the picture you want to use for the group's login picture in Workgroup Manager. To enter the path, open a Finder window and drag a picture file to the picture panel to the right of the Name text box.

- ■ **Comment**   Type any comment about the group in this text box.

- ■ **Enable The Following Services For This Group On**   In this pop-up menu, select the server that will provide the services. You can then select the check boxes for the services you want to provide. Use the two Allow pop-up menus to decide whether only group members, only some group members, authenticated users, or anyone can use these services.

 TIP   As with user accounts, you can save time with groups by creating presets and applying them as needed.

Choosing Members for a Group

To change the membership of a group in Workgroup Manager, click the Members tab, and then work in the Members pane (see Figure 7-31). Here, you can add users by clicking the + button and then dragging users or groups from the sidebar, or remove users by selecting them and then clicking the – button.

Figure 7-31.   Use the Members pane in Workgroup Manager to add members to a group or remove them.

Setting Up a Group Folder for a Group

Many groups benefit from having a shared folder to work in. To set up such a folder, use the controls in the Group Folder pane of Workgroup Manager (shown in Figure 7-32 with a folder added).

To set up a folder, click the + button, specify the folder's location in the dialog box that opens, and then click the OK button.

To set the owner for the folder, click the ellipsis (…) button to the right of the Short Name text box in the Owner area to display the sidebar, and then drag the owner to the Short Name text box. Mac OS X Server snaps the information into place.

Click the Save button when you've finished making changes to the group.

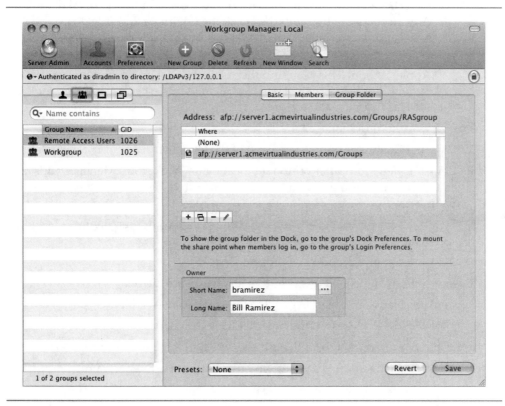

Figure 7-32.   Set up a group folder in the Group Folder pane in Workgroup Manager.

Creating Computer Accounts in Workgroup Manager

As I mentioned at the beginning of the chapter, you can also create accounts for computers in Workgroup Manager. A computer account enables you to manage a computer rather than a user.

To set up a computer account, follow these steps:

1. Find out the computer's name, its MAC address, and its hardware UUID:

   ■ **Computer name** It's usually easiest to use the name set in Sharing preferences on the Mac.

   ■ **MAC address** This is the hardware address of the computer's Ethernet card. To find it on the Mac, open System Preferences, click Network, and then click the Ethernet item. Click the Advanced button to display the Advanced dialog box, and then click the Ethernet tab. Write down the MAC address from the Ethernet ID readout at the top.

   ■ **Hardware UUID** This is the Mac's unique hardware address. Choose Apple | About This Mac, and then click the System Profiler button. In System Profiler, click the Hardware item in the left pane, and then look at the Hardware UUID readout.

2. Open Workgroup Manager.

3. Click the Computer button at the top of the left pane.

4. Click the New Computer button on the toolbar. Workgroup Manager adds a new computer and names it Untitled_1 in both the Name text box and the Short Name text box.

5. Type a descriptive name and a short name for the computer. Figure 7-33 shows these changes (and others) already made for a computer.

6. Add any comments and keywords needed.

7. In the Hardware UUID text box, type the hardware UUID.

8. Click the Network tab to display the Network pane (see Figure 7-34).

9. Type the MAC address in the Ethernet ID text box.

10. If the computer has a fixed IP address, type it in the IP Address text box.

11. Click the Save button to save the changes to the computer account.

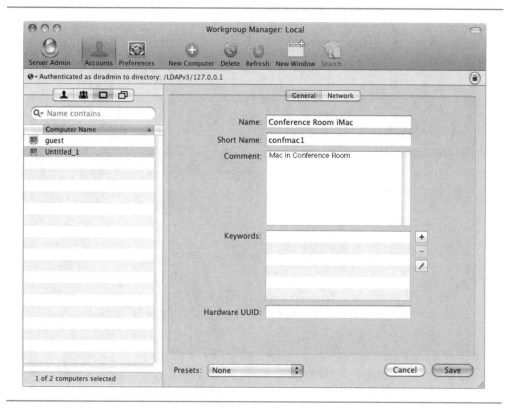

Figure 7-33.   Name the new computer in the General pane in Workgroup Manager.

Creating Computer Groups in Workgroup Manager

To manage the computer accounts you've created, you can place them in groups. By changing the settings for the group, you can then affect all its members.

To create a computer group, follow these steps:

1. Open Workgroup Manager.

2. Click the Computer Groups button at the top of the left pane.

3. Click the New Computer Group button on the toolbar. Workgroup Manager adds a new computer group, names it Untitled_1, and displays the Basic pane.

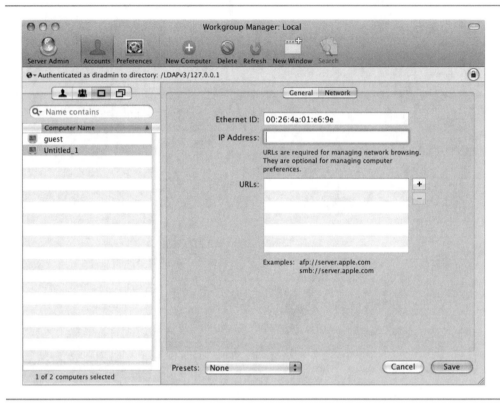

Figure 7-34.   Enter the computer's MAC address in the Ethernet ID text box in the Network tab.

4. Type the full name for the computer group in the Name text box.

5. Type the short name in the Short Name text box.

6. If necessary, change the group ID in the Group ID text box. Normally, you shouldn't need to change this number.

7. Type any comment needed for the group in the Comment text box.

8. Click the Members tab to display the Members pane.

9. Click the + button to display the sidebar.

10. Drag the appropriate computers to the group.

11. Click the Save button to save the computer group.

CHAPTER 8 | Add the iPhone or iPod touch to Your Network

These days, if you want to squeeze every bit of productivity out of your employees, you need to give them the best toys around. That means providing your best and brightest with the iPhone or the iPod touch, and connecting the devices to your network so that they can use them at any time—both when in the office and elsewhere.

To configure the iPhone or iPod touch to connect to the network, you can change the settings manually—but you can save time and effort by using Apple's iPhone Configuration Utility to automate the process. This chapter concentrates on using the iPhone Configuration Utility to set up the devices to connect to the network and use its services. For instructions on setting up the devices manually, see the section toward the end of the chapter.

Automating the Configuration of an iPhone or iPod touch

To configure an iPhone or iPod touch automatically, you use the iPhone Configuration Utility to create a configuration profile. You then apply that profile to the device, which picks up all the settings in the profile.

Let's take it from the top.

Getting and Installing the iPhone Configuration Utility

The first step is to get the iPhone Configuration Utility from the Enterprise page on Apple's iPhone support site. Point Safari (or your favorite browser) at www.apple .com/support/iphone/enterprise/, and then download the iPhone Configuration Utility for Mac OS X.

 NOTE   Apple also provides a version of the iPhone Configuration Utility for Windows. It runs on Windows XP Service Pack 3 or a newer version—Vista, Windows 7, Windows Server 2003, or Windows Server 2008.

The iPhone Configuration Utility comes as a disk image file. Your browser may open it for you and launch Installer; if not, double-click the disk image to open it, and then double-click the iPhoneConfigurationUtility.pkg file to kick Installer into life.

Follow through the Installer steps. Apart from swallowing or balking at the license agreement, your only decision is whether to change the install location from your server's hard disk (which is usually fine) to somewhere else.

 NOTE   You can run the iPhone Configuration Utility on any Mac, not just on your server. For simplicity, I'll assume you're using the server here.

Once you've installed iPhone Configuration Utility, run it from the /Applications/ Utilities/ folder. You'll see a window like the one in Figure 8-1. The Library section of the sidebar contains items for Devices, Applications, Provisioning Profiles,

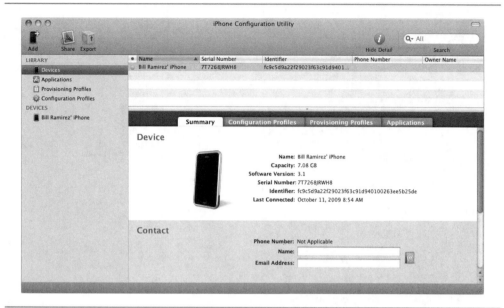

Figure 8-1.   iPhone Configuration Utility detects any iPhones or iPod touches connected to your Mac.

and Configuration Profiles. The Devices section lists each connected device (in the figure, an iPhone is connected).

Creating a Configuration Profile

To configure an iPhone or iPod touch automatically, you create a *configuration profile*. This is an XML file that contains details of what the device is and isn't allowed to do on your network. The configuration profile contains *payloads*, groups of settings for different aspects of the configuration. For example, a configuration file can contain one payload of e-mail settings and another payload of settings for virtual private networking.

TIP   Depending on your network's needs, you can either create a single configuration profile that contains every setting you want to apply to the iPhones and iPod touches or multiple profiles, each of which covers different aspects of configuration. Having multiple profiles often gives you more flexibility than a single profile, and so saves you time and effort.

To create a new configuration profile and set its General information, follow these steps:

1. In the Library section of the sidebar, click the Configuration Profiles item.

2. Click the New button on the toolbar. You can also press ⌘-N or choose File | New Configuration Profile. iPhone Configuration Utility creates a new configuration profile and displays the controls for editing it (see Figure 8-2).

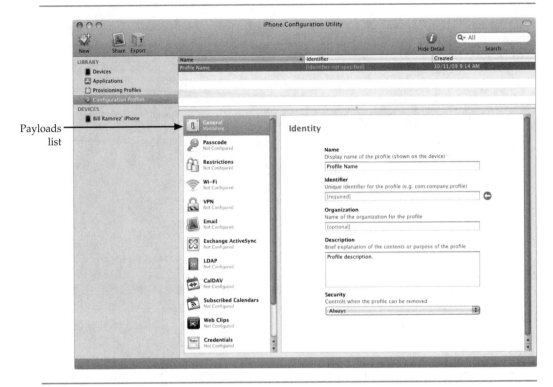

Payloads list

Figure 8-2. Ready to edit a new configuration profile in iPhone Configuration Utility.

3. With the General item selected in the payloads list, set the general information like this:

■ **Name** Type the name you want to use for the profile. This is the name that appears in the Name list in the upper pane.

■ **Identifier** Type the unique identifier you want to use for the profile—for example, **com.acmevirtualindustries.iphone1**. This identifier appears in the Identifier list in the upper pane.

■ **Organization** Type the name of your company or organization.

■ **Description** Type a description of this profile to help you distinguish it from the other profiles you create.

■ **Security** In this pop-up menu, choose how well you want to protect this profile against the user deleting it. Choose Never to prevent the user from deleting it (but allow updating with a newer profile), With Authorization to allow the user to delete it if they provide the correct password, or Always to allow the user to delete the profile. If you choose With Authorization, type the password in the Authorization Password text box that iPhone Configuration Utility displays.

After setting the General information like this, set the payloads by following the instructions in the upcoming sections as needed. For example, if you want to create a configuration profile that contains only Wi-Fi, VPN, and E-mail payloads, follow the instructions in only those sections.

Creating a Passcode Payload

If you want to protect the iPhone or iPod touch with a passcode that the user must enter to use the device, follow these steps:

1. Click the Passcode item in the payloads list. The right pane displays a Configure Passcode box. Click the Configure button to display the screen shown in Figure 8-3.

2. Select the Require Passcode On Device check box to activate the other controls.

3. Choose the settings for the passcode. Needs vary, but generally you'll want to clear the Allow Simple Value check box, select the Require Alphanumeric Value check box, set the Minimum Passcode Length pop-up menu to 6 or more, and set a short Auto-Lock period and Grace Period For Device Lock. If you use the Maximum Number Of Failed Attempts feature, set it to a number such as 10.

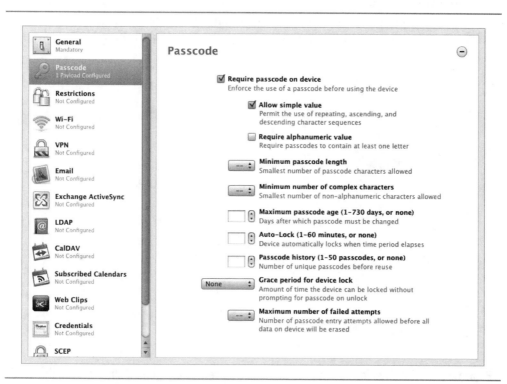

Figure 8-3.   To protect the iPhone or iPod touch, you'll probably want to lock it with a passcode.

Creating a Restrictions Payload

To restrict what the user can do on the iPhone or iPod touch, follow these steps:

1. Click the Restrictions item in the payloads list, and then click the Configure button in the Configure Restrictions box.

2. On the screen shown in Figure 8-4, clear the check box for each item you do not want to allow. You can:

   ■ Prevent the user from viewing content that's tagged as being explicit

   ■ Turn off Safari, YouTube, and the iTunes Store (referred to here in iPhone Configuration Utility as "iTunes Music Store")

   ■ Prevent the user from installing applications

   ■ Disallow the use of the iPhone's camera or the screen-capture feature on either the iPhone or the iPod touch

NOTE In case you haven't met the screen-capture feature—hold down the power button while you press the Home button to capture whatever the device's screen is showing.

Creating a Wi-Fi Payload

To set up the Wi-Fi network or networks the iPhone or iPod touch can connect to, click the Wi-Fi item in the payloads list, and then click the Configure button in the Configure

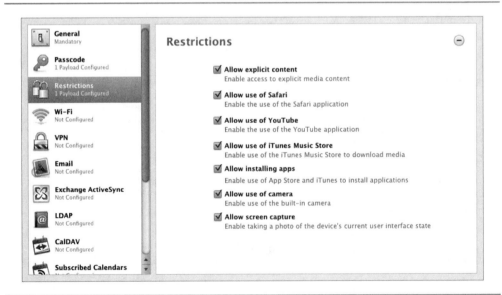

Figure 8-4. The Restrictions pane enables you to remove various distractions to the user's business-focused use of the iPhone or iPod touch.

Wi-Fi box. The Wi-Fi pane (shown in Figure 8-5 with settings already chosen) appears. Follow these steps to add a network:

1. In the Service Set Identifier (SSID) text box, type the SSID or network name.

2. Select the Hidden Network check box if you've set the access point to suppress broadcasts of the network's SSID.

3. Open the Security Type pop-up menu and choose the wireless security type the network uses—for example, WPA/WPA2.

4. In the Password text box, type the password for the wireless network.

To add another network, click the + button in the upper-right corner of the Wi-Fi pane, and then follow the preceding steps again.

Creating a VPN Payload

To set up the virtual private network (or networks) the iPhone or iPod touch can connect to, click the VPN item in the payloads list, and then click the Configure button in the Configure VPN box. In the VPN pane (shown in Figure 8-6 with some settings chosen), you can then set up the VPN connection like this:

1. In the Connection Name text box, type the name the user will see for the connection—for example, your company name and VPN.

2. In the Connection Type pop-up menu, choose the security protocol for the connection: Layer 2 Tunneling Protocol (L2TP), Point-to-Point Tunneling Protocol (PPTP), or IP Security (IPSec).

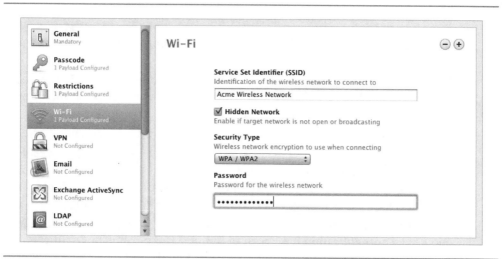

Figure 8-5.   Use the Wi-Fi pane to add the details for one or more wireless networks to the iPhone or iPod touch.

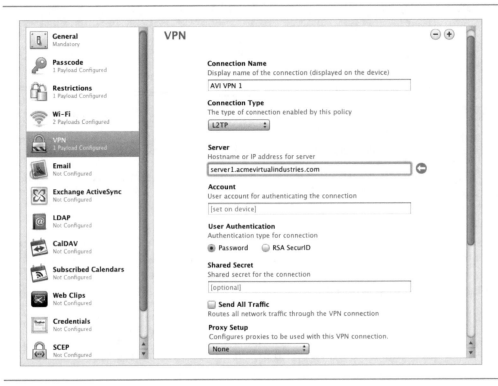

Figure 8-6. In the VPN pane, set up one or more virtual private network connections for the iPhone or iPod touch.

3. In the Server text box, type the hostname or IP address of the VPN server that the connection accesses.

4. In the Account text box, optionally type the user account for the VPN connection. Leave this text box blank if you want to have the user fill in the account.

5. For an L2TP connection or a PPTP connection, select the Password option button or the RSA SecurID option button, as appropriate, in the User Authentication area.

6. For a PPTP connection, open the Encryption Level pop-up menu and choose the strength of encryption to use. Automatic is normally the best choice, but you can also choose Maximum (128-Bit) to allow only connections with 128-bit encryption. Avoid using the None choice—all VPN connections need encryption.

7. For an IPSec connection, open the Machine Authentication pop-up menu and choose the authentication type: Shared Secret/Group Name or Certificate. If you choose Certificate, you will need to add a credential to the Credentials payload, as described later in this chapter. The VPN pane displays extra controls, as shown in Figure 8-7. Select the Include User PIN check box if the user will

Figure 8-7. When you choose to secure an IPSec VPN connection with a certificate, the VPN pane displays extra controls for controlling whether the user must provide a PIN and for allowing the device to establish a VPN on demand.

need to supply a personal identification number when connecting. You can also select the Enable VPN On Demand check box and build a list of domain names and host names that can set up a VPN connection.

8. For an L2TP connection or an IPSec connection, optionally type the shared secret in the Shared Secret text box. This preshared key is the same for all users of the VPN (unlike the account name and password, which are unique to each user).

To add another VPN, click the + button in the upper-right corner of the VPN pane, and then follow the preceding steps again.

NOTE See Chapter 15 for instructions on connecting client Macs to a VPN.

Creating an E-mail Payload

To set up e-mail for the iPhone or iPod touch, click the Email item in the payloads list, and then click the Configure button in the Configure Email box that appears. In the Email pane (see Figure 8-8), you can then set up e-mail like this:

1. In the Account Description text box, type the descriptive name by which the user will identify the account.

2. Open the Account Type pop-up menu and choose IMAP or POP, as appropriate.

Figure 8-8.   You can set up one or more e-mail accounts for the iPhone or iPod touch in the Email pane.

3. For an IMAP account, optionally type the path prefix in the Path Prefix text box.

4. If you're setting up a profile for a single user, type the account name in the Account Name text box and the e-mail address in the Email Address text box. If you're setting up a profile for multiple users, leave each of these text boxes set to "[set on device]".

5. In the Incoming Mail area, enter the details of the incoming mail server and authentication. Normally, you'll want to leave the User Name text box set to "[set on device]" to have the user set it.

6. Click the Outgoing Mail tab to display the Outgoing Mail controls, and then enter the details of the outgoing mail server and authentication. The available settings are the same as for the Incoming Mail area except for the addition of the Outgoing Password Same As Incoming check box, which you can select to use the same password for the outgoing mail server as for the incoming mail server.

To add another e-mail account, click the + button in the upper-right corner of the Email pane, and then follow the preceding steps again.

Setting Up an Exchange ActiveSync Payload

If your iPhones or iPod touches will need to connect to a server running Microsoft Exchange, you can set up an Exchange ActiveSync payload for the configuration file. Click the Exchange ActiveSync item in the payloads list, and then click the Configure button in the Configure Exchange ActiveSync box that appears.

 NOTE   Unlike with regular e-mail accounts, an iPhone or iPod touch can have only one Exchange account at a time.

You then see the Exchange ActiveSync pane (see Figure 8-9), in which you can choose settings like this:

1. In the Account Name text box, type the descriptive name the user will see for the account.

2. In the Exchange ActiveSync Host text box, type the hostname or IP address of the Exchange server.

3. Select the Use SSL check box if you want to secure the communications with Secure Sockets Layer—usually a good idea.

4. Optionally, type the domain in the Domain text box. Leave this text box blank and the User text box set to "[set on device]" to make the iPhone or iPod touch prompt the user to enter the user name.

5. If you're setting up a single account, type the e-mail address in the Email Address text box. Otherwise, leave it blank.

6. Similarly, you'll usually want to leave the Password text box blank.

7. To add to the payload a certificate for identifying the user, follow these steps:

   a. Click the + button below the Authentication Credential text box to display the Keychain dialog box shown in Figure 8-10.

   b. Select the certificate you want to use.

   c. Click the Choose button to close the dialog box and apply the certificate. iPhone Configuration Utility displays the dialog box shown in Figure 8-11.

   d. Type a passphrase in the Passphrase text box and the Verify text box, and then click the OK button. The certificate then appears in the Authentication Credential box, and its name appears in the Authentication Credential Name text box.

   e. If you want to include the passphrase rather than have the iPhone or iPod touch prompt the user for it, select the Include Authentication Credential Passphrase check box.

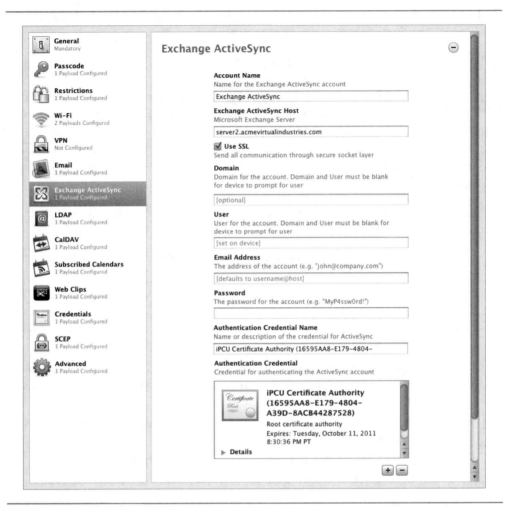

Figure 8-9. Set up an Exchange account in the Exchange ActiveSync pane.

Figure 8-10. In the Keychain dialog box, select the certificate to use for identifying the user.

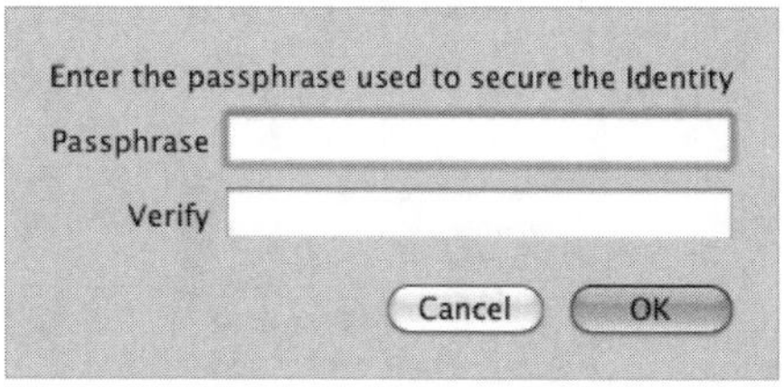

Enter the passphrase used to secure the Identity

Passphrase

Verify

Cancel   OK

Figure 8-11.   In this dialog box, secure the certificate with a passphrase.

Setting Up an LDAP Payload

If the iPhone or iPod touch will need to connect to an LDAP directory, configure an LDAP payload to set it up. Click the LDAP item in the payloads list to display the Configure LDAP box, and then click the Configure button. In the LDAP pane (see Figure 8-12), choose settings like this:

1. Type a friendly name for the account in the Account Description text box—for example, **Company Directory**.

2. Optionally, type the username in the Account Username text box and the password in the Account Password text box.

3. Type the hostname or IP address of the LDAP server in the Account Hostname text box.

4. Select the Use SSL check box if you want to secure the connection using Secure Sockets Layer, as is usually wise.

5. In the Search Settings list box, double-click the default name for the first entry, and then type the name you want to use. In the Scope column, use the pop-up menu to set the scope of the search: Base (searching only the base object), One Level (searching one level below the base object), or Subtree (searching the base object and all objects descended from it).

NOTE   You can click the + button below the Search Settings list box to add another search setting.

If necessary, click the + button in the upper-right corner of the LDAP pane to add another LDAP item, and then follow the above steps to choose settings for it.

Setting Up a CalDAV Payload

You can also set up the iPhone or iPod touch to connect to a calendaring server that uses the CalDAV protocol.

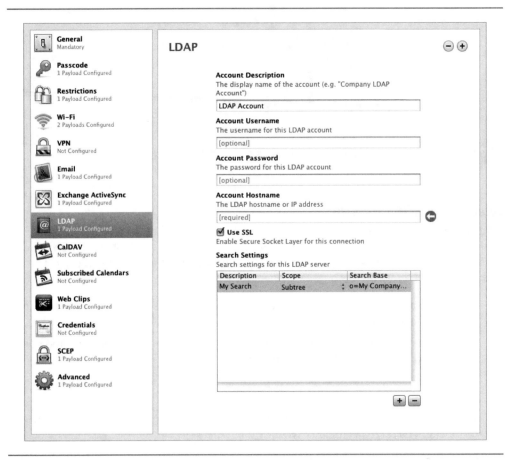

Figure 8-12.   You can set up an LDAP payload to enable the iPhone or iPod touch to connect to an LDAP directory.

Click the CalDAV item in the payloads list to display the Configure CalDAV box, and then click the Configure button. Follow these steps to choose settings in the CalDAV pane (see Figure 8-13):

1. Type a descriptive name in the Account Description text box—for example, **Company Calendars**.

2. Type the CalDAV server's hostname or IP address in the left Account Hostname And Port text box, and change the port in the right text box if necessary.

3. To direct the iPhone or iPod touch to a particular URL, enter it in the Principal URL text box.

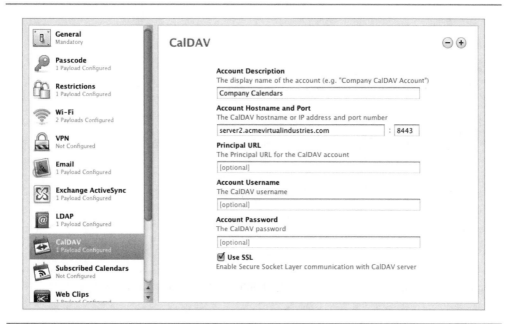

Figure 8-13.   Use the CalDAV pane to set up an iPhone or iPod touch to connect to your CalDAV server.

4. Optionally, type the CalDAV user name in the Account Username text box and the corresponding password in the Account Password text box.

5. Select the Use SSL check box if you want to secure the connection with Secure Sockets Layer—again, usually wise.

If you want to add another CalDAV item, click the + button, and then repeat the above steps.

Setting Up a Subscribed Calendars Payload

To subscribe the iPhone or iPod touch to one or more calendars, click the Subscribed Calendars item in the payloads list to display the Configure Subscribed Calendars box, and then click the Configure button. You can then choose settings in the Subscribed Calendars pane (see Figure 8-14) like this:

1. Type a descriptive name in the Description text box.

2. Type the calendar's URL in the URL text box.

3. Optionally, type the username in the Username text box, and the password in the Password text box.

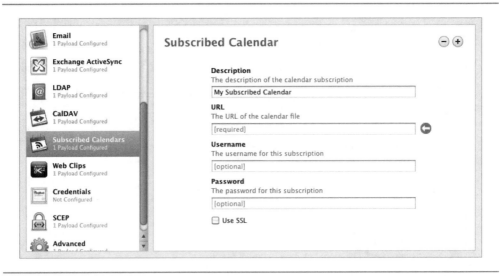

Figure 8-14.   You can also subscribe the iPhone or iPod touch to published calendars.

4. Select the Use SSL check box if you want to secure the connection with Secure Sockets Layer. For a company calendar, you'll probably want to use SSL; for a public calendar (for example, a calendar of public holidays), you probably won't.

If you want to add another subscribed calendar, click the + button, and then repeat the above steps.

Setting Up a Web Clips Payload

If you use an iPhone or iPod touch, you're probably familiar with Web clips—URLs you add as icons to the home screen (by using the Add To Home Screen command) so that you can access the pages instantly without dredging through your bookmarks in Safari. You can also add a payload of Web clips to a configuration profile to give users direct access to corporate, educational, and motivational pages (or any others you fancy).

To set up a payload of Web clips, click the Web Clips item in the payloads list to display the Configure Web Clips box, and then click the Configure button. In the Web Clip pane (see Figure 8-15), you can then quickly add as many clips as you need by following these steps:

1. In the Label text box, type the name to display on the home screen. Keep it succinct.

2. Type or paste the page's URL in the URL text box.

3. If you want the user to be able to remove the Web clip from the home screen, select the Removable check box. Clear this check box to prevent the user from removing it.

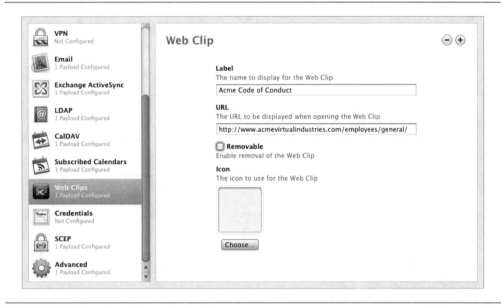

Figure 8-15.   Web Clips let you add shortcuts to useful web pages directly to the iPhone's or iPod touch's home screen.

4. Add an icon to the Icon text box. You can drag it from a Finder window or from iPhoto; alternatively, you can click the Choose button, pick the picture in the resulting dialog box, and then click the Open button.

To add another Web clip, click the + button in the upper-right corner of the Web Clip pane, and then repeat these steps.

Setting Up a Credentials Payload

If you need to use a certificate or identity to authenticate the iPhone or iPod touch with your network, use the Credentials payload to install the necessary credential. Follow these steps:

1. Click the Credentials item in the payloads list to display the Configure Credentials box.

2. Click the Configure button to display the Add Credential dialog box.

3. Select the credential, and then click the Open button. iPhone Configuration Utility displays the Credential pane (see Figure 8-16) with the details of the credential.

To add another credential, click the + button in the upper-right corner of the Credential pane, and then repeat these steps.

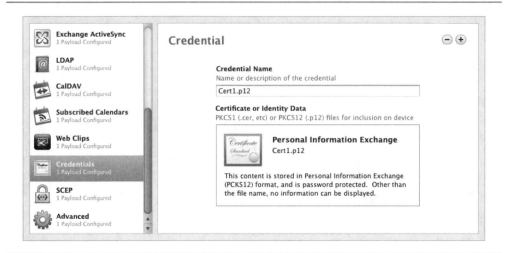

Figure 8-16. The Credential pane appears only when you have added a credential to the Credentials payload.

NOTE The SCEP item in the payloads list lets you set up a Simple Certificate Enrollment Protocol (SCEP) payload containing the information needed for the iPhone or iPod touch to obtain certificates from a CA. The Advanced item lets you change the way the iPhone connects to the cellular network. I won't cover these settings here, as it's not likely that you will need to configure them.

Applying a Configuration Profile

You can apply a configuration profile to an iPhone or iPod touch in three ways:

- **Directly** Connect the iPhone or iPod touch to your Mac, and apply the profile to the device.

- **By e-mail** Send the profile to the user's iPhone or iPod touch, and have the user apply it.

- **By download** Post the profile to a website, and have the user download it and apply it.

Applying a Configuration Profile Directly

The easiest way to apply a configuration profile is directly—by connecting the iPhone or iPod touch to your Mac and using iPhone Configuration Utility to put the profile on it. To do so, follow these steps:

1. Launch iPhone Configuration Utility if it's not already running.
2. Connect the device to your Mac with a USB cable. Your Mac detects the device and adds it to the Devices list in iPhone Configuration Utility.

3. Click the device in the Devices list to display its configuration screens.

4. Click the Configuration Profiles tab to display the Configuration Profiles pane (see Figure 8-17).

5. Click the Install button for the configuration profile you want to install.

6. The device displays the Installing Profile screen (shown on the left in Figure 8-18), where you can click the More Details button to display details about the profile (as shown on the right in Figure 8-18).

7. To install the profile, click the Install button on the Installing Profile screen, and then follow through the prompts.

Applying a Configuration Profile via E-mail

The second way of applying a configuration profile to an iPhone or iPod touch is via e-mail. As long as the device already has an e-mail account set up, this is easy for both you (the administrator) and the user. So once you've set up your iPhones or iPod touches with e-mail (perhaps by applying a profile directly), you may want to use this method to apply other configuration profiles or updates.

When you send a configuration profile via e-mail, the user receives a message containing the configuration profile. The user opens the message, touches the button for the attachment, and then sees the Install Profile screen you met in the previous section.

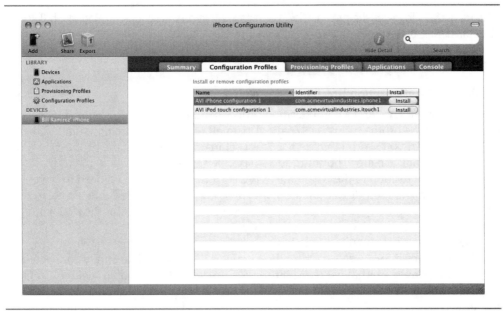

Figure 8-17.   Click the Install button in the Configuration Profiles pane of iPhone Configuration Utility to apply a profile to an iPhone or iPod touch.

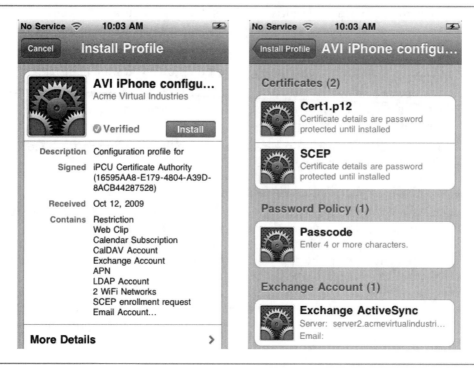

Figure 8-18.   To install the profile, click the Install button on the iPhone or iPod touch (left). To see the details of the profile (right), click the More Details button.

Applying a Configuration Profile from a Web Page

The third way of applying a configuration profile to an iPhone or iPod touch is by downloading the profile from a web page. This method bypasses the potential problems with e-mail (that you need to have an account set up in order to get the profile that will set up your e-mail account), but introduces a problem of its own: Unless the user already has a secure connection to the web page (which typically means you'll need to have applied a profile to their device already), they may have problems establishing a secure connection. You could send them an e-mail message with the URL and the password—but only if you've set up secure e-mail already.

These limitations mean than applying a configuration profile from a web page usually works best for updates: Once the iPhone or iPod touch is securely connected to your company's internal network, it can pick up an updated profile securely from an intranet page. When the user touches the button to open the file, they see the Install Profile screen.

Setting Up an iPhone or iPod touch Manually

If the users of your network have only a few iPhones or iPod touches, you may decide that creating configuration profiles and pushing them out to the devices is more work than setting them up manually. In this case, either you or the devices' users can set them up manually with the settings they need to access your network and the services the devices require.

To set the iPhone or iPod touch up, you'll need to provide most of the same pieces of information discussed earlier in this chapter; the only difference is that you're inputting the information directly on the device rather than in a file that you'll then apply to the device.

The setup process is straightforward if a bit laborious with one- or two-fingered typing. The main difficulty is finding the settings screens, as they're buried in different parts of the device's interface. To get you started, here is a brief summary of where you will find the most important settings you'll need to get the device working with your network:

- **Wi-Fi**   Choose Settings | General | Network | Wi-Fi to display the Wi-Fi Networks screen, and then touch Other. On the resulting screen, enter the name of the network, touch the Security button, and then choose the encryption type on the Security screen.

- **VPN**   Choose Settings | General | Network | VPN, and then touch Add VPN Configuration. On the Add Configuration screen, you can add the details of the VPN. If the VPN connection requires a certificate, you must install the certificate before you can set up the VPN connection.

NOTE   You cannot set up a VPN On Demand directly on the iPhone or iPod touch—for this feature, you need to use a configuration profile.

- **E-mail**   Choose Settings | Mail, Contacts, Calendars, and then touch Add Account. Touch the Other button to reach the Other screen. Then touch Add Mail Account to display the New Account screen.

- **Exchange**   Choose Settings | Mail, Contacts, Calendars, and then touch Add Account. Touch the Microsoft Exchange button on the Add Account screen to display the first of the Exchange settings screens.

- **LDAP**   Choose Settings | Mail, Contacts, Calendars, and then touch Add Account. Touch the Other button to reach the Other screen, and then touch Add LDAP Account to display the LDAP screen.

- **Calendars**   Choose Settings | Mail, Contacts, Calendars, and then touch Add Account. Touch the Other button to reach the Other screen. To add a CalDAV account, touch the Add CalDAV Account and work on the CalDAV screen. To add a subscribed calendar, touch Add Subscribed Calendar, and then enter the details on the Subscription screen.

- **Credentials**   Attach the credential to an e-mail that you send to the device, or download the credential to the device from a website (for example, an intranet site). When the Install Profile screen appears, verify the details of the certificate and make sure it's signed; then touch the Install button to install it.

- **Web Clips**   These you need to add manually. Steer Safari to the website, touch the + button at the bottom of the screen, and then touch Add To Home Screen.

Activating Your iPhones

Before you can use any of the iPhone's telephony features, you need to connect it to a computer that's running iTunes and walk through the activation process.

Ideally, each user of an iPhone or iPod touch will have iTunes on their Mac, as they'll need iTunes to synchronize the corporate battle anthems and educational podcasts onto the devices along with their bookmarks and any applications you permit them. In this case, iPhone users can handle the activation process themselves; you just hand over the USB cables and iPhones, remembering to pop the SIM card into each iPhone, and let the users get on with it.

If yours is a puritan workplace whose management has decreed that iTunes is a tool of sloth and inertia, you can activate each of the iPhones using your server or another Mac (and perhaps enjoy a spot of sloth while you do). Simply insert the SIM card first, then connect the iPhone to the Mac, and follow through the prompts.

PART II | Provide Services and Applications

CHAPTER 9 | Configure the Web Service and Control Internet Access

If your Mac OS X Server network is connected to the Internet, each client picks up an Internet connection automatically through the network. And they're up and away, surfing unsuitable websites with Safari, insulting your clients via e-mail (the subject of the next chapter), and perhaps even hauling down highly questionable files from FTP sites.

You may want to rein the users in a bit by pointing them at proxy servers that can take some of the sting out of raw Internet content. In this chapter, you'll learn how to do that—but first, you'll learn to set up your web server and create websites, because you'll need to do both in order to get a proxy server to work.

You'll also learn how to disable Internet Sharing to prevent users from adding their own, unauthorized devices to the network.

Setting Up the Web Server on the Web Service

Mac OS X Server includes a powerful, built-in web server based on the widely used Apache web server. Apache gets its name from a pun on the number of *patches* (fixes) the early versions needed ("a patchy server"), but these days it's renowned for its stability.

To get the web server working, you must first make sure the Web service is turned on. You can then configure the Web service with the settings you need.

 NOTE The Web service will be turned on if you selected the Web check box on the Services screen during installation. If you didn't, you'll need to turn the service on manually.

To get started, fire up Server Admin and connect to the server:

1. Open Server Admin. For example, click the Server Admin icon in the dock.
2. In the Servers list on the left, double-click the server to which you want to connect.
3. Type your user name and password if you haven't told your Mac to remember them, and then click the Connect button.

Turning On the Web Service

To turn on the Web service, follow these steps:

1. With the server selected in the Servers list box, click the Settings button to display the Settings pane.
2. Click the Services tab to display the Services pane.
3. In the Select The Services To Configure On This Server list box, select the Web check box.
4. Click the Save button to save the changes.

The Web service appears in the list of services beneath the server, and you can configure it as described next.

Configuring the Web Service

Now that you've turned the Web service on, you may need to configure it to make it work the way you want. Click the Web item in the services list under the server in the Servers pane of Server Admin, and then click the Settings button on the toolbar to display the Settings pane. You can then work through the following subsections, changing settings as needed. Most of the settings have sensible defaults, so you may not need to make changes to begin with.

NOTE   This section skips the settings in the Proxy pane (because we'll discuss these settings later in this chapter when setting up proxying) and the Modules pane (because it's beyond the scope of this book). If you're experienced with Apache, you can change the selection of modules used by working in the Modules pane. You can also edit the Apache configuration files manually—but make a backup first, just in case you don't get the results you're looking for.

Choosing General Settings for the Web Service

Click the General tab of the Settings pane to display the General pane (see Figure 9-1). You can then set the following settings:

- **Maximum Simultaneous Connections**   In this text box, type the maximum number of simultaneous connections your server is to accept.

NOTE   If you don't have a specific reason to change the settings in the General pane, leave them at their defaults. These are pretty safe for a start.

- **Connection Timeout**   In this text box, type the number of seconds a visitor may sit there doing nothing before the connection times out.
- **Minimum Spare Servers**   In this text box, type the minimum number of spare servers to keep in reserve. These aren't physical servers—Apple doesn't expect you to have dozens of spare servers dozing in the background, waiting for the world and its dog to visit your website. They're software processes for handling web traffic. The web server adds another server per second when demand requires it.

NOTE   It's hard to know at first how many spare servers your site will need. Start with the default settings that Mac OS X Server suggests, and use the Graphs pane to monitor usage. Adjust the numbers upward or downward as needed.

- **Maximum Spare Servers**   In this text box, type the maximum number of spare servers.

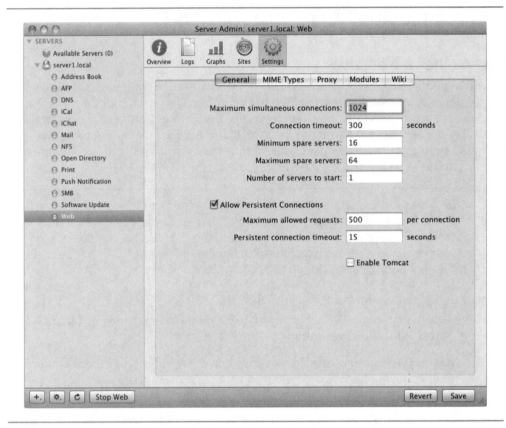

Figure 9-1. The General pane of Web service settings lets you control connections and the number of server threads.

- **Number Of Servers To Start** In this text box, type the number of servers you want to start when you launch the Web service. After that, the web server adds servers as needed.

- **Allow Persistent Connections** Select this check box if you want to allow clients to establish persistent connections to the web server.

 NOTE A *persistent connection* is a connection that allows the web server to respond to multiple requests from the same client without closing the connection after each request. Persistent connections are also called *keep-alive connections*. Web browsers typically request persistent connections, as they give better performance, so you'll normally want to allow persistent connections.

- **Maximum Allowed Requests**   In this text box, enter the maximum number of persistent connections you want to allow.

- **Persistent Connection Timeout**   In this text box, enter the number of seconds to wait before timing out a persistent connection.

- **Enable Tomcat**   Select this check box if you want to enable Tomcat, a feature for running JavaServer Pages (JSP) and Java servlets on your web server.

Choosing MIME Types Settings for the Web Service

Click the MIME Types tab to display the MIME Types pane of Web service settings (see Figure 9-2). This pane is where you add, delete, or edit MIME Type mappings and Content Handlers:

- **MIME Type mapping**   A MIME Type mapping tells the Web service the suffix or suffixes that correspond to a particular type of content. For example, the suffixes mov and qt come mapped to the video/quicktime MIME Type by default.

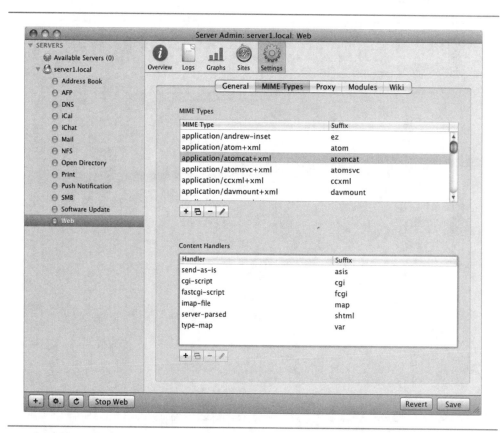

Figure 9-2.   If necessary, you can change MIME Type mappings and Content Handlers in the MIME Types pane of Web service settings.

■ **Content Handler**   A Content Handler tells the Web service the suffix or suffixes that correspond to a particular Content Handler. For example, the suffix cgi comes mapped to the cgi-script handler.

At first, you will probably not need to change MIME Types or Content Handlers. When you do need to change them, use the four buttons below the MIME Types list box or the Content Handlers list box to add, copy, remove, or edit items (looking at the buttons from left to right).

Choosing Wiki Settings for the Web Service

Click the Wiki tab to display the Wiki pane of Web service settings (see Figure 9-3). This pane provides the following settings for configuring wikis on your server:

■ **Data Store**   In this text box, enter the folder that you want to store the wikis in. The default is the /Library/Collaboration/folder. To change folder, click the Choose button, click the folder in the resulting dialog box, and then click the Choose button.

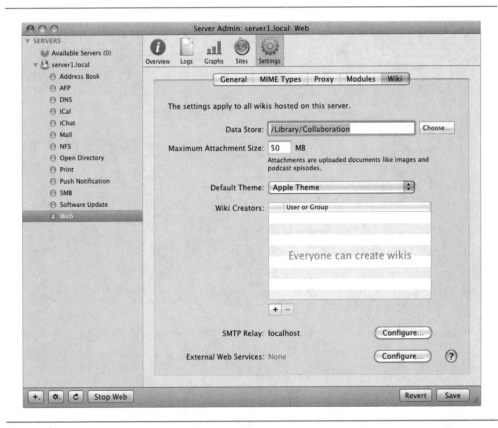

Figure 9-3.   In the Wiki pane of Web service settings, choose where to store wikis, the default theme, and who can create them.

- **Maximum Attachment Size**   In this text box, type the maximum size for files that users can attach to the wiki. You're probably safe starting with the default size, 50MB.

- **Default Theme**   In this pop-up menu, choose the theme that will give the overall look of the wikis. Users can override this setting, but your choice makes a starting point.

- **Wiki Creators**   Use this list box to set up a list of users and groups who can create wikis. The default setting, with this box blank, lets everyone create wikis, which works well for various situations. If you need to batten down the hatches, click the + button below the Wiki Creators list box to pop open the Users & Groups window, and then drag the appropriate users and groups to the Wiki Creators list box.

Saving the Changes You've Made to the Web Service

When you've finished making changes to the Web service, click the Save button to save the changes.

Starting the Web Service

After choosing settings, start the Web service by clicking the Start Web button.

Setting Up a Website

Now that the Web service is running, you have a working web server on which to set up a website. Proceed as described in this section.

NOTE   If you turned on the Web service and specified your domain name during setup, Mac OS X Server may have set up your website for you.

Putting Your Files in the Web Folder

Mac OS X Server provides a folder named /Library/WebServer/Documents/ for the documents that make up your website. You put your files in this folder or its subfolders to make them available on your website.

NOTE   Each user has their own mini website that appears on your web server under the username. For example, for a user named csmith, the website appears at http://webserv. acmevirtualindustries.com/~csmith/. To put content on this mini website, the user places the files in the Sites folder inside their home folder.

If you open a Finder window and peek into this folder, you'll see that it already has a couple of default pages—index.html and error.html—plus some cascading style sheets and graphics. Your first move should be to replace the index.html file with the home page for your website, and then add the pages to which that page links.

Setting Up the Website in Server Admin

After adding the content to your site's folders, you can create the website like this:

1. Open Server Admin. For example, click the Server Admin icon in the dock.

2. In the Servers list on the left, double-click the server to which you want to connect.

3. Type your user name and password if you haven't told your Mac to remember then, and then click the Connect button.

4. Expand the list of services, and then click the Web service.

5. Click the Sites button on the toolbar to display the Sites pane (shown in Figure 9-4 with a website added and the General pane displayed).

6. Click the + button above the General tab to add a website.

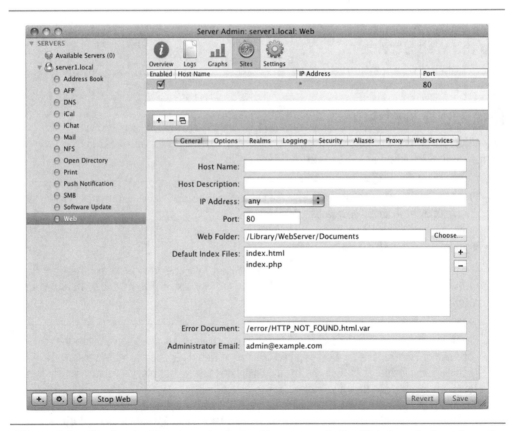

Figure 9-4. Display the Sites pane to start setting up a website. Click the + button above the General tab to add a website.

You can now configure the main aspects of the website by following the instructions in the next few subsections. These instructions skip advanced topics, such as building realms and setting up a reverse proxy.

Choosing General Settings for the Website

Click the General tab to display the General pane (shown in Figure 9-4), which provides the following settings:

- **Host Name** Type your website's fully qualified DNS name in this text box— for example, **www.acmevirtualindustries.com**.

NOTE When setting up a website, you need to register your domain name with a domain name authority so that other computers on the Internet know where to find your domain.

- **Host Description** In this text box, type the name that you want to use to refer to the website.

- **IP Address** In this pop-up menu, set the IP address at which to find the website. Normally, you'll want to pick the correct IP address from the pop-up menu, but you can choose Any if the IP address may change. The third choice, Other, is for when you're not ready to commit to an IP address yet—for example, because you don't know which IP address to choose.

- **Port** In this text box, type the port the website will use. Usually, you'll want to use port 80, the default port for HTTP, or 443, the default port for HTTP with SSL.

- **Web Folder** In this text box, enter the path to the folder that contains the website. If you've left the website in the /Library/WebServer/Documents/ folder, you don't need to make a change here; otherwise, click the Choose button, click the folder in the resulting dialog box, and then click the Choose button in the dialog box. You can put the folder pretty much anywhere on your server—for example, on a drive that has more free space.

- **Default Index Files** In this list box, create or edit the list of files to use as default pages when the user comes to your website without specifying a web page. Click the + button to add an entry, and then type the page's filename; to remove an existing entry, click it, and then click the – button. Drag the pages into the order you want the website to use them, putting your number one page at the top of the list.

- **Error Document** In this list box, type the address and name of the page to display when a user tries to reach a page that isn't there.

- **Administrator Email** In this text box, type the address to which you want the server to send any website error messages that occur. You'll probably want to direct these to a separate account than your main account.

Choosing Options Settings for the Website

Click the Options tab to display the Options pane (the populated part of which appears in Figure 9-5), and then choose the options you need:

- **Folder Listing** Select this check box if you want the server to display a list of folders when a visitor hits a missing page. The user can then click a link to open one of those folders. Showing the folder listing can be useful for internal websites, but for publicly accessible sites it tends to compromise security by giving visitors too much information when a page is missing.

- **WebDAV** Select this check box if you will use Web Distributed Authoring and Versioning (WebDAV) on. WebDAV enables users to edit pages on the server while it's up and running. Normally, you will want to leave this check box cleared. If you select this check box, you will need to set access privileges for the website. To set access privileges, you use realms, which are beyond the scope of this chapter.

- **CGI Execution** Select this check box if you will need to run Common Gateway Interface (CGI) scripts on your server.

- **Server Side Includes (SSI)** Select this check box if you want to include SSI directives in your web pages to include dynamic content.

- **Allow All Overrides** Select this check box if you want the Web service to check the web folder for additional configuration files to override default settings.

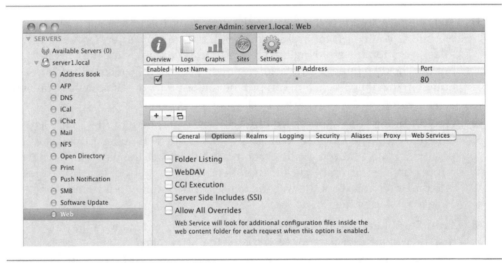

Figure 9-5. The Options pane provides a handful of options for controlling your website's behavior.

Choosing Logging Options

Click the Logging tab to display the Logging pane (see Figure 9-6), and then choose which items to log:

- **Enable Access Log**   Select this check box to turn on logging of accesses to the web server. You'll almost certainly want to turn on logging at first so that you can see how much attention the server is getting.

- **Access Log: Archive Every *N* Days**   To have the web server automatically archive the log file, keeping the current one down to size, select this check box and type the number of days in the text box.

- **Access Log: Location**   In this text box, tell the web server where to store the access log. The default location is usually fine; if not, click the Choose button, and follow the regular drill.

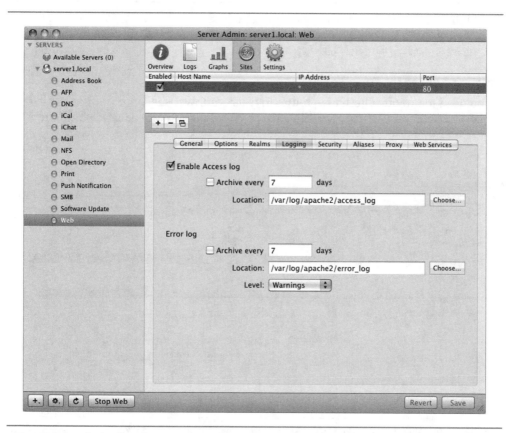

Figure 9-6.   In the Logging pane, choose whether to log accesses to your web server and what level of errors to log.

- **Error Log: Archive Every N Days**   As for the access log, you can have the web server automatically archive the error log after the number of days you choose.

- **Error Log: Location**   Also as for the access log, tell the web server where to store the error log. Again, you may not need to change the default location; if you do, click the Choose button.

- **Level**   In this pop-up menu, choose the level of error message you want to log: Emergency, Alert, Critical, Errors, Warnings (the default), Notices, Information, or Debug.

Turning On Secure Sockets Layer

If you want to use SSL to secure your website, click the Security tab to display the Security pane (the top part of which is shown in Figure 9-7). Select the Enable Secure Sockets Layer (SSL) check box, and then choose the certificate from the pop-up menu.

 NOTE   When you turn on SSL with the port set to 80, Server Admin warns you that it is switching the port to 443. Similarly, when you turn off SSL with the port set to 443, Server Admin notifies you that it is switching the port to 80.

Creating Aliases for Your Website

If you need to provide alternative routes to reach your website, or redirect particular requests to different URLs, click the Aliases tab to display the Aliases pane (see Figure 9-8).

Figure 9-7.   You can quickly apply SSL to your website using the controls in the Security pane.

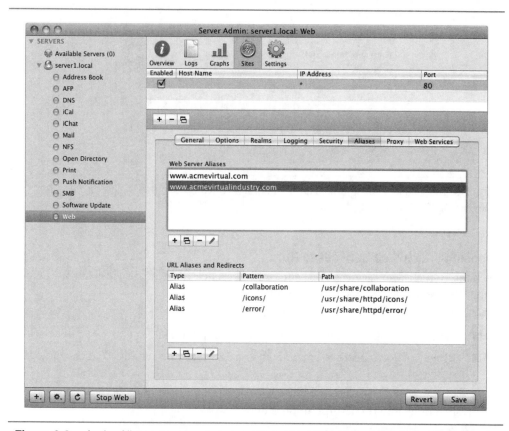

Figure 9-8. In the Aliases pane, set up any aliases and URLs your website needs to function properly.

In the Web Server Aliases list box, build a list of any aliases you want to direct to your website. For example, if your company has secured several similar URLs (or common typos for your main URL), you can add them as aliases for the main URL.

In the URL Aliases And Redirects list box, add any redirects needed. A redirect sends the visitor to a different URL than the URL they have entered or chosen. To add a redirect:

1. Click the + button under the URL Aliases And Redirects list box to display the dialog box shown in Figure 9-9.

2. In the Type pop-up menu, choose Redirect.

3. In the Pattern text box, enter the URL term you want to match.

4. In the Path text box, enter the URL to which you want to redirect the browser.

5. Click the OK button to close the dialog box and add the redirect to the list.

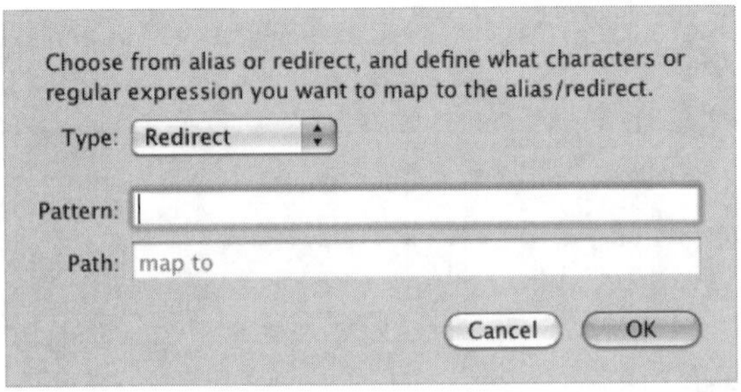

Choose from alias or redirect, and define what characters or
regular expression you want to map to the alias/redirect.

Type: Redirect

Pattern:

Path: map to

Cancel   OK

Figure 9-9. Use this dialog box to create redirects to send visitors to a different URL than they one they have entered.

Choosing Which Web Services to Run

To choose which web services your site provides, click the Web Services tab, and work in the Web Services pane (see Figure 9-10).

Select the check boxes for the services you want to run:

- **Wikis**   Enables the users to share data using wiki sites.

- **Blogs**   Allows users to create web logs, with entries arranged in chronological order.

- **Calendar**   Lets users create group calendars to help them avoid awkward meetings and duck difficult deadlines.

 NOTE   Click the arrow next to Wikis, Blogs, or Calendar to open that item in your web browser.

- **Mail**   Enables the users to get their message via webmail rather than through a regular e-mail client.

If you have turned on SSL, you can select the Configure Server-Side Mail Rules check box if you want users to be able to set up mail rules. You can also select the Change Their Password check box if you want them to be able to change their password.

Saving the Changes to Your Website

To save the changes you've made to your website, click the Save button.

If the Web service is running, and your changes include turning on SSL, Server Admin prompts you to restart the Web service to make the changes take effect (see Figure 9-11). Click the Restart button to restart the service. If this is a really bad time for restarting the service, click the Don't Restart button, and then restart it manually as soon as is convenient by using the Stop Web button (at the bottom of Server Admin when you have selected the Web service) and the Start Web button that replaces it.

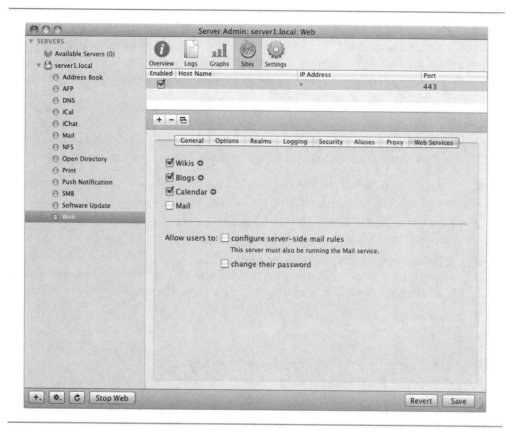

Figure 9-10.   In the Web Services pane, you can turn on and off the services for wikis, blogs, calendar, and mail.

Figure 9-11.   You will need to restart the Web service if you have turned on SSL.

Setting Up Proxying for Internet Access

To tighten security and speed up workgroup web access, you can use the caching web proxy system built into the web server. This section shows you how to set up a proxy server that will save frequently needed data from the Web to its hard disk so that it can provide it instantly when a client needs it.

Caching frequently needed data not only reduces the amount of thrashing your Internet connection gets but also transfers the data to the clients more quickly, so that line managers finish checking the sports scores more quickly and get back to work.

To make proxying work on your network, you need to do three things:

- **Create a website for the proxy**   You'll typically want to put this website on the default web port, port 80. Set the site up as described earlier in this chapter.

- **Configure the forward proxy settings for the Web service**   The forward proxy settings tell the web server how to handle proxy requests.

- **Tell the client which proxy server to use**   The client can be either a computer or a user. If the client is the computer, the proxy setting affects the user who is using it. If the client is the user, the proxy setting affects the computer they're using.

Understanding Forward Proxy and Reverse Proxy

Mac OS X Server offers both forward proxy and reverse proxy features:

- **Forward proxy**   A forward proxy sits between your client computers and the Internet, handling outbound traffic from the clients. Instead of requesting a web page from the web server as usual, a client computer asks the proxy server for the web pages. If the proxy server has the page in its cache, it supplies the page from there; if not, it gets it from the Internet, and then supplies it. The proxy server can also filter content—for example, denying requests to unapproved websites. On Mac OS X Server, you set up the forward proxy by using the Proxy pane under the Settings pane for the Web service.

- **Reverse proxy**   A reverse proxy sits between your web server and the Internet, handling inbound traffic intended for the web server. The reverse proxy can separate the web server from the Internet, reduce its load by caching frequently demanded content, or even distribute incoming requests among multiple web servers to balance the load. On Mac OS X Server, you set up a reverse proxy by using the Proxy pane under the Sites pane for the Web service. This chapter does not cover setting up a reverse proxy.

Configure the Forward Proxy Settings for the Web Service

Once you've got the website set up, configure the forward proxy settings for the Web service like this:

1. In Server Admin, click the Web service in the list of services under the server.

2. Click the Settings button to display the Settings pane.

3. Click the Proxy tab to display the Proxy pane (see Figure 9-12).

4. Select the Enable Forward Proxy check box.

5. If you see the message "Forward Proxy will not function properly with current Sites configuration," as shown in Figure 9-13, click the OK button. We'll deal with this problem shortly.

6. If you want to restrict access to the proxy server to only your network's users, select the Control Access To Proxy check box and type your domain name in the Allowed Domain text box. Doing this is usually a good idea.

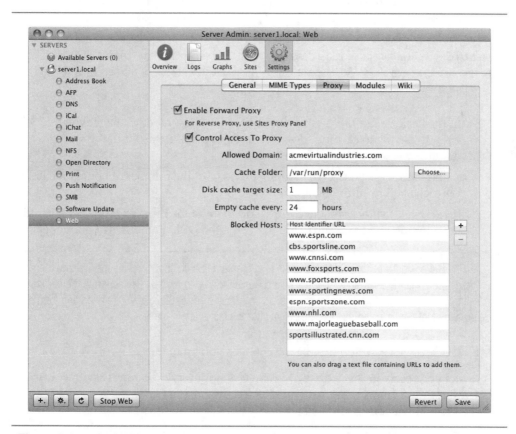

Figure 9-12.   In the Proxy pane, choose settings for the proxy server.

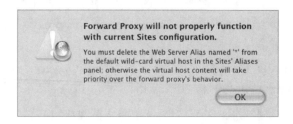

Figure 9-13. You may see this warning message when you select the Enable Forward Proxy check box. If so, just click the OK button for now.

7. In the Cache Folder text box, enter the folder in which to cache the data. Normally it's easiest to accept Server Admin's default suggestion, the /var/run/proxy/ folder. If you want to use a different folder, click the Choose button, select the folder in the resulting dialog box, and then click the Choose button.

NOTE The /var/run/proxy/ folder doesn't exist until you set up the proxy service for the first time and click the Save button. At that point, Server Admin creates the folder and sets its owner and group to www, giving them Read and Write privileges.

8. In the Disk Cache Target Size text box, enter the number of megabytes you want to devote to caching files. When the cache hits this limit, the server discards files on a first-in-first-out basis.

9. In the Empty Cache Every *N* Hours text box, set the number of hours to maintain the cache before emptying it.

10. If you want to block some websites, add them to the Blocked Hosts list box. Click the + button to add an entry, and then type the URL. Lather, rinse, and repeat.

TIP The easiest way to list blocked hosts is to create a text file that contains the list, and then drag it from the Finder window to the Blocked Hosts list box. In the text file, separate the entries with commas, tabs, or line breaks; line breaks are usually easiest unless you're exporting from a spreadsheet. Make sure there's a line break after the last entry in the list.

11. Click the Save button to save the changes you've made.

Now, if you received the "Forward Proxy will not function properly with current Sites configuration" message when you selected the Enable Forward Proxy check box, you need to take the following steps:

1. Click the Sites button on the toolbar to display the Sites pane.

2. In the tab bar, click the Aliases button to display the Aliases pane.

3. In the Web Server Aliases list box, click the * entry.

4. Click the – button under the Web Server Aliases list box to delete the entry.

5. Click the Save button to save the changes. Your forward proxy will now work.

Telling Users and Computers Which Proxy Servers to Use

After setting up the proxy server, you need to tell the clients to use it for web browsing—otherwise they'll just go straight past it to the Web, where they can be joyously sidetracked by sports sites, filth, and every other time sink the human imagination has produced.

 NOTE   You can also set up proxying for other services, such as FTP, SOCKS, and (delicate shudder) Gopher. This section assumes you're setting up web proxying, but you can apply the same technique to set up other proxies as needed.

You can set proxying for a user account, a group of user accounts, a computer account, or a group of computer accounts. Seeing this list, you'd probably guess that the tool for configuring proxy services is Workgroup Manager—and you'd be right.

To configure proxy services, follow these steps:

1. Open Workgroup Manager. For example, click the Workgroup Manager icon in the dock.

2. In the Workgroup Manager Connect dialog box, enter the server's address, your user name, and password, and then click the Connect button.

3. Click the lock icon at the right end of the authentication bar to open the Authenticate To Directory dialog box, type your administrator name and password, and then click the Authenticate button.

4. Click the user, computer, or group you want to affect.

5. Click the Preferences button to display the Preferences pane.

6. Click the Network icon to display the Network pane.

7. If the Proxies tab is not already selected, click it to display the Proxies pane (shown in Figure 9-14 with settings chosen).

8. In the Manage bar, select the Always option button to enable the controls.

9. In the Select A Proxy Server To Configure list box, click the proxy server you want to set up. Workgroup Manager displays text boxes to the right of the Select A Proxy Server To Configure list box.

10. Enter the details of the proxy server in these text boxes. For example, for a web proxy server, type the server's address in the Web Proxy Server text box, and the port number in the second text box.

11. In the Select A Proxy Server To Configure list box, select the check box for the proxy server to activate it.

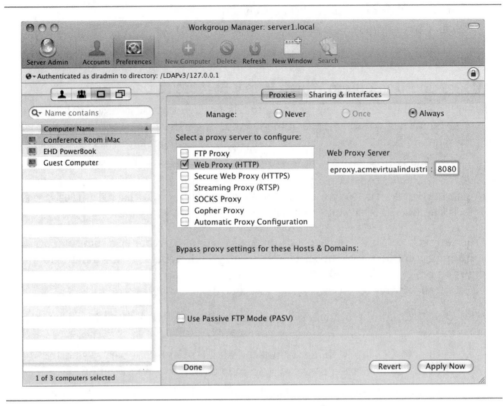

Figure 9-14. Use the Proxies pane in Workgroup Manager to set up proxy servers for a user account, group, or computer.

12. Repeat the previous three steps to configure the other proxy servers the account needs.

13. In the Bypass Proxy Settings For These Hosts And Domains text box, type the addresses of hosts and domains that the user or computer should connect to directly rather than going through the proxy.

   ■ You can enter a target server's name (such as server2.acmevirtualindustries. com), an IP address (such as 10.0.0.27), or a domain name (such as acmevirtualindustries.com).

TIP When you add a domain name, the bypassing is only for that domain—not for any of its subdomains. To add an entire website and all its subdomains, put an asterisk before it—for example, ***.acmevirtualindustries.com**.

- ■   To create an easy-to-read list, put each item on a new line. Alternatively, separate items with commas, semicolons, or spaces.

14. Select the Use Passive FTP Mode (PASV) check box if you want the user or computer to use passive FTP mode for FTP.

15. Click the Apply Now button to apply the changes.

16. Click the Done button to return to the Preferences pane.

Checking That Proxying Is Working

Now check that proxying is working as it should:

1. Log in to a client Mac using an account you haven't exempted from proxying.

2. Open Safari and try to access a site you put on your blocked list. Make sure the server prevents you from accessing the website.

3. Try to access a site you haven't blocked, such as the McGraw-Hill Professional website (www.mhprofessional.com). Make sure the proxy server doesn't block the site.

Disabling Internet Sharing

Internet Sharing is a neat Mac OS X feature that's great for home and ad-hoc situations where you need to share a Mac's Internet connection with other computers. For example, if you find yourself in a hotel room that offers only a single Ethernet port, you can hook your Mac into that, turn on Internet Sharing through the AirPort, and then connect your family's other computers to the Internet as well.

Internet Sharing is occasionally useful in a business context, but it's not the kind of thing you typically want running on a business network—unless your business encourages users to bring in their own devices and hook them up to the network.

To disable Internet Sharing, follow these steps:

1. In Workgroup Manager, click the computer or group of computers that you want to affect.

2. Click the Preferences button to display the Preferences pane.

3. Click the Network icon to display the Network pane.

4. Click the Sharing & Interfaces tab to display the Sharing & Interfaces pane (shown in Figure 9-15 with settings chosen).

5. In the Manage bar, select the Always option button.

6. Select the Disable Internet Sharing check box to disable Internet Sharing.

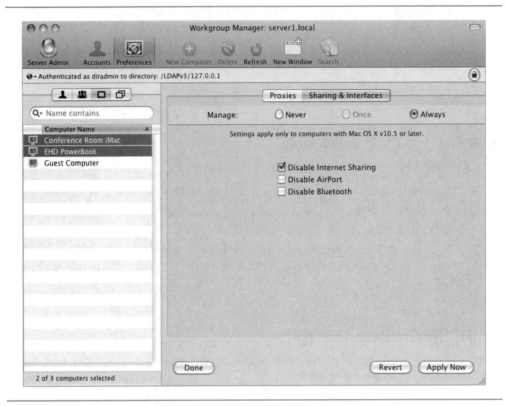

Figure 9-15. Use the Sharing & Interfaces pane to turn off Internet Sharing for one or more computers.

NOTE From the Sharing & Interfaces pane, you can also disable a Mac's AirPort (by selecting the Disable AirPort check box) and Bluetooth (by selecting the Disable Bluetooth check box). Turning these off is useful in some situations but tends not to increase your popularity.

7. Click the Apply Now button to apply the change.

8. Click the Done button to close the Sharing & Interfaces pane.

CHAPTER 10 | Set Up E-mail

E-mail is vital to both business life and home life these days—so it's no surprise that Mac OS X includes a full-fledged e-mail service for sending, receiving, and storing e-mail.

Apple would like e-mail setup to happen with a snap of the fingers, and it sometimes does—or so I'm told. Other times, you'll need to change several different categories of settings manually to get things working the way you want.

In this chapter, we'll start by looking at how e-mail works, because you may need to understand the essentials of this in order to get the mail service set up and working. After that, we'll look at how to turn on and configure the mail service and get it running correctly. Finally, we'll examine how you connect your network's users to e-mail.

Understanding How E-mail Works

If you've already got your domain and DNS in place when you set up Mac OS X Server, you may find that everything simply snaps into place: You enter the details of your mail server's address; users connect to the server, and set up their e-mail clients in the blink of an eye; and the messages start winging their way happily to and from your server.

Other times, things don't run as smoothly.

To work effectively with e-mail on Mac OS X Server, it helps to understand the essentials of how e-mail works. Otherwise, you may find yourself grappling in the dark with a multi-headed beast more than capable of biting whichever part of your anatomy you've left unattended.

Looking at E-mail from the User's Point of View

From the end user's point of view, e-mail is usually wonderful: You send a message, and the recipient gets it, often just moments later, even if they're halfway around the world. The recipient sends a detailed reply within minutes—and your mail server kicks out an auto-reply that you've just left on a six-month sabbatical to study the greater-crested moths of Machu Picchu.

Everything's nice and easy because the user is using just an e-mail client. All the client needs to do is hand off its outgoing mail to the server, pick up the incoming messages from the server, and generally enjoy the benefits.

From the administrator's end, things look much more complex. Let's take a peek.

Understanding How an E-mail Message Travels Between Servers

When an outgoing e-mail message leaves the client, the server has to deal with it. Most outgoing mail servers send mail using the Simple Mail Transfer Protocol (SMTP).

When you send an e-mail message, you normally use an e-mail address involving a domain name—brzezicki1@me.com, admin@acmevirtualindustries.com, or whatever—rather than an IP address. That means the outgoing mail server needs to look up the destination mail server (say, me.com) to find out where its Mail Exchange (MX) server is.

I say "mail server" there, but domains that get boatloads of mail tend to have multiple MX servers. That way, the servers can share the load, and the administrators can take a server offline for maintenance without all the users having to go cold turkey on e-mail. Each server has a number indicating its priority, with the lowest numbers indicating the highest priority. When sending a message, the SMTP server tries the highest-priority mail server first, then treks down the priority list until it gets a bite.

In an ideal world, the SMTP server would then shunt the message straight to the destination server across the Internet. In the real world, that can happen, but normally the message goes through several other servers on the way. Each server adds its name and a time stamp, so there's a trail you can follow back if Hansel or Gretel get lost in the woods.

One way or another (if you were born in the 1960s, imagine Debbie Harry growling that phrase), the message reaches the mail server (or one of the mail servers) at the recipient's domain. The mail server stores the message in a file until the recipient checks for messages.

Understanding How POP and IMAP Work

These days, most e-mail applications can use either of two mail protocols, POP and IMAP. Both work well, but they work in significantly different ways from each other—which means that one of your first decisions about e-mail is choosing between POP and IMAP.

Post Office Protocol (POP)

POP is the acronym for Post Office Protocol. With POP, e-mail messages stay on the server only until a mail application downloads them to a computer. So each time you check for messages, POP downloads them for you.

From the server's point of view, this is an efficient way to handle messages, because the server gets rid of the wretched things as soon as possible. POP is also good for people who use a single computer for e-mail, because most of their messages are stored on that computer and so are instantly accessible even if the computer is not connected to the network or Internet. By contrast, if the users use different computers to check e-mail, they're much better off with IMAP.

Internet Mail Access Protocol (IMAP)

IMAP is the acronym for Internet Mail Access Protocol. With IMAP, e-mail messages stay on the server until the user moves them elsewhere. As a result, a user can check e-mail from multiple different computers without getting their messages in a tangle. Each computer sees the same messages in the inbox, because each is looking at the user's inbox on the server rather than an inbox on the local computer.

IMAP is great for anyone who checks their messages from more than one computer. For the server, though, it's not so great, for two reasons:

- **The server needs more storage** Because all the messages are stored on the server, the server tends to silt up with messages. You can alleviate this problem by applying quotas to the users (and, preferably, explaining that the quotas are there for a practical reason rather than general cussedness).

■ **The server needs more horsepower** Whereas a POP client connects to the server, grabs its messages, and then disconnects, an IMAP client tends to stay connected. For example, when you delete a message in a POP client, the server doesn't have to do anything, because you've already downloaded the message to your computer. But when you delete a message in an IMAP client, the server must react immediately, deleting the message from whichever mailbox it was skulking in.

If your server has plenty of storage and grunt, IMAP is usually the better choice for e-mail these days. Apart from giving the users the freedom to check their messages from anywhere you permit, having the mail stored on the server also enables you to back it up more easily—and get rid of the backups when they are no longer required.

 NOTE Apple's MobileMe service uses IMAP for e-mail. That's why you can access your MobileMe mail from your iPhone, iPod touch, and every Mac that's still working, and still see the same mailbox.

Knowing How Your Mail Server Makes Its Presence Felt On the Internet

To work on the Internet, your server needs to have its DNS configured properly. There are two main parts to this.

The first part is that the mail server must have a public IP address—one that's accessible to the Internet. There are two main ways that you can give your mail server a public IP address: by connecting the mail server to an external port on your router or firewall, or by setting up a port-forwarding rule. You'll find the details of these arrangements in the following subsections.

The second part is that your domain's DNS records must include your mail server's address and mail exchanger record (MX for short). This is simply so that other mail servers can find your mail server. For example, when you send a message from your MobileMe account to ann@acmevirtualindustries.com, the MobileMe mail server has to find out which mail server handles mail for acmevirtualindustries.com.

Connecting the Mail Server to an External Port on Your Router or Firewall

In this arrangement, you open a port on your router (for example, a DSL router) or firewall, and then connect the mail server to it. The mail server then has a presence on the Internet, which it doesn't when it's connected solely to your internal network.

The ports you'll normally need to open are TCP ports 25 (SMTP), 110 (POP), and 143 (IMAP). If you configure mail to use custom ports, open those ports instead.

Setting Up a Port-Forwarding Rule

Instead of connecting your server to a port on the router, you can set up a port-forwarding rule from your public IP address to the mail server's internal IP address.

This arrangement is similar to the previous one but different. In this arrangement, you give your network's public IP address as the mail server's contact address, but then

Should You Host Your E-mail or Outsource It?

The alternative to hosting your own e-mail is to use an Internet service that hosts it for you. For many small companies, this is a tough choice.

Third-party e-mail hosting is especially helpful when you have a small network, an even smaller support staff, and insufficient time to set up e-mail and chase down the problems that inevitably rear their dearly beloved little heads. Your host handles the mail, the backups, and the headaches, and you provide just the master prescription and the cash to cover it.

On the downside, if you have someone else host your e-mail, you don't have full control over it. This can be problematic in ways that range from niggles about how exactly the e-mail is managed (someone else is managing it for you, so you don't have ultimate control) to larger concerns about keeping copies of e-mail safe for however long your regulators demand and losing them smartly and irretrievably after that.

direct any traffic to the mail ports on that IP address to your mail server's IP address on the internal network.

Depending on your router, you may be able to specify a "default server" that receives any incoming traffic that's not specifically directed elsewhere (which is easy to set up but dangerous, as your server may receive traffic that you'd ideally drop into a deep, dark oubliette).

If you can't (or won't) specify a "default server," you will need to configure port forwarding for each port that you want items to be forwarded from. For example, SMTP traffic is normally directed to port 25, so you would tell your firewall to pass along any traffic on port 25 to your mail server.

Turning On and Configuring the Mail Service

To set up mail, you need to turn on the Mail service (if it's not already running) and configure it (if it's not configured). This section shows you how to turn on Mail, configure it using the Server Configuration Assistant, and configure it further manually.

Turning On the Mail Service

See if the Mail service is running, and turn it on if it isn't. Follow these steps:

1. Open Server Admin. The easiest way to do this is to click the Server Admin icon in the dock.

2. In the Servers list on the left, double-click the server that you want to connect to.

3. Type your user name and password if you haven't told your Mac to remember them, and then click the Connect button.

4. In the Servers pane on the left, double-click the server to display the list of services. If the Mail service appears in the list, skip the remaining steps in this list.

5. Click the Settings button on the toolbar to display the Settings pane.

6. Click the Services tab to display the Services pane.

7. Select the Mail check box.

8. Click the Save button to apply the change.

The Mail service appears in the list of services in the Servers pane. Keep Server Admin open so that you can configure the Mail service, as described next.

Performing Essential Configuration with the Server Configuration Assistant

The Mail service has a vast number of settings, but normally you'll need to configure only some of them, leaving the rest with their default values. Usually, the best way to get started is to use the Server Configuration Assistant to perform the basic configuration for you, then open up the Settings pane so that you can poke and tweak other settings as needed.

To launch the Server Configuration Assistant, follow these steps:

1. In Server Admin, click the Mail service in the services list under the server in the Server's pane.

2. Click the Overview button on the toolbar to display the Overview pane (if it's not displayed by default).

3. Click the Configure Mail Service button.

The first screen of the Server Configuration Assistant is the Introduction screen, which tell you about the features that the mail server provides. Marvel briefly, and then click the Continue button.

On the Mail Service: General screen (see Figure 10-1), choose settings for the following options:

- **Enable POP**   Select this check box if you want users to be able to use POP to get their mail.

- **Enable IMAP**   Select this check box if you want users to be able to use IMAP to get their mail.

NOTE   Your mail server can run both POP and IMAP at the same time, so you can support both means of getting mail if you so choose. For example, you may want users whom your company keeps chained to a particular workstation to use POP while providing IMAP for knowledge workers who need to be able to check their e-mail from anywhere they can grab a connection.

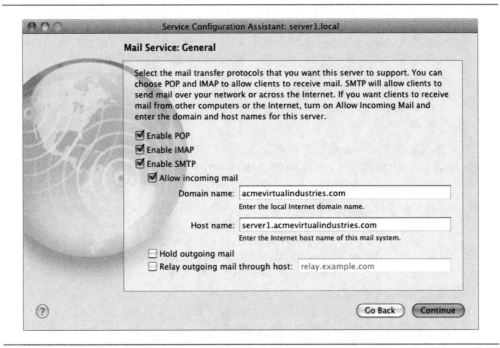

Figure 10-1. On the Mail Service: General screen of the Server Configuration Assistant, choose which mail transfer protocols to use and enter your domain name and host name.

- **Enable SMTP** Select this check box to turn on SMTP so that your server can send mail. You'll normally want to keep this check box selected unless you need to turn off the sending of mail so that you can troubleshoot problems.

- **Allow Incoming Mail** Select this check box if you want the server to accept incoming mail. You'll normally want to select this check box too unless you're dealing with a mail problem—for example, a deluge of spam.

- **Domain Name** In this text box, type the local Internet domain name—for example, **acmevirtualindustries.com**.

- **Host Name** In this text box, enter the mail server's host name—for example, **server1.acmevirtualindustries.com**.

- **Hold Outgoing Mail** Select this check box only when you need to stop the mail server from trying to send messages. If you lose your Internet connection, select this check box to enable the server to keep on accepting outbound messages from the mail clients but to stack them up in a queue instead of sending them. When the Internet connection is firing on enough cylinders again, you clear this check box, and the server starts chugging its way through the stacked-up messages.

■ **Relay Outgoing Mail Through Host**   Select this check box if your mail server relays e-mail through another server rather than sending the messages itself. The usual reasons for relaying mail are that your ISP handles the actual sending for you (often the case with smaller companies) or that you have a full-time mail server connected to the Internet to handle the sending, and this server is one that relays messages to that server (this arrangement happens more in larger companies). If you select this check box, type the mail server's name in the text box.

Click the Continue button, and you'll see the Mail Service: Filters screen (see Figure 10-2). This screen lets you choose how aggressively to target spam and how to handle viruses:

■ **Scan Email For Junk Mail**   If you want to try to filter out spam from incoming mail, select this check box, and then drag the Minimum Junk Mail Score slider to a suitable position on the Least–Moderate–Most continuum. Least flags mail as junk with only one hit (so be careful with this setting), Moderate needs six hits, and Most requires 40 hits.

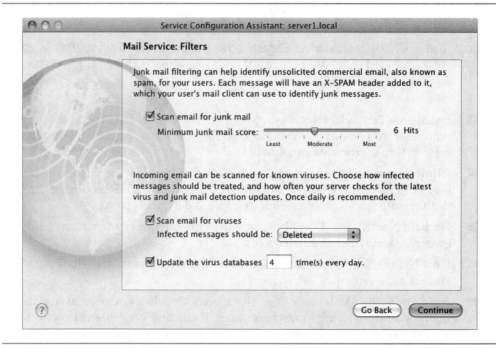

Figure 10-2.   On the Mail Service: Filters screen of the Server Configuration Assistant, choose how to handle junk mail and viruses.

■ **Scan Email For Viruses** If you want to scan incoming e-mail messages and their attachments for viruses, select this check box. Then, open the Infected Messages Should Be pop-up menu and choose how to handle the guilty: Deleted (the default), Bounced (back to the sender), or Redirected (so that you can examine them and pronounce your verdict).

■ **Update The Virus Databases *N* Time(s) Every Day** To update the definitions for junk and viruses automatically, select this check box, and then type the frequency in the text box. Automatic updating is usually a good idea.

Click the Continue button to mosey along to the Mail Service: Security screen (see Figure 10-3).

If you don't have a degree in secure methods of authentication, the Mail Service: Security screen can seem daunting. Here's what you need to know to navigate it successfully:

■ You can choose separate means of authentication for sending mail via SMTP, collecting mail via IMAP, and collecting mail via POP. Use the check boxes in the first column for SMTP, the second column for IMAP, and the third column for POP.

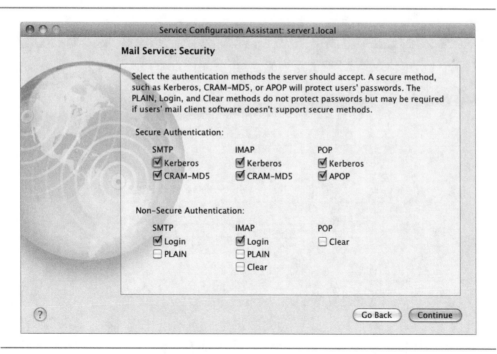

Figure 10-3. On the Mail Service: Security screen of the Server Configuration Assistant, choose which authentication protocols to use.

■ For each connection method, you can choose secure means of authentication, non-secure means, or both, by selecting the appropriate check boxes. Normally, you'll want to stick with the secure means unless you've got a client that can't handle them—in which case, provide only the non-secure means of authentication that the client needs.

■ Of the three secure methods of authentication, Kerberos is the most secure, but it's normally available only to computers you've bound to Open Directory. CRAM-MD5 and APOP are available on pretty much any e-mail client.

CAUTION   The problem with the Plain and Clear options is that they send the authentication information without adequate encryption to protect it from anyone who can intercept the data on the network.

When you've nailed down the security settings, click the Continue button to move along to the Mail Service: Mail Storage screen of the Server Configuration Assistant (see Figure 10-4).

By default, the mail server keeps the mail store in the /var/spool/imap/dovecot/ mail/ folder (Dovecot is one of the applications that run the mail service in the background). If you want to move it (for example, to a drive that has more storage space),

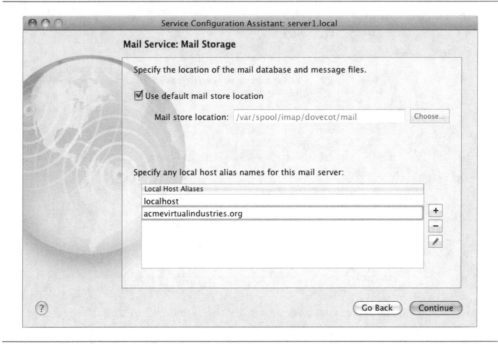

Figure 10-4.   On the Mail Service: Mail Storage screen of the Server Configuration Assistant, you can move your mail store and add local host alias names for the mail server.

clear the Use Default Mail Store Location check box and click the Choose button. In the resulting dialog box, select the folder, and then click the Choose button.

If you need the mail server to accept mail for any other domains than the one you specified on the Mail Service: General screen, add them to the Specify Any Local Host Alias Names For This Mail Server list box. To add an entry, click the + button, and then type the domain name.

Click the Continue button to display the Mail Service: Confirm Setup screen (see Figure 10-5), which summarizes the choices you've made.

Check that everything looks right (if not, click the Go Back button and fix the problem), and then click the Continue button.

The Server Configuration Assistant applies the settings you've chosen and starts the Mail service. When it has finished it displays the Service Configuration Complete screen, which tells you to use Server Admin to make any changes from now on.

Click the Close button to close the Server Configuration Assistant, and you'll pop right back into Server Admin. You can then make any further changes as discussed in the following sections.

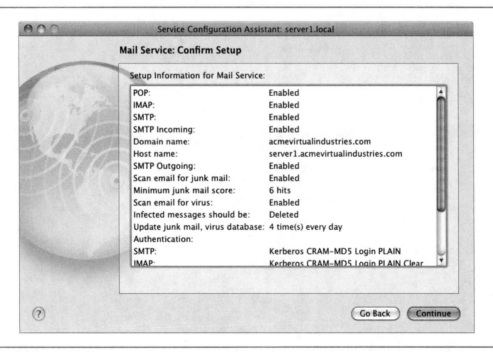

Figure 10-5.   On the Mail Service: Confirm Setup screen, check your settings, and then click the Continue button.

Configuring Your Mail Server Further Using Server Admin

The Server Configuration Assistant usually does enough to get your mail up and running, but you may need to choose further settings in the Settings panes for the Mail service in Server Admin. This section focuses on the settings you'll typically need to configure.

The place where you'll probably want to start making changes is the General pane (see Figure 10-6), so click the Mail service in the services list, click the Settings button on the toolbar, and then click the General tab.

You'll recognize most of these settings from earlier in the chapter. Here's what you need to know about the settings you haven't yet met:

- **Push Notification Server** To add a server that will push out mail notifications to clients such as the iPhone and iPod touch, click the Add button. Choose the server in the Server menu in the resulting dialog box, authenticate yourself, and then click the Connect button. The server's name then appears in the Push Notification Server readout.

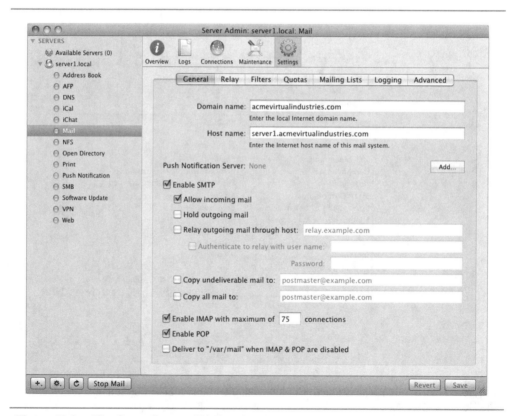

Figure 10-6. The General pane of Mail settings is where you enter your domain name and host name and choose whether clients can use POP, IMAP, or both.

- **Relay Outgoing Mail Through Host**   If you need to set up relaying, select this check box, and then type the address of the relay server. If the relay server requires authentication, as relay servers typically do, select the Authenticate To Relay With User Name check box, type the username in the text box, and add the password in the Password text box.

- **Copy Undeliverable Mail To**   Select this check box if you want to send copies of undeliverable messages to the address you enter in the text box. Normally, you'll want to use this option, as it enables you to field both messages sent to nonexistent addresses at your domain (for example, queries from customers who haven't found your Contact Us page) and messages sent to formerly valid addresses (such as those of people who've been fired or "rationalized").

- **Copy All Mail To**   Select this check box if you want to automatically copy every single message sent by users, sending the copies to the account you designate. Some companies and organizations require this Total Information Awareness approach for legal reasons, but if you use it, make absolutely clear to users that all their e-mail is being monitored. (Normally, you'll want to have Human Resources do this as part of a legally bombproof Computer Use policy that each employee signs.)

- **Enable IMAP With Maximum Of *N* Connections**   This check box will be selected if you selected the Enable IMAP check box in the Server Configuration Assistant. In the text box, enter the maximum number of connections your server will support; the default number is 1000, but you will probably want to change this number so that it just covers the number of e-mail accounts your company has or the number of them that you allow to use IMAP.

CAUTION   A single IMAP user typically has multiple connections to the server at the same time. Look at the Connections pane for the Mail service in Server Admin to work out what typical usage is before you reduce the maximum number of connections.

- **Deliver To "/var/mail" When IMAP & POP Are Disabled**   Select this check box if you want incoming mail to go to the /var/mail/ folder if you disable both POP and IMAP.

Choosing Relay Settings for the Mail Service

The Relay pane in Mail service settings (see Figure 10-7) enables you to limit the hosts and networks from which your mail server accepts messages.

To designate SMTP relays from which your server should accept messages, select the Accept SMTP Relays Only From These Hosts And Networks check box, and then build the list in the list box. As usual, click the + button to add an entry, and then type the details in the resulting dialog box.

To block specific hosts and networks, select the Refuse All Messages From These Hosts And Networks check box, and then assemble the list in the list box.

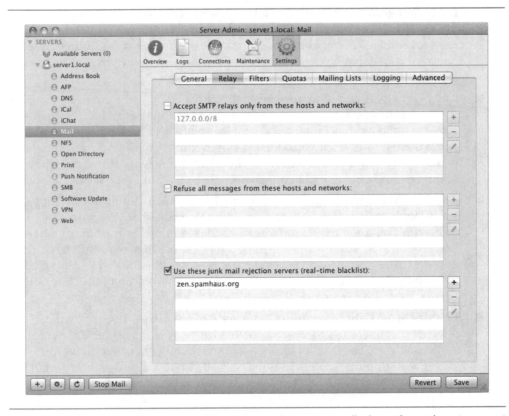

Figure 10-7. In the Relay pane of Mail service settings, you can list hosts from whom to accept or refuse messages.

To use real-time blacklisting of spam senders, select the Use These Junk Mail Rejection Servers, and then list them in the list box.

Choosing Filters Settings for the Mail Service

The Filters pane in Mail service settings (see Figure 10-8) adds additional filtering capabilities to those in the Server Configuration Assistant.

You'll recognize many of these settings from the Server Configuration Assistant, but here you can also do the following:

■ **List acceptable languages for e-mail** In the Accepted Languages text box, enter the two-character code for each language that's okay for incoming e-mail. To change the list, click the Edit button to its right, and then select and clear the check boxes in the resulting dialog box. For example, if you keep getting spam in Quechua or Rhaeto-Romance, you can suppress it here by clearing those two check boxes.

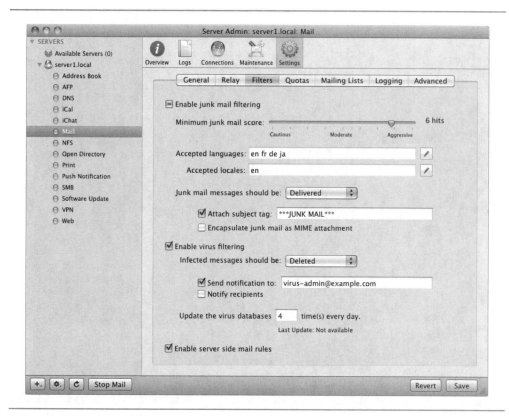

Figure 10-8. In the Filters pane of Mail service settings, you can choose further options for filtering and handling junk mail.

- **List acceptable locales for e-mail**   In the Accepted Locales text box, enter the two-character country code for each locale from which you'll accept messages. The available locales are English (en), Japanese (ja), Korea (ko), Thai (th), Chinese (zh), and Cyrillic (ru).

- **Choose how to mark junk mail**   If you choose to deliver junk mail to its recipients rather than bouncing it or sending it to the great bit-bucket in the sky, select the Attach Subject Tag check box and enter the warning text in the text box (the default text is ***JUNK MAIL***).

- **Turn on server-side mail rules**   To use server-side filtering to process e-mail before delivering it to mailboxes, select the Enable Server Side Mail Rules check box. You can then apply scripts in the Sieve mail-filtering language.

Choosing Quotas Settings for the Mail Service

Click the Quotas tab to display the Quotas pane (see Figure 10-9), and then choose how severely to restrict messages.

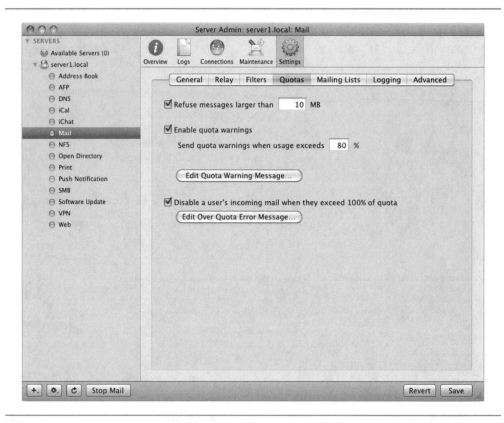

Figure 10-9. Use the controls in the Quotas pane to restrict the amount of space your users' mail can take up.

Bouncing Large Messages Back to Their Senders Mail servers tend to get unhappy if you give them huge messages to heave about, so you'll probably want to set a size limit for messages. Select the Refuse Messages Larger Than *N* MB check box to make your server bounce overstuffed messages back to their senders, and type the trigger size in megabytes in the text box.

The default setting is 10MB, which provides a reasonable balance between allowing your users to shift data by e-mail and letting them bring your server to its knees. If ten-meg messages (or, strictly speaking, messages whose attachments bulk them up to near that size) cause your server to choke, ratchet the limit downward until the users complain they can't transfer essential files.

NOTE E-mail is a great way of getting small and medium-size files from one person to another, but discourage your network's users from using e-mail as their standard means of transferring multi-megabyte files. If they must transfer files larger than your mail server can comfortably handle, set up an FTP server for them. You will need to communicate the limit for e-mail messages clearly (and in most cases repeatedly) to your network's users.

Siccing Quotas on Mail Accounts If you find your mail server is gradually silting up with messages, you can turn on quota warnings or even disable a user's account when they hit the limit.

To turn on quota warnings, select the Enable Quota Warnings check box, and then type the percentage in the Send Quota Warnings When Usage Exceeds N % text box. The default threshold is 80%. If you disable incoming e-mail at 100%, you'll probably want to set a lower threshold to give the users more warning.

NOTE The mail server filling up with messages tends to be more of a problem with IMAP servers than with POP servers, because POP clients download mail to the local machine.

Click the Edit Quota Warning Message button to display the dialog box shown in Figure 10-10. Type in the sender, message subject, message body, and then click the OK button.

If you want to enforce the quotas in a way that users will notice, select the Disable A User's Incoming Mail When They Exceed 100% Of Quota check box. Enforcing quotas like this is sometimes necessary, but it seldom feels friendly: You can probably imagine how much you'd enjoy life if the US Mail, FedEx, and UPS all decided to boycott you. (Then again, all they bring is bills and demands these days…)

Either way, you should explain why you've cut the user off. Click the Edit Over Quota Error Message button, set up the "you're over the legal limit" message in the dialog box

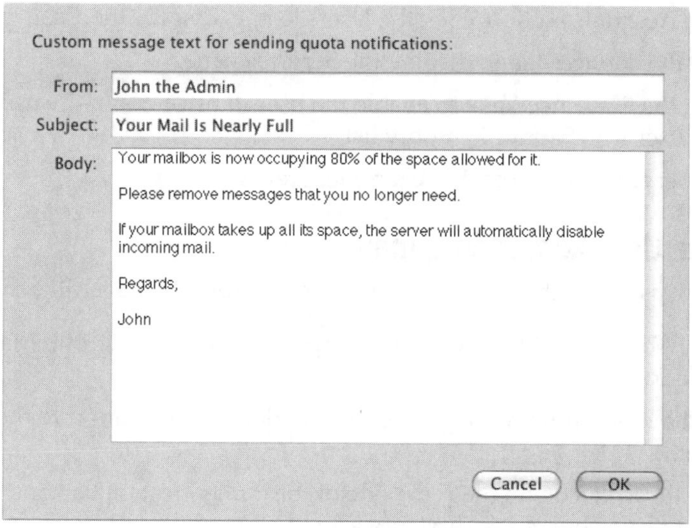

Custom message text for sending quota notifications:

From: John the Admin

Subject: Your Mail Is Nearly Full

Body: Your mailbox is now occupying 80% of the space allowed for it.

Please remove messages that you no longer need.

If your mailbox takes up all its space, the server will automatically disable incoming mail.

Regards,

John

Cancel   OK

Figure 10-10. In this dialog box, create a custom message warning users that they are running out of space for mail.

that opens, and then click the OK button. This dialog box has the same controls as the dialog box shown in Figure 10-10, but a different prompt.

Connecting Users to E-mail

By this point, the mail server is probably feeling lonely and looking for friendly faces on the network. Before it makes friends with any shady avatars, you need to set up the users to use e-mail.

Setting up the users with e-mail takes three steps:

1. Enable the users to use e-mail at all.

2. Decide whether they use POP or IMAP for accessing e-mail.

3. Connect the user to the mail server, either automatically or manually.

Let's take it from the top. Count us in…

Enabling a User to Use E-mail

The master switch to enable e-mail for users is in Server Preferences. Chances are that you turned the Mail service on for users during setup, but if not, you can turn it on (or off) for any user like this:

1. Open Server Preferences. For example, click the Server Preferences icon in the dock.

2. In the Accounts section, click the Users icon to display the Users pane.

3. Click the Services tab to display the Services pane.

4. Select the Mail check box to enable the user to use e-mail. (Clear this check box if the user's on Santa's Naughty list.)

5. Quit Server Preferences. For example, press ⌘-Q.

Choosing How a User Accesses E-mail

To choose how users get their e-mail, you use Workgroup Manager like this:

1. Open Workgroup Manager. For example, click the Workgroup Manager icon in the dock.

2. Use the Workgroup Manager Connect dialog box to connect to the appropriate server.

3. Click the lock icon on the right side of the authentication bar, and then authenticate yourself as directory administrator.

4. In the left pane, click the Users button if it's not already comprehensively clicked.

5. In the toolbar, click the Accounts button if the Preferences button is currently selected.

6. Click the Mail tab in the tab bar to display the Mail screen (shown in Figure 10-11 with settings chosen).

7. Click the user whose mail access you want to set.

8. In the Mail line below the tab bar, select the Enabled option button.

NOTE   From the Mail pane, you can also forward a user's e-mail to a different address. Select the Forward option button in the Mail line, and then type the address in the Forward To text box. This option is especially useful for taking care of e-mail for someone whom Security has just escorted from the premises.

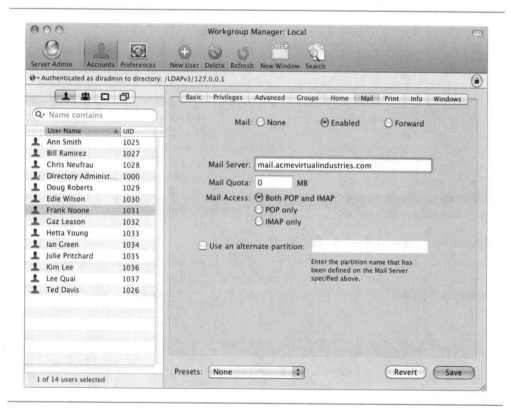

Figure 10-11.   Use Workgroup Manager to decide whether a user can use POP, IMAP, or both to gather their e-mail.

9. Verify that the Mail Server text box shows the right mail server.

10. In the Mail Access area, select the Both POP And Internet Mail Access Protocol (IMAP) option button, the POP Only option button, or the IMAP Only option button, as needed.

11. Click the Save button to save the changes to the user account.

12. Repeat steps 7 through 11 for each user whose mail settings you want to adjust, and then quit Workgroup Manager or find some other form of entertainment in it.

Connecting Users to Your Mail Server

Now that you've permitted the users to use e-mail and decided whether they can use POP, IMAP, or both, you need to actually connect the users to the mail server.

You can do this either automatically or manually. I'm guessing you'll prefer automatically, so we'll start there.

Connecting a User to the Mail Server Automatically

When a user connects to the network for the first time, Mac OS X automatically displays a dialog box offering to set up services for them. The exact dialog box depends on the situation (such as whether the user is connecting a Mac to the network for the first time or simply logging in themselves), but Figure 10-12 shows an example—the Mac OS X Server Invitation dialog box.

If the user click the Set Up button (or the local equivalent), Mac OS X sets up the services that the server is offering and then displays a dialog box to convey the good news. Figure 10-13 shows an example of this dialog box.

From here, the user usually needs to log out to make the changes take effect. They can then run Mail (or one of the other automatically configured applications), find the settings already snapped into place, and start accessing their messages.

Connecting a User to the Mail Server Manually

Instead of having a user connect to the mail server automatically as described in the previous section, you may need to set up the mail manually. To do so, open Mail by clicking the Mail button in the dock, and then set up the account by typing in its details.

Figure 10-12.   Mac OS X automatically prompts the user to set up applications such as Mail.

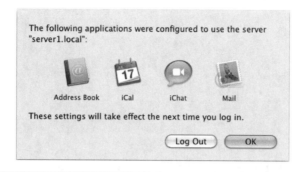

The following applications were configured to use the server "server1.local":

Address Book   iCal   iChat   Mail

These settings will take effect the next time you log in.

Log Out   OK

Figure 10-13.   After Mac OS X has set up key applications (such as Mail) to use the server, the user usually needs to log out and back in.

If Mail has no e-mail account configured, it displays the Welcome To Mail dialog box (see Figure 10-14), which walks you through the process of setting up the account. If Mail already has one or more accounts set up, you can kick the Assistant for creating a new account into life by choosing File | Add Account. The Assistant is then named Add Account, but it works the same way as the Welcome To Mail dialog box.

Welcome to Mail

Welcome to Mail

You'll be guided through the steps to set up your mail account.

To get started, provide the following information:

Full Name: Hetta Young

Email Address: hyoung@acmevirtualindustries

Password: ••••••••••••••••••

Cancel   Go Back   Continue

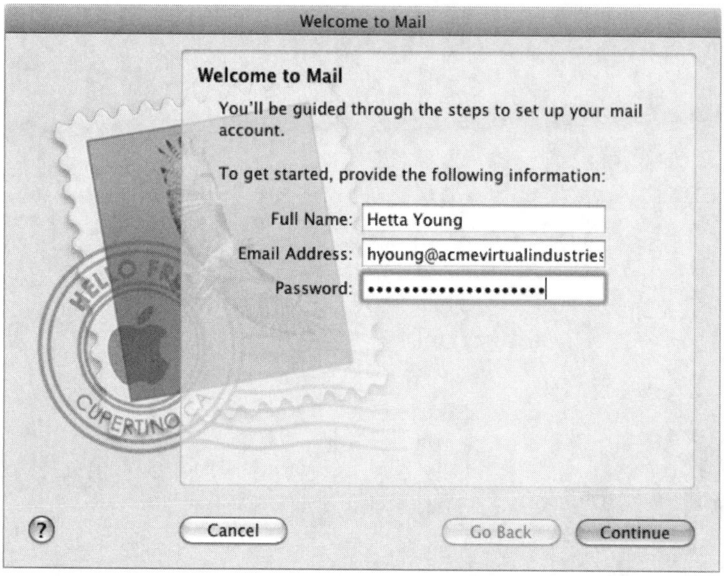

Figure 10-14.   To create an account manually, type the details in the Welcome To Mail dialog box (shown here) or the Add Account dialog box.

CHAPTER 11 | Set Up File Services

To transfer data across the network, your servers and clients use protocols—standardized ways of communicating. During setup, Mac OS X Server automatically starts enough protocols to get your network going, so you can start connecting Macs to it immediately. After that, though, you may need to run other protocols to enable other types of clients to communicate with the servers; and you may need to configure the protocols that are already running.

When you've sorted out the protocols, it'll be time to create share points to share folders and volumes on the network. I'll show you how to see which share points Mac OS X Server has set up for you automatically, how to add further share points, and how to configure share points.

After that, we'll go through how to set up home folders for users, either on the network or in Mac OS X's flexible mobile and external accounts that let users take their files and settings with them.

Sorting Out Your File Service Protocols

As I mentioned at the beginning of the chapter, to communicate with other computers, a computer uses one or more *protocols*—formalized ways of communicating. In this section you'll learn about Mac OS X Server's four protocols for file services, when to use each of them, and how to turn the protocols on and off as needed.

Understanding the Protocols That Mac OS X Server Can Use

Mac OS X Server can use four protocols for file services. Table 11-1 tells you what you need to know about them.

Seeing Which Protocols Your Server Is Using

Mac OS X Server provides a service to run each protocol—the AFP service, the FTP service, and so on. Depending on the installation options you choose, Mac OS X Server automatically sets up the AFP service, and may set up the SMB and NFS services as well. As a result, you have a working network—but you may need to change the services that are running.

You may also need to turn on the FTP service. FTP is primarily used for file transfer across the Internet, and is the least secure of the four protocols for file services—so don't turn it on unless you actually need it.

To see which protocols your server is using, open Server Admin and look at the services that are running:

1. Open Server Admin. For example, click the Server Admin icon in the dock.

2. In the Servers list on the left, double-click the server that you want to connect to.

3. Type your user name and password if you haven't told your Mac to remember them, and then click the Connect button.

Abbreviation	Full Protocol Name	Default Port	Used For	Comments
AFP	Apple Filing Protocol	548	Macs	Mac OS X Server sets up AFP automatically.
SMB	Server Message Block/ Common Internet File System	137, 138, 139	Windows or Windows-compatible computers	Macs can use SMB too, but AFP is far preferable. Use SMB only if needed.
FTP	File Transfer Protocol	21	File transfer, usually across the Internet	Use FTP only if you need to provide file transfer services across the Internet.
NFS	Network File System	2049	UNIX and other NFS clients	Macs can use NFS too, but AFP is much preferable.

Table 11-1.   Mac OS X Server's Protocols for File Services

4. Expand the list of services in the Server pane, and see whether AFP, FTP, NFS, and SMB appear with green lights next to them (see Figure 11-1). Alternatively, look at the Services list in the Overview pane. If a service doesn't appear, it's not set to run.

Turning a Protocol's Service On or Off

To turn a protocol's service on or off, first connect to the server using Server Admin:

1. Open Server Admin and connect to the server.
2. Click the server's entry in the Servers pane.

Turning a Protocol's Service On

To turn a protocol's service on, follow these steps in Server Admin:

1. Click the Settings button to display the Settings pane.
2. Click the Services tab to display the Services pane.

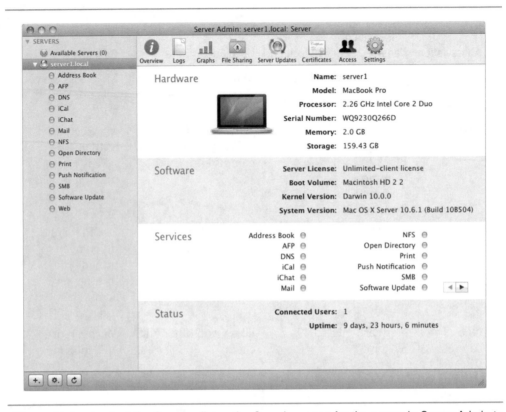

Figure 11-1.   Look at the Services list or the Overview pane for the server in Server Admin to see which protocols your server is using.

3. In the Select The Services To Configure On This Server list box, select the AFP check box, the FTP check box, the NFS check box, or the SMB check box, as appropriate.

4. Click the Save button to save the changes.

The service appears in the list of services beneath the server, and you can configure it as described later in this chapter.

Turning a Protocol's Service Off

The best way to stop using a protocol is to boot off any clients that are using the protocol's service, giving them a few minutes warning. Here's what to do:

1. In Server Admin, expand the server's entry, and then click the service in the services list.

2. Click the Connections tab to display the Connections pane (shown in Figure 11-2 for the AFP service).

Figure 11-2.   The Connections pane shows you how many users are connected to your server by a particular protocol, what they're doing, and how idle they are.

3. If clients are connected, click the Stop button to display the dialog box shown in Figure 11-3.

 NOTE   The Stop button you click in step 3 is the one at the bottom of the Connections pane, not the Stop button for the protocol (for example, the Stop AFP button) below the Servers pane.

4. In the Default Message box, adjust the number of minutes as needed.

5. Type any additional message in the Additional Message text box. For example, you might want to tell users to close their files.

6. Click the Stop button. Server Admin sends the message to the users (who see a countdown as shown in Figure 11-4), and then disconnects them after the specified time.

Figure 11-3.   Before stopping a service, send the connected users a message announcing their impending doom.

NOTE   After you click the Stop button, Server Admin makes that button unavailable to indicate that it is waiting to shut down the service. After shutting down the service, Server Admin changes the Stop button for the protocol to the Start button for the protocol.

Instead of giving the clients a countdown to disconnection, you can simply click the Stop button for the protocol. It's best not to do this if any clients are connected, because there's a good chance you'll cost them work and yourself grief. But if nobody is connected, go ahead and click the Stop button for the protocol. Server Admin displays the Stop Service Now dialog box (shown in Figure 11-5 for NFS), warning you that clients may lose their connection. (There's no "may" about it—they *will* lose their connection.)

After disposing of the clients, you can turn off the protocol's service:

1. In Server Admin, click the server's entry in the Servers pane.
2. Click the Settings button to display the Settings pane.

Figure 11-4.   Connected users see a minute-by-minute countdown of the time left before the server (in fact, the service) shuts down.

Figure 11-5. If nobody is using the service, you can simply damn the torpedoes and shut it down.

3. Click the Services button to display the Services pane.

4. Clear the check box for the service.

5. Click the Save button to save the change. Server Admin removes the service from the Services list in the Servers pane.

Choosing AFP Settings

Mac OS X Server automatically sets up AFP when you install your server, on the basis that you will want to use this protocol for communication among the Macs on your network. Chances are you won't want to turn AFP off, but you may want to adjust its settings, as described here.

Click the AFP item in the services list under the server in Server Admin, and then click the Settings button in the toolbar to display the Settings pane.

Choosing General Settings for AFP

Click the General tab to display the General pane (see Figure 11-6), and then choose settings as needed:

- **Encoding For Older Clients** If you still have Macs running System 8 or System 9—well, congratulations, but it's honestly time to buy new hardware. Until you do, use this pop-up menu to choose the encoding to use for them. Choose Roman unless you know you need a different encoding, such as Arabic, Cyrillic, or Japanese.

- **Login Greeting** In this text box, enter any greeting you want to display to each user who logs into the server. Press OPTION-RETURN to create a new line.

 NOTE Users don't see the greeting when logging into their home folder.

- **Do Not Send Same Greeting Twice To The Same User** Select this check box if you want each user to see the login greeting only once—for example, because you're using the message to provide general information that won't need repeating.

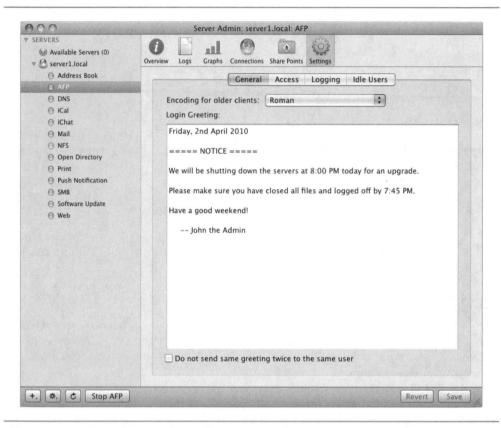

Figure 11-6.   You can set up a login greeting in the General pane of AFP settings.

Choosing Access Settings for AFP

Click the Access tab to display the Access pane (the top half of which appears in Figure 11-7, the lower part being blank), and then choose settings as needed:

- **Authentication**   In this pop-up menu, choose the authentication method to use. Your choices are Any Method (the default), Standard, or Kerberos.

- **Enable Guest Access**   Select this check box to allow guest access to AFP share points. Normally, you won't want to do this.

- **Enable Administrator To Masquerade As Any Registered User**   A clear winner for Best-Named Option In Mac OS X Server. Select this check box to enable yourself and other administrators to log in using a user's name but with your administrator password to see how AFP works for the user. This is a handy troubleshooting tool.

Figure 11-7.   The options in the Access pane in AFP settings include authentication, guest access, and the maximum number of connections.

■   **Maximum Connections**   On the Client Connections line, either select the Un-limited option button if you want the server to accept as many connections as your Mac clients can throw at it, or select the other option button and type the upper limit in the text box. If you selected the Enable Guest Access check box, choose settings on the Guest Connections line as well. Typically, you'll want many fewer guest connections than client connections.

Choosing Logging Settings for AFP

Click the Logging tab to display the Logging pane (see Figure 11-8), and then choose settings for what to log:

■   **Enable Access Log**   Select this check box to enable logging of access to the server via AFP.

■   **Archive Every *N* Days**   Select this check box to automatically archive the log after the number of days you specify. Archiving helps keep the log's size down, enabling you to find more easily the items you need in it.

■   **Select Events To Include In The Access Log**   In this area, select the check box for each item you want to include in the log: Login, Logout, Open File, Create File, Create Folder, or Delete File/Folder.

■   **Error Log: Archive Every *N* Days**   Select this check box to automatically archive the error log after however many days you enter.

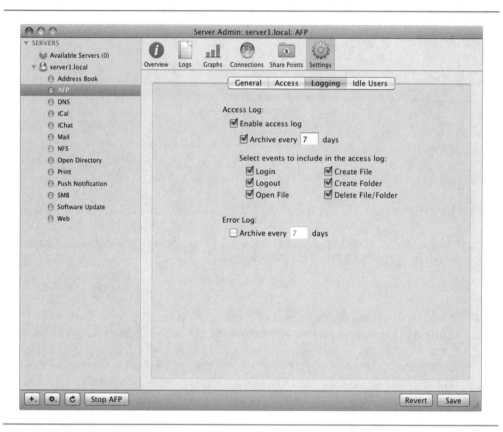

Figure 11-8.   The Logging pane in AFP settings lets you configure the access log and error log.

Choosing Idle Users Settings for AFP

Click the Idle Users tab to display the Idle Users pane (see Figure 11-9), and then choose how to handle idle users connected to your server.

- **Allow Clients To Sleep N Hours**   Select this check box if you want to allow clients to remain connected even if they're asleep. Type the number of hours in the text box.

- **Disconnect Idle Users After N Minutes**   Select this check box if you want to disconnect clients that remain idle but don't go to sleep. Type the number of minutes in the text box.

- **Except**   If you select the Disconnect Idle Users After N Minutes check box, select the check boxes for users you want to exempt from disconnection through idleness: Guests, Administrators, Registered Users, or Idle Users Who Have Open Files.

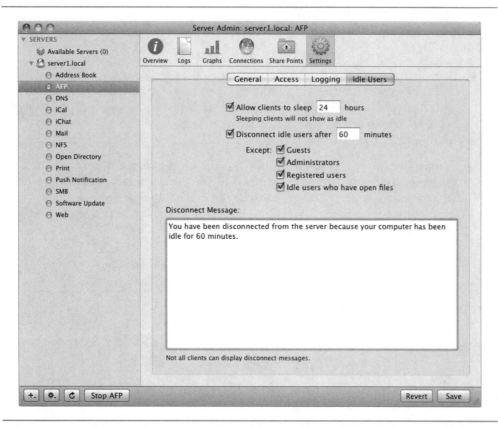

Figure 11-9.   In the Idle Users pane of AFP settings, choose whether to disconnect persistently idle users from your server.

■ **Disconnect Message**   To display a message explaining the disconnection, type it in this text box. Press OPTION-RETURN to create a new line.

After you finish making changes to the AFP service, click the Save button to save the changes.

Setting Up SMB

If your network has Windows clients, run the SMB service to provide file services for them. After you've started the service using the technique explained earlier in this chapter, you can set it up as described here.

In Server Admin, click the SMB item in the services list under the server, and then click the Settings button on the toolbar to display the SMB settings screens. You can then change the options detailed in the following sections.

Choosing General Settings for SMB

Click the General tab to display the General pane (see Figure 11-10), and then choose suitable settings:

- **Role** In this pop-up menu, choose the role the server plays on the Windows network: Standalone Server, Domain Member, Primary Domain Controller (PDC), or Backup Domain Controller (BDC). See Chapter 5 for a discussion of what a PDC and BDC do on the network.

- **Description** Type the description that the user should see for this server.

- **Computer Name** Type the NetBIOS name for the server. You can use up to 15 characters: letters and numbers only, with no punctuation, special characters, or spaces. Ideally, you'll make this name match the server's unqualified DNS name—for example, **server1** for a server fully qualified as **server1.acmevirtualindustries.com**.

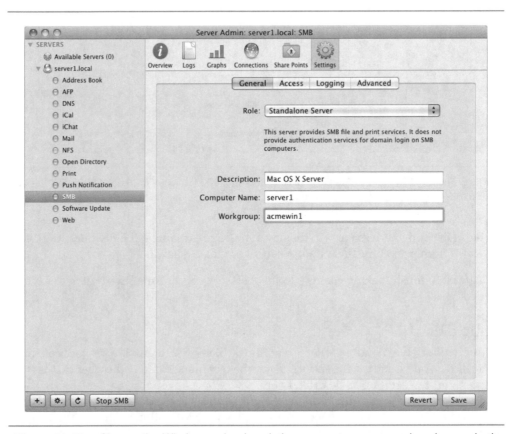

Figure 11-10. Choose the Windows role, description, computer name, and workgroup in the General pane of SMB settings.

■   **Workgroup**   Type the name of the domain that the Windows PCs are using. The name can be up to 15 characters long, and it must not be "workgroup."

Choosing Access Settings for SMB

Click the Access tab to display the Access pane of SMB settings (see Figure 11-11), and then choose settings for the following options:

■   **Allow Guest Access**   Select this check box to allow users to connect to the SMB share points without authentication. Normally, you will not want to do this.

■   **Client Connections**   In this area, select the Unlimited option button if you want the network's users to be able to connect to the SMB service without restriction. In a small network, this is reasonable; but in a larger network, you will probably want to set some ground rules by selecting the *N* Maximum option button and typing the appropriate number in the text box.

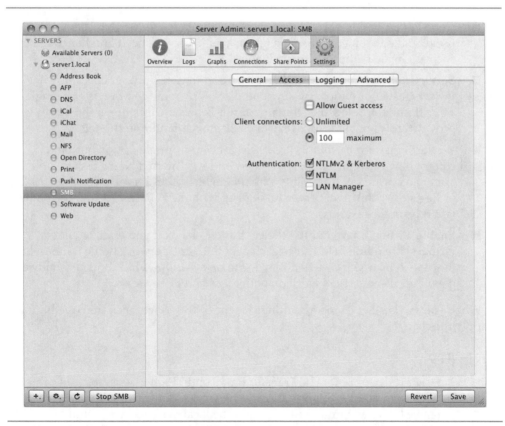

Figure 11-11.   In the Access pane of SMB settings, choose whether to allow guest access, how many client connections to accept, and which methods of authentication to use.

- **Authentication**   In this area, select the check box for each authentication method you want to use: NTLMv2 & Kerberos (the most secure option), NTLM (next most secure), or LAN Manager (grossly insecure, so best avoided unless you have clients running Windows 95).

Choosing Logging Settings for SMB

Click the Logging tab to display the Logging pane of SMB settings, and then choose the appropriate setting in its single control, the Log Level pop-up menu: High, Medium, or Low. You'll probably want to start with Medium, whose logging includes authentication failures, warning messages, and error messages; if this doesn't produce the level of information your heart desires, try High, which includes details of the files that SMB users access.

Choosing Advanced Settings for SMB

Click the Advanced tab to display the Advanced pane of SMB settings (see Figure 11-12), and then choose settings for the following options:

- **Code Page**   In this pop-up menu, choose the character set that clients should use. Use the Latin US code page unless you know you need another code page, such as Greek, Baltic, or Korean Hangul.

- **Services**   In this area, select the Workgroup Master Browser check box if the server will provide browsing and discovery of the computers in a single TCP/IP subnet. Select the Domain Master Browser check box if the server will provide browsing and discovery of computers in multiple subnets.

- **WINS Registration**   In this area, select the appropriate option button to control how the server appears to the Windows Internet Name Service (WINS). Your choices are Off (to disable WINS), Enable WINS Server (to enable WINS), or Register With WINS Server (to register with the WINS server whose name you type in the text box).

- **Enable Virtual Share Points**   Select this check box if you want to enable virtual share points. This gives each user the same network home folder when they log in on a Mac as when they log in on a Windows box, and is usually a good idea if some users work on both Macs and PCs.

When you've finished choosing settings for the SMB service, click the Save button to apply the changes.

Setting Up FTP

Mac OS X Server fully supports File Transfer Protocol (FTP), the venerable old protocol for shifting files from point A to point B across networks. But because you've got AFP, SMB, and maybe NFS for shunting files around the local network, you should use FTP only for transferring files across the Internet. Mac OS X Server leaves FTP off until you turn it on.

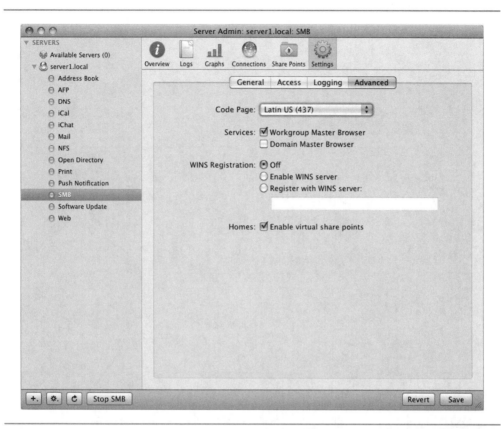

Figure 11-12.   In the Advanced pane of SMB settings, choose the code page, browsing details, WINS registration, and whether to enable virtual share points.

If you do need FTP to fill a hole in your protocol portfolio, turn on the FTP service as described earlier in this chapter. Then click the FTP item in the services list under the server, and set options as described in the following subsections.

Choosing General Options for FTP

To start configuring FTP, click the General button and choose settings in the General pane (see Figure 11-13):

- **Disconnect Client After *N* Login Failures**   In this text box, type the number of strikes you'll allow before barring the user from logging in. The default setting is the traditional three.

- **FTP Administrator Email Address**   In this text box, type the contact address for the FTP administrator.

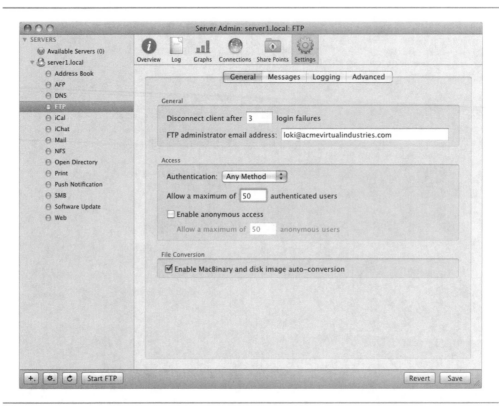

Figure 11-13. Most of the action happens in the General pane of FTP settings.

- **Authentication** In this pop-up menu, choose the authentication method: Any Method, Kerberos, or Standard.

- **Allow A Maximum Of *N* Authenticated Users** In this text box, set the maximum number of authenticated users the server is allowed to handle. Beyond this number, users receive a message saying that the server is busy.

- **Enable Anonymous Access** Select this check box if you will allow users to access the server under the user names "anonymous" or "ftp."

- **Allow A Maximum Of *N* Anonymous Users** If you allow anonymous access, type in this text box the maximum number of anonymous users the server may handle.

- **Enable MacBinary And Disk Image Auto-Conversion** Select this check box if you want FTP clients to be able to use automatic file conversion when transferring files.

Choosing Messages Settings for FTP

Now click the Messages tab to display the Messages pane (see Figure 11-14) and set up any messages you need:

- **Show Welcome Message** Select this check box if you want the server to show a welcome message when the FTP client logs in. Type the message in the text box.

- **Show Banner Message** Select this check box if you want the server to show a message when the FTP client first contacts the server (before login). Type the message in the text box.

Choosing Logging Settings for FTP

Now click the Logging tab to display the Logging pane (the top part of which appears in Figure 11-15; the lower part is blank), and choose which items to log. You can log the following four items for anonymous access, authenticated access, or both:

- **Uploads** Select this check box to record details of files that users upload to your server. You'll usually want to track these.

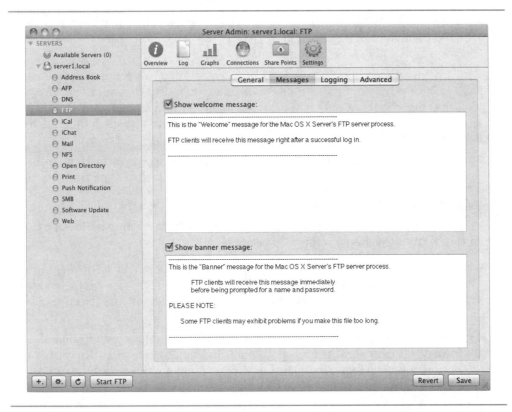

Figure 11-14. You can set up a welcome message and a banner message in the Messages pane of FTP settings.

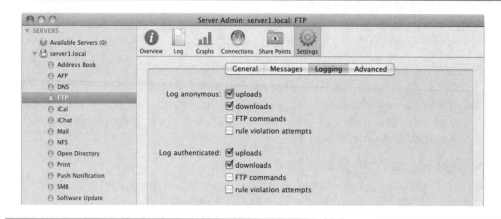

Figure 11-15.   In the Logging pane of FTP settings, choose whether to record uploads, downloads, commands, and rule violation attempts.

- **Downloads**   Select this check box to record the list of files that users download from your server. You'll usually want to keep tabs on these too, as it lets you see which files are most in demand.

- **FTP Commands**   Select this check box to record the FTP commands that users use. This is typically more information than you'll usually want to capture, so select this check box only when you think there's something to see. For example, if FTP users seem to be flailing, you can see where they go in their attempts to find files.

- **Rule Violation Attempts**   Select this check box to record permission errors—for example, when a user tries to access an item and is denied permission.

Choosing Advanced Settings for FTP

Click the Advanced tab to display the Advanced pane (whose exciting parts appear in Figure 11-16), and then choose settings as needed:

- **Authenticated Users See**   In this pop-up menu, choose which FTP items you want authenticated users to see: FTP Root With Share Points gives the greatest access, Home Folder With Share Points gives the next most, and Home Folder Only limits each user to seeing their home folder.

- **FTP Root**   If necessary, you can change the FTP root folder from its default location, /Library/FTPServer/FTPRoot/. To change the folder, click the Choose button, select the folder in the resulting dialog box, and then click the Choose button.

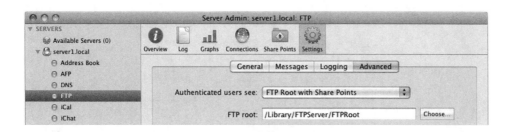

Figure 11-16. In the Advanced pane of FTP settings, you can choose which folders authenticated users see. You can also change the FTP root folder if necessary.

When you've finished choosing settings for the FTP service, click the Start FTP button at the bottom of the Servers pane to fire up the FTP service. Then crank up FileZilla, CyberDuck, or your favorite FTP client and make sure you can establish a connection to the server. Check that your welcome message and banner message are intelligible and appropriate.

Turning On and Setting Up NFS

If your network includes UNIX or Linux clients, as well as Mac clients and Windows clients, you will probably want to use the Network File System (NFS) protocol as well as AFP and SMB. If you don't have UNIX or Linux clients, make sure that NFS is turned off; while your Mac clients *can* use NFS, they're better off using AFP, and your server can do without the extra overhead that NFS entails.

To turn NFS on or off, follow the procedures explained in the section "Turning a Protocol's Service On or Off," earlier in this chapter.

To configure NFS, click the NFS item in the services list under the server, and then click the Settings button on the toolbar to display the Settings pane (the upper part of which is shown in Figure 11-17; the lower part is blank). Compared to the other protocols, this pane contains mercifully few options:

- **Use *N* Server Threads** In this text box, type the number of threads (daemons) you want to use for the NFS service. The more threads you use, the more clients NFS can handle—but the more effort your server has to devote to it. You'll probably want to start with the default setting, 20 server threads.

- **Serve Clients Via** In this area, select the option button for the protocol you want to use for NFS: the TCP And UDP option button, the TCP option button, or the UDP option button.

NOTE Transmission Control Protocol (TCP) gives clients better performance, while User Datagram Protocol (UDP) puts less strain on the server. Normally, it's best to use both TCP and UDP, unless the server is struggling to keep the clients fed and watered—in which case, switch to UDP, and maybe think about adding another server.

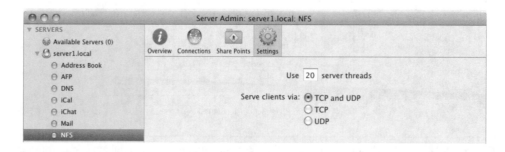

Figure 11-17. In the Settings pane for NFS, choose how many server threads to use and whether to use TCP, UDP, or both.

Creating Share Points to Share Folders and Volumes

Apart from surfing the Internet, blasting off e-mails, and creating wikis, your network's users will likely need to share files and folders on the network.

To set up volumes and folders that users can access, you create share points in Server Admin. To prevent people from sharing things they shouldn't, you apply suitable permissions to the volumes and folders. And to prevent people from being greedy, you can assign quotas of disk space on each share point as needed.

NOTE You set up each share point to work with the protocols that the clients will use to access it. For example, if only Macs will access the share point, you can set it up to share only via AFP. But if Windows boxes will access the share point too, you need to set it up for sharing via both AFP and SMB.

Seeing Which Share Points You Already Have

Share points tend to be essential to having happy network clients, so Mac OS X Server automatically sets up several share points for you during installation, depending on the choices you make. These may be all you need, at least to start with, so begin by reviewing the troops and seeing if they pass muster or need further drilling.

To see which share points you already have, open Server Admin (for example, click the Server Admin icon in the dock) and then connect to the server, authenticating yourself as necessary.

Click the File Sharing button on the toolbar to display the File Sharing pane. As you can see in Figure 11-18, this pane has a bar at the top under the toolbar with two pairs of visibility buttons: a Volumes button and a Share Points button, and a List button and a Browse button. There's also a toggle button farther to the right that switches between Share and Unshare, depending on whether the item is currently unshared or shared.

Normally, when you display the File Sharing pane at first, the Volumes button and the List button are selected, so you see the list of volumes. Click the Share Points button

Figure 11-18.   The File Sharing pane in Server Admin first shows your server's volumes and permissions.

to display the list of share points, as in Figure 11-19. Below it is a pane with tab buttons for toggling between showing options for the selected share point and permissions for the selected share point.

These are the share points that are already set up on your server. Let's see what we've got here:

- **Backups**   Mac OS X Server creates this share point if you choose to use Time Machine. In the Share Point pane below the list box, you'll see that the Enable As Time Machine Backup Destination check box is selected.

- **Groups**   Mac OS X Server creates this share point for sharing folders among groups.

- **NetBootClients0**   This share point contains data for booting diskless NetBoot clients (see Chapter 6 for information about Netboot).

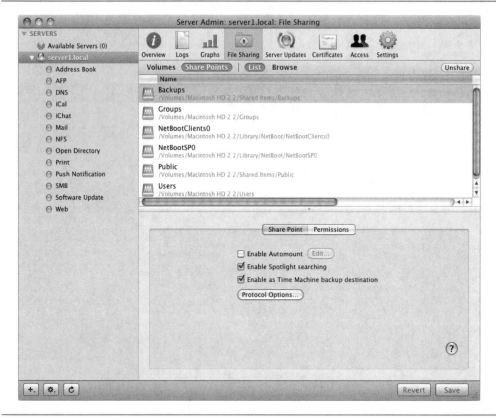

Figure 11-19.   Click the Share Points button to display the list of share points.

- ■ **NetBootSP0**   This share point is where you put disk image files for NetBoot and NetInstall (again, see Chapter 6 for details).

- ■ **Public**   This share point is for sharing files and folders with everyone at large on your network. This capability is useful on some networks, but on others, you may not need it.

- ■ **Users**   This share point is for user home folders.

So far, so good—but what about the icons in the Share Points list between the Name column and the Disk Space column? These indicate, from right to left:

- ■ **NetBoot status**   The icon appears in the first column if the share point provides NetBoot services for diskless workstations.

- ■ **Automount status**   The icon appears in the second column if the share point is configured to mount automatically.

- **Spotlight status**   The Spotlight icon (come on, you know it by now) appears if you've set Spotlight to search the share point.

- **Time Machine**   The Time Machine icon (you know this curling-arrow icon too) appears if you've configured the share point to accept Time Machine backups.

To configure an existing share point, you select it, and then use the controls in the Share Point pane or the Permissions pane. We'll look at these controls, and what they do, in a moment. But first, let's go through how to add another share point if you need one.

Adding Further Share Points

Now, if you need to add further share points, add them like this:

1. Open the File Sharing pane in Server Admin. (You should already be here.)

2. If the Volumes button isn't already selected, click it to display the list of volumes.

3. Choose whether to share the whole volume or just a folder on it:

   - **Share an entire volume**   Click the volume to select it.

   - **Share a folder on the volume**   Click the volume to select it, and then click the Browse button to display the column browser panes (see Figure 11-20). If you want to create a new folder, click the folder in which to create it, click the New Folder button, type the name in the dialog box that appears, and then click the Create button. Otherwise, click an existing folder.

4. Click the Share button to share the volume or folder.

5. Click the Save button to make Server Admin apply the change.

If you switch back to the list of share points by clicking the Share Points button, you'll see your new share point appears.

You can now configure the options and permissions for the share point, as discussed next. (Actually, you can configure them before clicking the Save button in step 5 above—but let's leave that technicality aside.)

Changing the Options Used for a Share Point

When you create a share point as described in the previous section, Server Admin sets it up for sharing with default options via AFP and SMB (if you're running SMB). These settings work fine for many share points, but for others, you may need to change them, as described here.

Start by clicking the share in the Share Points list in the File Sharing pane in Server Admin. (If the Volumes button is selected, click the Share Points button to display the list of share points.) Then make sure the Share Point tab in the lower pane is selected, so that you see the Share Point pane.

You can then set the options discussed in the following subsections.

Figure 11-20. Use the column browser panes to select the folder you want to share, and then click the Share button.

Choosing Whether to Use Automount on a Share Point

Select the Enable Automount check box if you want client Macs to automatically mount the share when a user logs in to the network. Auto mounting is great for users' home folders, but you may also want to use it on share points that provide resources all users should always be able to access when connected to the network.

After enabling the automount, click the Edit button to display the dialog box shown in Figure 11-21. You can then choose the following settings:

- **Directory**   In this pop-up menu, choose the directory in which the automount appears.

- **Protocol**   In this pop-up menu, choose the protocol to use for the automount. You will normally want to use AFP, but you can also use NFS.

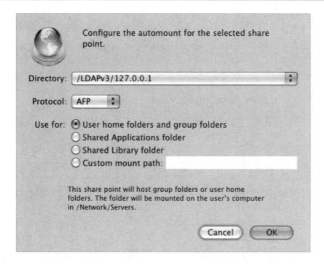

Figure 11-21. You can change the protocols and usage for an auto mounting share point in this dialog box.

- ■ **Use For**   In this area, select the option button that represents the purpose of the automount.

  - ■ **Home folders and group folders**   Select the User Home Folders And Group Folders option button. Clients mount the share point in the /Network/Servers/ folder.

  - ■ **Shared applications**   Select the Shared Applications Folder option button. This share point shows up in the /Network/Applications/ folder.

  - ■ **Shared library files**   Select the Shared Library Folder option button. This share point then surfaces in the /Network/Library/ folder.

  - ■ **Custom mount path**   Select the Custom Mount Path option button, and then type the mount path in the text box. This share point then appears on the user's Mac in the folder you chose.

When you've finished choosing settings for the automount, click the OK button to close the dialog box. If Server Admin displays the Authenticate dialog box for the directory domain (see Figure 11-22), type the directory administrator's name and password, and then click the OK button.

Choosing Whether to Train Spotlight on the Share Point

If you want Spotlight to search and index the contents of the shared folder, select the Enable Spotlight Searching check box.

You'll probably want to have Spotlight search many of your shared folders so that users can find the documents they contain. The disadvantage to using Spotlight

Figure 11-22.   If prompted, authenticate yourself as directory administrator in the Authenticate dialog box.

is that it increases the amount of work the server must do, and so it may degrade performance—so if a share point contains items that users will never need to search, clear the Enable Spotlight Searching check box. For example, there's no reason to use Spotlight on your NetBootClients0 and NetBootSP0 share points.

Choosing Whether to Enable a Share Point as a Time Machine Backup Destination

If you want to use the share point for Time Machine backups, select the Enable As Time Machine Backup Destination check box. See Chapter 18 for more information on backing up data with Time Machine.

Changing the Protocols Used for a Share Point

The next thing you can change about a share point is the protocols used. As I mentioned, Server Admin sets up each share point with AFP and SMB (if you're running SMB), so from the get-go the share point is configured for Macs, Windows boxes, and other SMB-capable clients to access.

If you have only Macs, you may want to turn off SMB. It's also possible—but less likely—you may want to use FTP or NFS on the share point. Or you may want to change the settings for AFP or SMB.

To make any of these changes, open up the Protocol Options dialog box like this:

1. In the File Sharing pane in Server Admin, click the share point you want to change. (If the Volumes button is selected, click the Share Points button to display the share points.)
2. In the lower pane, click the Share Point tab if it's not already selected.
3. Click the Protocol Options button.
4. Click the tab for the protocol you want to configure—AFP, SMB, FTP, or NFS.

You can then choose settings as described in the following sections.

Choosing AFP Options

The AFP pane (whose top part appears in Figure 11-23) contains only three settings:

- **Share This Item Using AFP**   Select this check box to use AFP on the share point, as you'll almost certainly want to do.

- **Allow AFP Guest Access**   Select this check box only if you want people to be able to connect to the share point without authentication. Normally, you'll want this only on a public folder.

- **Custom AFP Name**   If you want to change the AFP name for this share point, type the new name in this text box.

Choosing SMB Options

The SMB pane (see Figure 11-24) contains the following settings:

- **Share This Item Using SMB**   Select this check box to use SMB on the share point. If your network doesn't need SMB (for example, because all the clients use AFP), clear this check box to turn off SMB sharing.

- **Allow SMB Guest Access**   Select this check box only if you want people to be able to connect to the share point without authentication. Normally, you'll want this only on a public folder.

- **Custom SMB Name**   If you want to change the SMB name for this share point, type the new name in this text box.

- **Enable Oplocks**   Select this check box to enable opportunistic file locking on the share point. Opportunistic file locking is handy for clients, as it enables an application to lock the file on the share point so that nobody else can open it, cache the file's data on its hard disk, and work with it there. But not all applications support opportunistic locking.

- **Enable Strict Locking**   Select this check box to enable standard locking on files—when one person opens a file, the server locks it against other people opening it.

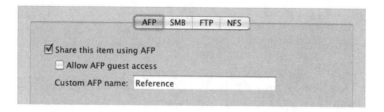

Figure 11-23. In the AFP pane of the Protocol Options dialog box, you can turn on guest access or customize the AFP name.

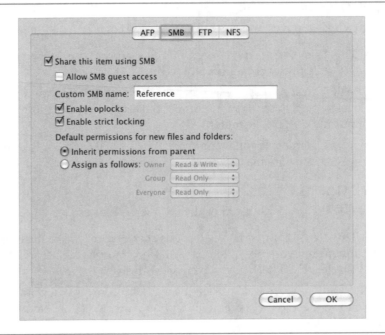

Figure 11-24. In the SMB pane of the Protocol Options dialog box, you can control guest access, locking, and permissions for new files and folders.

■ **Default Permissions For New Files And Folders**   In this area, select the Inherit Permissions From Parent option button if you want new files and folders to get the same permissions as the folder that contains them. This is usually the simplest arrangement, but if you want to use custom permissions, select the Assign As Follows option button, and set up the permissions you want in the Owner pop-up menu, Group pop-up menu, and Everyone pop-up menu. For example, you can give the owner Read & Write permission, the owner's group Read Only permission, and everyone else No Access.

Choosing FTP Options

The FTP pane (shown truncated in Figure 11-25) contains the same three settings as the AFP pane:

■ **Share This Item Using FTP**   Select this check box only if you want to use FTP on the share point.

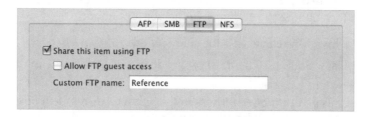

Figure 11-25.   In the FTP pane of the Protocol Options dialog box, you can turn on guest access or customize the FTP name.

- **Allow FTP Guest Access**   Select this check box only if you want people to be able to connect to the share point without authentication. The normal use for this is to provide downloads—for example, of your company's manuals.
- **Custom FTP Name**   If you want to change the FTP name for this share point, type the new name in this text box.

Choosing NFS Options

The NFS pane (see Figure 11-26) lets you not only share the share point but also configure who can do what with it.

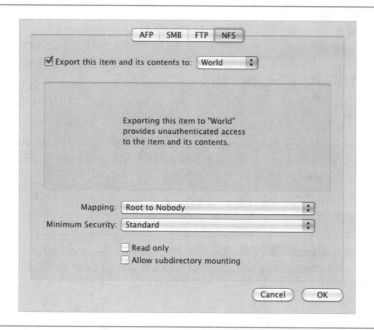

Figure 11-26.   In the NFS pane of the Protocol Options dialog box, choose whether to share the share point with the World (everyone), a Client List, or a Subnet.

To share the share point via NFS, select the Export This Item And Its Contents To check box, and then choose the audience in the pop-up menu:

- **World**   Everyone can access the share point.
- **Client List**   Build the client list by IP address or DNS name in the pane that appears.
- **Subnet**   Type the subnet address in the Subnet Address text box and the mask in the Subnet Mask text box that appears.

In the Mapping pop-up menu, choose the privilege mapping for the share point. You have four options here:

- **Root To Root**   Select this item to give a remote client's root user full privileges on the share point.
- **All To Nobody**   Select this item to give remote users only minimal privileges.
- **Root To Nobody**   Select this item to give a remote client's root user only minimal privileges.
- **None**   Select this item to avoid mapping any privileges.

In the Minimum Security pop-up menu, select the security level to use: Standard, Any, Kerberos v5, Kerberos v5 With Data Integrity, or Kerberos v5 With Data Integrity And Privacy. (The And Privacy item encrypts the data during transmission.)

Select the Read Only check box if you want to prevent the users from changing the items on the share point.

Select the Allow Subdirectory Mounting check box if you want to let clients mount the share point's subfolders as well as only being able to mount the share point itself.

Setting Permissions for a Share Point

To control who can do what with a share point, you can set permissions for it. To do so, follow these steps:

1. In the File Sharing pane in Server Admin, click the share point you want to change. (If the Volumes button is selected, click the Share Points button to display the share points.)

2. In the lower pane, click the Permissions tab to display the Permissions pane (shown in Figure 11-27 with the Users & Groups window displayed).

 NOTE   The **root** account is the all-powerful system account. The **wheel** group is an administrative group created automatically by Mac OS X that has lower privileges than the **root** account, but more than user accounts.

Figure 11-27. Use the Permissions pane to set permissions for a share point.

3. To add a user or group to the list:

    a. Click the + button to display the Users & Groups window.

    b. Click the Users button or the Groups button, as needed.

    c. Drag the user, group, or multiple items to the ACL list.

    d. In the Type pop-up menu, choose Allow or Deny, as appropriate.

    e. In the Permission pop-up menu, choose the permission level: Full Control, Read & Write, Read, Write, or Custom. If you choose Custom, the dialog box shown in Figure 11-28 opens. Choose the exact permissions you want to apply, and then click the OK button.

4. To remove a user or group from the list, click their entry, and then click the – button.

5. To change an existing permission, click it, and then choose a different item in the Type pop-up menu or the Permission pop-up menu.

6. When you have finished changing the permissions, click the Save button to apply the changes.

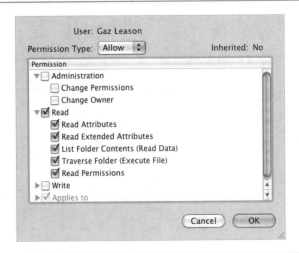

Figure 11-28. On rare occasions, you may need to set up custom permissions for a user or group.

Setting Up Home Folders for Users

To give each user a place to store documents safely, you create a home folder for the user. For a user who uses a Mac that stays attached to the network, you create a home folder on the network, where the user can access it from any Mac and can back it up. For a user who carries a MacBook, you create a mobile account—one stored on the MacBook, so that the user can work when not connected to the network. And for a user who needs the ultimate in portability, you can create an external account—one stored on an external drive such as a USB stick. No matter which Mac they plug the USB drive into, their entry appears on the login screen, and their files and settings are right there.

 TIP In a multi-server network, you can improve performance by locating users' home folders on servers close to the users' Macs rather than having all the home folders in the default location. In a small network, having the home folders in the default location works fine.

Mac OS X Server automatically creates the Users share point for storing users' home folders on your server. If you're planning to use this share point for the home folders, take a moment in Server Admin to make sure that it's set up correctly:

1. In Server Admin, click the File Sharing tab to display the File Sharing pane.
2. Click the Share Points button to display the list of share points.
3. Click the Users share point to display its settings in the lower pane.

4. Click the Share Point tab in the lower pane if the Permissions tab is currently selected.

5. Make sure the Enable Automount check box is selected.

6. Click the Edit button to display the dialog box for configuring the automount. (If the Enable Automount check box was cleared, and you select it, Server Admin displays this dialog box for you.)

7. In the Protocol pop-up menu, select the protocol you want to use. For Mac clients, use AFP.

8. In the Use For area, make sure the User Home Folders And Group Folders option button is selected.

9. Click the OK button to close the dialog box.

10. If you've made changes in the above steps, click the Save button to save them.

NOTE   There's no obligation to put the home folders in the Users share point—you can create another share point as needed. Make sure that the full pathname to the share point contains 89 characters or fewer and that it does not have any spaces.

Creating Mobile Accounts and External Accounts

As well as local accounts (on individual Macs) and network accounts for users who will normally be tethered to the network, Mac OS X Server also lets you create mobile accounts and external accounts.

■ **Mobile account**   A mobile account has a portable home directory that the user can cache on their Mac. The mobile account enables the user to work while not connected to the network. This is great for any network user who needs a Mac for company. You'll probably want to give yourself a mobile account—and maybe an external one.

■ **External account**   An external account is an even-more-mobile version of a mobile account. The account is external because it's stored on an external drive—either a USB stick or SD card, or one of those clunky, spinning-platter things that some people still use. (Just kidding.) An external account is a fantastic troubleshooter for administrators, so I'm betting you'll want to give yourself one. Knowledge workers and power users will probably demand them too.

NOTE   You can store an external account on any drive that's ejectable and is formatted with HFS Plus or FAT32. If you have the choice, go for HFS Plus rather than FAT32. You can also store an external account on a Mac (ideally a MacBook Pro, but a plain old MacBook if you're less lucky), connect it to another Mac in Target Disk mode, and use the external account on the other Mac from there. A USB drive is usually the best choice, because you can carry your entire operating environment on a device that you could swallow without medical intervention, but Target Disk mode lets you use a (usually) portable Mac as both your normal computer and a way to take over another Mac easily (by mounting your Mac as a portable disk containing an external account).

You create mobile accounts and external accounts in almost the same way, so we'll look at them both together here.

To turn a network account into a mobile account or an external account, follow these steps:

1. Open Workgroup Manager. For example, click the Workgroup Manager icon in the dock.

2. In the Workgroup Manager Connect dialog box, enter the server's address, your user name, and password, and then click the Connect button.

3. Click the lock icon at the right end of the authentication bar to open the Authenticate To Directory dialog box, type your administrator name and password, and then click the Authenticate button.

4. Click the user you want to affect.

5. Click the Preferences button on the toolbar to display the Preferences pane.

6. Click the Mobility icon to display the Mobility pane (shown in Figure 11-29 with options already chosen).

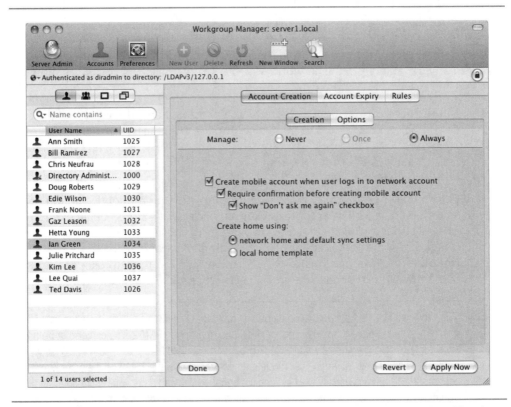

Figure 11-29. To create a mobile account, select the Create Mobile Account When User Logs In To Network Account check box in the Creation pane of Mobile preferences.

7. Make sure that the Account Creation tab is selected in the upper tab bar.

8. Make sure that the Creation tab is selected in the lower tab bar.

9. In the Manage bar, select the Always option button to enable the controls in the pane.

10. Select the Create Mobile Account When User Logs In To Network Account check box.

11. Select the Require Confirmation Before Creating Mobile Account check box if you want to get the user's assent to creating the mobile account.

12. Select the Show "Don't Ask Me Again" Checkbox check box if you want to let the user decline to create the mobile account and avoid further prompts for it.

13. In the Create Home Using area, select the Network Home And Default Sync Settings option button if you want the network home folder to replace the local home folder on the Mac. Usually, this is the best choice. The alternative is to select the Local Home Template option button, which bases the local home folder on the local home template.

14. If you need to apply encryption to the account or turn it into an external account, click the Options tab in the lower tab bar. Workgroup Manager displays the Options pane (shown in Figure 11-30 with settings already chosen).

15. In the Manage bar, select the Always option button to enable the controls in the pane.

16. To encrypt the account, follow these steps:

    a. Select the Encrypt Contents With FileVault check box.

    b. Select the Use Computer Master Password, If Available option button if you want to ensure that the account uses FileVault. This is usually the better option. The alternative is to select the Require Computer Master Password option button, which may let a user log in using a network account if no master password has been set.

    c. If you want to clamp down on the size of the home folder, select the Restrict Size check box. You can then either select the To Fixed Size option button and type the number of megabytes in the text box, or (if you've applied a quota to the network home folder) select the To Percentage Of Network Home Quota option button and type the percentage in the text box.

17. In the Home Folder Location area, choose where to store the home folder:

    ■ **Mobile Account** Select the On Startup Volume option button to place the account on the Mac's hard disk.

    ■ **External Account** Select the User Chooses option button, and then choose Any External Volume in the pop-up menu. This will make the user save the home folder to a removable drive.

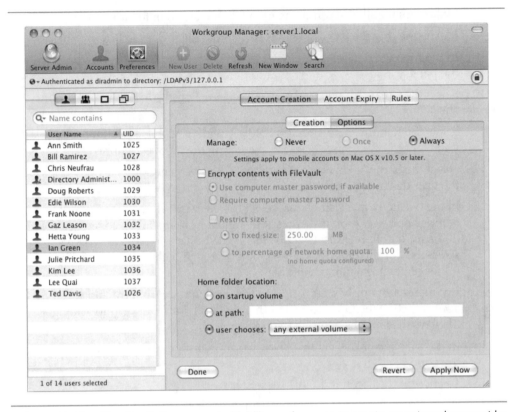

Figure 11-30. Use the Options pane in Mobility preferences to create an external account by locating the home folder on an external volume.

NOTE Apart from the Any External Volume item, the User Chooses pop-up menu offers the choices Any Volume and Any Internal Volume. You can choose the Any Volume item if you want the user to be able to choose whether to create an external account or an account on the Mac. But in most cases it's best to constrain the user to either placing the home folder on the startup volume or on an external volume.

18. Click the Apply Now button to apply the changes to the account.

Assigning a Home Folder to a User Account

To give a user a home folder on the network, you first set up a suitable share point using Server Admin, as discussed earlier in this chapter. This share point can be the Users share point that Mac OS X Server automatically creates for you, or a share point in a location that you find more convenient. You then use Workgroup Manager to assign a home folder to a particular user account—so if you create separate share points for different sets of users, Workgroup Manager is the tool you use for pointing the users to the right share points.

To assign a home folder to a user account, follow these steps:

1. Open Workgroup Manager. For example, click the Workgroup Manager icon in the dock.

2. In the Workgroup Manager Connect dialog box, enter the server's address, your user name, and password, and then click the Connect button.

3. Click the lock icon at the right end of the authentication bar to open the Authenticate To Directory dialog box, type your administrator name and password, and then click the Authenticate button.

4. In the left pane, click the user you want to affect.

5. Click the Home tab to display the Home pane (shown in Figure 11-31 with the creation of a Home folder underway).

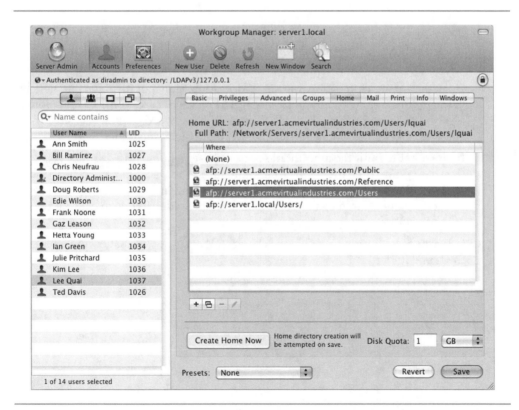

Figure 11-31.   Use the Home pane in Workgroup Manager to assign a home folder to a user account.

Setting Disk Quotas for Users on Other Share Points

As you saw in the previous section, you can set a disk quota for a user's home directory by using the Disk Quota text box and the megabyte-or-gigabyte pop-up menu next to it in the Home pane of the user's entry in Workgroup Manager.

You can use the same technique to set a disk quota for any other share point:

1. In Workgroup Manager, click the user you want to straitjacket.

2. With the Accounts button on the toolbar selected, click the Home tab to display the Home pane.

3. In the list of share points, click the share point for which you want to set the quota.

4. Enter the quota number in the Disk Quota text box, and select GB or MB (come on, be reasonable) in the pop-up menu.

5. Click the Save button to save the changes.

6. In the list box, click the share point on which you want to create the home folder.

7. Click the Create Home Now button. Workgroup Manager displays the message "Home directory creation will be attempted on save" next to the Create Home Now button (as you can see in the figure). In other words, when you save the changes, Workgroup Manager will try to create the home folder there.

8. If you want to limit the amount of space the user's home folder can devour on the share point, type the appropriate number in the Disk Quota text box, and choose GB in the pop-up menu. (The pop-up menu also offers an MB choice, but setting quotas in megabytes for users' home folders tends to cause grief nowadays.)

9. Click the Save button to save your changes. Workgroup Manager now creates the home folder.

CHAPTER 12 | Install and Manage Applications

Connecting your Macs to the network and giving the users accounts on them is all well and good, but sooner or later the users will start demanding to get some work done—or their bosses will.

In this chapter, we'll look at how you can provide users with the applications they need and prevent them from running the applications they shouldn't use—even if those applications are already on the Mac the user's logged in to.

Installing and managing applications tends to break down into three main steps:

- **Installing an initial set of applications onto the Mac** As discussed in Chapter 6, you can automatically install an initial slew of applications when you're setting up Mac OS X. In this chapter, I'm going to assume that you've taken this step; if not, move rapidly 150 pages to the left.

- **Choosing which applications the user may and may not run** Some power users may need to run any software they can get their hands on. But most users benefit from delicate encouragement in the right direction.

- **Getting additional applications and updates onto the Macs** Like the great churning river of Time (or was it Space?), software refuses to stand still. After you've deployed your Macs, ten to one you'll need to install further applications on at least some of the Macs, and updates on all of them.

In this chapter, we'll look at the second and third steps of this tango.

NOTE Chapter 17 discusses how to use Software Update to keep Mac OS X itself and Apple applications up-to-date.

Controlling the Applications a User Can Run

Power users tend to revel in having free rein on their Macs, but other users benefit from your restriction of the applications and widgets they can run. By providing less of a cornucopia of software, you reduce the risk of the user wasting time trying to choose among similar applications, and you prevent them from running applications that are guaranteed to waste time.

NOTE Okay, cards on the table—the users *may* benefit from having a restricted choice of software, but *you* certainly benefit. You don't want to support every application in sight, just those that suit your company's needs best.

Getting Ready to Restrict the Applications and Widgets

To restrict the applications and widgets a user can run, you use Workgroup Manager, as you'd probably imagine. But there's a wrinkle here: To restrict the applications effectively by using digital signatures to identify the applications, you need to be able to show Workgroup Manager the applications that you want to permit. That means the applications need to be installed on the Mac you use to set up the restrictions. Unless you've installed your regular suite of applications on your server, this means using a client Mac—one that has the Server Administration Software installed (see Chapter 5 for instructions on how to do this).

To get ready to restrict the applications and widgets, take these steps to launch Workgroup Manager and get to the Applications pane:

1. Log in to a Mac that has all the applications you want to permit, plus the Server Administration Software.

2. Click the Workgroup Manager icon on the Dock to open Workgroup Manager.

3. Connect to your directory server.

4. Authenticate yourself as directory administrator if Workgroup Manager doesn't do this for you automatically.

5. Click the user or group you want to affect.

6. Click the Preferences button to display the Preferences pane.

7. In the Overview pane, click the Applications icon to display the Applications pane.

NOTE   You can also control applications for a Mac or a group of Macs in Workgroup Manager. For example, if you provide Macs that can be used by anyone who can physically access them (for instance, in a library setting), you may want to restrict the applications they can run.

You're now ready to set restrictions for the user as discussed in the following sections.

Restricting the Applications the User Can Run

You can restrict the applications a user can run in three ways:

- **Allow only specific applications**   You can build a list of the applications the user is allowed to run.

- **Block applications in specific folders**   You can designate one or more folders as no-go zones.

- **Allow applications in specific folders**   You can tell Mac OS X that applications in one or more particular folders are okay, even if you don't know which applications are actually there.

You can mix and match these three approaches to produce the combinations of permitted and blocked applications you need.

Allowing Only Specific Applications

To choose the applications the user can run, follow these steps:

1. Display the Applications pane in Workgroup Manager by clicking the Applications tab.

2. In the Manage bar, click the Always option button to activate the other controls. Figure 12-1 shows the Applications pane open with a list of permitted applications underway.

3. Select the Restrict Which Applications Are Allowed To Launch check box.

4. With the lower Applications tab selected, add the permitted applications to the Always Allow These Applications list box like this:

   a. Click the + button to open a dialog box for adding applications.

   b. Select the application or applications. SHIFT-click or ⌘-click to select multiple applications at once.

   c. Click the Add button.

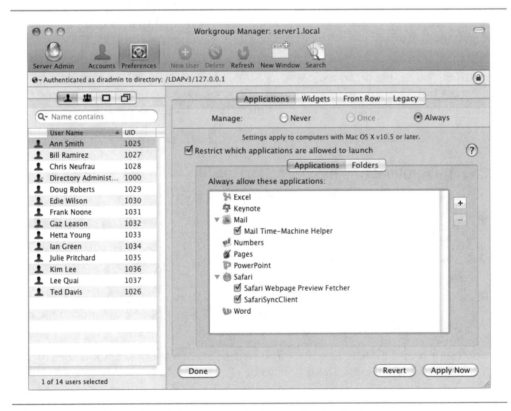

Figure 12-1. Set up a list of approved applications in the Applications pane.

d.   If the application has a digital signature applied to it, Workgroup Manager protects it using the digital signature. If the application doesn't have a digital signature, Workgroup Manager prompts you to add one (see Figure 12-2). Normally, you'll want to click the Sign button. This prevents users from renaming a restricted application as one of the applications you've allowed and running it under the radar.

5.   If a disclosure triangle appears to the left an application you add, the application has helper applications that you can disable. To do this, click the disclosure triangle to display the helper applications, and then clear the check box for each one you want to disable.

 NOTE   Normally it's best to leave the helper applications enabled unless you know users can cause grief with them. Disabling a helper application may make the application behave differently or become unstable.

Setting Up Allowed and Blocked Folders

To set up allowed and blocked folders of applications, follow these steps:

1.   In Workgroup Manager, with the Applications tab selected on the upper tab bar, click Folders on the lower tab bar to display the Folders pane (shown in Figure 12-3 with folders added).

2.   To bar applications in one or more folders, follow these steps:

a.   Click the + button to the right of the Disallow Applications Within These Folders list box.

b.   In the dialog box that opens, select the folder that contains the applications you want to block.

c.   Click the Add button.

d.   Repeat these bulleted steps to add other blocked folders as needed.

Figure 12-2.   Workgroup Manager prompts you to add a digital signature to an application that lacks one.

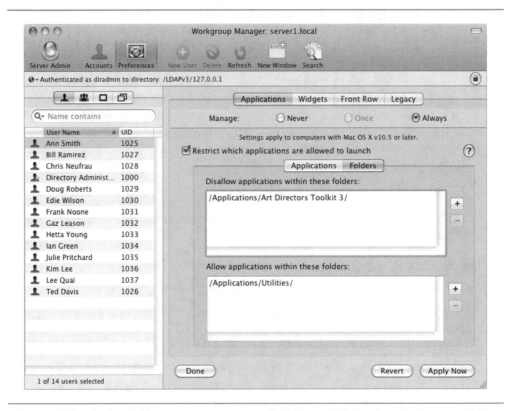

Figure 12-3. In the Folders pane, you can specify folders of blocked applications and folders of permitted applications.

3. To allow applications in one or more folders, follow these steps:

   a. Click the + button to the right of the Allow Applications Within These Folders list box.

   b. In the dialog box that opens, select the folder that contains the applications you want to permit the user to run.

   c. Click the Add button.

   d. Repeat these bulleted steps to add other allowed folders as needed.

4. If you've finished making changes to the software the user can run, click the Apply Now button. If you're going to change the settings for widgets, Front Row, or legacy applications, you may prefer to wait until you've finished changing the settings before you apply the changes.

Choosing Which Widgets the User Can Run

Depending on what the user is doing, widgets can be essential to a productive working day or the biggest time sink since YouTube and eBay combined (if you can imagine what a mess that would be). If prudence or the management counsels restraint, you may want to lock down the selection of widgets that users can run—or prevent them from running any widgets at all.

To control which widgets the user can run, follow these steps:

1. Click the Widgets tab in the upper tab bar in the Applications pane to display the Widgets pane.

2. In the Manage bar, select the Always option button to enable the controls in the lower pane (shown in Figure 12-4 with widgets selected for disabling).

3. Select the Allow Only The Following Dashboard Widgets To Run check box.

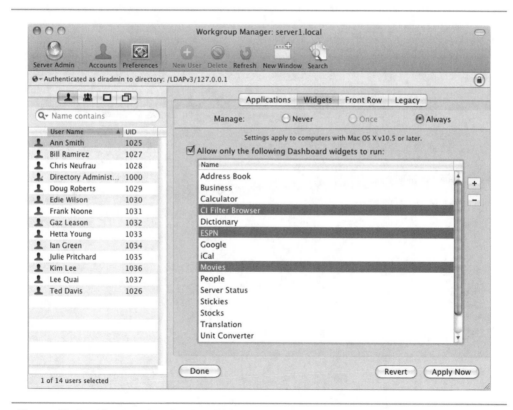

Figure 12-4. You can also choose which widgets to allow the user to run.

4. In the list box, select each widget that you want to prevent the user from running. As usual, click to select a single item, click the first item and then SHIFT-click the last item to select a contiguous range of items, or click the first item and then ⌘-click each other item to select separate items.

5. Click the – button to remove the selected items from the list.

6. If you need to add widgets to the list, click the + button, select the widget or widgets in the dialog box that opens, and then click the Add button.

7. If you've finished making changes to the software the user can run, click the Apply Now button. Otherwise, follow through the next two sections.

Choosing Whether the User Can Run Front Row

Front Row can be such a waste of time that Workgroup Manager provides a separate pane for turning it off easily. If you want to disable Front Row, follow these steps:

1. Click the Front Row tab in the upper tab bar to display the Front Row tab (see Figure 12-5).

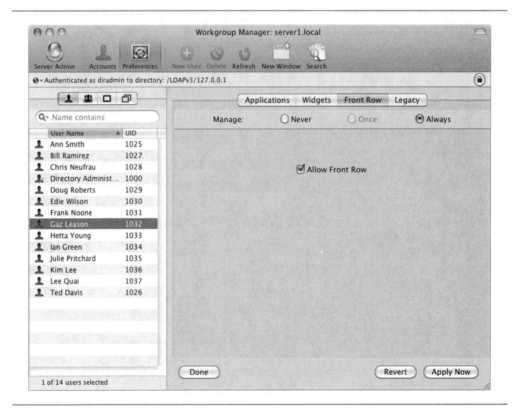

Figure 12-5. Front Row is such a serial offender that you can turn it off separately.

2. In the Manage bar, select the Always option button.

3. In the main part of the pane, clear the Allow Front Row check box.

Again, you can click the Apply Now button to apply the change immediately.

Controlling Which Legacy Applications the User Can Run

If your network has Macs still running Tiger (Mac OS X 10.4), you need to use the controls in the Legacy pane to specify which applications the users can run. Follow these steps:

1. Click the Legacy tab in the upper tab bar to display the Legacy pane (shown in Figure 12-6 with choices made).

2. In the Manage bar, select the Always option button.

3. Select the User Can Only Open These Applications option button or the User Can Open All Applications Except These option button, as appropriate.

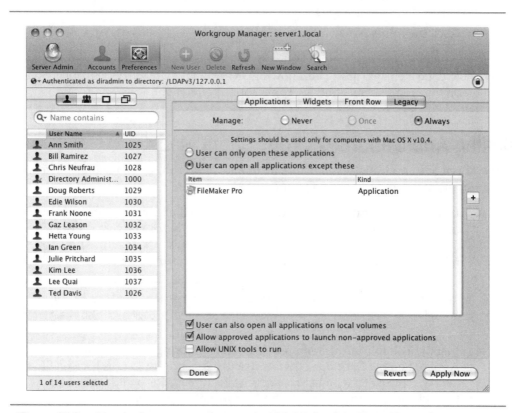

Figure 12-6. Use the Legacy pane to control which applications Tiger riders can run.

4. In the list box, build the list of permitted applications or blocked applications, depending on your choice in step 3. Either way, click the + button, select the application or applications in the resulting dialog box, and then click the Add button.

5. Select the User Can Also Open All Applications On Local Volumes check box if you want the user to be able to run any application on the Mac's hard disk. (If you're restricting applications, this setting is an invitation for trouble.)

6. Select the Allow Approved Applications To Launch Non-Approved Applications if you want the user to be able to run helper applications from the list of applications that you've specifically approved.

NOTE   Whether to allow helper applications is a vexed question. If you let the user run them, the user may also be able to run applications you want to block. But if you block helper applications, the permitted applications may not run correctly, and you may need to enable them by name.

7. Select the Allow UNIX Tools To Run check box if you want the user to be able to run UNIX applications.

8. Click the Apply Now button to apply the changes.

When you've finished choosing settings for applications, click the Done button. The Overview pane then appears again, showing an arrow in a circle next to Applications to indicate that you're managing the Applications preferences.

Installing Applications on Your Client Macs

Apart from any applications you install with Mac OS X itself, you have three main options for installing applications on your client Macs:

- **Install the applications directly**   You can go to the Mac, log yourself in, and install the application from a CD, DVD, USB stick, or network drive. This approach works fine for small networks—up to, say, a dozen or two dozen Macs—but involves too much labor and legwork for any network larger than that.

NOTE   Alternatively, you can have the users install the applications on their Macs for you. But you'll need to give them administrative privileges to do so, which I'm betting you won't want to do.

- **Install the applications remotely via Screen Sharing**   If you don't have Apple's Remote Desktop software (discussed next), you can use Screen Sharing to take control of a remote Mac and install applications on it. You're limited to working on a single Mac at a time, so installing the applications will take a while, but at least you're spared the trek to the other Mac, and you can perform other tasks on your local Mac while Installer chugs along.

■ **Install the applications through Apple Remote Desktop**   If you have Apple
Remote Desktop, you can use it to install applications on multiple Macs at
the same time from the comfort of your aerie. This is the fastest and most
convenient method—as long as you have Apple Remote Desktop.

NOTE   You can buy Apple Remote Desktop from the Apple Store (http://store.apple.com) or—often
for less—from other online retailers such as Amazon.com. For intimate networks, get the 10-client
version priced at $299; for larger gatherings of Macs, get the unlimited-client version priced at $499.

Installing the applications directly is straightforward if time-consuming. The following sections discuss the other two approaches.

Deploying Applications Through Screen Sharing

Screen Sharing is a poor man's version of Apple Remote Desktop: You can reach out
and take control of another Mac, and install software on it—but only one Mac at a time.

If this is enough for your network's needs, proceed as described in this section.
You'll need first to turn on Screen Sharing on each Mac that you want to reach out and
touch. Once you've done that, connecting to the Mac via Screen Sharing is easy as filching
candy from a baby.

Turning On Screen Sharing for a Client Mac

First, set up Screen Sharing on the client Mac like this:

1. Open System Preferences. For example, click the System Preferences icon in the
    Dock, or choose Apple | System Preferences.

2. In the Internet & Wireless section, click the Sharing icon to display the Sharing
    pane (shown in Figure 12-7 with settings chosen).

3. In the list box on the left, select the Screen Sharing check box.

4. Click the Computer Settings button to display the Computer Settings dialog
    box (see Figure 12-8) and then choose settings as needed:

    ■ If you want anyone to be able to ask for permission to control the screen,
       select the Anyone May Request Permission To Control Screen check box.
       Normally, you'll want to clear this check box.

    ■ If you want users of Virtual Network Computing (VNC) to be able to
       control the screen, select the VNC Viewers May Control Screen With
       Password check box, and then type the password in the text box. This
       check box, too, you'll normally want to clear.

5. In the Allow Access For area, you'll usually want to select the Only These
    Users option button rather than the All Users option button, and make sure
    the Administrators item appears in the list box. If not, click the + button, select
    Administrators in the dialog box that opens, and then click the Select button.

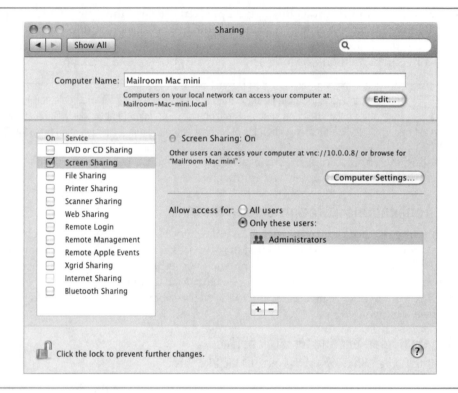

Figure 12-7.   Turn on Screen Sharing in the Sharing pane in System Preferences to give yourself remote control of a Mac.

(If you want to set yourself in a privileged position over other administrators, use the – button to remove Administrators from the list box. Then click the + button, choose your avatar in the dialog box, and click that Select button.)

6. When you're done, quit System Preferences. For example, press ⌘-Q or choose System Preferences | Quit System Preferences.

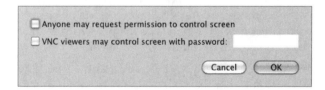

Figure 12-8.   Choose whether anyone can request control of the screen via Screen Sharing and whether VNC users get to join in the fun.

Connecting to a Client Mac via Screen Sharing

To connect to a client Mac via Screen Sharing, follow these steps:

1. Open a Finder window. For example, click the Finder button in the Dock, click the desktop and press ⌘-N, or use the mouse to lasso an already open window that's cantering aimlessly around your desktop.

2. In the sidebar, double-click the Shared category to expand it if it's currently collapsed. The list of accessible computers on your network appears.

3. Click the Mac to which you want to connect.

4. Click the Share Screen button. In the Finder's column view, the Share Screen button appears handily in the second column. In any of the three other views, it appears in the gray bar below the Search box.

5. The Screen Sharing application springs into life, pokes the remote Mac, and then prompts you for your user name and password for that Mac (see Figure 12-9).

6. In the Connect area, select the As A Registered User option button.

NOTE To connect by asking for permission, select the By Asking For Permission option button, and then click the Connect button. The user sees a Control Request dialog box. If they click the Share Screen button, you're in; if they click the Cancel button, you get an Authentication Failed message. This seems ambiguous, but the small print spells it out by telling you that the user declined your request.

7. Type your user name for the remote Mac in the Name text box and your password in the Password text box.

8. Select the Remember This Password In My Keychain check box if you want Mac OS X to store the password for future use.

Figure 12-9. Normally you'll want to connect to the remote Mac as a registered user rather than by asking for permission.

9. Click the Connect button. Screen Sharing establishes a connection to the remote Mac and displays a window showing whatever is happening on its desktop.

You now have control of the remote Mac, and can install software on it as if you were sitting at it.

Deploying Applications Through Apple Remote Desktop

If you have Apple Remote Desktop, you can manage your Macs not just singly, but in groups—even managing every single Mac on the network at the same time. It's no surprise that Apple charges as much for the unlimited-client version of Apple Remote Desktop as for Mac OS X Server itself.

NOTE You can install Apple Remote Desktop either on your server or on a Mac you use for administration.

Once you've installed Apple Remote Desktop, run it from the Applications folder. If you plan to use it frequently—and chances are that you will—CTRL-click or right-click the icon in the Dock and choose Options | Keep In Dock to anchor it there for eternity.

Turning On Remote Management for a Client Mac

To manage your client Macs via Apple Remote Desktop, the Remote Management feature in Sharing preferences needs to be turned on. If you've already turned this feature on during setup, you're riding high. If not, follow these steps on each client Mac to turn on Remote Management:

1. Open System Preferences. For example, click the System Preferences icon in the Dock, or choose Apple | System Preferences.

2. In the Internet & Wireless section, click the Sharing icon to display the Sharing pane (shown in Figure 12-10 with settings chosen).

3. In the list box on the left, select the Remote Management check box.

4. Click the Computer Settings button to display the Computer Settings dialog box (see Figure 12-11) and then choose settings as needed:

   - **Show Remote Management Status In Menu Bar** Select this check box if you want to display a Remote Management menu in the client Mac's menu bar. From this menu, the user can send a message to the administrator and can directly open Sharing Preferences.

   - **Anyone May Request Permission To Control Screen** Select this check box only if you want screen sharing to be available to other, non-administrator users too. Normally, you'll want to clear this check box.

NOTE The Anyone May Request Permission To Control Screen feature and VNC Viewers May Control Screen With Password feature are primarily used for Screen Sharing, which is based on the same technology as Apple Remote Desktop.

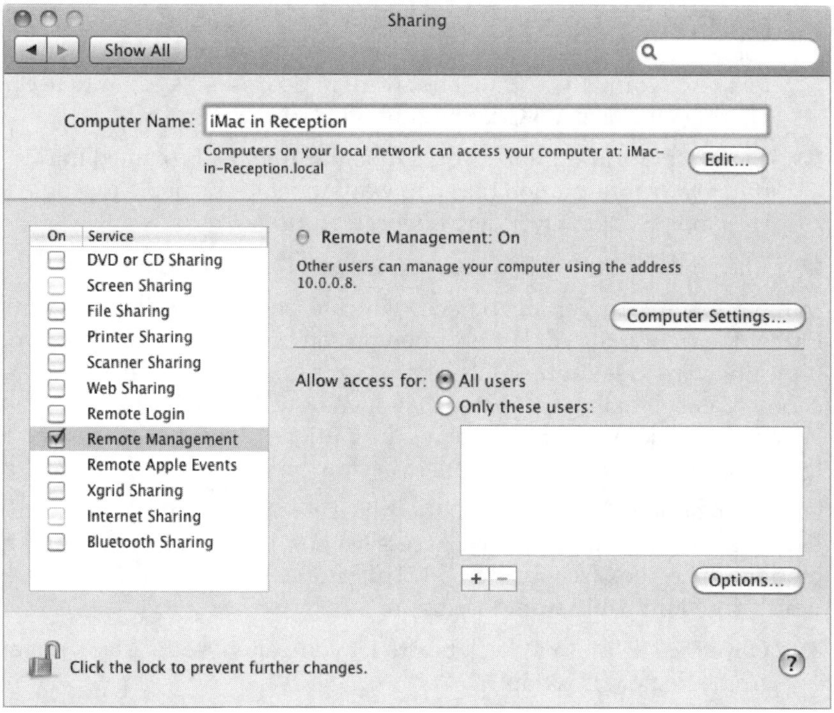

Figure 12-10. Turn on Remote Management in the Sharing pane in System Preferences to make a Mac manageable with Apple Remote Desktop.

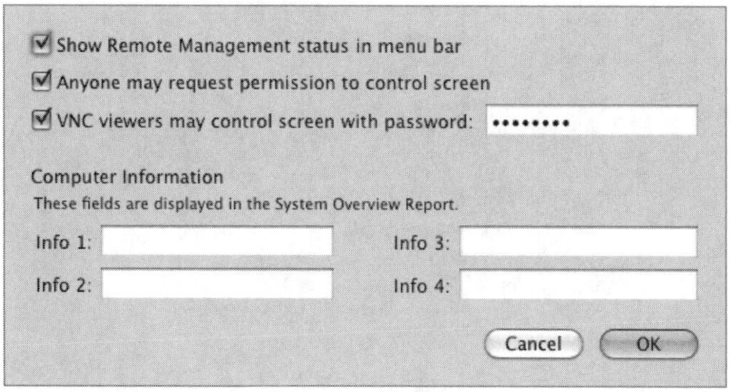

Figure 12-11. In the Computer Settings dialog box, choose whether to display a Remote Management menu in the menu bar and whether to allow VNC access.

■ **VNC Viewers May Control Screen With Password**   Select this check box if you want to allow Virtual Network Computing (VNC) clients to connect to Screen Sharing, and then type a tough-to-guess password in the text box. Normally, you will not want to do this—it's better to use Screen Sharing and keep VNC safely shut off.

■ **Computer Information**   Add to the four Info fields (named Info 1 through Info 4) any information that you want to make available to Apple Remote Desktop's System Overview Report feature.

■ Click the OK button to close the Computer Settings dialog box.

5. In the Allow Access For area, choose which users may access the Mac remotely. Rather than select the All Users option button as Mac OS X suggests, you will typically want to select the Only These Users option button, click the + button, choose yourself in the dialog box that opens, and then click the Select button. When you do so, Mac OS X displays the Options dialog box, discussed next, so that you can decide which powers to bestow on yourself.

6. To choose options for all users (if the All Users option button is selected) or a listed user selected in the Allow Access list box, click the Options button. The Options dialog box (see Figure 12-12) offers the following options, most of which you'll probably want to turn on:

■ **Observe**   Select this check box to let yourself view the Mac's screen via Apple Remote Desktop.

■ **Control**   When you've selected the Observe check box, you can select this check box to allow yourself to take control of the Mac without consulting the user.

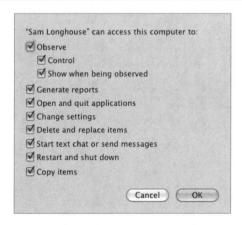

Figure 12-12.   You'll probably want to grant yourself a full set of powers in the Options dialog box for Remote Management.

■ **Show When Being Observed**   When you've selected the Observe check box, you can select this check box to give the user a visual cue when you're observing the Mac. The Remote Management menu icon changes from a pair of binoculars to a monitor showing a pair of binoculars, and the item at the top of the menu changes from Ready Mode to Controlled Mode.

 TIP   Even when you turn it on, Apple Remote Desktop's visual cue that you're observing the screen is subtle enough for many users to miss. Unless you're in an environment where monitoring is expected, such as in a lab during a computer training class, it's a good idea to warn the user with a text message that you are about to observe their screen.

■ **Generate Reports**   Select this check box to allow Apple Remote Desktop to generate reports including this Mac.

■ **Open And Quit Applications**   Select this check box to give yourself control over applications—useful when you will use Apple Remote Desktop to update them.

■ **Change Settings**   Select this check box to enable yourself to change settings such as system preferences.

■ **Delete And Replace Items**   Select this check box to allow yourself to delete files and folders, and to replace existing items. This capability is useful for upgrades, but tread carefully over the user's loved-and-wanted files.

■ **Start Text Chat Or Send Messages**   Select this check box to enable Apple Remote Desktop to chat with the Mac or send messages to it. Both capabilities are highly useful.

■ **Restart And Shut Down**   Select this check box to give yourself the power to restart the Mac or shut it down. Restarting is regrettably often necessary for software upgrades.

■ **Copy Items**   Select this check box to let yourself copy items from the Mac.

7. Quit System Preferences. For example, press ⌘-Q or choose System Preferences | Quit System Preferences.

Connecting to Client Macs Using Apple Remote Desktop

After you've set up the Remote Management service, you can connect to the client Macs quickly with Apple Remote Desktop.

Launch Apple Remote Desktop if it's not running, and then select the computers in the All Computers list (shown in Figure 12-13) or the Scanner list.

You can then click the Observe button on the toolbar to see what the Macs are doing. In Figure 12-14, the left Mac is visiting Wikipedia, while the right Mac is giving its screen saver an airing. In other words, both are ripe for an installation.

To take control of a Mac, click it, and then click the Control button on the toolbar. To keep the hemispheres of your brain from detaching themselves in disgust, you can take control of only one Mac at a time.

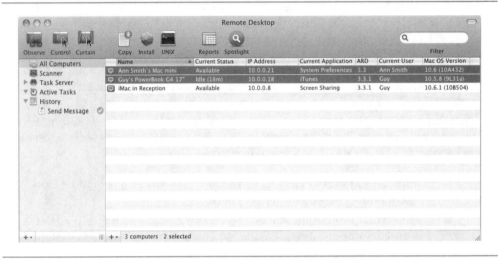

Figure 12-13.   In Apple Remote Desktop, select the client Macs you want to affect.

Installing Software via Apple Remote Desktop

Once you've taken control, you can configure the Mac as if you were sitting at it. For example, you can change System Preferences manually, drag an application to the Trash, or take any other action you're permitted to take directly on it.

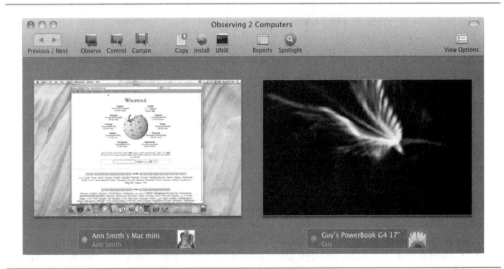

Figure 12-14.   Apple Remote Desktop lets you observe what one or more of your client Macs are doing.

NOTE To install software via Apple Remote Desktop, you need package files. If the software is not already in a package file, use PackageMaker as described in Chapter 6 to create your own custom package files.

Rather than configure a Mac by taking control of it, however, what you'll often want to do is use Apple Remote Desktop's feature for installing software on multiple Macs at the same time. To do so, follow these steps:

1. In the Remote Desktop window, select the Macs that you want to install the software on.

NOTE You can also start installing software from the Observing window in which you're observing one or more Macs. Just click the Install button on the toolbar to get started.

2. Click the Install button on the toolbar to display the Install Packages dialog box (see Figure 12-15).

3. Add packages to the Packages list at the top of the Install Packages dialog box. Either drag in packages from a Finder window or click the + button, select the package or packages in the resulting dialog box, and then click the Open button.

4. In the After Installation area, select the appropriate option button:

   ■ **Don't Restart** As long as the software you're installing doesn't require Mac OS X to be restarted afterward, this is always the best choice.

   ■ **Attempt Restart, Allow Users To Save Documents** Select this option button if the software requires Mac OS X to be restarted, but you want to give the users the chance to save any unsaved changes to documents they've been working on.

   ■ **Force An Immediate Restart** Select this option button if you absolutely need to restart the Macs straightaway, without even giving the users the chance to save unsaved changes.

5. In the Run This Task From area, select the This Application option button to run the installation from Remote Desktop. This is the normal way to run the installation, but it requires all the Macs that you're installing on to be online now. The alternative is to select the other option button, The Task Server On This Computer, which lets you use a designated Task Server to run the installation for computers that are currently offline. (Using a Task Server is a more advanced use that we won't get into here.)

6. On the If A Problem Occurs line, select the Stop The Copy On All Targets check box if you want to stop the copy operation if any of the Macs isn't present, correct, and responding. Leave this check box cleared to make the installation go ahead on as many Macs as possible, even if one of them chokes.

Figure 12-15. In the Install Packages dialog box, build the list of packages you want to install and choose options for installing them.

7. On the Security line, select the Encrypt Network Data check box if it's vital to keep the installation data secure as it passes across your network. Performance suffers when you encrypt the data, so don't encrypt it unless you have a good reason. If you have a wired network, and you're installing applications that aren't top secret, you probably don't need encryption.

8. On the Network Usage line, select the Limit To N Kilobytes Per Second check box, and type a suitable value in the text box, if you want to prevent the installation from hogging your network's bandwidth.

 NOTE If you want to install the software later, click the Schedule button and use the resulting dialog box to choose when to install it.

9. Click the Install button. Apple Remote Desktop closes the Install Packages dialog box and starts installing the software.

CHAPTER 13 | Run Windows Applications on Macs

I f you've decided to run Mac OS X on both your servers and your desktops, you're probably attached so strongly to Apple's operating systems that it would take brute force to pry the MacBook Pro from your cold, curled fingers. But needs must when the devil drives, and chances are that some of the people in your company will need to run Windows some of the time—on their Macs. You may even be one of them.

In this chapter you'll learn how to deal with this issue neatly and easily.

Understanding the Options for Running Windows Applications on Macs

When push comes to shove, any Mac built around an Intel chip can run Windows applications perfectly well. In fact, you have a choice of two main ways of running Windows applications on your Macs:

- **Boot Camp**   You create a separate partition on your Mac's hard drive and install Windows on it. You can then boot your Mac either to Mac OS X or to Windows.

- **Virtual Machine**   You use a virtual-machine application to create a fake PC running within Mac OS X. You can then install Windows on the virtual machine and run whichever Windows applications you need. (You can also install other operating systems, such as Linux—but here we'll assume Windows is the target.)

So it's a binary choice—or it would be if there wasn't a joker in the pack: Instead of using either Boot Camp or a virtual machine, you can use Remote Desktop Connection. Remote Desktop Connection enables your Mac to control a Windows PC across the network or the Internet. Once you're connected to the PC, you can run any application that is installed on the PC.

Which Means of Running Windows Is the Best for You?

Here are quick points for deciding which way of running Windows will suit you best:

- If you need to run Windows applications alongside your Mac applications, a virtual machine is the way to go.

- If you need the best possible Windows performance, use Boot Camp.

- If you need only occasional use of Windows applications, or if you need to share a single copy of an extortionately priced Windows application among multiple users, go for Remote Desktop Connection.

You'll find more details on the pros and cons of the different approaches in the following sections.

NOTE   You can also play mix-and-match with your options if you're feeling frisky. Some virtual-machine applications can run a Boot Camp installation of Windows, which lets you use your Boot Camp Windows from inside Mac OS X. And, you can use Remote Desktop Connection to connect to and control a virtual machine—if you genuinely need to.

Running Windows Applications Using a Virtual Machine

If you need to keep Mac OS X running while you're working in the Windows applications, use a virtual machine. You run the virtual machine as an application alongside your Mac applications, and you can even copy and paste data between applications in the virtual machine and your Mac applications.

The disadvantages to running a virtual machine are pretty straightforward:

- First, you have to pay for both the virtual-machine application (probably; more on this in a moment) and a copy of Windows.

- Second, you'll find that performance in the virtual machine ranges from moderate to downright mangy. This is no surprise, because the virtual machine is emulating a PC rather than running on actual physical hardware. Still, if your Mac can run Mac OS X at a decent speed, normal business applications in the virtual machine should run at a tolerable speed.

- Third, having to run the virtual machine may also slow your Mac down a bit—or a lot.

Choosing a Virtual-Machine Application

At this writing, there are three main virtual-machine applications for Mac OS X:

- **VMWare Fusion**   VMWare Fusion from VMWare, Inc. costs around $80 per workstation. Fusion lets you run most versions of Windows and many other operating systems; it can also run Mac OS X Server on top of Mac OS X (though it cannot run the client version of Mac OS X). You can run a virtual machine either inside a Fusion window or have its applications appear in Mac-like windows directly on your Mac desktop (but not contained by a Fusion window), a feature called Unity.

- **Parallels Desktop for Mac**   Parallels Desktop for Mac from Parallels costs around $80 per workstation. Parallels Desktop can run most versions of Windows and many versions of UNIX and Linux, but it cannot run Mac OS X. Parallels Desktop can import virtual machines from VMWare and VirtualBox, which is a neat trick. You can run a virtual machine either in a Parallels window or have each application appear in its own Mac-like window directly on your Mac desktop, which Parallels calls Coherence mode.

- **VirtualBox**   VirtualBox from Sun Microsystems (www.virtualbox.org) is a free open-source virtualization application. VirtualBox runs all current versions of Windows—Windows 7, Windows Vista, and Windows XP; Windows Server 2008 and Windows Server 2003—and many versions of UNIX and Linux.

VirtualBox has the advantage of being free and largely easy, and many Mac users seem to like it just fine. But in my experience, VirtualBox tends to act goofy sometimes for no discernible reason, losing network connections on both the virtual machine and the host, so I tend to use the other two applications instead.

VMWare Fusion and Parallels Desktop are pretty much neck and neck for features, and it's well worth trying both before buying either. Both VMWare, Inc. and Parallels offer a free trial version, so giving both a spin costs you nothing beyond virtual elbow grease. I tossed a virtual coin on which of the two to use for the screenshots in this chapter, and Parallels came down heads.

NOTE VMWare Fusion and Parallels Desktop can both create a virtual machine based on a Boot Camp partition. This capability lets you run the same copy of Windows in either a virtual machine or directly on your Mac's hardware, which is as handy as snow chains in a blizzard.

Installing the Virtual-Machine Application

Once you've downloaded the full version or the trial version of the virtual-machine application, installation is straightforward. For example, Figure 13-1 shows the disk image for Parallels Desktop. Double-click the Install icon, and you're off. You get to accept the license agreement, you can change the default installation location if you so choose, and you must authenticate yourself; but that's the full extent of the excitement.

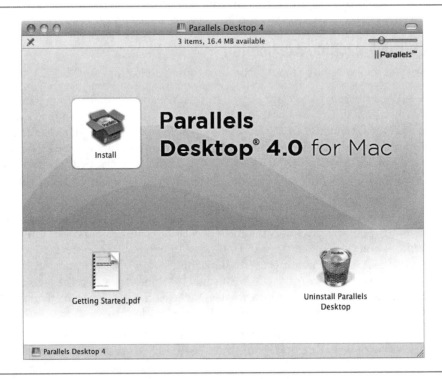

Figure 13-1. Primed and pumped to install Parallels Desktop.

NOTE   Keep the virtual-machine application's disk image. You will need it again if you want to uninstall the virtual-machine application.

Creating a Virtual Machine

After installing the virtual-machine application, you create a virtual machine so that you can then install Windows on it. Each of the applications walks you through the process of setting up the virtual machine. You'll usually want to select the option for creating a custom virtual machine, as shown for Parallels Desktop in Figure 13-2, so that you can pick the amounts of disk space and RAM the virtual machine has. Depending on the Mac you're using and the virtual-machine application, you can also choose the number of processors to give the virtual machine (see Figure 13-3).

Table 13-1 shows suggestions for the amount of disk space and RAM to devote to virtual machines running the versions of Windows you're most likely to want. As is traditional with such tables, the amounts of RAM are minimums; more is always better if you can spare it without hobbling your Mac. The amounts of disk space

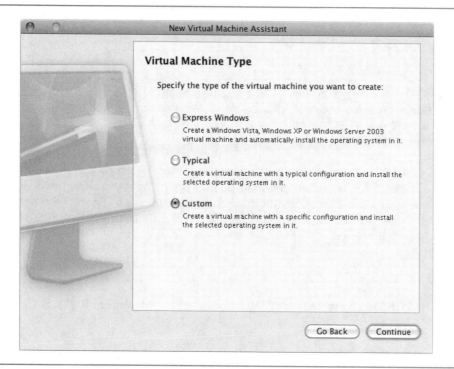

Figure 13-2.   Choosing the Custom option button on the Virtual Machine Type screen of the New Virtual Machine Assistant in Parallels Desktop lets you choose how to configure the virtual machine.

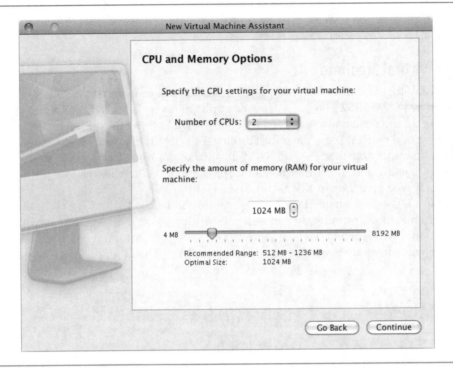

Figure 13-3. Setting the number of CPUs and the amount of RAM for a virtual machine in Parallels Desktop. You may well need to tweak these settings later when you find out how well—or otherwise—the virtual machine runs.

shown in the table are adequate for the operating system itself plus applications, but they assume that you will store most of the files on the network. If you will store them on the virtual hard disk inside the virtual machine, you'll need more space. Generally, though, it's better to keep the files on a real disk, from which you can back them up easily if needed.

Windows Version	Disk Space	Minimum RAM
Windows 7	16GB	1GB
Windows Vista	16GB	1GB
Windows XP	8GB	512MB

Table 13-1. Disk Space and RAM for Windows in Virtual Machines

Unless you have a Boot Camp partition that you want the virtual machine to pick up, or you already have a hard disk image file that you've created with another virtual-machine application, choose the option for creating a new hard disk image file. You'll then face choices such as those shown in Figure 13-4.

The terminology varies among the various applications, but there are three main choices to make here:

■ **How big to make the virtual hard disk**   Again, Table 13-1 offers some suggestions. If the Mac has plenty of disk space to spare, giving the virtual machine more space is often wise.

■ **Whether to split the virtual hard disk into 2 GB files**   This simplifies the process of backing up the virtual hard disk onto DVD. If you're planning to back the virtual hard disk up onto a honking hard drive, or if you're not planning to back it up, you don't need to select this option.

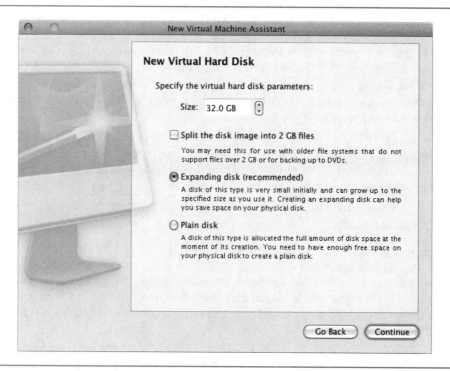

Figure 13-4.   Choosing settings for the virtual hard disk for a virtual machine. Again, this is in Parallels Desktop.

■ **Whether to create an expanding disk or a plain disk**   An *expanding disk* is a file that takes up only as much space on your Mac's hard disk as it actually needs, while pretending to the virtual machine to actually have however many gigabytes you allocated to the virtual hard disk. A *plain disk* is a file that actually grabs that amount of space on your Mac's hard disk and devotes it to the virtual machine, whether the VM uses it or not. A plain disk gives better performance—if your Mac can sacrifice all those gigabytes. If you're pressed for space, on either a laptop or desktop Mac, create an expanding disk.

Choosing How to Handle Networking

Your other main choice is how to handle networking for the virtual machine. You typically have four choices, of which the fourth doesn't really count:

■ **Shared Networking**   Shared networking lets the virtual machine tap into your Mac's network connections, so that it can access the network just as your Mac can. This gives you the greatest integration between the virtual machine and the Mac and is usually the best option to choose.

■ **Bridged Networking**   Bridged networking lets your virtual machine show up on the network as a separate computer with its own IP address. The advantage of this arrangement is that you can make the virtual machine accessible to other computers on the network without involving the host machine (your Mac). This is handy if you're running a server in the virtual machine, but it's usually less helpful if the virtual machine is just running Windows to provide you with applications.

■ **Host-Only Networking**   Host-only networking gives the virtual machine access to your Mac, but not to the rest of the network. Use this option when you're running two or more virtual machines as their own network on top of the Mac—for example, when testing software.

■ **No Networking**   This option (or non-option) runs the virtual machine in glorious isolation.

When you've made your choice, follow through the remaining screens to finish creating the virtual machine.

After that, installing Windows is nearly as easy as falling off a slack wire. You put the Windows DVD in the host's optical drive, tell the virtual machine to grab that drive, and then fire up the virtual machine. Accept the offer to boot from the DVD, and the installation starts to run.

Once the virtual machine pulls itself up by its bootstraps, you'll see the first Windows installation screen. The options available depend on the version of Windows, but the Windows 7 options shown in Figure 13-5 are pretty typical.

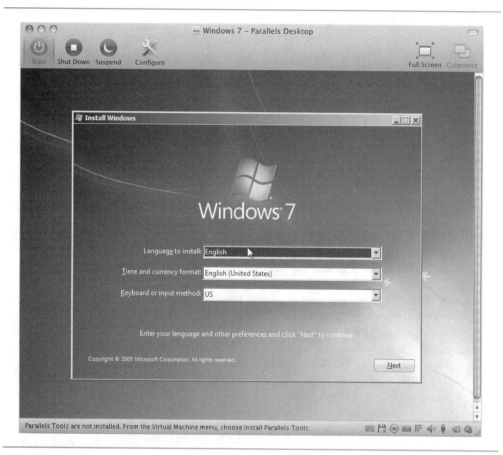

Figure 13-5.   Starting to install Windows 7 inside a virtual machine

The next decision is the key one: custom installation or upgrade installation? Unless you've got an existing version of Windows to upgrade in the same virtual machine, you'll want the custom installation—in other words, you'll install a fresh copy of Windows.

One other thing—in the relief of finding the license key, remember to clear the Automatically Activate Windows When I'm Online check box so that Windows doesn't glom onto your (virtual) hardware immediately. Instead, make sure that everything's working, and that you're satisfied with the way Windows runs on the virtual machine, before you let the limpet attach itself.

Installing the Virtual Machine Tools or Additions

After you get Windows running, you need to install the virtual machine tools—some of the virtual machine applications call them "additions"—that help integrate the virtual machine with Mac OS X and make it a good citizen. The tools give you seamless movement of the mouse pointer between the virtual machine and Mac OS X, which is worth having on its own. They also ginger up the graphics performance considerably, so you'll want to install them.

Here are the commands you need:

- **Parallels Desktop** Choose Virtual Machine | Install Parallels Tools.
- **VMWare Fusion** Choose Virtual Machine | Install VMWare Tools.
- **VirtualBox** Choose Devices | Install Guest Additions.

Installing Antivirus Software on the Virtual Machine

With the virtual machine tools in place, it's time to hamstring the virtual machine by installing antivirus software. You may be tempted to skip this step, because the virtual machine is hampered enough already by its lack of reality—but given that most malware targets Windows because of its market share, sashaying out on the Internet commando (as it were) tends to be a mistake.

Any of the antivirus applications should do the trick, but if you want to keep performance above the grotesque, avoid loading a kitchen-sink antivirus application that will drag the virtual machine deeper into torpor. For example, unless you'll use e-mail on the virtual machine, you can probably dispense with protection against phishing messages and scanning of e-mail attachments. Instead, go for a strictly minimalist approach, such as what's provided by free antivirus applications from the likes of Avast (www.avast.com) or AVG (http://free.avg.com). Protection against viruses and malware—yes. Six degrees of preservation against knuckle-dragging spam—no.

Updating Windows with the Latest Service Pack and Patches

Now that your virtual machine is protected against most online mischief, you need to update Windows with the latest Service Pack and then slap on all the patches that have been released since it was manufactured. Run Windows Update by choosing Start | All Programs | Windows Update, and then take an extended lunch break while Windows Update downloads the goods. Install all the updates, restart Windows one or more times, and your virtual machine will be ready for installing the applications that you actually want to run on it.

NOTE You may need to reinstall your virtual machine's tools or additions after installing a Service Pack. Microsoft has decreed that the fun never stop.

Installing and Running Applications

With Windows fully updated, install the applications that you need to run—plus any updates available for the applications. You don't need me to tell you how to do this—nor how to run the applications once you have installed them.

Most virtual-machine applications give you the choice of running the Windows applications either in the virtual machine window or integrated into Mac OS X. Using the virtual machine window (see Figure 13-6) helps you keep Windows and Mac apart and gives you a separate Windows desktop to work on, but integrating the windows (see Figure 13-7) tends to be easier when you need to switch from a Mac application to a Windows application, or vice versa.

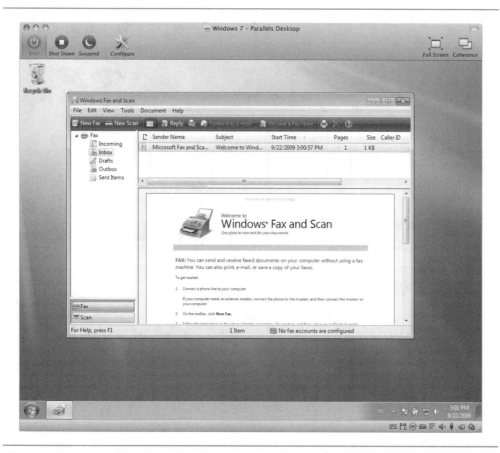

Figure 13-6.   Running a Windows application in the virtual machine's window gives you an almost genuine Windows desktop.

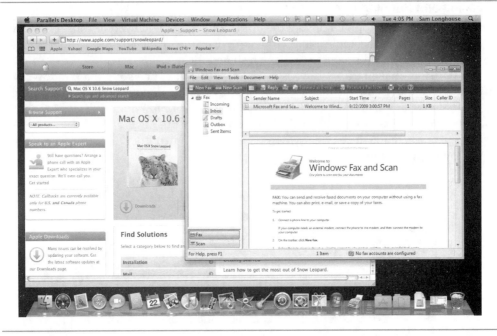

Figure 13-7.   Running a Windows application integrated into Mac OS X makes switching among applications easier. Windows and the Windows Fax And Scan application appear on the Dock with Parallels icons, and additional Parallels tools appear in the menu bar.

Running Windows Applications Using Boot Camp

Using Boot Camp lets you turn a Mac into a full Windows PC—and if you want, forget that Mac OS X is even installed on the Mac.

Where Boot Camp scores over a virtual machine is that you get to run Windows at the full speed your Mac can manage. This means Boot Camp occasionally makes sense for business applications that demand a lot of grunt—terrain mapping, video editing, and other high-end pursuits, though many of these tend to be the province of the Mac anyway—but it's seldom convenient to forsake all your Mac applications just to run a Windows application or two.

Okay, let's admit it: Who Boot Camp really appeals to is Mac-using gamers who want to play demanding Windows games.

There are three disadvantages to using Boot Camp:

■   **You must create a separate partition for Windows on the Mac's hard disk.**
Unless the Mac is severely short of space, this is more a minor nuisance than a serious hardship.

■ **You must reboot to switch between Mac OS X and Windows.** You can't use both operating systems, or their applications, at the same time. If you're actually trying to get business done rather than slice your way through Resident Evil 5, this can be a major bind.

■ **You must buy a full, licensed copy of whichever version of Windows you want to run.** You need a copy of Windows for a virtual machine as well, so this isn't too severe either.

Understanding the Process of Setting Up Boot Camp

Setting up Boot Camp is a three-stage process:

1. Use Boot Camp Assistant to create a new partition for Windows.
2. Install Windows on the new partition. (This stage runs on seamlessly from the first.)
3. Install the drivers for Windows to make all the hardware work.

 TIP You can install Windows using Boot Camp and then run it through VMWare Fusion or Parallels Desktop. This neat solution can give you the best of both worlds.

Using Boot Camp Assistant to Create a New Partition

To get started, use Boot Camp Assistant to create a new partition like this:

1. Click the desktop to activate the Finder, then open the Utilities folder by press ⌘-SHIFT-U or choosing Go | Utilities.
2. Double-click the Boot Camp Assistant icon to launch Boot Camp Assistant. The Assistant displays its Introduction screen (see Figure 13-8).
3. Before you click the Continue button to power your way to the next screen, click the Print Installation & Setup Guide button to print out a hard copy of the Boot Camp Installation & Setup Guide. This document is packed with all the knowledge and wisdom you'll long to be able to access when the Boot Camp process goes awry and you're unable to start your Mac—so it's a good idea to have a hard copy to hand. (If you have another computer available, print the document to a PDF, and then open the PDF for reference.)
4. Now click that Continue button. The Create A Partition For Windows screen appears (see Figure 13-9).
5. Choose how much space to devote to Windows in one of these ways:

   ■ Drag the divider bar to set a custom amount of space for each partition.
   ■ Click the Divide Equally button to divide the space equally between Mac OS X and Windows.
   ■ Click the Use 32 GB button to create a 32 GB partition for Windows. This is plenty of space for Windows 7 or Windows Vista, so it's a fair choice.

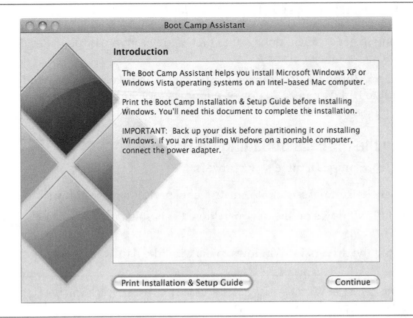

Figure 13-8.   Boot Camp Assistant walks you through the process of creating a Windows partition on your Mac's hard disk and installing Windows on it.

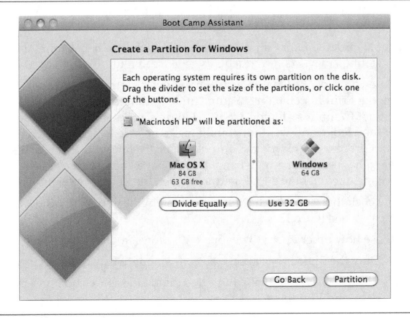

Figure 13-9.   Drag the divider bar on the Create A Partition For Windows screen to tell Boot Camp Assistant how much space to give Windows.

6. Click the Partition button. Boot Camp Assistant partitions the disk as you commanded without trashing your existing Mac OS X data, and then displays the Start Windows Installation screen (see Figure 13-10).

7. Slip the Windows CD or DVD into your Mac's optical drive and click the Start Installation button.

8. Your Mac restarts and launches the Windows installation.

9. Follow through the Windows installation, typing in your product key when prompted, and then accepting the license terms.

NOTE   When you enter the license key, clear the Automatically Activate Windows When I'm Online check box to prevent Windows from locking itself to your Mac. Check that Windows runs properly, and that you want to keep using Boot Camp, before you activate Windows. You have a 14- or 30-day grace period, depending on the version of Windows, so there's plenty of time to assess the performance.

10. On the Where Do You Want To Install Windows? screen, click the partition marked BOOTCAMP.

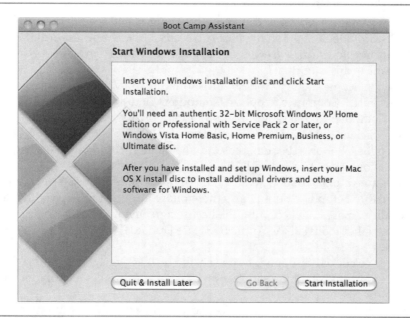

Figure 13-10.   From the Start Windows Installation screen, you can start installing Windows, or postpone the process until later.

11. If you're installing Windows Vista or Windows 7, you'll see a warning saying "Windows cannot be installed to this hard disk space. Windows must be installed to a partition formatted as NTFS." This message appears because Boot Camp Assistant has formatted the disk space as FAT32. To convert the partition, follow these steps:

    a. Click the Drive Options (Advanced) link to display a row of controls toward the bottom of the window.

    b. With the BOOTCAMP partition still selected, click the Format link. Windows displays an Install Windows dialog box warning that you're about to nuke all the data on the partition.

    c. Click the OK button. Windows formats the partition and removes the warning message.

12. Now make sure the BOOTCAMP partition is still selected (if it's not, you'll rue this day), click the Next button, and let the installation roll.

13. After Windows copies and expands the files, follow through the setup screens to create your initial user account, set a password, and pick a user account picture and desktop background.

Installing the Mac Hardware Drivers

Once you've logged on, you'll find Windows looking like it's been dragged through a hedge backward after a night on the tiles—the screen at low resolution and blurry with it, windows large and clumsy (see Figure 13-11), and half its hardware missing.

Don't panic—this is normal.

Close the Welcome Center window if it's squatting on your screen real estate, and then choose Start | Computer to open a Computer window. (In Windows XP, choose Start | My Computer to open a My Computer window.)

Control+click or right-click the optical drive, and then click Eject on the shortcut menu. When the Windows disc emerges into the daylight, blinking like a badger, replace it with your Mac OS X install DVD.

Up pops an AutoPlay dialog box for the Windows Support disc (see Figure 13-12).

Click the Run Setup.Exe button, and then follow through the steps of the Boot Camp Installer. Apart from accepting the license agreement, the only choice you have to make is whether to install the Apple Software Update For Windows. Normally, this is a good idea.

After you've clicked through the screens, the Installer gets to work. You'll hear various bleeps and grunts of digital satisfaction as your Mac installs the drivers it needs to make its hardware run properly.

When the Installer completes its tasks and you click the Finish button, you see the Boot Camp dialog box shown in Figure 13-13, telling you that you must restart the Mac. Click the Yes button to clear up all of Windows' hardware problems.

After Windows restarts, and you log on, your desktop appears at the correct resolution, and all your hardware should be working—well, your Mac's hardware, anyway.

Figure 13-11. On first boot in Boot Camp, Windows looks like it's been through the wringer.

Figure 13-12. Insert your Mac OS X install DVD and accept the offer to run the setup.exe application.

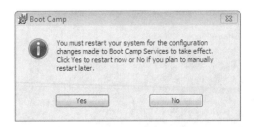

Figure 13-13. After installing the drivers, you'll need to restart the Windows PC.

Installing Antivirus Software

Your next move should be to install antivirus software on Windows to protect your PC from both local and Internet threats.

Because Windows is running directly on your Mac's hardware, you don't have the same performance concerns as for Windows running on a virtual machine, so you can safely load a full antivirus, antispyware, and antihalitosis package if you so choose. If you're the one who will run Windows, you may prefer to use an antivirus application that concentrates on viruses and malware, but trusts you to exhibit horse sense in your dealings with the Internet.

Updating Windows with the Latest Service Pack and Patches

Before you install Crysis and Halo, update Windows with the latest Service Pack and every relevant patch Microsoft has released since it.

Run Windows Update by choosing Start | All Programs | Windows Update, tell Windows to download everything it says is important, and then give it time to do so. Install all the updates, restart Windows when it prompts you, and you'll be ready to install the applications.

Installing the Applications You Need

Now install the applications you need to run in Windows. Check for updates to the applications to make sure you've got the latest fixes.

Returning to Normality

To return from Windows to Mac OS X, you can either quickly restart from the Boot Camp icon in the system tray or use the Boot Camp Control Panel to set the startup disk to your Mac OS X installation.

Restarting from the Boot Camp Icon

When you need to bounce straight into Mac OS X, click the Boot Camp icon in the system tray (the gray diamond-shaped icon) and click Restart In Mac OS X on the pop-up menu (see Figure 13-14). In the Boot Camp dialog box that opens, click the OK button.

Figure 13-14. The quick way to return to Mac OS X is to use the Boot Camp icon in the system tray.

Using the Boot Camp Control Panel to Set the Startup Disk

If you want your Mac to start in Mac OS X next time you boot it, rather than restart it now, use the Boot Camp Control Panel to change the startup disk. Follow these steps:

1. Click the Boot Camp icon in the system tray (the gray diamond-shaped icon), and then click Boot Camp Control Panel.

2. If the User Account Control dialog box opens, make sure it says Boot Camp, and then click the Continue button.

3. In the Boot Camp Control Panel (see Figure 13-15), click the Mac OS X item on the Startup Disk tab. This item has the name of your Mac's hard disk partition—for example, Macintosh HD.

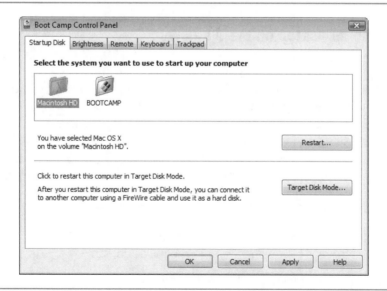

Figure 13-15. Use the Boot Camp Control Panel to change your startup disk to your Mac's Mac OS X partition.

4. Click the Apply button.

5. Close the Boot Camp Control Panel.

 NOTE To get back into Windows, choose Apple | System Preferences and click the Startup Disk icon. Click the Windows On BOOTCAMP icon, and then click the Restart button. Click the Restart button again in the confirmation dialog box that Mac OS X displays. Alternatively, restart your Mac, hold down OPTION at the startup chime, and then select the boot disk.

Running Windows Applications Using Remote Desktop Connection

The third way of running Windows applications on your Mac is by using Remote Desktop Connection to control a Windows PC. The Windows PC runs the applications, and you control it—and them—from your Mac.

Remote Desktop Connection is a solution that's worth considering when you're dealing with a Windows application (or several of the brutes) that you need occasionally rather than regularly. It's especially useful in small offices that need to share expensive applications among several users, each of whom will use them only occasionally—but there's no reason you shouldn't use it in bigger networks as well if you find it convenient.

Don't use Remote Desktop Connection to share everyday applications such as web browsers, e-mail clients, or office productivity applications. There are plenty of Mac applications for these purposes, so you shouldn't need to run them via Remote Desktop Connection.

Setting Up Remote Desktop on the Windows PC

To use Remote Desktop Connection, you must first set up Remote Desktop on the Windows PC. *Remote Desktop* is the Windows component that allows a remote computer to connect to the PC; *Remote Desktop Connection* is the application that you run on the remote computer (Mac or PC) to make the connection.

 NOTE Remote Desktop is the little brother of Terminal Services, a Windows Server feature that lets thin clients run their operating system off the server instead of off their own hard disks. If you have a Windows Server on your network, you can use Terminal Services for thick clients, such as your Mac desktops, as well. Setting up Terminal Services may make you feel like a priest or an undertaker, but you'll get used to it as soon as you start reaping the benefits.

Only the high-end versions of Windows include Remote Desktop—the "home" versions don't have it. The versions with Remote Desktop are:

- **Windows 7** Professional, Ultimate, Enterprise
- **Windows Vista** Business, Ultimate, Enterprise
- **Windows XP** Professional

To set up Remote Desktop in Windows 7 or Windows Vista, follow these steps:

1. Press WINDOWS KEY–BREAK to open the System window.
2. Click the Remote Settings link in the upper-left corner.
3. If the User Account Control dialog box opens to verify you're the one running the System Remote Settings feature, click the Continue button.
4. On the Remote tab of the System Properties dialog box (see Figure 13-16), select the Allow Connections From Computers Running Any Version Of Remote Desktop option button.

NOTE   Select the Allow Connections Only From Computers Running Remote Desktop With Network Level Authentication option button when you will use a Windows Vista or Windows 7 PC to connect to the remote computer.

5. Click the Select Users button to open the Remote Desktop Users dialog box (see Figure 13-17).
6. Click the Add button, and then use the Select Users dialog box to add the users needed.

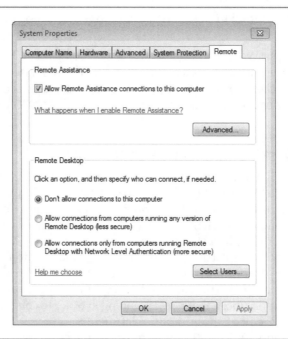

Figure 13-16.   Turn on Remote Desktop on the Remote tab of the System Properties dialog box.

Figure 13-17. Use the Remote Desktop Users dialog box to set up the list of people who can connect to the PC via Remote Desktop Connection.

7. Click the OK button to close the Select Users dialog box.
8. Click the OK button to close the Remote Desktop Users dialog box.
9. Click the OK button to close the System Properties dialog box.

NOTE To set up remote users in Windows XP, press WINDOWS KEY–BREAK to open the System Properties dialog box, and then click the Remote tab. Select the Allow Users To Connect Remotely To This Computer check box, then click the Select Remote Users button and use the Remote Desktop Users dialog box to build the list of users, as described nearby for Windows 7 and Windows Vista.

Installing Remote Desktop Connection on the Mac

Next, download the Remote Desktop Connection client from the Mactopia zone on the Microsoft website (www.microsoft.com/mac/). Click the Downloads link, click Remote Desktop in the Products section, and then click the latest version of Microsoft Remote Desktop Connection Client for Mac. You get a choice of languages, from English and Spanish through to Dutch, Swedish, and Japanese.

Once the download completes, open the disk image file and double-click the Remote Desktop Connection package file it contains (see Figure 13-18).

The rest of the installation is unremarkable, except that you may need to quit any of the Microsoft Office applications that you're running in order to complete the installation. Not only is this requirement straight out of left field, but the quit-these-applications message mentions only Office 2008—but in fact you need to quit the Office 2004 applications, too, if you've had the temerity not to upgrade to 2008.

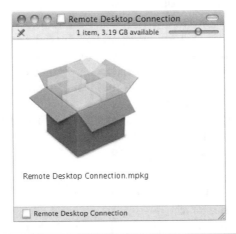

Figure 13-18. Double-click the package file in the Remote Desktop Connection download to run the installation.

Connecting via Remote Desktop Connection

After installing Remote Desktop Connection, launch it from the Applications folder. Up comes the uninformative little window you see in Figure 13-19.

 NOTE As with any other application, Control+click or right-click Remote Desktop Connection's Dock icon and choose Options | Keep In Dock if you plan to use it frequently.

Connecting Quickly

You can connect quickly by simply typing the PC's name or IP address in the Computer box and hitting the Connect button, but what you'll usually want to do is set up a connection to the computer so that you can easily connect in future. Remote Desktop Connection saves the connection in a file, and you can create as many connections as you need.

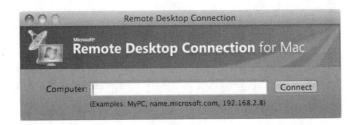

Figure 13-19. Remote Desktop Connection first opens as a small window like this.

Creating and Saving a Connection

The connection consists of the computer's name or IP address, your logon details for the computer (if you choose to store them), and all the settings you care to specify for how the connection should behave. (We'll get into these is a moment.)

To configure a connection, you create or open the connection, open the Preferences window, and pick the settings in it. Conceptually, this is a mess—the preferences are normally for an application, not what boils down to properties for a file—and if you use multiple connections, you need to keep an eye on which connection you currently have open to avoid confusion. But it does work.

Here's a quick run-through of the process:

1. If you've just opened Remote Desktop Connection for the first time, you'll have an empty connection open named Default.rdp. If you've used Remote Desktop Connection before, press ⌘-N or choose File | New Connection to create a new connection. Again, you get the little Remote Desktop Connection window shown in Figure 13-19.

2. Type the computer's name or IP address. (You need to enter this information before Remote Desktop Connection will let you save a connection.)

3. Press ⌘-SHIFT-S or choose File | Save As to display the Save As dialog box.

NOTE   If you've got the Default.rdp file open, you need to press ⌘-SHIFT-S rather than plain ⌘-S to display the Save As dialog box. Pressing ⌘-S simply saves the changes to Default.rdp.

4. Type the name for the connection, and then click the Save button to save it and close the dialog box.

NOTE   Remote Desktop Connection automatically saves your connections in a folder called RDC Connections in your Documents folder (~/Documents/RDC Connections/). This is usually a good place to keep the connections, but you can choose a different folder if you prefer.

5. Press ⌘-COMMA or choose Remote Desktop Connection | Preferences to open the Preferences window.

6. If the Login pane (see Figure 13-20) doesn't appear at the front, click the Login button.

7. Type your user name, password, and domain (if necessary) for the Windows computer.

8. Select the Add User Information To Your Keychain check box if you want to store the details in your keychain. This move saves time, but it does reduce your security.

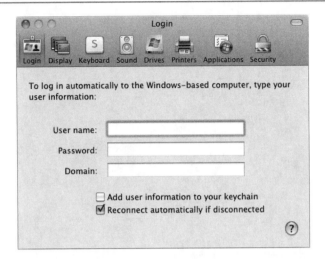

Figure 13-20.   Enter your login information for the Windows PC on the Login pane of Remote Desktop Connection's Preferences window.

9. Select the Reconnect Automatically If Disconnected check box if you want Remote Desktop Connection to automatically reestablish your connection if it gets disconnected. Usually this setting is helpful too.

10. Click the Display button to open the Display pane (see Figure 13-21).

11. In the Remote Desktop Size pop-up menu, choose the window size to use. You get a full range of resolutions from 640 × 480—pretty much a joke size these days—up to the highest resolution your Mac's screen can handle. Choose Full Screen if you want the Windows desktop to appear full screen.

12. In the Colors pop-up up menu, choose the number of colors to use:

    ■ **256 Colors**   Use this setting for dial-up connections only. All the colors will look vile.

    ■ **Thousands**   Use this setting to improve performance over Internet connections or saturated network connections. This setting works well for tasks that don't involve graphics.

    ■ **Millions**   Use this setting to see the display at full quality over a LAN connection. Try this setting if you're working with graphics on the Windows box.

13. If your Mac has multiple displays, use the Open Remote Desktop Window On pop-up menu to choose which display the Windows desktop appears on.

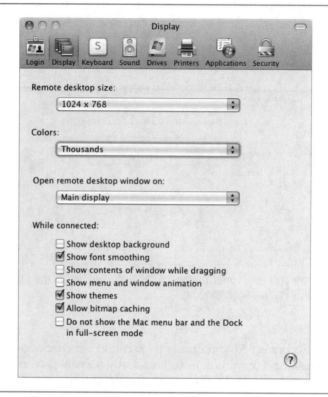

Figure 13-21. Use the Display preferences pane to set the remote desktop's size and number of colors and to choose performance options.

14. In the While Connected Area, clear the check boxes for any options you don't need. All the options except the last two affect the amount of data that Remote Desktop must pump across the network connection to your Mac, so the fewer options you use, the better performance you'll get—at the cost of looks.

   ■ **Show Desktop Background** Controls whether the Windows desktop background appears. This is useless but can be pretty.

   ■ **Show Font Smoothing** Controls whether the Mac shows the fonts smoothed or in all their jagged glory. You can safely turn off font smoothing unless working on designs.

   ■ **Show Contents Of Window When Dragging** Controls whether a window shows its contents when you drag or whether it appears as an empty frame. Turning off this setting is generally a good idea.

   ■ **Show Menu And Window Animation** Controls whether the Mac displays Windows' animations on menus and windows. You can easily dispense with these.

- **Show Themes**   Controls whether the Mac displays Windows' themes—the graphical looks and eye candy. If you turn off themes, you get better performance and the square-cornered Windows 2000 look—functional enough, but a bit industrial for some tastes.

- **Allow Bitmap Caching**   Controls whether your Mac stores partial screen pictures to help it redraw the screen more quickly. Caching improves performance but is technically a security threat, as someone could hack into your Mac and retrieve the bitmaps to see what you had been doing.

- **Do Not Show The Mac Menu Bar And The Dock In Full-Screen Mode**   Controls whether the menu bar and the Dock appear when you're running Remote Desktop Connection full-screen.

15. Click the Keyboard button to display the Keyboard pane (see Figure 13-22). Here, you can choose which Mac keys to use in place of Windows keys, such as the Windows key.

   - To turn off a shortcut, clear its check box.

   - To change a shortcut, click to select it, click in the Mac column, and then press the key or key combination you want to use.

16. Click the Sound button to display the Sound pane (see Figure 13-23).

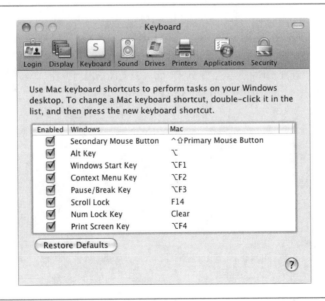

Figure 13-22.   Use the Keyboard pane to configure how to map your Mac's keyboard to the Windows keyboard.

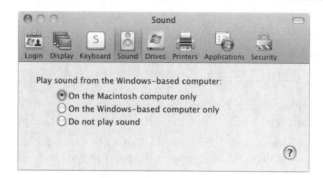

Figure 13-23. The Sound pane lets you bring the PC's sound to your Mac, play it on the PC, or suppress it.

17. Choose how to handle the sound by selecting the On The Macintosh Computer Only option button, the On The Windows-Based Computer Only option button, or the Do Not Play Sound option button.

18. Click the Drives button to display the Drives pane (see Figure 13-24).

19. If you want to share one or more of your Mac's drives or folders with the Windows PC, open the pop-up menu and make the appropriate choice. For example, choose All Disk Drives to share all disk drives.

20. Click the Printers button to display the Printers pane (see Figure 13-25).

21. If you want to be able to print from the Windows PC to a printer connected to your Mac, select the Use A Printer That Is Connected To The Mac check box, and then pick the printer in the pop-up menu.

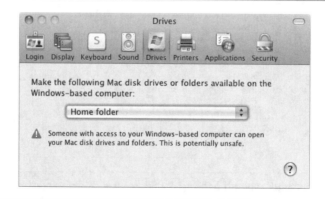

Figure 13-24. If necessary, you can share one or more of your Mac's drives or folders with the Windows PC.

Figure 13-25.   You can also print from the Windows PC to a printer connected to your Mac.

22. Click the Applications button to display the Applications pane (see Figure 13-26).

23. If you want Windows to launch an application automatically when you connect to the PC via Remote Desktop Connection, select the Start Only The Following Windows-Based Application When You Log In To The Remote Computer check box. Type the application's path and filename into the Application Path And File Name text box, and then type in the application's working directory in the Working Directory text box.

24. Click the Security button to display the Security pane (see Figure 13-27).

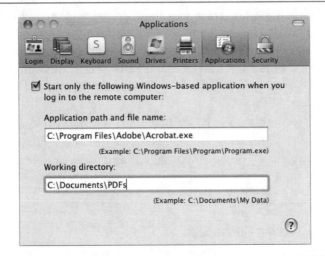

Figure 13-26.   The Applications pane lets you set an application to run automatically when you connect to the Windows PC via Remote Desktop Connection.

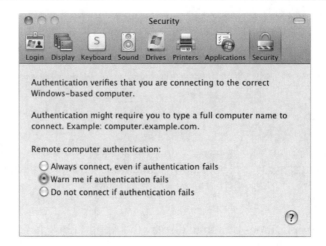

Figure 13-27.   In the Security pane, decide whether to require authentication to make sure you're connecting to the right remote computer.

25. Select the appropriate option button for your security needs:

   ■ **Always Connect, Even If Authentication Fails**   Select this option button if your priority is on connecting and you're confident you won't connect to an imposter.

   ■ **Warn Me If Authentication Fails**   Select this option button to have Remote Desktop Connection warn you about authentication problems and allow you to decide whether to go ahead with the connection. This is usually the most practical setting.

   ■ **Do Not Connect If Authentication Fails**   Select this option button to have Remote Desktop Connection refuse any connection that fails authentication. This is the safest setting.

26. Click the Close button (the red button on the title bar) to close the Preferences window.

27. Press ⌘-s or choose File | Save to save the changes you've made to your connection.

Your connection is now ready for use.

Connecting Using a Saved Connection

If you've just created a connection as described in the previous section, all you need do to connect to the Windows PC is click the Connect button.

If you don't have the right connection open, open it either from the File | Open A Recent Connection submenu or by choosing File | Open A Saved Connection (or pressing ⌘-O), clicking the connection in the Open RDC dialog box, and then clicking the Open button. Then click the Connect button in the Remote Desktop Connection window.

If you chose not to store your username and password in the connection, Remote Desktop Connection prompts you to provide them.

Type your credentials, and select the Add User Information To Your Keychain check box if you want to save them for future use. Then click the OK button.

NOTE   If you cannot connect to the Windows PC, you may need add an exception for Remote Desktop to Windows Firewall. Choose Start | Control Panel, and then open Windows Firewall. Click the Exceptions tab and make sure that the Remote Desktop check box is selected. Close the Windows Firewall dialog box and try the connection again.

Working on the Remote PC

Once you've connected to the remote PC, the Remote Desktop Connection window shows the PC's screen (or, if you chose to use Remote Desktop Connection full screen, you get the full-on PC experience). Figure 13-28 shows Remote Desktop Connection in a window.

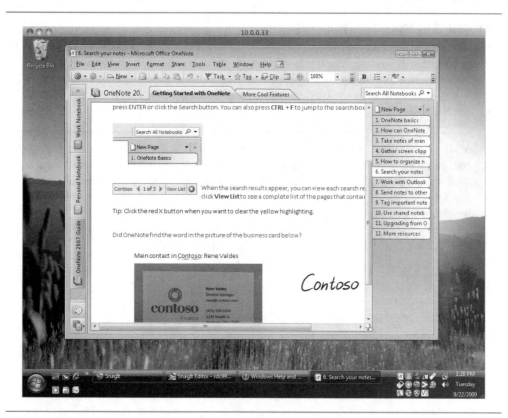

Figure 13-28.   A Remote Desktop Connection session open in a window

Figure 13-29.   Some versions of Windows check that you intend to disconnect your Remote Desktop Connection session.

You can now work much as if you were sitting at the remote PC. Use the keyboard shortcuts you chose in the Keyboard pane to issue keyboard commands, and wield your mouse as usual.

If you chose to share a printer with the PC, you'll find it in the Printers folder or Printers And Faxes folder (depending on the version of Windows). If you chose to share one or more drives or folders, you'll find them in Computer or My Computer (again, depending on the version of Windows) in the Other Drives category.

Disconnecting from the Remote PC

To disconnect from the remote PC, open the Start menu, and then click the Disconnect button. Depending on the version of Windows you're using, this button may be labeled Disconnect, or it may simply bear an X icon.

Windows may confirm the disconnection (see Figure 13-29) or may simply disconnect you. In either case, Remote Desktop Connection closes.

NOTE   To shut down or restart the remote PC, you need to use the Windows Security command on the Start menu. You can't shut down or restart directly from the Start menu, to prevent you from shutting down as if you were at the PC and then kicking yourself when you realize you're not.

CHAPTER 14 | Manage Printers

Reality is far from the paperless office that has been gracing administrators' dreams for thirty years now; printing remains a hard fact of daily life in almost every organization. So unless you're very much the exception, you'll need to provide printing services on your Mac OS X Server network.

In this chapter, you'll learn how to set up printing. There are five main steps:

- Get the printers and physically attach them to the network. We'll go through the various ways you can set them up.

- Configure the print service on your server so that you can manage the printing centrally from your administrative aerie. You can also create printer pools to distribute print jobs automatically to the printers that are looking for action.

- Choose which printer or printers each user may use. You can also set quotas to control how much the users can use the printers if you like. Many people like to print their drafts in full color and at high resolution. Most don't need to.

- Set up the Mac clients to use the printers. The gleaming, 40-page-per-minute beasts will be lonely until the users can send them print jobs.

- Manage your print queues. To keep everything running smoothly, you'll need to keep an eye on the print queues—for example, pausing them to fix printer problems—and remove any print jobs that turn out to be unnecessary.

You use Server Admin to turn on and configure the print service and to manage your print queues. You then use Workgroup Manager to set privileges for users and computers to access them.

Adding a Printer to Your Mac Network

Usually, the first step is to add your printers to your network. But before you do this, you have two main decisions to make:

- **Whether to use the print service** Normally, you'll want to use the print service to manage the printer—but in some cases you may need to set up a printer without the print service.

- **How to make the physical connection** You can connect a printer to the network in several different ways. We'll look at the four most useful ways.

Deciding Whether to Manage Your Printers with the Print Service

On your Mac OS X Server network, you can set up printing either using the print service or not using it. Normally, you'll want to use the print service to enable you to manage the printers effectively from a central point rather than leaving them to the users' questionably tender mercies.

If you simply connect a printer to your Mac network, you can set up the client Macs to use it more or less as if it were a local printer. Figure 14-1 shows a simplified diagram of printing without the print service.

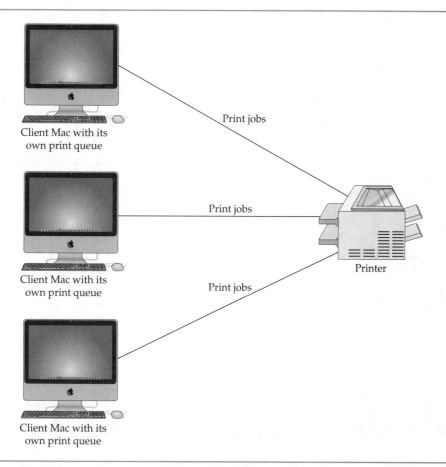

Client Mac with its
own print queue

Print jobs

Client Mac with its
own print queue

Print jobs

Printer

Print jobs

Client Mac with its
own print queue

Figure 14-1.   If you do not use the print service, client Macs send print jobs directly to the network printer.

In this arrangement, each Mac manages its own print jobs in its own print queue, with the print jobs going straight to the printer from there. If the printer runs out of paper or gets in a jam, the printer notifies only the user whose print job it's currently choking on, and other users have to wait until the printer becomes available. There's also no way to balance the load across printers except by a user choosing a different printer—for example, because they've noticed that one of their colleagues is up to their elbows in toner at the printer they would normally use.

NOTE   Instead of using the print service, you may be able to use remote-monitoring software provided by the manufacturer of your printers. For example, Konica Minolta supplies PageScope Enterprise, and HP provides Web JetAdmin.

This approach works in an office small enough to see your afflicted colleague or hear their curses, but usually you're better off using the print service. When you do, the print service creates a print queue for each printer and manages the printers, as shown in simplified form in Figure 14-2.

When one of the printers runs into a problem, you get a warning and can fix the problem—or redirect the print jobs waiting for the printer—before your colleagues hit the warpath. Better yet, you can set up printer pools to distribute the print jobs across different printers as needed, so that you don't have some printers idle while others are breaking rocks on the print gang. And (arguably best) you can set a page quota for each individual user on a particular print queue, which can be a great help in dissuading users from printing out rough drafts of business documents in full color and at photographic quality.

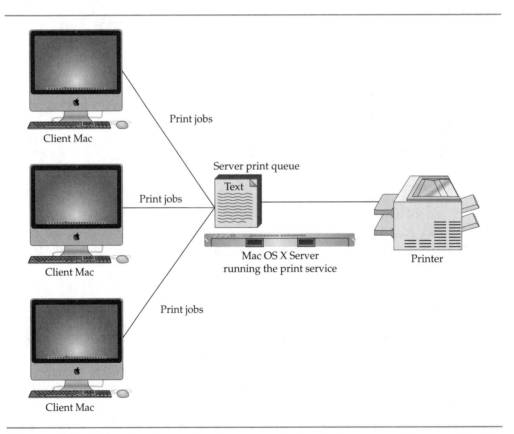

Figure 14-2. Using the print service gives you central control over your printers and the jobs they print.

NOTE Using the print service has a downside as well—when the server throws a hissy fit, nobody can print.

Deciding How to Connect the Printer to Your Network

There are four main ways to add a printer to your network:

- Connect the printer directly to a Mac
- Connect the printer to your server
- Connect the printer to an Ethernet switch
- Connect the printer to a print server or router

NOTE A fifth way to connect a printer to the network is wireless. Wireless network printers can be great in home and small-office setups, but are often a headache to configure. In larger networks, you're normally better off connecting a printer via cables to your network. If the network has no cabled section, connect the printer to your wireless access point or to your server.

The best approach depends on the type of printer and what you're trying to do with it, so let's look at each of these in turn.

Connecting a Printer Directly to a Mac

The simplest way to connect a printer to a Mac is to connect it directly, just like you'd do at home. For example, you can connect many standalone printers via USB or Ethernet (if the Mac has an Ethernet port that's twiddling its virtual thumbs). When you do this, the Mac normally detects the printer automatically, interrogates it about its ancestry and ambitions, and loads the driver for it without comment.

To see if the Mac has detected the printer correctly, open System Preferences (for example, click the System Preferences icon on the dock, or choose Apple | System Preferences) and click the Print & Fax icon in the Hardware area. If the printer appears in the Print & Fax pane, as in Figure 14-3, all is well.

If the printer doesn't appear in the Print & Fax pane, follow these steps:

1. Click the + button to display the Add Printer dialog box.
2. Click the Default tab to display the Default pane (see Figure 14-4).
3. Select the printer in the list. If the list is populated with networked printers, look for USB in the Kind column.
4. If necessary, edit the name and location Mac OS X suggests for the printer.
5. If the Print Using pop-up menu shows the right printer driver for the printer, you're set. Otherwise, open the pop-up menu and select the printer driver (you may need to search for it).

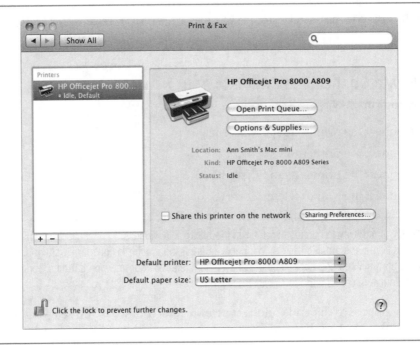

Figure 14-3. When you connect a printer directly to a Mac via USB, Mac OS X normally notices the printer and loads the driver automatically.

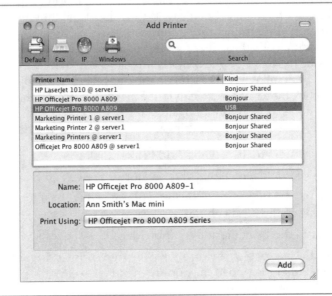

Figure 14-4. If the printer you're adding doesn't appear in Print & Fax preferences, use the Add Printer dialog box to add it.

6. Click the Add button. The Add Printer dialog box closes, and the printer appears in the Print & Fax pane.

7. Quit System Preferences. For example, press ⌘-Q.

Use this arrangement only when you need to dedicate the printer to a particular Mac. For example, knowledge workers who create confidential documents may need a printer at their workstation or in their office to prevent others from seeing sensitive data. They will also probably have the smarts to manage their own print queue and deal with everyday maintenance of the printer—for example, reloading the paper trays or replacing a toner cartridge.

While you *can* set a Mac that has a printer directly connected to it to share the printer with other Macs on the network, doing so is not usually a good idea. Instead, use one of the other ways of attaching the Mac to the network, as described in the rest of this chapter.

Connecting the Printer to Your Server

Perhaps the next easiest way to share a printer is to connect it directly to a USB port on your server and share it on the network from there using the print service. This arrangement works well as long as your server has USB ports to spare, and you're able to locate the printer or printers somewhere convenient for the users without compromising the server's security.

 NOTE When you connect a printer to your server, you must use the print service to share it.

To share a printer in this way, follow these steps:

1. Connect the printer to your server (for example, via USB) and power it on.

2. Open System Preferences. For example, click the System Preferences icon on the dock.

3. Click the Print & Fax icon in the Hardware area to display the Print & Fax pane.

4. If the printer appears, as in Figure 14-5, all is well. If not, add the printer as described in the previous section.

Once the printer is present and correct, Mac OS X Server automatically creates a print queue for it. You can then configure the print queue as described later in this chapter.

Connecting Your Printer to an Ethernet Switch

If your printer sports an Ethernet connection, you can connect it directly to an Ethernet switch, just like the computers on the network. Generally speaking, this is the best arrangement for a network printer, as you can connect the printer to any convenient Ethernet port.

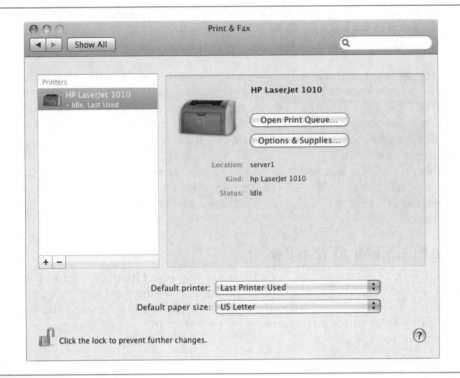

Figure 14-5. A printer connected to a server appears in the Print & Fax pane in System Preferences but does not have options for sharing.

You then use the printer's configuration software to assign the printer an IP address so that you can reach it on the network.

NOTE Many printers can pick up an IP address from a DHCP server, but assigning the printer a fixed IP address lets you manage the printer without having to hunt for it on the network. It also helps the users connect to the printer reliably if they've added it via its IP address rather than via Bonjour.

Connecting a Printer to a Print Server or Router

If your printer uses a different form of connection than Ethernet—typically USB these days, but you may be running a venerable old printer that has a parallel-port connection—you can connect it to a print server or router to make the connection to the network.

For example, if you use an AirPort Extreme in your network, you can connect a USB printer to the AirPort and share it easily on the network. The Printer shows up in the Printers pane of AirPort Utility (see Figure 14-6), which makes it automatically appear

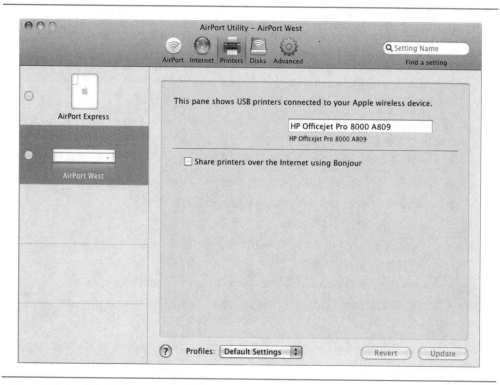

Figure 14-6.   The Print pane in AirPort Utility shows any printer you have connected to your AirPort's USB port. This printer is shared on the network.

on the network. You can then either simply let client Macs connect to it without the print service (which means the Macs manage their own print jobs and print problems) or set up a queue for it using the print service (which enables you to control printing from the server).

NOTE   Sharing a printer via an AirPort Extreme (or a similar device) is easy and convenient—as long as it works. But you may find that such connections are flaky enough to make you use a different means of printer sharing.

Setting Up the Print Service

After connecting your printers to the network, your next step is to set up the print service on your server.

You create a print queue for each printer and choose suitable print service settings for the way you want the printer to behave. You can also set up printer pools to spread the print load across the available printers.

Turning On the Print Service

Start by using Server Admin to turn on the print service if it's not already running. Follow these steps:

1. Open Server Admin. For example, click the Server Admin icon in the Dock.

2. Connect to the server, and authenticate yourself as needed.

3. In the Servers pane on the left, expand the list of services so that you can see whether the print service is running.

4. If the print service isn't running, start it like this:

   a. Click the Settings button on the toolbar to display the Settings pane.

   b. Click the Services tab to display the Services pane.

   c. Select the Print check box.

   d. Click the Save button to save the change. The print service appears in the list of services in the left pane.

5. Click the print service in the left pane to display its settings screens.

6. Click the Start Print button at the bottom of Server Admin to start the print service running.

Leave Server Admin open for now so that you can use it to do battle with print queues—after we run through how they work.

Understanding How Print Queues Work

Mac OS X Server lets you create print queues using three different printing protocols:

- **Internet Printing Protocol (IPP)**   IPP is the printing protocol you'll want to use normally, as it not only works with Mac OS X, Windows, and UNIX, but it also gives you the most management options and the tightest security. This chapter concentrates on printing using IPP

 NOTE   On an IPP print queue, a user can monitor and manage a print job—for example, the user can pause the print job or delete it. For users used to printing to local printers, this won't be exciting—but it's a big improvement on LPR and SMB print queues, where the print job is out of the user's sight and control the moment it's sent.

- **Line Printer Remote (LPR)**   LPR is a older printing protocol that you can use for UNIX and for ancient versions of Mac OS (for example, System 9).

- **Server Message Block (SMB)**   SMB is a widely used protocol for sharing files and printers. You can use SMB to enable Windows PCs to print on your Mac network, but you'll normally be better off using IPP.

NOTE One thing that's confusing with print queues is that you often use a different protocol for sharing the print queue than the print service is using to communicate with the printer. Mac OS X Server can communicate with printers using either LPR or Open Directory, but you use IPP, LPR, or SMB to share the print queue with the clients. LPR offers the greatest potential for confusion: Just because Mac OS X Server is using LPR to communicate with the printer doesn't mean you must use LPR to share the queue—in fact, you're normally better off using IPP.

Creating the Print Queues and Choosing Settings

You're now ready to create the print queues and choose settings. Follow these steps:

1. In the left pane of Server Admin, click the print service.

2. Click the Queues button on the toolbar to display the Queues pane (shown in Figure 14-7 with a print queue already created).

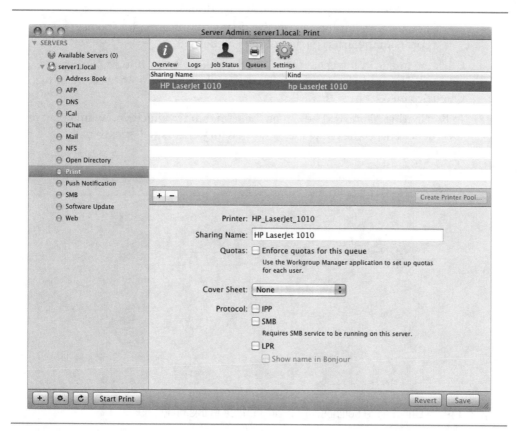

Figure 14-7. Use the Queues pane in Server Admin to create print queues.

3. If the printer is connected directly to the server, Mac OS X Server automatically creates a queue for it. Otherwise, follow these steps to create a print queue for the printer:

   a. Click the + button to display the dialog box shown in Figure 14-8.

   b. In the Specify A Printer To Use With the New Queue pop-up menu, choose the printer's type: LPR or Open Directory.

   c. For an LPR printer, type the host name or IP address in the Printer's Address text box. Then either leave the Use Default Queue On Server check box selected if you want to use the default print queue on the server, or clear this check box and type the queue name in the Queue Name text box. Click the OK button.

   d. For an Open Directory printer, when you select the Open Directory in the Specify A Printer To Use With The New Queue pop-up menu, the dialog box changes to show a list of Open Directory printers. Select the printer you want to use, and then click the OK button.

   e. Click the Save button to save the changes you've made. The new queue appears in the list at the top of the Queues pane.

4. Click the queue in the list at the top of the Queues pane if it is not already selected. The queue's details appear in the editing pane at the bottom of the Queues pane.

5. In the Sharing Name text box, type the name under which you want to share the queue. This is the name that your network clients will see, so make it descriptive.

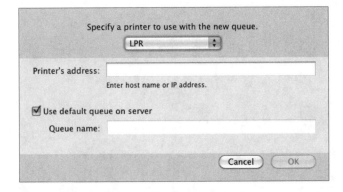

Figure 14-8. Choose the settings for the print queue in this dialog box.

NOTE   If you're sharing the queue via LPR or SMB, you need to keep the name down to 32 characters or fewer. You can use the letters a to z in either uppercase or lowercase, the numbers 0 to 9, and the underscore character. This means you'll often need to remove spaces from the default name, either deleting them or replacing them with underscores.

6. If you want to apply quotas to this print queue, select the Enforce Quotas For This Queue check box. You'll then need to set up quotas in Workgroup Manager as discussed later in this chapter.

NOTE   You can rename a print queue later if necessary, but it's best to avoid doing so: When you rename a print queue, each user who was using the queue must update their Mac to the new name in order to print. If they use the old name, their print jobs go to the great bit-bucket in the sky.

7. If you want the printer to print a cover sheet for each print job, choose which type in the Cover Sheet pop-up menu. Choose None if you want the print jobs unadorned.

8. In the Protocol area, select the check box for each printing protocol you want the clients to use. Normally, your best bet here is to select the IPP check box and leave the SMB check box and the LPR check box cleared.

NOTE   If you select the LPR check box, you can select the Show Name In Bonjour check box to make the LPR print queue show up in Bonjour. This can make it easier to set up your clients with the printer.

9. Click the Save button to save the changes you've made to the print queue.

Leave Server Admin open if you want to create one or more printer pools, as discussed next. Otherwise, press ⌘-Q to quit Server Admin.

Balancing the Print Load Across Multiple Printers

Even in an ideal world, you could hardly expect your network's users to magically choose to send their print jobs to the networked printer that was idling rather than one of the two busy printing their guts out. And in the real world, much less so—which is why Mac OS X Server gives you the option to create a printer pool. This is a way of balancing your users' printing needs across the printers available on your network, and it can save you a lot of time and grief.

A printer pool consists of two or more printers of the same type—the same make and model—so that the user gets the same print result no matter which printer handles the print job. Ideally, you'll locate the pooled printers in the same area so that the users can find their printouts easily without trekking around the building.

To create a printer pool, you first set up the printers you want to pool, and then take the following steps:

1. If Server Admin isn't open, launch it.
2. Connect to the server that manages the printers you want to pool.
3. In the Servers pane on the left, click the disclosure triangle to display the list of services.
4. Click the print service in the list of services.
5. Click the Queues tab to display the Queues pane.
6. Select the printer queues you want to pool.
7. Click the Create Printer Pool button. The dialog box shown in Figure 14-9 opens.
8. Type the name for the printer pool, and then click the OK button. Server Admin closes the dialog box and creates the printer pool.
9. With the printer pool selected in the list of printers, choose settings in the lower part of the Queues pane; as for a printer:
   - ■ Select the Enforce Quotas For This Queue check box if you want to apply quotas to the queue.
   - ■ In the Cover Sheet pop-up menu, choose whether to use a cover sheet.
   - ■ In the Protocol area, select the IPP check box, the SMB check box, or the LPR check box, as appropriate. As before, you're normally best off sticking with IPP unless you have a good reason to use SMB or LPR.
10. Click the Save button to save the changes you've made.
11. Quit Server Admin if you've finished using it.

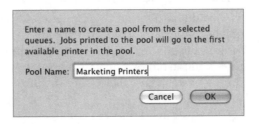

Figure 14-9. Name your printer pool in this dialog box.

Choosing Which Printers a User Can Print On

To choose which printers a user can print on, use Workgroup Manager like this:

1. Open Workgroup Manager. For example, click the Workgroup Manager icon in the dock or double-click the Workgroup Manager icon in the /Applications/ Server/ folder.

2. If Workgroup Manager doesn't authenticate you automatically, click the lock icon at the right end of the authentication bar and authenticate yourself as directory administrator.

3. In the left pane, click the user for whom you want to select printers.

 NOTE   You can also set printers preferences for a group of users, for a computer, or for a group of computers.

4. Click the Preferences button on the toolbar to display the Preferences pane.

5. Click the Printing icon to display the Printing panes.

6. If the Printers pane does not appear at the front, click the Printers tab to display it.

7. In the Manage bar, select the Always option button to enable the controls.

8. If the Printer List pane does not appear at the front, click the Printer List tab to display it. Figure 14-10 shows the Printer List pane with some settings chosen.

9. Add the printers the user may use to the User's Printer List box by selecting them in the Available Printers list box and then clicking the Add button. To remove a printer from the User's Printer List box, select it, and then click the Remove button.

10. Toward the bottom of the Printer List pane, select or clear the four check boxes as appropriate for the user:

   ■ **Allow User To Modify The Printer List**   Clear this check box if you want to prevent the user from changing the list of printers available to them.

   ■ **Allow Printers That Connect Directly To User's Computer**   Clear this check box if you want to restrict the user to network printers only. If you select the check box, you can give yourself some protection by selecting the Require An Administrative Password check box; without this setting, a user can wheel in their own printer and set it up on their Mac freely.

   ■ **Only Show Managed Printers**   Select this check box to make Mac OS X show only managed printers, not unmanaged ones.

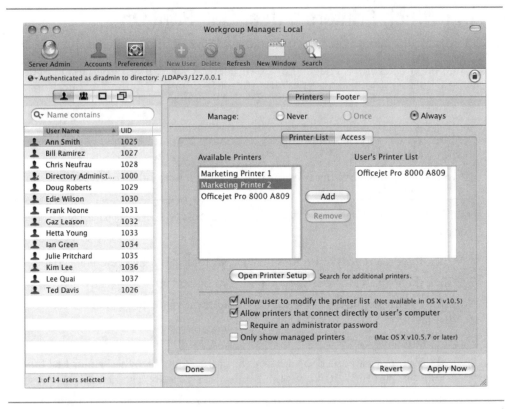

Figure 14-10. Use the Printer List pane to control which printers are available to the user and what the user can do with them.

11. Click the Access tab to display the Access pane (see Figure 14-11).

12. In the User's Printer List box, select the printer you want to make the default one, and then click the Make Default button. The list box shows an asterisk to the left of the printer's name to indicate that it is the default.

13. If you want to restrict access to a printer, select it in the User's Printer List box, and then select the Require An Administrator Password check box.

14. If you want the user's print jobs to include an identifying footer, follow these steps:

    a. Click the Footer tab to display the Footer pane (see Figure 14-12).

    b. In the Manage bar, select the Always option button to make the controls available.

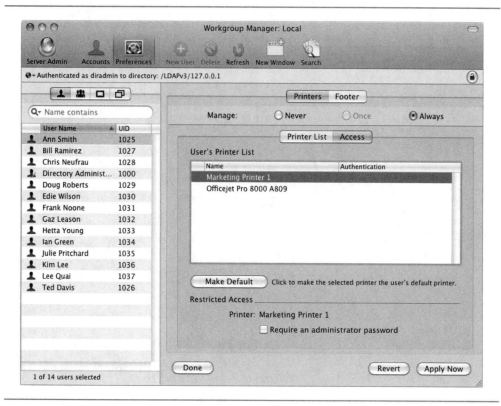

Figure 14-11.   Set the user's default printer in the Access pane.

    c.   Select the Print Page Footer (User Name And Date) check box.

    d.   Select the Include MAC Address check box if you want the footer to include the MAC address (the hardware address of the Ethernet card) of the Mac from which it was sent.

    e.   Choose the font in the Font Name pop-up menu.

    f.   Type the font size in the Font Size text box.

15.   Click the Apply Now button to apply the changes you've made to the user.

16.   Click the Done button to close the Printing pane.

Leave Workgroup Manager open if you want to set print quotas for users, as described next.

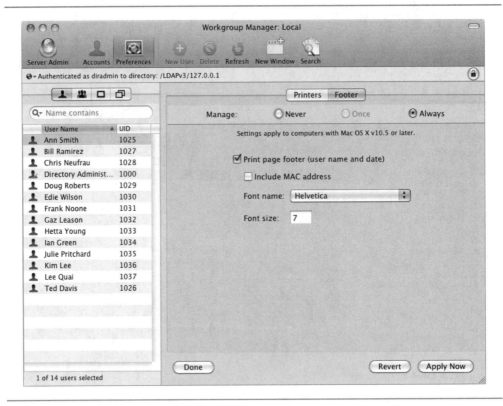

Figure 14-12.   You can also add a footer to each of the user's print jobs if necessary.

Setting a Print Quota for a User

To make sure that users don't use printers more than they should, you can set quotas for them—for example, 5 pages on the high-quality color printer and 100 pages on the boring old black-and-white printer per day.

CAUTION   Setting quotas can be a tricky business. Unless you know exactly what a person's job entails and can be certain they don't need to print substantial documents, err on the side of caution when setting quotas. You can also give a user an "unlimited quota" (that wavering, high-pitched sound you hear is the editor gibbering at this contradiction in terms) on a printer that's cheap to run so that they can print when they've run dry their quotas on the tastier printers.

To set quotas, use Workgroup Manager like this:

1. Open Workgroup Manager. For example, click the Workgroup Manager icon in the dock or double-click the Workgroup Manager icon in the /Applications/ Server/folder.

2. If Workgroup Manager doesn't authenticate you automatically, click the lock icon at the right end of the authentication bar and authenticate yourself as directory administrator.

3. In the left pane, click the user to whom you want to apply quotas.

4. Click the Print tab to display the Print pane.

5. To apply the same setting to each print queue, follow these steps:

   a. Select the All Queues option button. The Print pane displays the controls shown in Figure 14-13 (with settings already chosen).

   b. Type the number of pages in the Limit To N Pages text box.

   c. Type the number of days in the Every N Days text box.

6. To set a different quota for each print queue, select the Per Queue option button. The Print pane displays the controls shown in Figure 14-14. Follow these steps:

   a. In the Queue Name pop-up menu, select the print queue you want to affect. If the print queue isn't there, click the Add button and then type the name in the Queue Name text box.

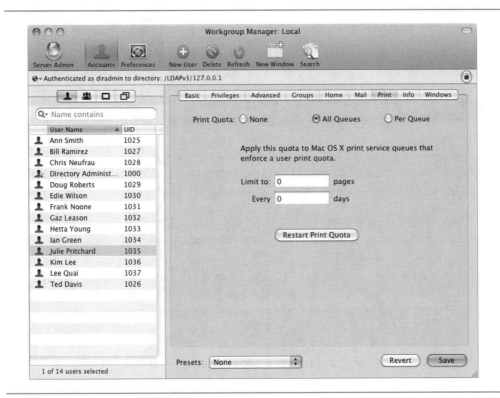

Figure 14-13. The quick way to set quotas is to apply the same quota to each print queue.

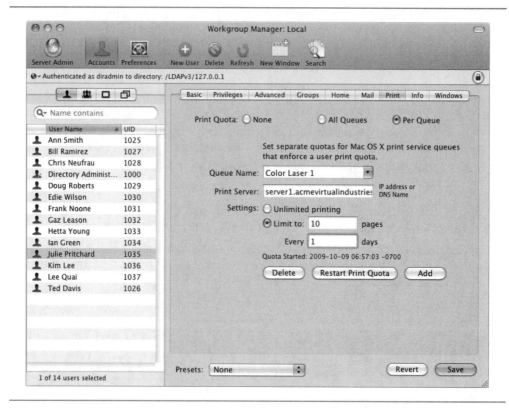

Figure 14-14. For greater control, you can set a different quota for each print queue.

 NOTE A print queue name appears in the Queue name pop-up menu only if you've selected the Enforce Quotas For This Queue check box for the queue in the Queues pane in Server Admin.

b.   In the Print Server text box, type the server's DNS name or IP address. If Workgroup Manager entered this information when you selected the print queue, you're set.

c.   In the Settings area, select the Unlimited Printing option button if this is the printer the user should be using for most documents. Otherwise, select the Limit To option button, and then enter the number of pages in the Limit To *N* Pages text box and the number of days in the Every *N* Days text box.

d.   Repeat these bulleted steps to set a quota for each other print queue.

NOTE If a user runs into their quota and comes to plead their case, you can grant a reprieve by clicking the Restart Print Quota button in the Print pane.

7. Click the Save button to save the quotas.

8. Pick another victim in the user list and set quotas for them.

9. Quit Workgroup Manager when you've finished setting quotas.

NOTE As usual with Workgroup Manager, you can save time and effort by creating presets loaded with your typical values and then applying them to user accounts.

Setting Up Printing on Your Clients

The next step is to set up your Mac clients to print on the print service.

NOTE You can also set up Windows PCs and UNIX boxes to print using the Mac OS X Server print service. This chapter assumes you're using Macs.

To set up a Mac client to print with the print service, you use a PostScript Printer Description file, or PPD for short. As its name suggests, the PPD gives the Mac the information it needs to use the printer's features—for example, details about its paper trays, and whether it has learned the dark art of duplexing documents.

NOTE Mac OS X (both the Server and the client versions) come with PPD files for many printers, and Apple provides new PPD files and printer drivers every so often via Software Update. As a result, your Macs may well already have the information they need to support your printer. But if the printer is a brand-new model, you may need to download a PPD installer from the printer manufacturer's website.

To add an IPP print queue to a client Mac, first arm yourself with the information you need:

■ **Server's host name or IP address** Either works, so use whichever you find easier to remember.

■ **The name of the print queue** You can skip the name to use the default print queue, but normally it's best to specify a queue. Some manufacturers use default queue names that are many furlongs short of intuitive.

Then follow these steps on the client Mac:

1. Choose Apple | System Preferences to open the System Preferences window.

2. In the Hardware category, click the Print & Fax icon to display the Print & Fax preferences pane (see Figure 14-15).

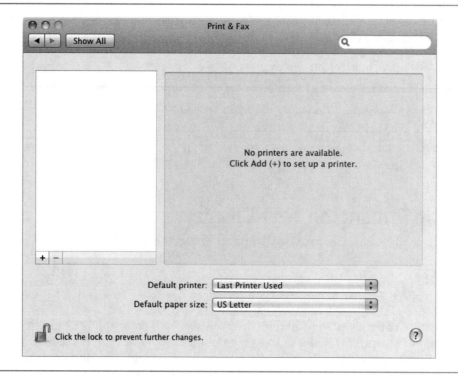

Figure 14-15. Click the + button in the Print & Fax preferences pane to start adding an IPP print queue to a Mac.

3. Click the + button below the printers pane on the left to display the Add Printer dialog box.

4. Click the IP button on the toolbar to display the IP pane (shown in Figure 14-16 with settings chosen).

5. Open the Protocol pop-up menu and choose Internet Printing Protocol – IPP.

6. In the Address text box, type the DNS name or IP address of the server. Mac OS X then gathers the printer information from the server and displays the available queues in the Queue pop-up menu.

NOTE You add the IPP print queue by telling the client Mac to look for the queue on the server. You don't need to point the client Mac directly at the printer.

7. In the Queue pop-up menu, select the print queue's name. If the name doesn't appear, you can type it in.

8. If you want, change the default name that appears in the Name text box.

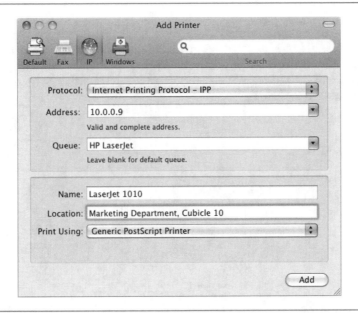

Figure 14-16. Use the IP pane of the Add Printer dialog box to add an IPP print queue to a client Mac.

9. Also if you want, edit the location in the Location text box. This information is to help the user find the printer, so make it as explicit as necessary.

10. In the Print Using pop-up menu, select the printer's type if you're certain what it is. If not, select Generic PostScript, as this works fine for most printers. The print service sends the print job along in the correct format for the printer.

11. Click the Add button. Mac OS X checks the printer information. If there are any choices to be made, the Installable Options dialog box appears. Choose the appropriate settings—for example, you can select the Duplex Printing Unit check box in the figure—and then click the Continue button.

12. After Mac OS X sets up the printer, the printer appears in the Print & Fax pane in System Preferences.

13. Add any other printers you need to add now.

14. In the Default Printer pop-up menu (see Figure 14-17), select the printer you want to use as the default. You can select the Last Printer Used item to use whichever printer you last printed on.

15. In the Default Paper Size pop-up menu, choose the default paper size to use for printing (for example, US Letter or US Legal).

16. Quit System Preferences. For example, press ⌘-Q or choose System Preferences | Quit System Preferences.

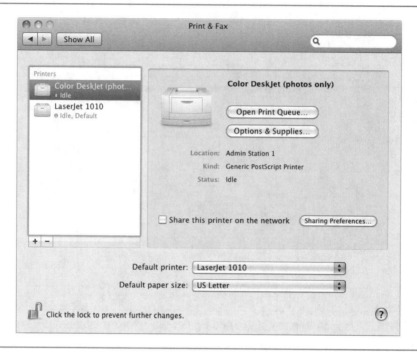

Figure 14-17.   After adding one or more print queues, choose the user's default printer. You can also set the default paper size.

Managing Your Print Queues

After you have set up your print queues and connected your clients to them, you can sit back and wait for things to go wrong. Or, more realistically, you can devote your attention to other aspects of administering your network until the print service starts waving flags and firing distress rockets in your general direction.

To manage your print queues, open Server Admin (come on—you know how by now), expand the server's list of services, and click the Print service in it. Then click the Job Status tab to display the Job Status pane, shown in Figure 14-18 with one printer sulking offline.

From here, you can take the following actions:

■   **Pause a print queue**   When you need to stop a queue from printing so that you can fix a problem with the printer, click the queue, and then click the Pause button below the list box. Fix the problem, and then click the Resume button to resume printing. If you interrupted a print job by pausing it, Mac OS X Server prints it again from the beginning, so you (or the user) may need to discard the first part of the aborted printout.

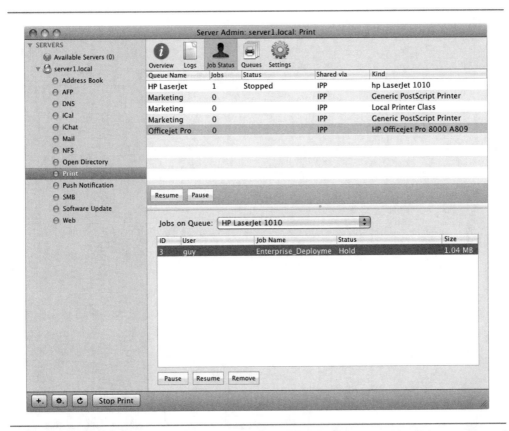

Figure 14-18. Use the Job Status pane in Server Admin to manage your print queues and sort out problems.

- **Pause a print job**   Click the queue to display the print jobs it contains. Then click the print job (or click one job and then ⌘-click each other print job you want to pause), and then click the Pause button. Click the Resume button when you want to set the print job or print jobs rolling again.

NOTE   By pausing a print job, you can make another job further down the print queue print sooner. But in general, you'll do better to create a high-priority queue (perhaps with a printer pool) for your lights-and-siren users rather than pausing other people's print jobs in a standard-priority queue.

- **Remove a print job**   When you realize that a user has started to print the entire Library of Congress, click the queue, click the print job, and then click the Remove button.

CHAPTER 15 | Allow Remote Access to Your Network

To keep competitive, but preserve some fragments of your home life, you and your colleagues will probably need to work outside the office as well as in it. Among its many features, Mac OS X Server includes virtual private networking that enables you (and them) to connect securely to your network from anywhere in the world that offers an Internet connection.

In this chapter, we'll make sure you understand the essentials of how virtual private networking works; you'll also go through the steps of setting up the server to accept VPN connections and deciding who's allowed to use it. After that, we look at how to connect your client Macs to the VPN—and how to connect the iPhone and iPod touch as well.

Understanding Virtual Private Networking

Virtual private networking uses an insecure public network to handle secure private networking. The network you create by using virtual private networking is called a *virtual private network*, logically enough, and both terms abbreviate to *VPN*—so whenever you see the term on its own, you need to decide whether it needs an "-ing" at the end.

Understanding What VPNs Are Good For

Usually, the Internet is the insecure public network that you want to create a secure connection across. Instead of needing to connect via dial-up and suffer the double pain of long-distance charges and modem speeds, a remote user can connect securely via VPN (with an "-ing") at the full speed of her Internet connection. Similarly, instead of paying the wallet-busting costs of a leased line to connect each satellite office to the mother ship, you can create a VPN (no "-ing") and connect each office via the Internet.

Those are typical uses, but you can also create a VPN across pretty much any other type of network that's not secure enough for your needs. For example, wireless networks are inherently less secure than wired networks because not only do the signals travel outside the building, but someone can perch on a hilltop several miles away, point an antenna at the building, and pick the network up loud and clear. To protect your valuable data, you can use VPN across the wireless network to ensure that snoopers can't read it. And if even a wired network isn't secure enough for your super-sensitive network traffic, you can create a VPN within it.

Understanding the Different Technologies for VPNs

Mac OS X can use three different technologies for VPNs, so you'll need to choose the one that best suits your needs. Here's what you need to know:

■ **L2TP Over IPSec** Layer 2 Tunneling Protocol (L2TP) over IP Security (IPSec) is usually the best choice for VPNs on Mac networks. This type of VPN uses strong encryption derived either from a signed digital certificate or from a *shared secret*, a sort of password that multiple people know (as opposed to most computer passwords, which are unique to each user—or supposed to be). Use L2TP Over

IPSec for your VPN unless you have a compelling reason to use PPTP or you have Cisco hardware that supports Cisco IPSec. This chapter shows L2TP in its examples, as L2TP is the VPN technology you're most likely to use.

NOTE For securing an L2TP VPN with IPSec, you can either buy a certificate from a certificate authority (CA) after going through the necessary checks or create your own certificate using the method explained in Chapter 4.

- **PPTP** Point-to-Point Tunneling Protocol is an older tunneling protocol that is much less secure than L2TP Over IPSec or Cisco IPSec. PPTP is secured by a password and uses either 128-bit encryption (which is fine) or 40-bit encryption (which is much too weak). Use PPTP only if you need to allow clients running Jaguar (Mac OS X 10.2) or Windows 2000 clients to connect to your VPN. (Nobody should be running these antediluvian operating systems—but of course some people are. You can use your VPN to force them to upgrade.)

- **Cisco IPSec** Cisco IP Security (IPSec) is a protocol mostly used in Cisco network routers. Cisco IPSec uses two-factor authentication, authenticating machines using either a shared secret (a password) or a certificate and authenticating users by account name and password, to provide tight security.

Setting Up a Virtual Private Network

To set up a VPN, you need to turn on the VPN service (if it's not already running) and configure it (if it's not configured). You can then start the service, and choose the users you will allow to connect to it.

Turning On the VPN Service

Now see if the VPN service is running, and turn it on if it isn't. Follow these steps:

1. Open Server Admin. For example, click the Server Admin icon in the dock.

2. In the Servers list on the left, double-click the server you want to connect to.

3. Type your user name and password if you haven't told your Mac to remember them, and then click the Connect button.

4. In the Servers pane on the left, double-click the server to display the list of services. If the VPN service appears in the list, skip the remaining steps in this list.

5. Click the Settings button on the toolbar to display the Settings pane.

6. Click the Services tab to display the Services pane.

7. Select the VPN check box.

8. Click the Save button to apply the change.

The VPN service appears in the list of services in the Servers pane. Keep Server Admin open so that you can configure the VPN service, as described next.

Configuring the VPN Service

Next, configure the VPN service as described in the following subsections. You first choose settings in the L2TP pane (or in the PPTP pane if you must use PPTP for your VPN). You then use the Client Information pane to set DNS, search, and routing information for the VPN clients, and finally choose whether you want to use chatty logging or laconic logging.

Setting Up an L2TP VPN

To set up an L2TP VPN, follow these steps:

1. In the Servers pane in Server Admin, click the VPN service in the list of services under the server to display the VPN screens.

2. Click the Settings button to display the Settings pane.

3. Click the L2TP tab to display the L2TP pane (see Figure 15-1).

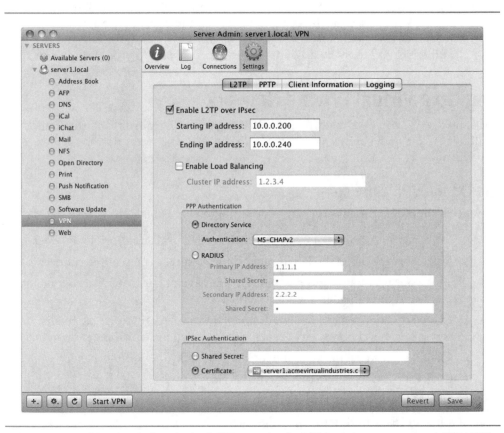

Figure 15-1.   Use the settings in the L2TP pane for the VPN service to set up an L2TP VPN.

NOTE   To set up a PPTP VPN, click the PPTP tab instead of the L2TP tab. The PPTP pane has fewer settings than the L2TP pane, but most of the settings it does have are similar to those in the L2TP pane, so you'll have no trouble figuring them out from the instructions here. The one setting that deserves mention is the Allow 40-Bit Encryption Keys In Addition To 128-Bit check box. Make sure this check box is cleared unless you are compelled to accept connections with 40-bit encryption, which is too weak to be safe.

4. Select the Enable L2TP Over IPSec check box to make the remaining controls in the pane available.

5. In the Starting IP Address text box, type the first IP address that you want to assign to clients that connect to the VPN.

CAUTION   You need to reserve a separate chunk of IP addresses for your VPN, and keep them firmly cordoned off from the rest of your network. (You can also use a separate subnet.) If you are using DHCP, do not let your VPN IP addresses overlap the range of IP addresses that your DHCP server is assigning. Apart from keeping your DHCP server happy and preventing clients from butting their virtual heads, this separation will enable you to identify your VPN clients easily and will save you any amount of confusion.

6. In the Ending IP Address text box, type the last IP address that you want to assign to VPN clients.

7. If you want to use load balancing on your VPN, select the Enable Load Balancing check box, and then type the balancing IP address in the Cluster IP Address text box.

8. In the PPP Authentication box, choose the authentication method for PPP:

   ■ **Directory Service**   Select this option button to have VPN clients authenticate via the directory service. Choose Kerberos in the Authentication pop-up menu if you've set up a Kerberos authentication server; choose MS-CHAPv2 if you haven't got Kerberos.

   ■ **RADIUS**   Select this option button to have VPN clients authenticate via a RADIUS server. Type the primary RADIUS server's IP address in the Primary IP Address text box and its shared secret in the Shared Secret text box, then enter the corresponding information for the secondary RADIUS server.

NOTE   RADIUS is the acronym for Remote Authentication Dial In User Service. You can turn on the RADIUS service in the Services pane of Server Admin.

9. In the IPSec Authentication box, choose how to authenticate VPN clients via IPSec:

   - **Shared Secret**   Select this option button to authenticate users via the password that you type in the text box. Make this password strong— 8 characters absolute minimum, 12 characters sensible minimum, including letters, numbers, and symbols.

   - **Certificate**   Select this option button to authenticate users via the certificate that you pick from the pop-up menu. The certificate provides greater security, but in many cases, the shared secret is so much easier to implement that it's the clear choice.

10. Click the Save button to save the changes you've made to the VPN service.

Setting DNS, Search, and Routing Information for Clients

Now set up DNS, search, and routing information for the VPN's clients:

1. In Server Admin, with the VPN service selected in the Servers pane, click the Settings button on the toolbar to display the Settings pane.

2. Click the Client Information tab to display the Client Information pane (shown in Figure 15-2 with settings chosen).

3. In the DNS Servers text box, type the IP address of the DNS server the VPN clients should use for resolving DNS queries after connecting to the VPN. (For traffic that doesn't go to the VPN, the VPN client continues to use its usual DNS server—for example, one on the client's local network or at their ISP.) To enter multiple servers, put each on a new line.

4. In the Search Domains text box, enter any search domains that the client will need after connecting to the VPN. (You may not need to enter any search domains.)

NOTE   The entries in the Network Routing Definition box tell the VPN clients which addresses are on the network to which they've connected via the VPN. This lets a client know whether to send the request across the VPN connection or across its regular network or Internet connection. For example, when the client needs to connect to a server on the network, that request should go through the VPN; when the client wants to visit Google, that request should go straight to the Internet rather than to the VPN and then out to the Internet.

5. In the Network Routing Definition list box, set up the network routing definitions that the VPN clients need. Follow these steps:

   a. Click the + button to display the dialog box shown in Figure 15-3.

   b. Type the network's IP address in the IP Address text box.

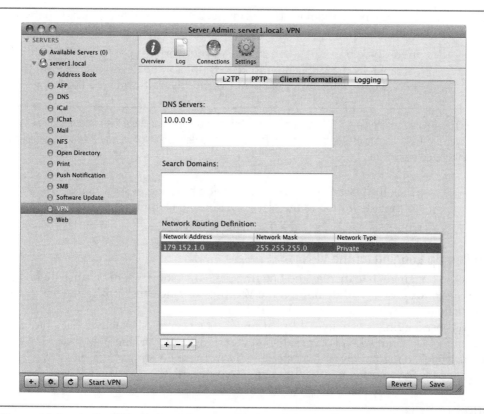

Figure 15-2.   In the Client Information pane for the VPN service, set the DNS server address, the search domains, and the network routing definitions.

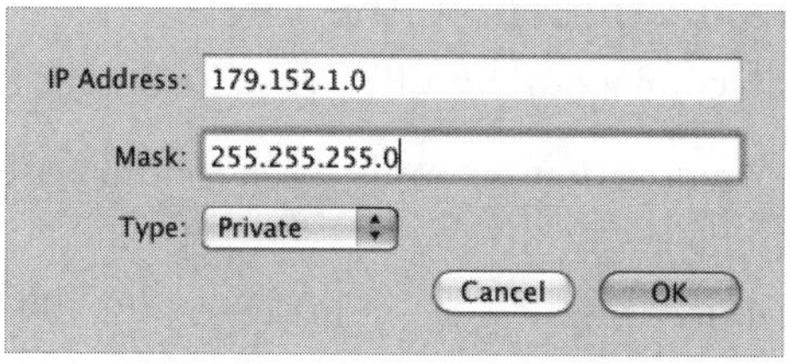

Figure 15-3.   Use this dialog box to create network routing definitions that tell the VPN clients which traffic belongs on the VPN and which doesn't.

c.   Type the network mask (for example, 255.255.255.0 for a Class C network) in the Mask text box.

d.   In the Type pop-up menu, choose the network's type: Private or Public. Private tells the VPN client to keep traffic for the destination within the VPN. Public tells the VPN client to send the traffic outside the VPN.

TIP   When setting up a VPN connection for clients who will connect via their Internet connection, you'll usually want to create one or more Private routing definitions for your network and let all other traffic go elsewhere.

e.   Click the OK button to close the dialog box. Server Admin adds the routing definition to the Network Routing Definition list box.

7.   Click the Save button to save the changes you've made.

Setting Up Logging for the VPN

Click the Logging tab to display the Logging pane (not shown here because there's only one check box to see), and then select the Verbose Logging check box if you want to see all the details of what happens on the VPN.

Verbose logging is usually helpful at first, as it lets you tell exactly what's happening on the VPN, but when you're satisfied that things are working okay, you may want to drop back to regular logging by clearing the Verbose Logging check box.

Click the Save button to save the changes you've made.

Starting the VPN

With all the settings in place, you can now start the VPN by clicking the Start VPN button at the bottom of the Server Admin window.

Server Admin shows a green light next to the VPN item in the services list to show that the VPN service is up and running.

Choosing Which Users Can Connect to the VPN

To choose which users can connect to the VPN, you use Server Preferences like this:

1.   Open Server Preferences. For example, click the Server Preferences icon in the dock.

2.   In the Accounts area, click the Users icon to display the Users pane.

3.   Click the user for whom you want to allow or deny VPN access.

4.   Click the Services button to display the Services pane (see Figure 15-4).

5.   Select or clear the VPN check box, as appropriate.

6.   When you have finished choosing VPN settings for users, quit Server Preferences. For example, press ⌘-Q.

Figure 15-4.   In the Services pane of Server Preferences, select the VPN check box to allow the user to use the VPN.

Connecting Your Client Macs to the VPN

Now that the server is ready to accept VPN connections, you can set up the client Macs and connect them to the VPN.

Setting a Client Mac to Connect to the VPN

To set up the client Macs to connect to the VPN, follow these steps:

1. Open the System Preferences window. For example, click the System Preferences icon in the dock, or choose Apple | System Preferences.

2. In the Internet & Wireless area, click the Network icon to display the Network pane.

3. Click the + button below the list of network to display the dialog box shown in Figure 15-5 (with settings already chosen).

4. Open the Interface pop-up menu and choose VPN. The dialog box adds the VPN Type pop-up menu.

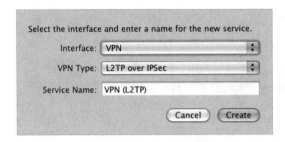

Figure 15-5. Use this dialog box to start setting up a VPN connection.

5. In the VPN Type pop-up menu, select the VPN type you need: L2TP Over IPSec, PPTP, or Cisco IPSec. This example uses L2TP Over IPSec. System Preferences enters a generic name derived from the VPN type in the Service Name text box—for example, VPN (L2TP).

6. In the Service Name text box, change the name as needed. For example, you may prefer a descriptive name, such as MonomaniaCorp VPN, rather than the dusty default name.

7. Click the Create button to close the dialog box. System Preferences adds the VPN entry to the list of network interfaces and displays its configuration screen (see Figure 15-6).

NOTE You can create multiple configurations for the VPN. This section assumes you're creating just a single configuration. To create another configuration, open the Configuration pop-up menu and choose Add Configuration. In the Create A New Configuration Called dialog box, type the name for the configuration, and then click the Create button. You can then set the details of the new configuration.

8. Leave the Default item selected in the Configuration pop-up menu for now.

9. In the Server Address text box, type the IP address of the server.

10. In the Account Name text box, type the user's account name for the VPN connection.

11. Click the Authentication Settings button to display the Authentication Settings dialog box (see Figure 15-7).

12. In the User Authentication area, select the appropriate option button: Password, RSA SecurID, Certificate, Kerberos, or CryptoCard. For a password, type it in the text box. For a certificate, click the Select button, click the certificate in the Choose An Identity dialog box that opens, and then click the Continue button.

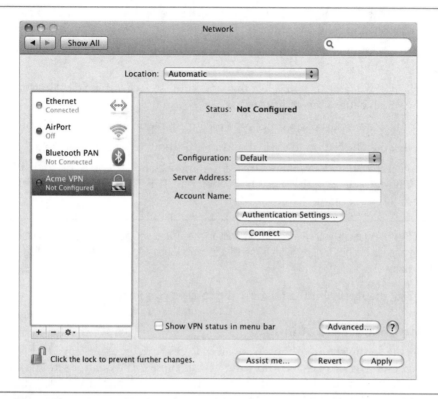

Figure 15-6. The VPN entry shows up in the network interfaces list as Not Configured, so your next move is to configure it.

User Authentication:
- Password: ••••••••••••••••••••••••••
- RSA SecurID
- Certificate [Select...]
- Kerberos
- CryptoCard

Machine Authentication:
- Shared Secret: ••••••••••••••••
- Certificate [Select...]

Group Name: [ ]
(Optional)

[Cancel] [OK]

Figure 15-7. In the Authentication Settings dialog box, choose the means of authenticating the user and the computer.

13. In the Machine Authentication area, select the option button for the means of authenticating the computer:

- **Shared Secret**   If you select this option button, type the password in the text box.

- **Certificate**   If you select this option button, click the Select button, and then choose the certificate.

14. If this Mac is part of a group, type the group name in the Group Name text box.

15. Click the OK button to close the Authentication Settings dialog box.

16. Select the Show VPN Status In Menu Bar check box if you want to display the VPN status icon in the Mac OS X menu bar. This is handy if you (or the user) use the VPN often.

 NOTE   The choices you've made in this section are all that you need for many VPN connections. If you need to choose further settings, see the section "Choosing Advanced VPN Settings," later in this chapter.

17. Click the Apply button to apply the choices you've made.

Choosing Advanced VPN Settings

As well as the settings you've chosen so far, Mac OS X includes advanced VPN settings that you can set to control exactly how the VPN behaves. The default settings work well for many VPNs, but if you find you need to choose advanced VPN settings, click the Advanced button in the VPN pane to display the Advanced Settings dialog box, and then work through the following subsections.

Choosing Settings in the Options Pane of Advanced Settings

Start by clicking the Options tab in the Advanced Settings dialog box to display the Options pane (see Figure 15-8). You can then choose settings for the following options:

- **Disconnect When Switching User Accounts**   Select this check box if you want Mac OS X to disconnect from the VPN when you switch user accounts. Normally, this behavior is useful, so that you don't leave the VPN connection open when you're not there to use it, but you may need to clear this check box if you work from multiple accounts on your Mac.

- **Disconnect When User Logs Out**   Select this check box if you want Mac OS X to disconnect from the VPN when you log out. This behavior, too, is usually what you want, but you can clear the check box if you need to maintain the VPN connection even when you log out.

- **Send All Traffic Over VPN Connection**   Select this check box if you want your Mac to direct all your network traffic over the VPN rather than just that traffic sent to addresses on the VPN. Normally, you would select this check box when using a VPN to protect traffic on a wireless or wired network rather than when using a VPN to connect remotely across the Internet.

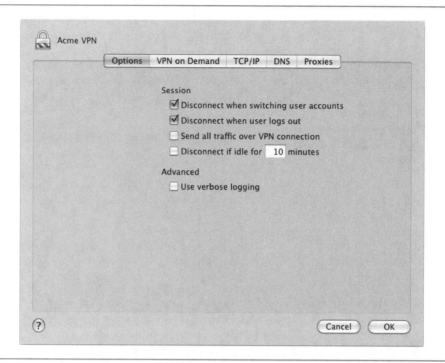

Figure 15-8.   The Options pane of the Advanced Settings dialog box lets you choose whether to disconnect automatically from the VPN and whether to use verbose logging.

■   **Disconnect If Idle For *N* Minutes**   Select this check box if you want Mac OS X to disconnect you from the VPN automatically after a period of inactivity. Type the number of minutes in the text box.

■   **Use Verbose Logging**   Select this check box if you want to log all the details of your VPN connections instead of just errors. Verbose logging is useful when the VPN is misbehaving, but regular logging is fine most of the time.

Choosing VPN On Demand Settings

Next, click the VPN On Demand tab to display the VPN On Demand pane (see Figure 15-9). Here, you can create a list of any domains for which you want to use the VPN, so that when you enter that domain in your web browser, Mac OS X automatically uses the VPN. If you have multiple VPN configurations, you can choose which VPN configuration a particular domain fires up.

To add a domain, click the + button below the list box. In the entry that Mac OS X adds to the list box, type the domain name, and then choose the configuration from the pop-up menu in the Configuration column. (If you've created only a Default configuration so far, that will be your sole choice here.)

To remove a domain from the list, click it, and then click the – button.

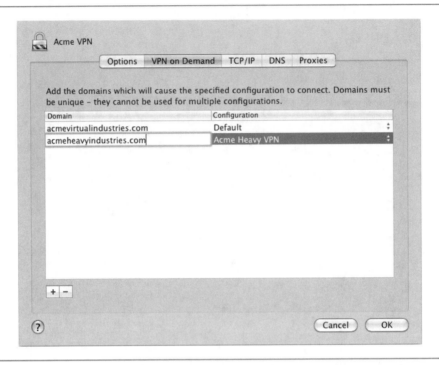

Figure 15-9. In the VPN On Demand pane of the Advanced Settings dialog box, you can specify domains for which Mac OS X should automatically use the VPN.

Configuring TCP/IP for the VPN Manually

In many cases, you can let Mac OS X handle the details of TCP/IP for the VPN connection, but sometimes you may need to choose settings manually. To do so, click the TCP/IP tab of the Advanced Settings dialog box, and then work in the TCP/IP pane (see Figure 15-10).

If you're using IPv4, as most of us still are, open the Configure IPv4 pop-up menu and choose Manually instead of Using PPP. Out spring the IPv4 Address text box, the Subnet Mask text box, and the Router text box, in which you can enter the details of the connection. Make sure the Configure IPv6 pop-up menu is set to Off.

If you're using IPv6, set the Configure IPv4 pop-up menu to Off, and then choose Manually in the Configure IPv6 pop-up menu. You can then fill in the details in the Router text box, the IPv6 Address text box, and the Prefix Length text box that appear.

Configuring DNS Servers and Search Domains for the VPN

If you need to set DNS servers or search domains for the VPN, click the DNS tab in the Advanced Settings dialog box, and then work in the DNS pane (see Figure 15-11). To add an item, click the + button below the DNS Servers list box or the Search Domains list box, and then type in the details. To delete an item, click it, and then click the – button.

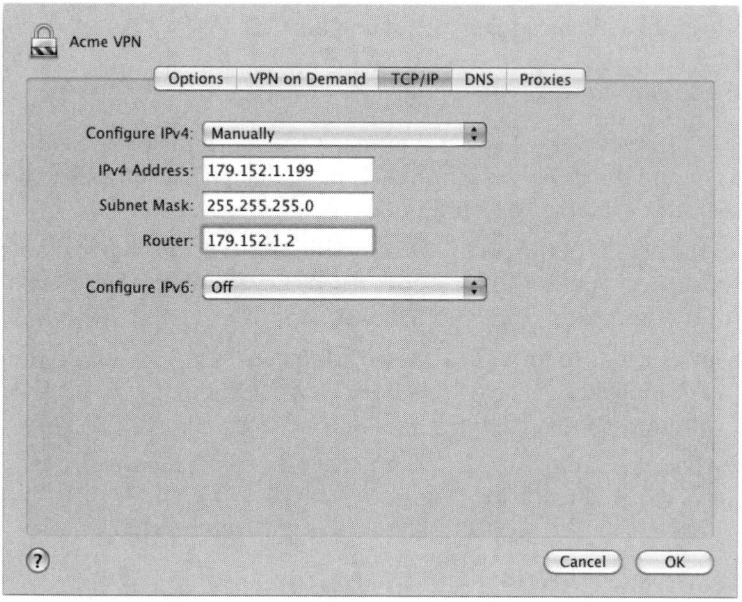

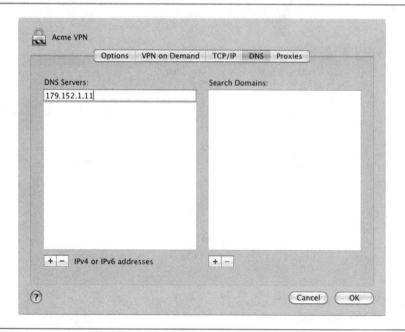

Figure 15-10. You can configure TCP/IP settings manually for a VPN connection.

Figure 15-11. The DNS pane of the Advanced Settings dialog box lets you specify DNS servers and search domains for a VPN connection.

Choosing Proxy Servers for the VPN

The final pane of the Advanced Settings dialog box, the Proxies pane (see Figure 15-12), enables you to set up proxy servers for the VPN.

Follow these steps to set up proxying:

1. In the Select A Protocol To Configure list box, click the protocol that you want to configure the proxy server for. The pane displays text boxes to the right of the Select A Protocol To Configure list box.

2. Enter the details of the proxy server in these text boxes. For example, for a web proxy server, type the server's address in the Web Proxy Server text box, and the port number in the second text box.

3. If the user needs to provide a password to use the proxy server, select the Proxy Server Requires Password check box. Type the username in the Username text box and the password in the Password text box.

4. In the Select A Protocol To Configure list box, select the check box for the protocol to activate the proxying.

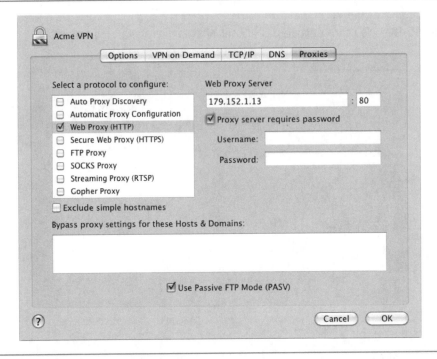

Figure 15-12. If your VPN connection needs proxy servers, set them up in the Proxies pane of the Advanced Settings dialog box.

5. Repeat the previous four steps to configure the other protocols for which the VPN needs proxying.

6. Select the Exclude Simple Hostnames check box if you want to avoid using proxying for simple hostnames.

7. In the Bypass Proxy Settings For These Hosts And Domains text box, type the addresses of hosts and domains that the Mac should connect to directly, rather than going through the proxy. You can enter a target server's name (such as server2.acmevirtualindustries.com), an IP address (such as 10.0.0.27), or a domain name (such as acmevirtualindustries.com); put an asterisk before the domain if you want to include all its subdomains (for example, *.acmevirtualindustries.com).

8. Select the Use Passive FTP Mode (PASV) check box if you want the Mac to use passive FTP mode for FTP.

Applying the Changes You've Made

When you've finished choosing advanced settings, click the OK button to close the Advanced Settings dialog box and return to the Network pane of System Preferences.

Click the Apply button to apply the changes you've made to the VPN connection. It's now ready for use.

Connecting a Mac to a VPN

To connect a Mac to the VPN, click the VPN status icon on the menu bar, and then click the Connect item for the appropriate VPN (see Figure 15-13). The VPN status icon displays the word "Connecting" as it establishes the connection, and then shows a readout of the time connected as a delicate reminder that the connection is up and running.

To disconnect, click the VPN status icon, and then click the Disconnect item on the menu.

Figure 15-13. Use the VPN status icon on the menu bar to quickly connect to the VPN and disconnect from it.

NOTE If you choose not to display the VPN status icon, you can connect to and disconnect from the VPN using the controls in the Network pane of System Preferences. Click the VPN interface in the interfaces list to display the controls.

Connecting an iPhone or iPod touch to a VPN

If your network's users connect their iPhones or iPod touches to the network, they'll probably want to connect them via VPN as well. You can set this up either automatically or manually.

Setting Up a VPN Automatically on an iPhone or iPod touch

If you need to configure more than a few iPhones or iPod touches, you'll probably want to automate the process by using iPhone Configuration Utility. See Chapter 8 for instructions on getting iPhone Configuration Utility, installing it, and creating payloads for VPN settings.

Choosing VPN Settings Manually on an iPhone or iPod touch

If you have only a few iPhones or iPod touches to configure, you may find it quickest to set them up manually. Follow these steps to choose VPN settings:

1. From the Home screen, choose Settings | General | Network to display the Network screen.

2. Touch the VPN button to display the VPN screen (shown on the left in Figure 15-14).

3. Touch the Add VPN Configuration button to display the Add Configuration screen, shown on the right in Figure 15-14.

4. Near the top of the screen, click the button for the security type the VPN uses: L2TP, PPTP, or IPSec. The iPhone or iPod touch displays a list of the information required for the connection.

5. Type in the details for the VPN configuration on the screen:

   ■ **Description** This is the name under which the VPN appears in the list of VPNs. Choose a descriptive name that suits you.

   ■ **Server** Type the computer name (for example, vpnserv .acmevirtualindustries.com) or IP address (for example, 216.248.2.88) of the VPN server.

   ■ **Account** Type the user's login name for the VPN connection.

   ■ **Password** If the user will use a password rather that a certificate (discussed next), you can enter it here and have the iPhone provide it each time the user connects. For greater security, you can leave the password area blank so that the user must enter the password manually each time they connect. This

Figure 15-14.   The VPN screen (left) contains the master switch for turning the VPN connection on or off. On the Add Configuration screen (right), enter the information for the connection, and then save it.

prevents anyone else from connecting using the iPhone, but it's laborious, especially if the password uses letters, numbers, and symbols (as a strong password should).

■ **RSA SecurID**   (L2TP and PPTP only) If the user will use an RSA SecurID token, move this switch to On to use it. The iPhone or iPod touch then hides the password field, because the token obviates the need for a password.

■ **Use Certificate**   (IPSec only) If you have installed a certificate for authenticating the user on the connection, move this switch to On. The switch is available only when a certificate is installed.

■ **Secret**   (L2TP only) Type the preshared key, also called the shared secret, for the VPN. This preshared key is the same for all users of the VPN (unlike the account name and password, which are unique to each user).

■ **Group name**   (IPSec only) Type the name of the group to which the user belongs for the VPN.

- **Send All Traffic**   (L2TP and PPTP only) Leave this switch set to On (the default position) if you want to route all network traffic to the VPN server. Turn this switch off to make connections to other parts of the Internet than the VPN go directly to those destinations.

- **Encryption Level**   (PPTP only) Leave this set to Auto to have the iPhone or iPod touch try 128-bit encryption (the strongest) first, then weaker 40-bit encryption, and then None. If you've set up your VPN to require 128-bit encryption (as you normally should do), choose Maximum here. Never use None.

6. If your VPN needs proxying, scroll down to the bottom of the configuration screen, touch the Manual button, and then enter the server and port. To use authentication, move the Authentication switch to the On position, and then type in the username and password.

7. When you've finished entering the information, touch the Save button to save the connection. The VPN connection then appears on the VPN screen.

The iPhone or iPod touch is now ready to connect to the VPN.

Connecting the iPhone or iPod touch to the VPN

If you've set up the iPhone or iPod touch with a single VPN connection, the user can connect by displaying the VPN screen (Settings | General | Network | VPN) and then moving the On/Off slider to the On position.

If you've set up two or more VPNs, the user needs to select the right VPN in the Choose A Configuration list on the VPN screen before moving the On/Off slider to the On position.

The iPhone or iPod touch then connects to the VPN. If you left the user to enter their password on each connection, the device prompts them to enter it.

To end the VPN connection, the user displays the VPN screen again, and then moves the On/Off slider back to the Off position.

PART III | Secure and Maintain Your Network

CHAPTER 16 | Secure Your Macs and Your Network

For humans, life is a terminal disease filled with threats, viruses, and vague premonitions of impending doom—so in our wisdom, we've inflicted much the same on our computers. The long, the short, and the ugly of it is that your Macs and your network will face constant threats until you consign them to digital oblivion, after which the problem passes to their replacements.

In this chapter you'll learn how to reduce the threats to your Macs and to your network. We'll start by taking a 30,000-foot view of the threats that you'll typically face, and then dig into the details of what you can do to improve things.

There's one thing I should mention before we start. Security is a huge topic, about which people write whole books, so this chapter hasn't a snowflake's chance at mid-summer in Death Valley of covering everything. What this chapter aims to do is point out the types of threats to your network that you will normally need to counter, and shows you straightforward countermeasures you can take against them.

Your Executive Overview of the Threats

Your network and its Macs face plenty of threats, including the following:

- **Intrusion**   If someone sidles into your workplace and sits down at an unattended workstation, they may be able to access sensitive material on the network. Or they may find themselves looking at a login screen the Mac has activated as soon as the user stepped away from it. You can choose which scenario you want.

- **Theft**   Someone might waltz into your workplace, slide a Mac Pro under their coat, and sidestep back out, but your colleagues would likely query anyone whose tailoring was that disastrous. Normally, it'll be your organization's MacBooks that are in danger of taking a walk on the wild side, and it's much more likely to happen when they're out of the building than in it. Either way, you need to protect your hardware against booting up if it falls into the wrong hands.

 NOTE   I was joking about the Mac Pro—but it's well worth asking your colleagues to query anything odd they see happening with hardware. The Australian Customs service lost a couple of high-powered servers a few years back when a pair of fake engineers in smartly logo-ed boiler suits wheeled them away on carts for "servicing" and failed to return them.

- **Attack across a network**   Any computer that's connected to a network can be attacked across it—so any computer that's connected to a network needs protection against attack. You'll need to protect your network with a firewall to keep out Internet threats.

- **Viruses and malware**   Mac OS X's underlying UNIX code base generally has better security than the snails and puppy-dog tails (or whatever) that Microsoft has stirred into the foundations of Windows. Besides, fewer malefactors and virus writers create malware for Mac OS X because it is a much smaller target than Windows PCs. But there *is* malware that targets Macs, so you'll need to protect against it by running antivirus software on your Macs.

■ **User error** No amount of baked-in UNIX goodness can protect your network's Macs against users taking, ah, *unwise* actions. But you can reduce users' scope for error by tightening the security on your Macs and removing from System Preferences any items that you don't want users to experiment with.

■ **Phishing** No matter how good your e-mail filtering, it's almost inevitable that your network's users will receive e-mail messages that try to get valuable information from them one way or another. You'll want to educate your network's users to recognize phishing messages and delete them rather than follow their suggestions. And you'll want to persuade or prevent (or both) the users from connecting unauthorized media devices such as iPods or USB drives to their computers.

Securing Your Network's Macs

In a default configuration, a standalone Mac has many features that make it easier and more fun to use, but that are less secure than administrators would like them to be. Many of these features are available after you connect a Mac to your network as well.

This section shows you how to choose more secure settings for a Mac, starting with setting an Open Firmware password to protect the Mac during bootup. After that, you can lock down System Preferences, install antivirus software, and choose security options for your web browsers. For managed Macs, you can also use Workgroup Manager to apply restrictions to user accounts.

Setting an Open Firmware Password

When you turn a Mac on, and it plays the startup chime and starts thinking about booting, you can press several different keys to change the way it starts up:

■ Press OPTION to display Startup Manager, which shows a list of all available boot devices that you can choose from.

■ Press C to start the Mac from the optical drive (if there's a suitable CD or DVD in it).

■ Press N to start the Mac from a NetBoot server (assuming there's one available).

■ Press T to start up in Target Disk Mode, mounting the Mac as an external drive on the Mac to which you've connected it via FireWire.

■ Press ⌘-V to start up in Verbose mode. Verbose mode shows you the commands the operating system is trying to execute and the results it's getting. This is useful for troubleshooting boot problems. If all is well, Verbose mode ends when the Mac displays the blue screen during bootup.

- Press ⌘-S to start up in single-user mode. Single-user mode boots to the root account in text mode for troubleshooting. From single-user mode, you type **exit** and press RETURN to reboot the Mac.

- Press ⌘-OPTION-O-F to start up in Open Firmware mode, where you can muck about with startup and hardware settings.

- Press ⌘-OPTION-P-R to reset the Parameter RAM (PRAM), a troubleshooting move you may need to perform when your Mac starts pondering existential questions (such as "Do I really have to start up today?"). Chucking the toys out of the pram should reset the baby's temper.

All of these maneuvers are useful at the right time, but you don't want unauthorized people pulling them on your Macs. To prevent them, you enter an Open Firmware password, a password that the person must enter before they're allowed to do any of the above.

NOTE   You can set an Open Firmware password for both client Macs and servers. Do both.

To set an Open Firmware password, follow these steps:

1. Insert the Mac OS X DVD in the Mac's optical drive.

2. Restart the Mac.

3. Press C at the startup chime to boot from the DVD.

4. On the Mac OS X screen, select your language (for example, English), and then click the arrow button to continue.

5. On the Install Mac OS X (or Install Mac OS X Server) screen, choose Utilities | Firmware Password Utility from the menu bar to launch Firmware Password Utility.

6. On the first screen, which tells you about Open Firmware passwords, click the New button.

7. Select the Require Password To Start This Computer From Another Source check box.

8. Type a strong password in the Password text box and the Verify text box.

NOTE   For the Open Firmware password, you can use only letters and numbers—you can't use symbols. This means you'll need at least 10-12 characters to create a strong password.

9. Click the OK button.

10. Click the Quit button to quit Firmware Password Utility.

11. Choose Mac OS X Installer | Quit Mac OS X Installer or press ⌘-Q. Installer displays a dialog box asking if you've taken leave of your senses.

12. Click the Restart button to restart the Mac.

13. At the startup chime, press OPTION to display the list of available boot devices. Verify that the Mac prompts you for the Open Firmware password before it lets you see them.

Locking Down System Preferences on a Mac

Once the Mac is running, an Open Firmware password doesn't give any protection. So you need to make sure any would-be intruder must provide a login password.

The way you do this is by locking down System Preferences on the Mac. We'll start with the most important settings for security and then look at the others that can make a difference.

Open System Preferences by clicking the System Preferences icon in the dock or by choosing Apple | System Preferences. Then work your way through the following subsections.

Choosing General Security Settings

The best place to start locking things down is Security preferences, so click the Security icon in the Personal area of the System Preferences window. Then click the General tab to display the General pane (see Figure 16-1).

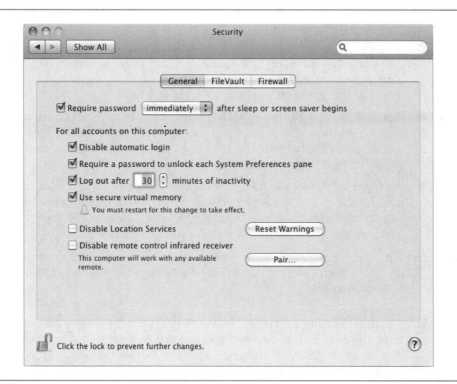

Figure 16-1. The General pane of Security preferences is the place to start when locking down a Mac.

1. If the lock icon in the lower-left corner is closed, click the icon, type your user name and password in the resulting dialog box, and then click the OK button. Mac OS X opens the lock and enables the options.

2. Choose the settings the Mac needs:

   - **Require Password After Sleep Or Screen Saver Begins** Select this check box if you want the user to provide their password each time they wake the Mac from sleep or from daydreaming with its screen saver. Choose Immediately or one of the shortest times—5 Seconds or 1 Minute—in the pop-up menu to make this security mechanism effective.

NOTE If you select the Require Password After Sleep Or Screen Saver Begins check box, visit the Energy Saver pane in System Preferences and set the Computer Sleep slider to a short time, such as 10 minutes. Then go to the Desktop & Screen saver pane, and set the Start Screen Saver slider to start the screen saver after an even shorter period of inactivity (such as three minutes). Then visit the Exposé & Spaces pane, click the Exposé tab, and set up one or more hot corners for starting the screen saver easily with the mouse pointer.

   - **Disable Automatic Login** Select this check box to prevent any user from setting up automatic login (where Mac OS X automatically logs in with the designated user account).

   - **Require A Password To Unlock Each System Preference Pane** Select this check box if you really want to lock down System Preferences. This straitjacket is good for Macs shared in a public location, such as in a library or social club, but tends to grate on regular users.

   - **Log Out After *N* Minutes Of Inactivity** Select this check box to make Mac OS X automatically log out a user who has been idle for the length of time you specify in the text box. This can be a good security measure, though forced logouts often annoy users.

   - **Use Secure Virtual Memory** Select this check box to make Mac OS X encrypt the temporary files used for virtual memory. Temporary files can include passwords and other sensitive data, so using secure virtual memory is a good move.

CAUTION After turning on the Use Secure Virtual Memory option, you need to restart the Mac to make the change take effect.

   - **Disable Location Services** Select this check box to prevent the Mac from using Wi-Fi signals to determine where in the world it is. (The Mac does this to set the time zone automatically, not because the National Security Agency is on your case.)

   - **Disable Remote Control Infrared Receiver** Select this check box to prevent anyone using the Mac's infrared receiver for remote control.

Encrypting a Mobile Account with FileVault

If you create mobile accounts for your users, you can force Mac OS X to encrypt the contents of the mobile accounts with FileVault. To do this, select the Encrypt Contents With FileVault check box in the Options pane within the Account Creation pane in Mobile preferences when setting up the account.

Choosing FileVault Security Settings

If a Mac is at risk of being lost or stolen, you should set it to encrypt users' home folders so that they cannot be read by anyone who doesn't know the password. Otherwise, someone can connect the Mac to another Mac via FireWire cable, boot it in target disk mode, and simply read the files off it.

To encrypt the users' home folders, you use the FileVault feature. FileVault encrypts the user's home folder using the user's password as the key. When you turn on FileVault, you must set a master password for the Mac so that you can recover the user's data if they forget their password.

Click the FileVault tab is the Security pane in System Preferences to display the FileVault pane (see Figure 16-2).

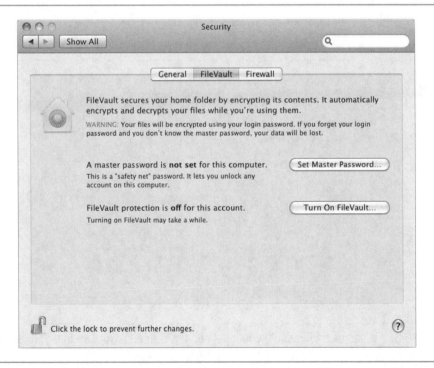

Figure 16-2. FileVault encrypts the contents of a user's home folder so that they cannot be read without a password.

CAUTION   Turning on FileVault involves logging the current user out, so save any unsaved work and close all applications before you start.

You can then set up FileVault like this:

1. If the readout says "A master password is not set for this computer," set the master password like this:

    a. Click the Set Master Password button to display the dialog box shown in Figure 16-3.

    b. Type a strong password in the Master Password text box and the Verify text box. If you want help choosing a strong password, click the key icon to the right of the Master Password text box, and then use the Password Assistant (see Chapter 3 for details).

    c. If you must create a password hint, type it in the Hint text box. A hint compromises the password's security, so it's best not to create one.

    d. Click the OK button.

2. Click the Turn On FileVault button. Mac OS X prompts you to enter the password for the user account.

3. Type the password, and then click the OK button. FileVault displays the dialog box shown in Figure 16-4.

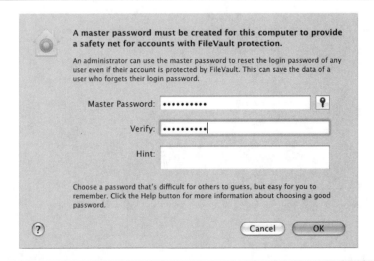

Figure 16-3.   When using FileVault, you must set a master password so that you can decrypt the encrypted data if a user forgets their password.

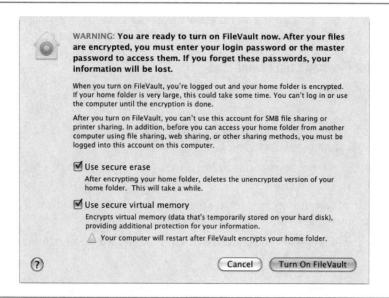

Figure 16-4. When you turn on FileVault, you will normally want to use both Secure Erase and Secure Virtual Memory to keep your data safe.

4. Make sure the Use Secure Erase check box and the Use Secure Virtual Memory check box are selected.

5. Click the Turn On FileVault button. FileVault logs you out, encrypts the home folder, and securely erases the unencrypted version of the home folder.

FileVault then displays the login screen, from which you can log in as usual. You see a warning that your previous home folder has been securely erased (see Figure 16-5), and if you try to use Spotlight, you'll find that it's busily reindexing the new home folder. Once that's done, everything works as usual, but in the background, FileVault is encrypting and decrypting the files in your home folder as you use them.

Figure 16-5. After you log back in, FileVault tells you that it has securely erased your previous home folder.

CAUTION   When you apply FileVault to a user's Mac, make sure they know they should save all their files within their home folder so that FileVault will encrypt them.

Setting Up the Firewall on a Client Mac

To protect the client Macs, you can set up the firewall that comes with Mac OS X. Follow these steps:

1. In the Security pane in System Preferences, click the Firewall tab to display the Firewall pane (see Figure 16-6).

2. Look at the Firewall readout in the upper-left corner to see if the firewall is on or off.

3. Click the Start button to start the firewall. The Firewall readout changes to On, and the Advanced button becomes available.

4. Click the Advanced button to display the dialog box shown in Figure 16-7.

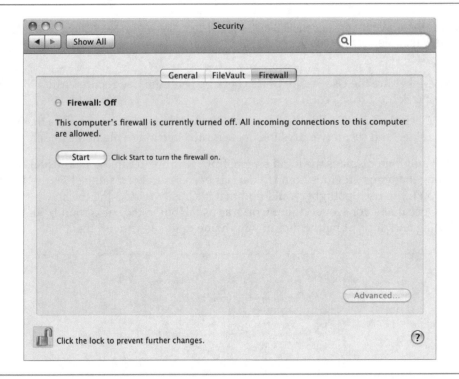

Figure 16-6.   Turn on the firewall to protect a Mac from unwanted incoming connections.

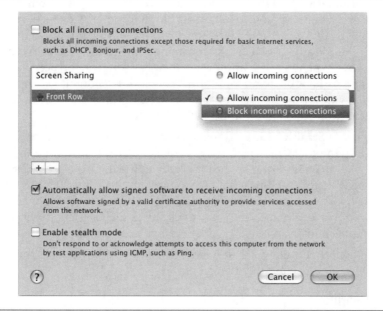

Figure 16-7. In this dialog box, choose which incoming connections the firewall should block and which it should allow.

5. Choose which services to block and which to allow:

   ■ **Block All Incoming Connections** Select this check box if you want to block all connections apart from vital network services, such as DHCP (for acquiring a network address), Bonjour (for finding other Macs and devices such as printers), and IPSec (for security). When you select this check box, Mac OS X makes the list box and the two lower check boxes unavailable.

CAUTION Blocking all incoming connections prevents you from connecting to a Mac via Screen Sharing or Remote Management.

   ■ **[List of Allowed and Blocked Connections]** If you've left the Block All Incoming Connections check box cleared, you can create a list of allowed connections and blocked connections in the list box. To add an application, click the + button, select the application in the dialog box that opens, and then click the Add button. After adding the item, click the pop-up menu and choose Allow Incoming Connections or Block Incoming Connections, as needed.

- **Automatically Allow Signed Software To Receive Incoming Connections** If you've left the Block All Incoming Connections check box cleared, select this check box if you want software signed by a valid certificate authority to accept incoming connections. This is a compromise between naming each application that may (or may not) accept connections (and perhaps blocking some applications you've forgotten to approve) and allowing any application at all to accept incoming connections. In effect, you're outsourcing the approval to the CA.

- **Enable Stealth Mode** Select this check box if you want the firewall to drop Internet Control Message Protocol (ICMP) packets straight into oblivion instead of responding civilly to them. This is a good security measure for machines that are exposed on the Internet, but for Macs on a network that is protected by a firewall, you will probably want to leave Stealth Mode off so that you can use tools such as Ping to check network connectivity.

6. When you've chosen which services the troll will allow to pass the bridge, click the OK button to close the dialog box.

Turning Off Sharing

Mac OS X includes a fantastic range of sharing capabilities that enable you to share everything from your files to your Internet connection or your screen. You can even let someone else take over your Mac fully via either Screen Sharing or Remote Management (discussed in Chapter 12).

These sharing capabilities are great when you're using the Mac at home or in a peer-to-peer network (see Chapter 20), but in other situations, they reduce the Mac's security—so you'll probably want to turn most of them off.

 NOTE The one Sharing feature you should keep running is the Remote Management feature; run this only if you use Remote Desktop to manage the Mac remotely. Use the Allow Access For settings to restrict the use of Remote Management only to yourself and other administrators who will manage this Mac.

To turn off the Sharing features, click the Sharing icon in the Internet & Wireless area of the System Preferences window, and then clear each of the check boxes in the list box on the left of the Sharing pane (see Figure 16-8).

Preventing CDs and DVDs from Running Automatically

Normally, when you insert a CD or DVD, Mac OS X automatically opens it for you. This is helpful, but your Macs will be more secure if you set them to ignore CDs or DVDs until the user actually opens them.

To do so, click the CDs & DVDs icon in the Hardware area of the System Preferences window. In the CDs & DVDs pane, choose Ignore in the When You Insert A Music CD pop-up menu, the When You Insert A Picture CD pop-up menu, and then When You Insert A Video DVD pop-up menu.

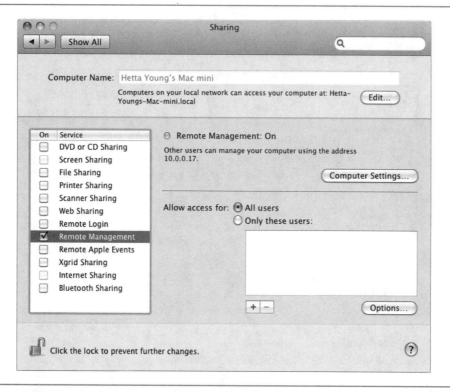

Figure 16-8.   In the Sharing pane in System Preferences, turn off every Sharing feature that you are not using.

Tightening Security in Accounts Preferences

The last place to visit in System Preferences is the Accounts pane, which you reach by clicking the Accounts icon in the System area of the System Preferences window. Click the Login Options item at the bottom of the accounts list to display the Login Options pane (see Figure 16-9), authenticate yourself if the padlock is slammed shut, and then choose settings:

- ■   **Automatic Login**   Set this pop-up menu to Off. (If the control is disabled, someone else is managing your settings.)

- ■   **Display Login Window As**   Select the Name And Password option button to force each person to provide the user name rather than picking it from the list.

- ■   **Show The Restart, Sleep, And Shut Down Buttons**   Clear this check box if you want to strip the login window down to its essentials. This prevents someone from restarting the Mac, putting it to sleep, or shutting it down without either logging in or using its power button. (Okay, or interrupting the building's power supply…)

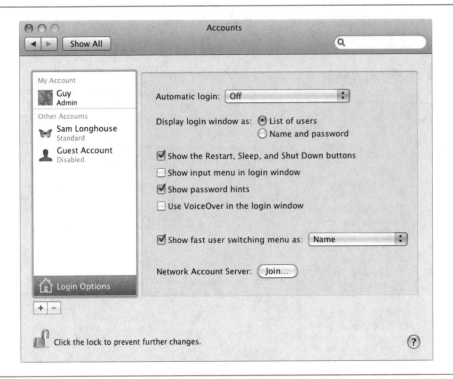

Figure 16-9. You can tighten security on the Login Options pane in Accounts preferences.

 NOTE The Show Input Menu In Login Window check box controls whether the login window includes the input menu, which lets you switch among the different keyboard layouts the Mac is set up to use (for example, U.S. and Dvorak). The Use VoiceOver In The Login Window check box controls whether users can use the VoiceOver feature (announcing aloud which controls are available) to navigate the login window. Neither poses a security threat, so select these check boxes if users will need these features.

- **Show Password Hints** Clear this check box to turn off the display of password hints, as these could help someone break into a user account.
- **Show Fast User Switching Menu As** Clear this check box to turn off Fast User Switching.

Once you've finished choosing System Preferences, quit System Preferences by pressing ⌘-Q.

Installing Antivirus Software

Even though Macs effortlessly resist most malware targeted at Windows PCs, you will normally need to run antivirus software to keep Macs safe against malevolent software designed to run on Mac OS X.

Most of the major antivirus vendors offer Mac OS X versions of their antivirus suites—for example, McAfee (www.mcafee.com) makes VirusScan for Mac, Symantec (www.symantec.com) sells Norton AntiVirus for Mac, and Kaspersky (www.kaspersky.com) creates Kaspersky Anti-Virus for Mac. There are also Mac-specific antivirus vendors, such as Intego (www.intego.com), which provides VirusBarrier X6.

So you have a good choice—but if you prefer not to pay, that's an option too. ClamXav (www.clamxav.com) is a free virus checker for Mac OS X that's more limited than the full antivirus suites, but can provide enough protection for managed Macs that aren't allowed to rampage around the seedier quarters of the Internet.

Securing Web Browsers

Web browsers are responsible for a multitude of sins, so it's worth taking a few moments to restrict the damage that your browser can do.

NOTE This section assumes you're dealing with Safari, as that's the browser Apple includes with Mac OS X. If you've sprung for an alternative browser, such as Firefox or Camino, you'll need to dig out similar settings in it.

To protect Safari, you need to set suitable preferences. Open the Preferences window by pressing ⌘- (⌘ and the COMMA key), or by choosing Safari | Preferences. You can then choose settings as discussed in the following subsections.

Choosing General Preferences for Safari

In the General pane (see Figure 16-10), you'll normally want to set the Home Page to somewhere useful or educational rather than the hottest sports-betting site. But the key setting here is the Open "Safe" Files After Downloading check box, which you should make sure is clear. "Safe" is in double quotation marks because the file types that this option automatically opens or mounts (in the case of disk images) are only notionally safe rather than practically safe.

Choosing AutoFill Preferences for Safari

In the AutoFill pane (see Figure 16-11), you'll normally want to clear all three check boxes. Autofilling data can be helpful for users who need to deal with many web forms, but allowing Safari to autofill sensitive data raises the risk of entering it in a form unintentionally.

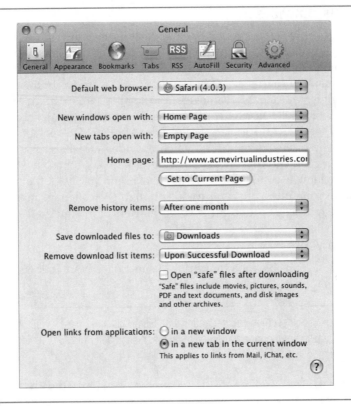

Figure 16-10. In the General pane of Safari preferences, clear the Open "Safe" Files After Downloading check box.

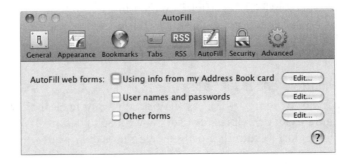

Figure 16-11. While Autofilling data in web forms can save time and effort, it increases the possibility that Safari will provide data where it shouldn't.

Choosing Security Preferences for Safari

The Security pane of Safari's preferences (see Figure 16-12) is where you have the most choices to make. These are the options in the Security pane:

- **Warn When Visiting A Fraudulent Website**   Select this check box to turn on Safari's anti-phishing features—usually a good idea.

- **Enable Plug-Ins**   Normally, you'll want to select this check box to enable Safari to play multimedia contents such as audio and video.

- **Enable Java**   Select this check box if you want Safari to execute Java code on website. Some website require Java code for extra features, so you may lose functionality by clearing this check box—but malicious Java code can threaten your Mac's security.

- **Enable JavaScript**   Select this check box to allow Safari to execute scripts in the JavaScript web-programming language. Some sites require these scripts to provide full functionality, so clearing this check box may prevent certain features from working.

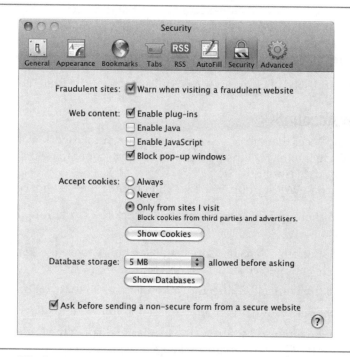

Figure 16-12.   The Security pane in Safari preferences includes a handful of important security settings.

■ **Block Pop-Up Windows**   Select this check box to make Safari block pop-up windows from websites. Blocking pop-ups is usually a good idea, as pop-up windows tend to be either advertising or attempts to sabotage your browser. If you need to permit pop-ups temporarily for a particular website, you can choose Safari | Block Pop-Up Windows to remove the check mark from this menu item; give the same command again when you want to reinstate the blocking.

 NOTE   Blocking pop-up windows is an area where some other browsers score over Safari. For example, Firefox lets you permit some sites to display pop-up windows while suppressing pop-ups from all other sites. This is much better than having to turn blocking off when you need to see pop-ups consistently for a site.

■ **Accept Cookies**   For security, select the Only From Sites I Visit option button rather than the Always option button (which also accepts cookies from third-party sites, one affiliated with sites you visit). Selecting the Never option button provides tighter security, but it prevents many websites from working correctly, so it's not usually a practical choice.

■ **Ask Before Sending A Non-Secure Form From A Secure Website**   Select this check box to make Safari warn you when a secure website you've accessed tries to send a data form in a non-secure way. This warning is often helpful, but many reputable sites (such as Google's Gmail) trigger the warning.

After you've finished choosing settings for Safari, close the Preferences dialog box.

Restricting User Accounts

For the users and Macs that are directly connected to your network, you can use Workgroup Manager to restrict the preferences for an account to help keep the user or the computer out of trouble.

Start by launching Workgroup Manager and opening the Preferences pane like this:

1. Open Workgroup Manager. For example, click the Workgroup Manager icon in the dock.

2. In the Workgroup Manager Connect dialog box, choose the server you want to connect to, and then click the Connect button.

3. Authenticate yourself as directory administrator so that you can make changes.

4. Select the user account or computer account you want to affect.

5. Click the Preferences button on the toolbar to display the Preferences pane. Normally, the Overview pane will appear here (see Figure 16-13), but if the Details pane has elbowed its way to the front, click the Overview tab to fix things.

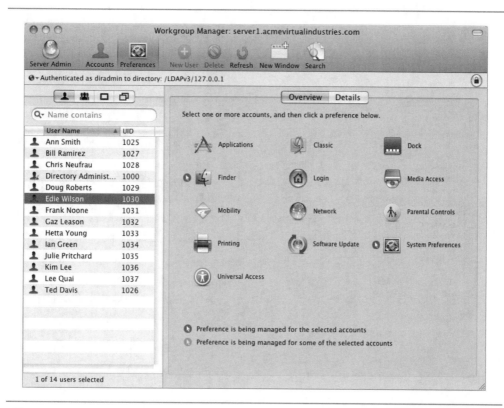

Figure 16-13.   From the Overview pane in Preferences in Workgroup Manager, you can restrict what users can do with their Macs.

From here, you can make a vast number of changes by clicking the appropriate icon in the Overview pane and working with the pane or panes that you reach. The following subsections discuss the three categories of settings that tend to be most immediately helpful for keeping users out of trouble.

Restricting the Finder

Start by clicking the Finder icon in the Overview pane, and then clicking the Commands tab in the tab bar to display the Commands pane (see Figure 16-14). Select the Always option button in the Manage bar, and you can then choose whether to include commands such as Connect To Server, Restart, and Shut Down in the user interface. Clear the check box for each command you want to remove, click the Apply Now button to apply the change, and then click the Done button to return to the Overview pane.

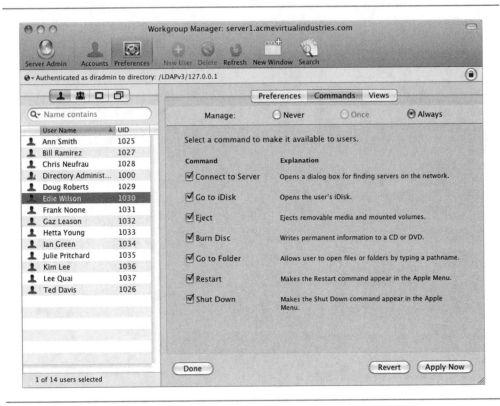

Figure 16-14. In the Commands pane within Finder preferences, you can remove commands that you do not want the user to use.

Restricting Media Access

Next, click the Media Access icon in the Overview pane, and then click the Disc Media tab to display the Disc Media pane (see Figure 16-15). Here, you can clear the Allow check box to prevent the user from using particular media (such as DVDs) or select the Require Authentication check box to require them to get an administrator's approval before using a certain type of media. You can also select the Eject All Removable Media At Logout check box if you want the Mac to do its best toaster impression when the user logs out.

So far, so controlling—but you're not done yet. Click the Other Media tab to display the Other Media pane (see Figure 16-16), select the Always option button in the Manage bar, and then choose which internal and external disks the user may use, whether they need to bring attention to themselves by seeking authentication, and whether any media is read only.

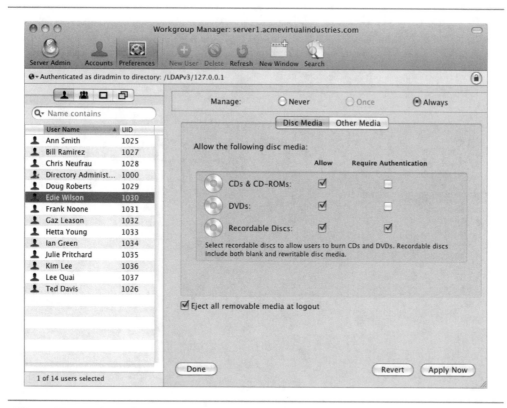

Figure 16-15. In the Disc Media pane within Media Access preferences, you can choose which discs the user may use with or without authentication.

Again, click the Apply Now button to apply the change, and then click the Done button to return to the Overview pane.

Restricting System Preferences

System Preferences can be a minefield, as the same window gives access to everything from changing the desktop background (almost always harmless, although questions of taste do arise) to creating new user accounts (often the opposite). Mac OS X helps you by locking the more sensitive preferences, but you'll probably also want to use Workgroup Manager to remove categories of preferences that you don't want the user messing with.

So click the System Preferences icon in the Overview pane in Preferences, select the Always option button in the Manage bar of the System Preferences pane (see Figure 16-17), and then clear the check box for each item that you want to suppress.

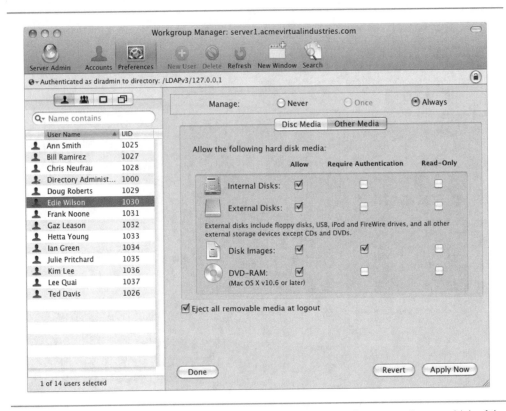

Figure 16-16. In the Other Media pane within Media Access preferences, choose which of the internal and external disks the user may use, whether they must authenticate, and whether the disks are read only.

You can take the nuclear option by clicking the Show None button, but in most cases you'll do better to weed out the harmful preferences while leaving the harmless but useful ones for the user. For example, making the Appearance, Desktop & Screen Saver (subject to an agreed standard of taste), Dock, Exposé & Spaces, and Spotlight preferences available gives the user decent control over the user interface without threatening the stability of the corporate boat. (If the user uses non-standard input, include Language & Text preferences as well.)

Once more, click the Apply Now button to apply the changes, and then click the Done button to return to the Overview pane.

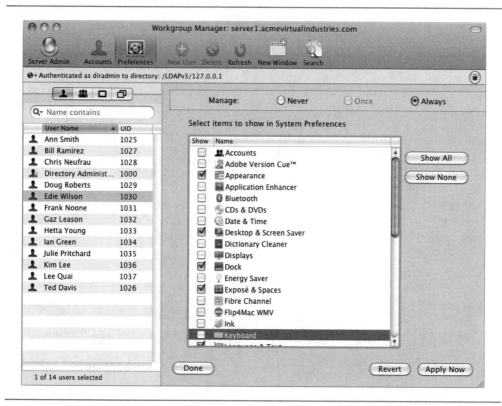

Figure 16-17.   In the System Preferences pane, choose which items to strip out of the user's System Preferences window.

Keeping Your Company's iPhones and iPod Touches Safe

If your company provides some of its workers with iPhones and iPod touches to encourage them to think out of the box and play inside it, it's vital that you lock the devices down as far as possible.

iPhones and iPod touches are especially vulnerable because not only do people tend to carry them everywhere (fair enough—that's the point of the devices), but they're small enough for the light-fingered to slip in their pocket or secrete about their person (also part of the point). They can also carry a huge amount of data, can access e-mail and shared information, and even connect remotely on the company's network via VPN. So if someone lifts one of your company's iPhones or iPod touches, you need to neutralize it as soon as possible.

Your main line of defense for the iPhone or iPod touch is the passcode lock that prevents anyone from using the device without tapping in the correct passcode. You can set the passcode lock either via a configuration policy (as discussed in Chapter 8) or manually through the Set Passcode screen (shown on the left in Figure 16-18), which you access by choosing Settings | General | Passcode Lock.

On the Passcode Lock screen (shown on the right in Figure 16-18), which appears after you have set the passcode and confirmed it, set the Require Passcode setting to Immediately to make sure the lock is applied as soon as the user switches the device off (putting it to sleep). If this is too restrictive, choose one of the shortest periods of time: After 1 Minute or After 5 Minutes. The longer periods (After 15 Minutes, After 1 Hour, and After 4 Hours) render the passcode lock more or less useless if the device is lost or stolen.

To make the locking effective, you must also set the Auto-Lock setting to a short time, such as 1 Minute or 2 Minutes rather than 5 Minutes or Never. This reduces the chance of the iPhone or iPod touch being stolen while unlocked through simply being on.

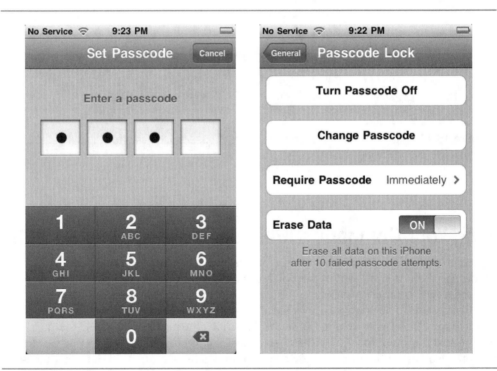

Figure 16-18. On the Set Passcode screen (left), set the passcode to protect the iPhone or iPod touch against unauthorized access. On the Passcode Lock screen (right), require the passcode immediately and move the Erase Data switch to On.

Anyone determined enough to get at your data (or cunning enough to enlist a child) can simply keep whaling on the passcode until they get the right one, so you must also move the Erase Data switch to the On position to make the device erase all its data after 10 failed attempts to enter the passcode. When you do this, the device pops up a warning panel at the bottom of the screen, and you must touch the Enable button to go ahead with the setting.

Securing Your Network

Securing your network's Macs and handheld devices is a good start, but you'll also need to secure your network if you haven't already done so. In this section, we'll go over the security measures you should put in place for a wireless network and for a wired network. After that, we'll look at how to secure your network's Internet connection, which is likely to be its weakest link.

Securing a Wireless Network

If you've set up a wireless network, as discussed in Chapter 2, you should already have taken the first big step toward securing it—using Wi-Fi Protected Access (WPA) to prevent unauthorized people from breaking users' passwords and logging in themselves.

You can secure the wireless network further by limiting the MAC addresses that can join it, and by running a VPN across it.

Limiting Your Wireless Network to Approved MAC Addresses

To help make sure that no unauthorized computer can access the wireless network, you can set the wireless access point to accept connections only from approved MAC addresses, the addresses of the wireless network cards in the computers. How you do this depends on the wireless access point you're using, but here's what to do on an AirPort Extreme:

1. Open AirPort Utility. For example, click the Spotlight icon at the right end of the menu bar, type **airp**, and then click the appropriate hit.

2. If you have multiple AirPorts or Time Capsules, click the one you want to affect.

3. Click the Manual Setup button to get your greasy mitts on the vital controls.

4. Click the AirPort button in the toolbar if it's not already clicked.

5. Click the Access tab in the tab bar to display the Access pane (shown in Figure 16-19 with a list underway).

6. In the Mac Address Access Control pop-up menu, choose Timed Access.

 NOTE   You can also control MAC access through RADIUS. We won't investigate this option here.

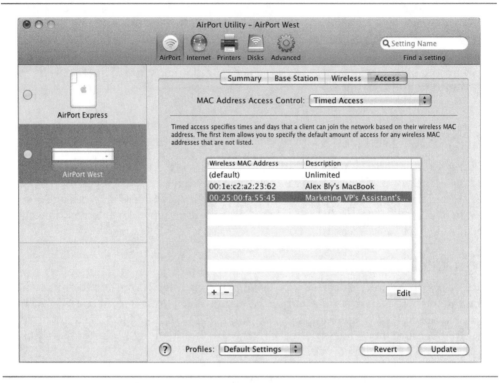

Figure 16-19. To restrict an AirPort to accepting connections from only approved MAC addresses, use the Access pane in AirPort Utility.

7. Create the list of addresses in the list box like this:

a. Click the + button to display the Timed Access Control Setup Assistant dialog box (see Figure 16-20).

b. Type the MAC address of the permitted computer in the MAC Address text box. If you're running AirPort Utility on the computer you're adding, click the This Computer button to pop the computer's address in the text box.

TIP You can just hammer in the MAC address's hex characters without bothering about the colons—Mac OS X inserts them for you automatically after each pair of characters.

c. In the Description text box, type the name by which you will identify the computer—for example, Alex Bly's MacBook.

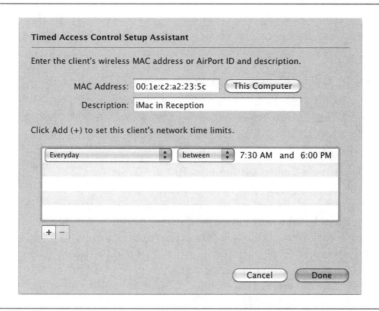

Figure 16-20.   Use the Timed Access Control Setup Assistant dialog box to decree which MAC address can connect to the wireless network when.

    d.   In the list box that occupies most of the dialog box, set up the times when the computer with this MAC address may and may not connect to the network. In the first pop-up menu, choose the day: Everyday, Mondays, Tuesdays, Wednesdays, Thursdays, Fridays, Saturdays, Sundays, Weekdays, or Weekends, if you're feeling generous; choose No Access if you're feeling grumpy. In the second pop-up menu, choose All Day if you're feeling free and easy, or Between if you want to set start and end times with the controls that pop up.

    e.   If you need to add another set of time restrictions, click the + button below the list box, and then repeat the previous step.

    f.   Click the Done button when you've finished setting up the MAC straitjacket. AirPort Utility adds the details to the list in the Access pane.

  8. When you've finished creating the list of approved MAC addresses, click the Update button, and then click the Continue button in the dialog box that AirPort Utility displays.

Protecting Your Wireless Network with a Virtual Private Network

If you need tighter security on your wireless network, set up a virtual private network (VPN) to carry the traffic across it. The VPN encrypts the data, which means that anyone who uses a wireless sniffer to capture the data on your network will get gobbledygook rather than useful data. See Chapter 15 for instructions on setting up a VPN.

NOTE One security suggestion you'll often see for wireless networks is to create a closed network by preventing the access point from broadcasting the network's SSID (the service set identifier to those of the wireless persuasion, or the network's name to mere mortals). Turning off SSID broadcasts doesn't give you much security, as anybody who points a wireless sniffer at your building will see the network's packets flying through the coffee fumes and the curses, and will be able to detect the network's name. What turning off SSID broadcasts will do is deter casual freeloaders looking for a wireless network to glom onto. If they can't see your network, they'll try someone else's.

Securing a Wired Network

Unlike a wireless network, a wired network doesn't extend invisibly in all directions past the boundaries of the building that houses it—so in most cases physical security is less of an issue than with wireless networks. Even so, you'll want to make sure that nobody plugs you're your wired network who shouldn't, and that nobody gets creative by connecting a switch or a wireless access point to an Ethernet port.

Beyond that, security on a normal wired network usually involves making sure bad traffic doesn't spread from one computer to another and that nothing evil comes in across the Internet connection (as discussed in a moment) or any other network to which your network is connected.

If the traffic on your wired network is especially sensitive, you can secure it by running a VPN on the network.

Securing Your Internet Connection with a Firewall

The foolproof way to protect your network from Internet threats is not to connect the network to the Internet, but sadly this is a viable option for only the most specialized networks these days. If you're not part of a military network that daren't speak its name, or a government agency whose name others daren't speak, it's pretty much certain that you'll need to provide full-on Internet connectivity for your network's users.

To secure your Internet connection, you use one or more firewalls. Depending on your network setup, the firewall may be on any of four devices:

- **Internet router** Most Internet routers include a firewall that you configure either using a web browser or a custom utility supplied by the manufacturer.

- **Separate firewall** To provide extra protection, you can use a separate hardware firewall. To configure the firewall, you'll use either a web-based interface or a custom utility.

- **Wireless access point** Many wireless access points include built-in firewalls. For example, the AirPort Extreme includes automatic firewall capabilities that are turned on by default.

- **Your server** If your server is acting as the Internet gateway for your network, you can run the Mac OS X firewall on the server to protect the network from Internet threats.

If you are using the firewall on your server to protect the network, set it up like this:

1. Open Server Preferences. For example, click the Server Preferences icon in the Dock.

2. In the System area of the Server Preferences window, click the Security icon to display the Security pane (shown in Figure 16-21 with some settings chosen).

3. If the master switch is off, move it to the On position to turn the firewall on.

4. In the Expose These Services On My Firewall list box, list the services you want to allow to pass through the firewall. To add a service, click the + button, choose the service in the Add Service pop-up menu in the resulting dialog box, and then click the Add button. To remove a service, click it in the list box, and then click the – button.

5. When you've finished setting up the firewall, quit System Preferences. For example, press ⌘-Q.

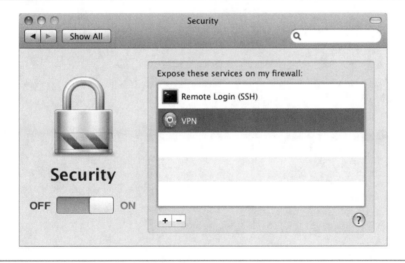

Figure 16-21.   Use the Security pane in System Preferences to set up the Mac OS X Server firewall and control which services can pass through it.

CHAPTER 17 | Keep Your Client Macs Up to Date

To keep Mac OS X and your Apple applications up to date on your client Macs, you'll need to run Software Update. As you'll know from using it on your server (if not elsewhere), Software Update can automatically check for and download updates, then shepherd the user through the process of installing them.

Choosing Where to Get Software Updates

Your Macs can get their software updates from either of two sources:

- **Download from Apple's servers**   As you saw in Chapter 4, your server can download the available updates from Apple's servers and apply them to itself. This works well not only for your main server, but also for any Macs that must operate on their own—for example, MacBooks that spend most of their time disconnected from the corporate network. These Macs can download the updates across the Internet connection, just as if they were standalone Macs in, say, a home setting.

- **Download from one of your servers**   You can set up your server, or one of your servers, to provide updates to the Macs on the network. This approach has two main advantages: First, it saves huge amounts of bandwidth on your Internet connection, as each update needs to be downloaded only once (to the server) rather than once to each Mac that needs it. Second, it enables the Macs on your network to get the updates far more quickly across the network than if they had to download them. In other words, everyone wins—after you've done some careful setup.

On the basis that it's best to have the computers do as much of your work as possible, we'll look first at the automatic option.

Setting Your Server to Provide Software Updates

To set up your server to provide Software Updates, follow these steps:

1. Open Server Admin. For example, click the Server Admin icon on the Dock.
2. Connect to the server by double-clicking it in the Servers list. Authenticate yourself if necessary.
3. Click the disclosure triangle to expand the list of services.
4. If the Software Update service does not appear in the list of services, follow these steps to turn it on:
   a. Click the Settings button on the toolbar to display the Settings pane.
   b. Click the Services tab to display the Services pane.

    c. In the Select The Services To Configure On This Server list box, select the Software Update check box.

    d. Click the Save button. The Software Update service appears in the list of services.

5. In the list of services, double-click Software Update.

6. Click the Settings button on the toolbar to display the Settings pane (see Figure 17-1).

7. If you want to limit the amount of bandwidth clients can consume, select the Limit User Bandwidth To check box, type the value in the text box, and then choose KB/second or MB/second in the pop-up menu.

8. In the Store Updates In text box, enter the folder in which to store the updates. The default folder, /var/db/swupd/ is fine unless your system volume is short of space—in which case, click the Choose button, use the Choose A Folder Where You Would Like To Store Software Updates dialog box to pick the folder, and then click the Choose button.

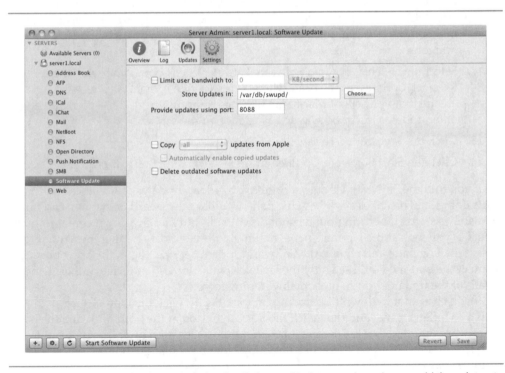

Figure 17-1.   In the Settings pane for the Software Update service, choose which updates to copy and whether to limit the user bandwidth.

CAUTION Software Updates can take up many gigabytes on your server. Make sure the volume you choose has plenty of free space.

9. In the Provide Updates Using Port text box, enter the port to use. Stick with the default port, 8088, unless you actively prefer a different vintage.

10. If you want your Software Update server to automatically copy updates from Apple's Software Update servers, select the Copy Updates From Apple check box. In the pop-up menu, choose All or All New, as appropriate.

NOTE The alternative to having your server copy all (or all new) updates from Apple's servers is to choose the updates manually. Having the server get all the updates automatically is usually easiest, provided that you have the bandwidth to download the updates without discomfort and your server has space to store them. But if your network's Macs have a largely standardized configuration, you can save space by picking only the updates you actually need.

11. If you choose to download updates automatically, you can select the Automatically Enable Copied Updates check box if you want the server to make the updates available automatically to your Mac clients. The alternative is to enable updates manually—for example, after vetting them for stability and suspect political opinions.

12. Select the Delete Outdated Software Updates check box if you want the server to knock updates on the head when their shelf life is over. As long as you ensure that your client Macs grab updates promptly from the server, deleting older updates is a good way to save space on the server.

13. Click the Save button to save the changes.

14. Click the Start Software Update button to start using Software Update.

If you told the Software Update service to download updates automatically, it now starts doing so. This takes a while, so be patient. What's awkward is that you can't immediately see that it's sorting out a list of downloads and hauling down copies of them: In fact, if you look at the Updates pane, nothing will seem to be happening. And if you look at the Log pane and choose the Software Update Service Log in the View pop-up menu at the bottom, you'll see only the laconic "Sync Started" message, rather than details of the updates you're presumably hoping to get.

If you chose not to download updates automatically, click the Updates tab to display the Updates pane, and then click the Refresh button at the bottom. When the list of software updates appears (again, it takes a while), select the updates you want to grab (see Figure 17-2), and then click the Copy Now button at the bottom of the Server Admin window.

NOTE To choose which version of a software update the server offers to clients, click the Choose Version button, choose the version in the resulting dialog box, and then click the Save button.

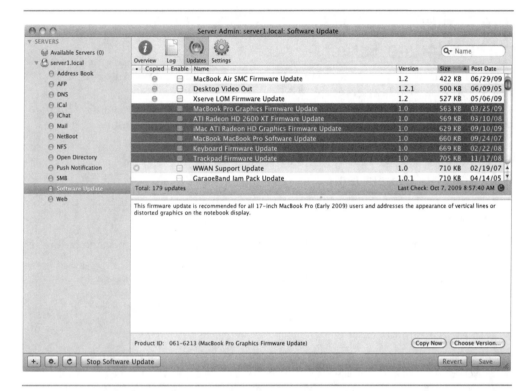

Figure 17-2.   If you've chosen to manage Software Updates manually, select the items you want to download, and then click the Copy Now button.

When you've downloaded an update, the Copied column shows a blue button next to it. You can then select the Enable check box to make the update available to the Macs on your network.

NOTE   You can set up multiple servers to provide software updates, each to different clients. But at this writing, you can't set your Software Update servers to communicate with each other—for example, sharing files. Each Software Update server needs to download its own copies of each update file, which is a good reason for keeping down the number of Software Update servers your network uses.

Setting a Client Mac to Download Updates from Your Update Server

Now you need to tell your Macs to use your Software Update server rather than Apple's Software Update servers.

For managed client computers, you do this using Workgroup Manager. For unmanaged client computers, you need to use the defaults command in Terminal.

Setting a Managed Client Mac to Download Updates from Your Update Server

To set a managed client Mac to download updates from your Software Update server, follow these steps:

1. Open Workgroup Manager. For example, click the Workgroup Manager button on the Dock.

2. Connect to the server, authenticating yourself as needed.

3. Click the Computers button to display the Computers pane, or click the Computer Groups button to display the Computer Groups pane, on the left of Workgroup Manager.

 NOTE You can also apply the Software Update settings to a user account or a group of user accounts. Usually, though, it's more effective to apply them to a computer or group of computers.

4. In the left pane, click the computer or computer group you want to affect.

5. Click the Preferences button to display the Preferences pane for the computer or group.

6. If the Overview pane is not already displayed, click the Overview tab to display it.

7. Click the Software Update icon to display the Software Update pane (shown in Figure 17-3 with settings chosen).

8. In the Manage box at the top, select the Always option button.

9. In the Software Update Server To Use text box, type the address of your server that is providing Software Updates. Put the address in this format:

   `http://server:port/index.sucatalog`

10. Click the Apply Now button to apply the change.

11. Click the Done button to finish making changes to the Software Update service.

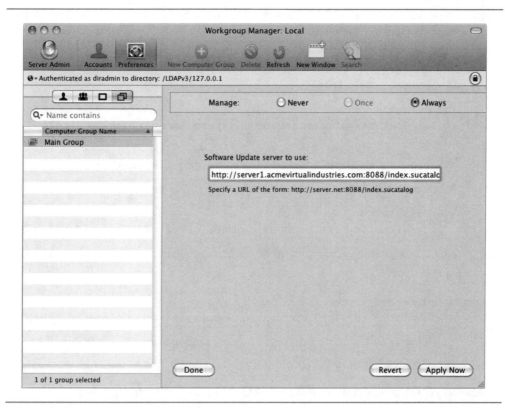

Figure 17-3.   Use the Software Update settings in Workgroup Manager to set a Mac to use your Software Update server.

Controlling Where an Unmanaged Client Mac Gets Its Updates

To control where an unmanaged client Mac gets its updates, you use Terminal on the client. You'll need to be working on the client—either at the keyboard or through remote access, such as Remote Login, Remote Desktop, or Screen Sharing—not through management software.

Setting an Unmanaged Client Mac to Download Updates from Your Update Server

To set an unmanaged client Mac to download updates from your Software Update server, follow these steps:

1. Open Terminal. For example, click the Desktop, choose Go | Utilities, and then double-click Terminal in the Utilities folder.

2. Type the appropriate **defaults write** command for the version of Mac OS X the client is running, replacing the placeholder *yourdomain* with your domain name (for example, acmevirtualindustries.com). Each of these is a single command, even though the book shows them wrapped onto a second line:

    ■ **Snow Leopard (10.6)**

    ```
    defaults write ¬
        /Library/Preferences/com.apple.SoftwareUpdate CatalogURL

    http://su.yourdomain:8088/¬
        index-leopard-snowleopard.merged-1.sucatalog
    ```

    ■ **Leopard (10.5)**

    ```
    defaults write ¬
        /Library/Preferences/com.apple.SoftwareUpdate CatalogURL

    http://su.yourdomain:8088/index-leopard.merged-1.sucatalog
    ```

    ■ **Tiger (10.4)**

    ```
    defaults write ¬
        /Library/Preferences/com.apple.SoftwareUpdate CatalogURL

    http://su.yourdomain:8088/index.sucatalog
    ```

3. Press RETURN to apply the command.

Checking Where an Unmanaged Client Is Getting Its Software Updates

To check where an unmanaged client is getting its software updates, follow these steps:

1. Open Terminal. For example, click the Desktop, choose Go | Utilities, and then double-click Terminal in the Utilities folder.

2. Type a defaults read command for the CatalogURL information in the com.apple.SoftwareUpdate preferences:

    ```
    defaults read /Library/Preferences/com.apple.SoftwareUpdate ¬
    CatalogURL
    ```

3. Press RETURN to display the server address.

Returning an Unmanaged Client to the Apple Software Update Server

To make an unmanaged client use the Apple Software Update server again instead of your Software Update server, use Terminal to delete the CatalogURL information in the com.apple.SoftwareUpdate preferences. Follow these steps:

1. Open Terminal. For example, click the Desktop, choose Go | Utilities, and then double-click Terminal in the Utilities folder.

2. Type a defaults delete command for the CatalogURL information in the com.apple.SoftwareUpdate preferences:

```
defaults delete /Library/Preferences/com.apple.SoftwareUpdate ¬
CatalogURL
```

3. Press RETURN to run the command.

Configuring Software Update to Check for Updates

To configure Software Update to check for updates, follow these steps:

1. Choose Apple | System Preferences to open the System Preferences window.

2. In the System category, click the Software Update icon to open the Software Update pane.

3. If the Scheduled Check tab isn't selected, click it now to bring the Scheduled Check pane to the front (see Figure 17-4).

4. For most client Macs, you'll want to select the Check For Updates check box, and then choose either Weekly or Daily in the pop-up menu. Daily updates keep your client Macs safest, but put the greatest strain on your server or Internet connection, and frequent prompts to apply updates may distract users. Monthly updates, while convenient for users, tend to leave the clients without the benefit of the latest fixes and updates for too long.

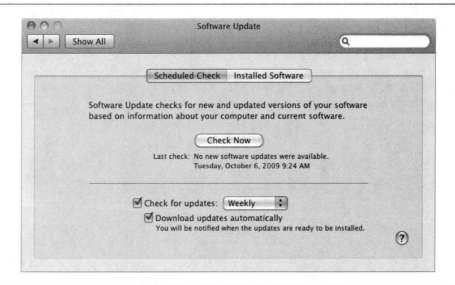

Figure 17-4. Normally it's a good idea to set Software Update to check for updates either daily or weekly, and to download the available updates automatically.

5. If you select the Check For Updates check box, select the Download Updates Automatically check box if you want the client to download the update files automatically from the server. Normally, this is most convenient for the users, as the updates are ready to roll when Software Update prompts the user to install them. But if your server is the one providing the updates, and your network is fast, you can clear the Download Updates Automatically check box and have the client pull the files across from the server only when they are needed.

6. When you've made your choices, press ⌘-Q or choose System Preferences | Quit System Preferences to quit System Preferences.

Installing the Updates

When you've set Software Update to check automatically for updates, it prompts you to install any it has found. If you prefer to check manually, choose Apple | Software Update to launch Software Update and make it check for updates.

From here, you can simply click the Install And Relaunch button to install the updates and restart the Mac, or the Install button to install the updates if none of them requires the Mac to be restarted afterward.

NOTE   If one or more updates require the Mac to be restarted, Software Update first installs those updates that do not require a restart. Software Update then prompts you to restart the Mac, logs you out, and then installs the updates.

Normally, though, you'll want to see what your Mac is getting. To do so, click the Show Details button. The Software Update dialog box expands to show the available updates.

Clear the check box for any update you do not want to install, and then click the Install Items button (its name includes the number of items—for example, Install 5 Items). If Mac OS X prompts you to restart your Mac to complete the installation, do so as soon as is convenient.

CHAPTER 18 | Back Up and Restore Data

W hile your company's knowledge workers focus on creating data, manipulating it, and squeezing value out of it, you as the administrator must focus on keeping the data safe for them. This means backing up all the data that's valuable in case something goes wrong, and restoring the data from backup when something *does* go wrong.

Backup and restore can be a game of high stakes, and to save you from tripping up and getting impaled on them, Mac OS X Server provides a powerful feature called Time Machine for backing up data automatically and restoring it easily. You just have to make sure Time Machine is turned on and pointing in the right direction so that you're in a good position to restore that valuable data after Humpty Dumpty discovers gravity.

To that end, in this chapter you'll learn how Time Machine works. After that, I'll show you how to set up your backup disk on the server and point the clients to it, and then point the server to its own backup disk. We'll then look at how to recover data from a Time Machine backup the easy way (on either a client or a server), followed by a glance at the hard way of recovering the server from a Time Machine backup.

Understanding How Time Machine Backups Work

Time Machine automatically backs up the data from a Mac (client or server) to a designated drive so that, when push comes to shove, you can pop back to the past, grab the files you need to recover, and then forward again to the future.

Understanding How Incremental Backups Work

A backup is essentially a copy of the files you want to keep safe. You can create a quick backup of valuable files by simply using a regular Copy command to copy them to another location—for example, to a USB flash drive that you carry with you. This could hardly be easier, either conceptually or practically.

The problem with backing up files by simply copying them is the amount of space the backups take (because you get every file every time) and the length of time the process of making the copies takes (likewise). Time Machine streamlines the backup process by automatically copying only the files needed to protect those files you've chosen to back up. So when a file has not changed since the last backup, Time Machine saves disk space (and time) by not copying it again.

This kind of backup is called an *incremental* backup. Here are the details of how Time Machine implements incremental backups:

- **First backup: Full backup**   After you turn Time Machine on, it makes a full backup of all the files you've chosen to back up. (You can exclude particular drives and folders from the backup. We'll get to this later in the chapter.) This takes a while.

- **Hourly backups**   After that first backup, Time Machine makes hourly backups of files that have changed since the last backup. On a normal system, most files won't have changed, so the hourly backup goes pretty quickly.

- **Daily backups**   Each day, Time Machine makes an incremental daily backup—in effect, consolidating the day's hourly backups into a daily backup. Time Machine keeps a month's worth of daily backups.

- **Weekly backups**   Once you get further than a month in the past, it becomes less likely that you will need the daily backups. So Time Machine keeps weekly incremental backups after a month.

Even incremental backups consume disk space rapidly, so when your backup disk starts running out of space, Time Machine automatically deletes the oldest backups. This first-in, first-out culling makes perfect sense, as it's normally the more recent copies of files that you'll want to restore when trouble strikes.

Understanding How You Set Up Time Machine

Here's how you set up Time Machine to back up your clients and your server:

- **Choose a Time Machine drive on the server**   First, you tell Time Machine on the server which drive to use as a backup location for networked users.

- **Point the client Macs toward the Time Machine drive on the server**   Second, you configure Time Machine on the clients to back up data to the Time Machine drive on the server. So if the clients lose data, you will be able to restore it from the Time Machine backups on the server.

- **Set Time Machine to back up the server itself**   So far, you've consolidated your point of failure on the server, which leaves you asking the classic question, "Who guards the guards?" To back up your server and the backups on it, you set up Time Machine on the server to back up the data from the server to an external drive. So if the server loses data (including the client data it has been saving), you can restore that data to the server.

 NOTE   You may also need to set up individual backup solutions for users who rarely connect to the network—for example, users who work mainly at home. For such users, you can set up Time Machine using an external drive connected to the Mac, as if the Mac were a standalone one. You set up the Mac with its external drive the same way as you set up the server with its external backup drive, as described later in this chapter.

Setting Up Time Machine in Server Preferences

If you chose a Time Machine drive on the Client Backup screen during setup, Time Machine should be up and humming by now. If not, use Server Preferences to set up Time Machine now. Follow these steps:

1. Open Server Preferences. For example, click the Server Preferences icon in the dock.

Figure 18-1. The Time Machine pane in Server Preferences looks like this when Time Machine is not yet turned on.

2. In the System area, click the Time Machine icon to display the Time Machine pane (see Figure 18-1).

3. Click the Select Backup Disk button to display the Choose Destination Volume For Client Time Machine Backups dialog box (see Figure 18-2).

4. Click the disk you want to use.

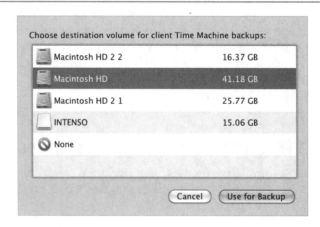

Figure 18-2. Choose the disk on which to store the Time Machine backups for your client Macs.

Figure 18-3.   The Time Machine pane adds the disk you chose and turns on the master switch.

5. Click the Use For Backup button. Server Preferences closes the dialog box, displays the disk in the Time Machine pane, and slides the Time Machine master switch from Off to On (see Figure 18-3).

6. To choose which users can back up using Time Machine, follow these steps:

    a. Click the arrow button to the right of Configure User Access to display the Users pane.

 NOTE   To open the folder that Time Machine stores the backups in, on the drive that you chose, click the lower arrow button in the Time Machine pane.

    b. Click the Services button to display the Services pane (see Figure 18-4).

    c. Click the user you want to affect.

    d. Select or clear the Time Machine check box, as appropriate.

    e. When you've finished choosing the users, click the Back button in the upper-left corner corner of the Server Preferences window if you want to return to the Time Machine pane, or simply press ⌘-Q if you're ready to quit Server Preferences.

Figure 18-4. Use the Services pane in Server Preferences to control whether a user may back up to the server using Time Machine.

Moving Time Machine Backups to Another Disk

Backups tend to take up lots of space, and unless your backup disk is as large and empty as North Dakota, you may find it filling up. You can clear older items off it, or let Time Machine automatically quietly knock the oldest backups on the head and drop them overboard, but given the inevitable march of terabytes, sooner or later you'll probably want to replace the backup disk with another disk instead.

To switch to another backup disk, all you need to do is open the Time Machine pane in Server Preferences and use the Choose Destination Volume For Client Time Machine Backups dialog box to tell Time Machine which disk to use, just as you did when setting up Time Machine at first.

So far, so easy—but there's a complication: When you switch to another disk, Time Machine doesn't copy your old backups to the new disk. It just leaves them where they were.

This means two things:

■ First, when users run their next backup, Time Machine will be making a full backup rather than an incremental backup. The backup will take that much longer—so you should warn them ahead of time.

> ■ Second, if you want to keep some of those backups, you may want to
> copy them from the old disk to somewhere safe.
>
> You can handle both these issues easily enough—but you'll probably want to
> postpone them for as long as possible. So there's all the more reason to make sure
> that your backup disk is large enough to begin with.

Setting Time Machine to Back Up a Client's Data

Now that you've set up the Time Machine disk on the server and chosen which user
accounts to enable, you need to point the client Macs to use the Time Machine disk as
their backup location.

Automatically Setting Time Machine to Back Up a Client's Data

When a user who does not yet have Time Machine set up logs in to the network, Mac
OS X automatically prompts them to use the Time Machine disk you've designated
as their backup location. If the user accepts the invitation (and you should encourage
them to do so), Mac OS X sets up Time Machine to use that disk and starts creating
backups.

Manually Setting Time Machine to Back Up a Client's Data

If a user is unable to set up Time Machine using the automated process, you can set up
Time Machine manually by using System Preferences. To do so, use the same technique
described for setting up Time Machine to back up the server in the section "Setting the
Server to Back Up with Time Machine," later in this chapter.

Preventing Users from Changing Time Machine Settings

When Time Machine is set up, you may want to prevent users from turning it off or
pointing it to another drive. You can head them off at the pass by removing Time
Machine from System Preferences as described here.

To remove Time Machine from System Preferences, follow these steps:

1. Open Workgroup Manager. For example, click the Workgroup Manager icon in
   the dock.

2. In the Workgroup Manager Connect dialog box, enter the server's address,
   your user name and password, and then click the Connect button.

3. Click the lock icon at the right end of the authentication bar to open the
   Authenticate To Directory dialog box, type your administrator name and
   password, and then click the Authenticate button.

4. Click the user you want to affect.

5. Click the Preferences button to display the Preferences pane.

6. Click the System Preferences icon to display the System Preferences screen (shown in Figure 18-5 with settings chosen).

7. In the Manage bar, select the Always option button.

8. Clear the Time Machine check box.

 NOTE   While you're here, you may want to clear the check boxes for other System Preferences that you don't want the user to mess with, such as Startup Disk.

9. Click the Apply Now button to apply the change.

10. Click the Done button to close the System Preferences pane.

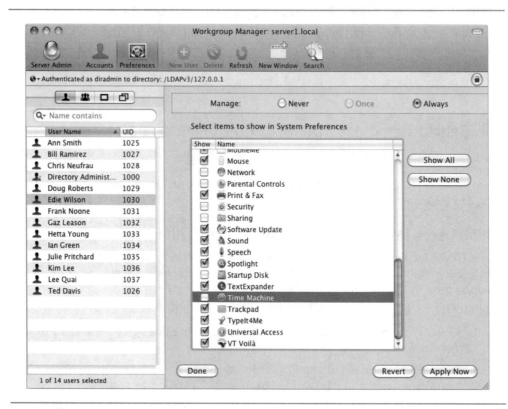

Figure 18-5.   Workgroup Manager lets you remove Time Machine from System Preferences to prevent users from messing with its settings.

Running a Backup Manually

Usually, it's most convenient to leave Time Machine in peace to back up your systems at its regular intervals. But when you rarely connect to the network, you may want to force a backup at a convenient time, even if it's not when Time Machine is scheduled to run. Similarly, you may choose to run a backup right this instant if you have a premonition of disaster.

To run a backup now, click the Time Machine status icon on the menu bar and choose Back Up Now from the menu. If you didn't put the Time Machine status icon on the menu bar, CTRL-click or right-click the Time Machine icon in the dock and choose Back Up Now from the shortcut menu.

NOTE   If you need to stop a backup (for example, because you're about to about to slam your MacBook shut and race to the airport), click the Time Machine status icon on the menu bar and choose Stop Backing Up from the menu.

Setting the Server to Back Up with Time Machine

Your clients' data is valuable to them, but the data on your server is important to both you *and* them. That means you'll need to back up the server as well so that you can restore it if anything goes amiss.

Once again, the tool you use is Time Machine. This time, though, you're setting Time Machine on the server itself, so you work in System Preferences rather than in Server Preferences. And you'll almost certainly want to store the backup on an external drive rather than an internal drive.

NOTE   You can follow these same steps to set up a client Mac's Time Machine manually. The main difference is that the dialog box for choosing the backup destination will include the backup drive you've designated on the server. Normally, you will want to point the clients to this drive.

To set up Time Machine on the server, follow these steps:

1. Open System Preferences. For example, click the System Preferences icon in the dock or choose Apple | System Preferences.

2. In the System area, click the Time Machine icon to display the Time Machine pane (see Figure 18-6).

3. Click the Select Backup Disk button to display the dialog box shown in Figure 18-7.

NOTE   If you see the message "Reformat required (incompatible filesystem)" next to a drive in the dialog box for choosing the Time Machine backup disk, the problem is usually that the disk uses the FAT32 file system, which Time Machine can't use for backups. If you select such a drive for Time Machine, Mac OS X prompts you to erase its existing contents so that you can use it. Click the Erase button if you want to go ahead and get rid of everything on the drive; make sure the data is expendable first, because you won't be seeing it again. Mac OS X reformats the drive using the Mac OS X Extended file system.

Figure 18-6. Use the Time Machine pane in System Preferences to set up Time Machine backups on your server or on a standalone Mac.

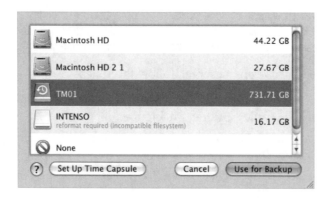

Figure 18-7. In this dialog box, select the drive to use for Time Machine.

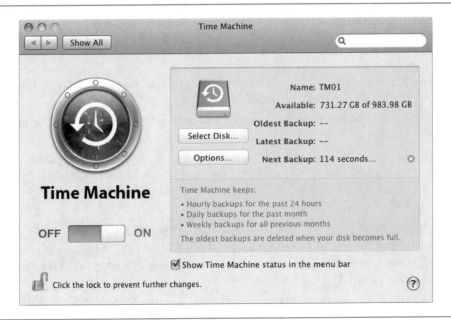

Figure 18-8.   Click the Options button to configure options for Time Machine. Click the X button if you want to stop the first backup from running immediately.

4. Click the disk you want to use for Time Machine, and then click the Use For Backup button. Mac OS X closes the dialog box, displays the drive in the Time Machine pane, and starts counting down to the first backup (see Figure 18-8).

5. Click the Options button to display the Options dialog box (see Figure 18-9).

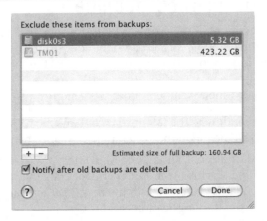

Figure 18-9.   In the Options dialog box, choose which items to exclude from backups.

NOTE On a MacBook, the Options dialog box also includes a Back Up While On Battery Power check box. Clear this check box if you want Time Machine to wait until you're back on power from a socket before it runs.

6. Add to the Exclude These Items From Backups list box each drive or folder you do not want to include in Time Machine backups:

   a. Your Time Machine drive appears here from the start, and you cannot remove it.

   b. To add a drive or folder, click the + button. select the drive or folder in the dialog box that opens; select the Show Invisible Items check box if you need to select a hidden folder. After making your selection, click the Exclude button.

   c. To remove an item from the list, click it, and then click the – button.

   d. Select the Notify After Old Backups Are Deleted check box if you want Time Machine to alert you after it has deleted older backups (to make space for new ones).

   e. When you've finished creating the list, click the Done button to close the dialog box and return to the Time Machine pane.

7. Select the Show Time Machine Status In The Menu Bar check box if you want to display a Time Machine icon in the menu bar. This icon spins when Time Machine is working; provides commands for starting and stopping backups, entering Time Machine, and opening Time Machine preferences; and is generally useful.

8. Quit System Preferences. For example, press ⌘-Q.

Recovering Data Using Time Machine

If a user finds they've accidentally sent one of their precious files to sleep with the fishes, or you discover that you've mislaid a vital folder from your server, you can use the Time Machine application to recover them. This works the same way on both client Macs and the server.

To recover data using Time Machine, follow these steps:

1. Open a Finder window to the folder that contains the files you want to recover. For example, click the Finder button in the dock, and then navigate to the folder.

2. Launch Time Machine. Click the Time Machine icon in the menu bar and choose Enter Time Machine from the menu, or click the Time Machine icon in the dock. (If you've suppressed both the menu bar icon and dock icon, launch Time Machine from the Applications folder.)

3. On the star-field screen that Time Machine displays, click the Finder window you opened. Time Machine displays a stack of available versions of that folder, stretching back to the event horizon (see Figure 18-10).

4. Navigate to the version you want to recover:

   ■ Click the title bar of a window down the stack to bring it to the front.

   ■ Click the upward arrow in the lower-right corner of the screen to display the next older window, or click the downward arrow to display the next newer window.

   ■ Move the mouse pointer over the timeline on the right side of the screen to display the dates and times of available backups, and then click the line for the backup you want.

5. Click the files or folders you want to recover.

6. Click the Restore button to restore them to their previous location.

Figure 18-10. Time Machine displays the available versions of the folder in date order, with the latest at the front.

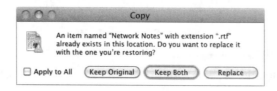

Figure 18-11. When restoring files, you may need to tell Time Machine how to resolve file conflicts.

7. If the items you are restoring will overwrite existing files with the same name, Time Machine displays the Copy dialog box (see Figure 18-11) to check whether you want to do this. Make the appropriate choice:

- **Keep Original** Click the button to cancel the restore operation. You can then check out the current version of the file, see if it's worth keeping, and run Time Machine again if it's not.

- **Keep Both** Click this button to have Time Machine rename the current version of the file by adding "(original)" to its name, and then restore the older version without changing its name. (This isn't "original" in any recognizable sense, but never mind.)

- **Replace** Click this button to have Time Machine replace the current version with the older version.

- **Apply To All** Select this check box if you want to take the same action with each of the items you're restoring that causes a file conflict.

After restoring the items, Time Machine automatically closes, leaving you to work with the restored items.

Recovering the Server Using Installer

If things go drastically wrong with the server, you may need to restore the whole thing from a Time Machine backup. Here's how to do that.

1. Insert your Mac OS X Server DVD in the optical drive, and then restart the server.

2. Hold down c at the startup sound to boot the server from the DVD.

3. On the first screen, choose the installation language, and then click the arrow button.

4. On the Install Mac OS X Server screen, choose Utilities | Restore System From Backup to display the Restore Your System screen.

5. Click the Continue button to display the Select A Backup Source screen.

6. In the Backups list box, click the disk that contains the backup.

7. Click the Continue button, and then follow through the prompts to perform the restoration.

CHAPTER 19 | Automate Routine Tasks with AppleScript

With the world economy imitating a roller coaster, it's great to have a job these days. But it's even better if you can get someone else to do your work for you.

Actually, make that some*thing* rather than some*one*. This is because both the server and client versions of Mac OS X include the powerful scripting language called AppleScript, which you can use to automate routine tasks on your network so that you don't have to perform them manually.

This chapter introduces you to some of the possibilities that AppleScript offers for streamlining your work life and taking chunks out of your workload:

■ In the first part of this chapter, you'll learn where to find AppleScript Editor, how to use it, how to dig out the commands you need, and several of the more essential programming structures that AppleScript uses.

■ In the second part of the chapter, we'll look at five quick examples of what you can do with AppleScript to lighten your load. Unless you're phenomenally lucky, these won't all be things you want to do, but they should give you some idea of the possibilities.

NOTE   For a comprehensive introduction to AppleScript, and detailed examples of how to use AppleScript to script widely used applications, from the Finder and Apple Mail to Microsoft Office's Word, Excel, and Entourage, see *AppleScript: A Beginner's Guide*, also published by McGraw-Hill, written by this same fool, and available from any fine bookshop you can identify online or off.

Getting Up and Running with the AppleScript Editor

The tool you use for working with AppleScript is AppleScript Editor, which you'll find in the /Utilities/ folder. You can fire AppleScript Editor up from there easily enough by clicking the desktop and choosing Go | Utilities to open the Utilities folder, but it's often quicker to press ⌘-SPACEBAR, type **apples** into the Spotlight field, and then hit the AppleScript Editor result that usually pops up right at the top.

TIP   When AppleScript Editor is open, nail its icon to the Dock so that you can launch it instantly. CTRL-click or right-click the AppleScript Editor icon in the Dock, click or highlight Options, and then choose Keep In Dock from the shortcut menu.

Once you've launched AppleScript Editor, you'll see a script window titled (so to speak) Untitled, containing an unsaved script with no contents. Figure 19-1 shows an example of an Untitled script window, with the key items labeled to make sure we're on the same page.

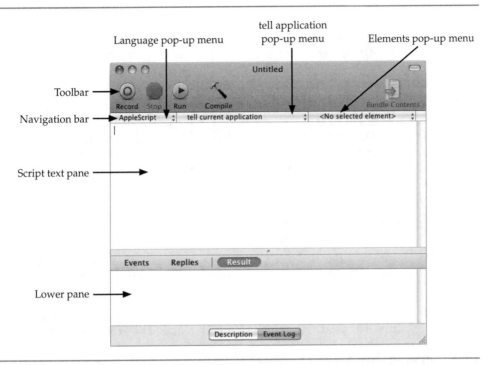

Figure 19-1.   AppleScript Editor automatically opens a new script window so that you can get right to work creating a script.

Most of the interface is pretty straightforward, but let's make sure you know what's what:

- **Toolbar**   The toolbar contains buttons for the commands you're most likely to need frequently. As usual, you can customize the toolbar by CTRL-clicking or right-clicking it, choosing Customize Toolbar in the pop-up menu, and then working in the dialog box that opens.

- **Navigation bar**   The navigation bar is the thin horizontal strip under the toolbar. At its left end, the language pop-up menu lets you switch between AppleScript and other scripting languages that AppleScript Editor supports; normally, you'll want to leave this menu set to AppleScript. On the right is the elements pop-up menu, which you can use to select elements (such as variables or properties) that you've defined in the script. Until you select an element, the elements pop-up menu shows "<No selected element>," as shown in the figure. In the middle, you can display the tell application pop-up menu, which lets you quickly direct a **tell** block to a particular application without having to set up the block in your code. (You'll meet tell blocks shortly.)

NOTE   To display the tell application pop-up menu, choose AppleScript Editor | Preferences, and then click the Editing button in the toolbar to display the Editing pane. Select the Show "Tell" Application Pop-Up menu check box, and then close the Preferences window.

- **Script text pane**   This pane is where you create and edit each script.

- **Lower pane**   This pane displays two main different types of information, depending on which of the tabs at the bottom of the window is selected. When the Description tab is selected, the pane displays the description of the script—text you write to explain what the script is and what it does. When the Event Log tab is selected, the pane displays the event log. The event log contains three different categories of information, which you can switch among by clicking the three visibility buttons:

  - **Events**   Click this visibility button to see the events the script has sent. This helps you keep track of exactly what's happening in the script.

  - **Replies**   Click this visibility button to see the values the script has returned for the events. This information helps you see the information the script is getting.

  - **Result**   Click this visibility button to see the result of running the script—for example, which button in a dialog box the user clicked.

Creating and Running a Script

To create a script, you type commands in the script window, and then compile them. Try this quick example:

1. Type **system info** in the script window. Unless you've customized AppleScript Editor, the letters appear in purple monospaced font, which indicates that it's new text that hasn't been compiled yet.

2. Compile the script by clicking the Compile button on the toolbar or (if you prefer to keep your fingers on the keys) pressing ⌘-K. AppleScript Editor checks out your code (all two words of it), finds that it will compile just fine, and changes it to a different font and color. The different font indicates that the code has been compiled; the color indicates what type of code component the words are. AppleScript Editor uses different font colors for different types of code components. In this case, **system info** appears in boldface in one of the subtler shades of purple, which indicates that it is a command name in AppleScript's Standard Additions suite.

NOTE   You can run a script without compiling it first. If you do this, AppleScript Editor compiles all uncompiled parts of the script before running it.

3. Run the script by clicking the Run button on the toolbar or pressing ⌘-R. AppleScript Editor executes the **system info** command and returns the result in the Result pane (see Figure 19-2).

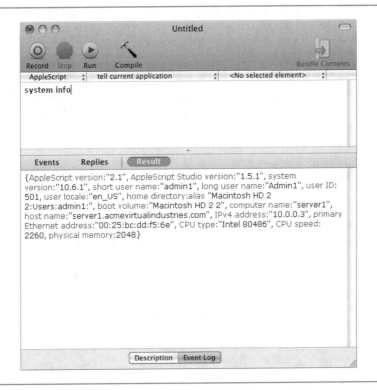

Figure 19-2. AppleScript Editor displays the result of the system info command in the Result pane.

As you can see, there's a whole slew of information, which is useful for getting an overview of the system—everything from the version of AppleScript (**AppleScript version**) to the long user name (**long user name**—AppleScript is straightforward about things like this) and the amount of RAM (**physical memory**). But what you'll often need to do is *return*, or *get*, a particular piece of information from the list. We'll do that next.

Finding Out What Version of Mac OS X Is Running

To get a single piece of information from the **system info** command, use the **get** command, tell AppleScript the item you want, and put the **system info** command in parentheses. For example, the following command returns from the **system info** command the **system version** property, which contains the version of Mac OS X the Mac is running:

```
get the system version of (system info)
```

When you press ⌘-K or click the Compile button this time, you'll notice that Apple-Script Editor applies different colors to the text: **get the** and **of** receive black boldface that indicates they're keywords in the AppleScript language, **system info** becomes bold purple as before, and **system version** goes purple without the bold—timid purple, if you will—to show that it's a property in the Standard Additions suite.

> **NOTE** I'll stop going on about the colors now, but you can find a full list of what's what in the Formatting pane in AppleScript Editor preferences (press ⌘-, or choose AppleScript Editor | Preferences). You can also change the colors and fonts that AppleScript Editor uses for different categories of AppleScript terms.

Run the script by pressing ⌘-R or clicking the Run button, and you'll see the result in the Result pane—for example:

```
"10.6.2"
```

AppleScript puts the information inside double quotes to indicate that it's a string of text (a sequence of text characters) rather than a number. You can create your own strings as needed by typing text between double quotes, and you can join two strings together by using the concatenation operator, & (the ampersand character).

> **NOTE** Unlike many programming and scripting languages, AppleScript lets you use the word "the" in your scripts to make the language sound more natural. You can put it anywhere you want in your scripts—AppleScript simply ignores it, so there's no right or wrong place for it. (If you prefer to omit "the," that's fine too.)

Displaying a Dialog Box and Returning the Result

Getting information like you've just done is useful, but you'll usually need to do something with the information rather than just make it appear in the Result pane in AppleScript Editor.

One thing you'll often need to do is display information in a dialog box. AppleScript makes this easy with the **display dialog** command. The basic syntax for the command looks like this:

```
display dialog prompt [with title title] [buttons list_of_buttons]
    [default button default_button] [cancel button cancel_button]
```

The **prompt** parameter is required—the dialog box has to contain some text. All the other items are optional (which is why they're in brackets), but you'll probably want to use most of them in many of your dialog boxes.

For example, the following code snippet displays the dialog box shown in Figure 19-3:

```
set msgVersion to "Your Mac is running Mac OS X version " ¬
    & (get the system version of (system info)) & "."
set msgTitle to "Mac OS X Version Information"
display dialog msgVersion with title msgTitle ¬
    buttons {"OK"} default button "OK"
```

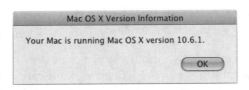

Figure 19-3. A single-button message box with a prompt and a title.

NOTE Two quick things here: First, the set **msgVersion to** statement creates a variable named **msgVersion** and then assigns the string of text to it, using ampersands to concatenate the different parts of the string. The **display dialog** command then uses the variable's contents as its prompt. Second, the ¬ character indicates that the same statement continues on the next line. You enter this character and start a new line by pressing OPTION-RETURN, or enter the character on its own by pressing OPTION-L.

This type of dialog box is useful for displaying information—for example, to warn the user about what a script is going to do, or to let them know that a script has finished running and that they can now resume their version of normality. But what you'll often need to do with a dialog box is let the user make a choice among two or three courses of action. To do so, add two or three buttons to the dialog box, return the button the user has clicked, and then take action accordingly.

To add the buttons to the dialog box, you provide the list of buttons needed as strings of text in a list, starting with the first button. For example, the following code snippet displays the dialog box shown in Figure 19-4, which has a Yes button, a No button, and a Help button:

```
set msgVersion to "Your Mac is running Mac OS X version " & ¬
    (get the system version of (system info)) & "." & return ¬
    & return & "Do you want to upgrade to Mac OS X version 10.6.2?"
set msgTitle to "Mac OS X Version Information"
display dialog msgVersion with title msgTitle buttons ¬
    {"Yes", "No", "Help"} default button "Yes"
```

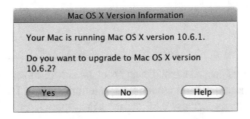

Figure 19-4. Use a two-button or three-button dialog box to let the user make decisions in scripts.

TIP   You can create a dialog box with an OK button and a Cancel button by omitting the **buttons** argument. But usually it's clearest to include the argument and specify the buttons you want.

When the user clicks one of the buttons, AppleScript closes the dialog box and returns the result, which it stores in a predefined variable called **result**. To find out which button the user clicked, you check the **button returned** property of the **result**:

```
the button returned of the result
```

To do something with that button, you need to use a condition in your script.

Using a Condition to Direct a Script

For making decisions, AppleScript gives you several different kinds of condition based on if:

■ **if... then**   If the condition is **true**, then take the following actions.

■ **if... then... else**   If the condition is **true**, then take the following actions. If the condition is **false**, take the actions after the **else** statement.

■ **if... then... elseif... else**   If the condition is **true**, then take the following actions. If the condition is **false**, evaluate the **elseif** condition; if it's **true**, take the actions after it. Otherwise, take the actions after the **else** statement.

NOTE   In an **if... then... elseif... else** condition, you can use as many **elseif** statements as you need.

For example, the script would more sensibly check to see if the system version was earlier than the 10.6.2 version it offers. Here's an example:

```
set myVer to the system version of (system info)
ignoring numeric strings
    if myVer is less than "10.6.2" then
        display dialog "Your Mac is running Mac OS X version " ¬
            & myVer & "." & return & return & ¬
            "Do you want to upgrade to version 10.6.2?" ¬
            with title "Mac OS X Upgrade Available" ¬
            buttons {"Yes", "No"} default button "Yes"
    end if
end ignoring
```

NOTE   I'm sure you've noticed the odd thing about the previous example—the **if** statement is wrapped up in an **ignoring numeric strings... end ignoring** block. This **ignoring** statement is needed to compare strings such as 10.6.2 correctly. See *AppleScript: A Beginner's Guide* for details on **ignoring** statements—and their opposite, **considering** statements.

Similarly, the script would normally use an **if... then... else** statement to deal with whichever of the buttons the user had clicked:

```
if the button returned of the result is "Yes" then
    -- take actions for Yes button
else -- the user clicked the No button
    -- take actions for No button (or do nothing)
end if
```

Getting User Input with a Dialog Box

Having the user make a decision in a dialog box is useful, but you may also need the user to provide textual information. You can do this by adding the **default answer** parameter to the **display dialog** statement. The **default answer** parameter displays a text box that you can either leave empty to allow the user's genius free expression or pre-fill with a default answer or sample text to get the user thinking in the right direction.

For example, the following code snippet displays the dialog box shown in Figure 19-5.

```
display dialog "Type your user name and click OK:" ¬
    default answer "" ¬
    with title "Enter Your User Name" ¬
    buttons {"OK", "Cancel"} ¬
    default button "OK"
```

AppleScript stores the contents of the text box in the **text returned** property of the **result**, so you can get at it like this:

```
text returned of the result
```

Finding Information in a Dictionary File

To find information about the AppleScript objects you need to work with in an application, you open the application's AppleScript dictionary file in AppleScript Editor. Choose File | Open Dictionary from AppleScript Editor to display the Open Dictionary dialog box, click the application you want, and then click the Choose button.

Figure 19-5.   Add a text box to a dialog box to get user input.

NOTE   If the application you want doesn't appear in the list in the Open Dictionary dialog box, click the Browse button to open a dialog box that lets you browse the Mac's file system for the application.

The Dictionary Viewer then opens, showing the dictionary for the application you chose. Figure 19-6 shows the dictionary file for Server Preferences open in the Dictionary Viewer. You use the three panes at the top to browse the available information to find the details of what you need. When you select an item in the upper panes, Dictionary Viewer displays the details in the lower pane. For example, in the figure, the lower pane shows the information about the Connect command.

Telling an Application What to Do

To pass a AppleScript command to an application or other object, you use a **tell** block. This is a block of code that starts with the keyword **tell** and the name of the application or object, and ends with the **end tell** keywords.

For example, if you want to tell Server Preferences to do something, you create a **tell** block to the **application** object named "**Server Preferences**" like this:

```
tell the application "Server Preferences"
    -- you put the commands here
end tell
```

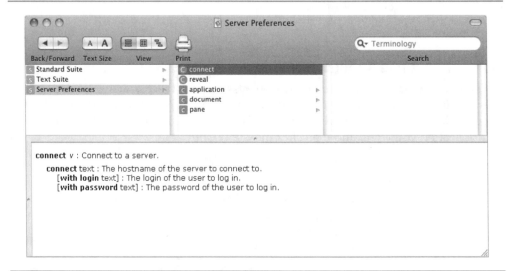

Figure 19-6.   Open the dictionary file in AppleScript Editor's Dictionary Viewer to find information about an application's AppleScript objects and commands.

NOTE To make a note in a script, you add a *comment*. You can create what's called an *inline comment* by putting two hyphens (--) before the text you want AppleScript to ignore on that line; putting the whole comment on its own line, as in the example, is usually easiest. Or you can create a multiline comment that starts with the **(*** characters and ends with the ***)** characters.

This code snippet uses the **connect** command to tell Server Preferences to connect to a specified server, using the **with login** parameter to specify the login name and the **with password** parameter to provide the corresponding password. It then uses the **activate** command to bring Server Preferences to the front, so that it is visible:

```
tell the application "Server Preferences"
    connect "server1.acmevirtualindustries.com" ¬
        with login "admin2" with password "donttrythisatwork"
    activate
end tell
```

Repeating Actions

Often, in your code, you'll need to repeat one or more actions, either a set number of times (for example, five times) or until a condition becomes true. For repeating actions, AppleScript provides a half-dozen different **repeat** loops, of which these three tend to be the most useful:

- **repeat with a counter variable** Repeats a set of actions using a counter variable you specify. The counter variable starts at a start value, increases or decreases on each repetition, and ends the loop when it reaches the end value. Here's an example:

```
repeat with myCounter from 1 to 5
    -- actions here
end repeat
```

- **repeat for each item in a list** Repeats a set of actions for each item in a list you define. For example, if you create a list of employees like the **employees** list here, you can repeat the actions for each **employee** item in the **employees** list in turn. This code snippet uses the **make new folder** command to create a new folder on the desktop for each employee in the list, so you end up with a folder named Smith, a folder named Ramirez, and a folder named Kim:

```
set employees to {"Smith", "Ramirez", "Kim"}
repeat with employee in employees
    set this_employee to contents of employee
    tell application "Finder"
        mak new folder at desktop with properties ¬
            {name:this_employee}
    end tell
end repeat
```

■ **repeat as long as a condition is true** Runs a set of actions if a condition is **true** and keeps repeating the actions as long as the condition remains **true**. For example, the following snippet tells Microsoft Word to close the back document as long as the **count of documents** (the number of open documents) is greater than 1:

```
tell the application "Microsoft Word"
    repeat while (count of documents) is greater than 1
        close the back document
    end repeat
end tell
```

Examples of Using AppleScript for Administration

This section shows you a handful of examples of using AppleScript for administering Macs.

Mounting and Unmounting Network Volumes

To give your network clients access to files on the network, you may need to mount network volumes on the Macs. Once a volume is mounted, you can either leave it mounted until the user logs out or shuts down the Mac (which then ejects the volume automatically), or unmount the volume via AppleScript when it is no longer needed.

Mounting a Volume

To mount a network volume in a script, use the **mount volume** command. This command takes the following parameters:

■ **volume_name** This parameter is required. It gives the name or URL of the volume—for example, **smb://10.0.0.5/ or afp://server.local/public/**.

■ **on server** This parameter is optional. When you use it, the parameter gives details of the server that contains the volume. What you'll often do is include the server name in the **volume_name** parameter, in which case you can omit the on server parameter.

■ **in AppleTalk zone** This parameter is optional. When you use it, the parameter specifies the AppleTalk zone in which to find the server. If you've entered the full network path in the **volume_name** parameter, you can omit the **in AppleTalk zone** parameter.

■ **as user name** This parameter is optional, but you'll normally want to use it. The parameter gives the user name under which to log on to the server. If you omit this parameter, Mac OS X tries to log on as a guest user; if the server doesn't allow guest access (and most of your servers probably don't), Mac OS X cannot mount the volume.

Figure 19-7.   When mounting a volume in a script, you'll normally want to supply the password. Otherwise, Mac OS X prompts the user to enter the password.

- **with password**   This parameter is optional, but you'll want to use it if you use the **as user name** parameter. This parameter gives the password to use for authenticating the user name. If you omit the **with password** parameter, the server prompts the user for the password (see Figure 19-7), just as if they were connecting manually.

For example, the following command uses AFP to mount the volume named Documents on the server named server1.local, providing a user name and a password:

```
mount volume "afp://server1.local/Documents" as user name ¬
    "droberts" with password "n0acc3ss"
```

NOTE   If you specify a server but not which volume on it to mount, Mac OS X prompts the user to choose among the available volumes.

Unmounting a Volume

When your script has finished using the volume you've mounted, you can unmount the volume by telling the Finder to eject it. For example, the following statement ejects the volume named "Documents":

```
tell application "Finder"
    eject alias "Documents"
end tell
```

Finding Out the Version of an Application

To find out which version of an application a Mac has, use the **version** command. For example, the following command returns the version of the Numbers application from the iWork suite:

```
get the version of application "Numbers"
```

Setting Up an SMTP Server in Mail

Apple's Mail application is fully programmable, so you can use AppleScript to do everything from creating a message automatically to configuring user accounts. This example creates a new SMTP server that uses SSL encryption:

```
tell application "Mail"
    set smtpserver to "smtp.acmevirtualindustries.com"
    set smtpuser to "djones"
    set new_smtp to make new smtp server with properties ¬
        {server name:smtpserver, uses ssl:true}
    tell new_smtp
        set authentication to password
        set user name to smtpuser
        set password to "trythisathome"
    end tell
end tell
```

Setting Up Microsoft Office File Paths on a Client Mac

After setting up Microsoft Office on a Mac, you may find that you need to set custom file paths to tell the Office applications where to find templates, clip art, and other useful items. The following example is for Microsoft Word. It sets the user templates path (the path to the user's own templates) to a folder on the local hard drive and the workgroup templates path (the path to the folder in which an administrator can make additional templates available) to a folder on the server:

```
tell the application "Microsoft Word"
    set default file path file path type user templates path ¬
        path "macintosh hd:users:don:documents:templates"
    set default file path file path type workgroup templates path ¬
        path "server1:Templates:Word"
end tell
```

That example shows where AppleScript's "natural-language" approach to programming syntax becomes as strained as a good consommé. In case your brain is rebelling against parsing it, here's the breakdown:

- **set default file path**   This is the command for setting the default file path.

- **file path type**   This announces that the next item will specify the type of file path.

- **user templates path** (or **workgroup templates path**)   This specifies the type of file path.

- **path**   This introduces the string that gives the path.

    See? As clear as mud (or that consommé).

CHAPTER 20 | Create Peer-to-Peer Mac Networks for Small Offices

J ust as you thought the end was drawing nigh… so far in this book, we've been looking at networks based on servers running Mac OS X Server tied together with Open Directory. And as you've seen, they work great and give you easy administration and tight control over the network and the computers on it.

But if you have only a handful of Macs, you may not need a server in order to have an effective Mac-based network—and you may well prefer not to drop the dough needed for a copy of Mac OS X Server and a Mac to run it on.

Instead of building a server-based network, you can put together a peer-to-peer network—a network in which each Mac can share items, such as a folder, a printer, or an Internet connection, as needed with the other Macs. In this chapter, you'll learn how to plan and set up a peer-to-peer network using Macs.

Planning Your Peer-to-Peer Network

Start by planning your peer-to-peer network. Draw up a list of the Macs you want to connect to the network and the devices you will share on the network. If it's a tiny network, it's fine to make the list in your head, but if you're dealing with more than a couple of handfuls of Macs, you'll probably want to put it down on paper. You may also want to sketch out the network so that you can easily see what's where.

Specifically, you'll need to decide:

- **Which Macs you will connect to the network**   Usually, you'll want to connect all of them so that everyone can share and enjoy, but in some circumstances, you may need to keep some machines separate. For example, the managing director may deem his files so precious that he requires a standalone workstation—or you may rate him such a threat to shared files that you decide to cordon him off entirely. (You could also allow him on the network but apply a permissions straitjacket to him.)

- **Which Mac will share which item**   Each Mac that's sharing files, printers, or an Internet connection will need to be up and running all the time that those items are required. In most offices, this means that Mac will need to be running throughout office hours—and maybe halfway through the night as well.

- **How the Macs will connect to the Internet**   In most cases, the easiest way to share the Internet connection is through the network switch or router, but in some cases you may prefer to use Mac OS X's built-in Internet Sharing feature (which is covered later in this chapter).

Figure 20-1 shows an example of a simple network on which one Mac is sharing a printer, another Mac is sharing files, and everyone else is freeloading like fury. The Internet connection is shared through a router.

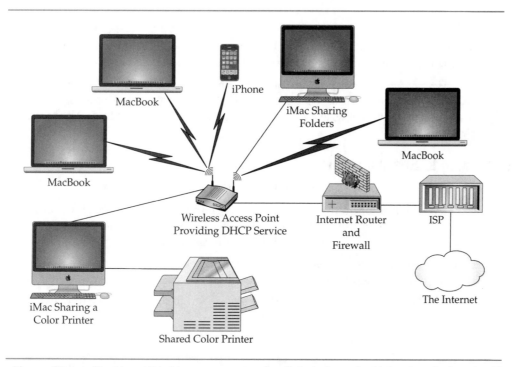

Figure 20-1.   Decide which Macs your network will include and which other devices it will share.

NOTE   When planning your network, you'll probably be forcefully reminded of the advantages that a server offers—rather than having to keep several Macs running the whole time to provide files, printing, and so on, you could simply have a server. One solution is to consolidate the sharing on as few of your Macs as possible—perhaps on the Mac that you use—so that you can easily make sure that everything's available and retain control of the sharing. You'll need to make sure the Mac is powerful enough to handle the demands, though, or you'll get a glacial response when you're using it. At this point, you're halfway to setting up a server-based network: You've got client Macs accessing another Mac that's acting as a server, even though it's not running the server version of the operating system and it's not directly managing the other Macs on the network, just controlling what they can access.

Enough planning. Let's look at how you actually get the Macs sharing with each other. We'll start with printing.

Sharing Printers

As you'd imagine, you first tell the Mac that's connected to the printer that you want it to play nice and share. You then tell the other Macs where the printer is.

NOTE   If you're buying a printer for a peer-to-peer network, look at getting a model that connects to the network via Ethernet, so that you can connect the Macs directly to it without a Mac having to share it.

Setting a Mac to Share a Printer

To share a printer with other Macs on the network, follow these steps:

1. Install the printer on the Mac that will make the printer available for sharing. For example, connect the printer to the Mac via a USB cable, and let Mac OS X automatically choose and load the driver to use for the printer.

2. Open System Preferences. For example, click the System Preferences icon in the dock or choose Apple | System Preferences.

3. In the Hardware area, click the Print & Fax icon to display the Print & Fax pane (see Figure 20-2).

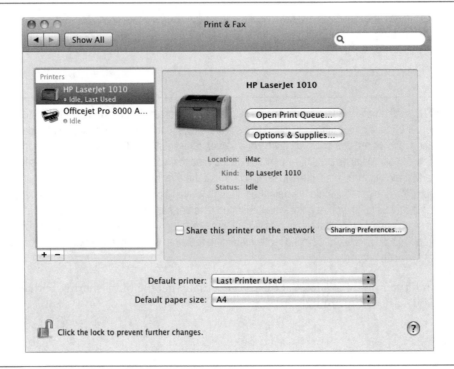

Figure 20-2.   To share a printer, select the Share This Printer On The Network check box in the Print & Fax pane in System Preferences.

4. Look at the Location readout and the Kind readout below the printer, and see if they make clear which printer this is, where it's located, and what it's for. If you want to improve the information, click the Options & Supplies button, enter more informative details in the General pane of the dialog box that opens (see Figure 20-3), and then click the OK button.

5. Select the Share This Printer On The Network check box to turn on sharing.

NOTE When you select the Share This Printer On The Network check box, the Print & Fax pane may display a warning icon and the message "Printer sharing is turned off." That's no problem; we'll fix it next.

6. Click the Sharing Preferences button to display the Sharing pane of System Preferences (shown in Figure 20-4 with settings chosen). System Preferences automatically selects the Printer Sharing item in the Sharing list box so that you can see which printers you're currently sharing.

7. If the Printer Sharing check box is currently cleared, select it to turn on printer sharing.

8. In the Printers list box, click the printer for which you want to set permissions.

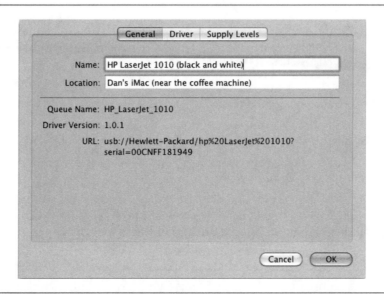

Figure 20-3. Use the Name text box and Location text box in this dialog box to make clear which printer this is and where your colleagues will find it.

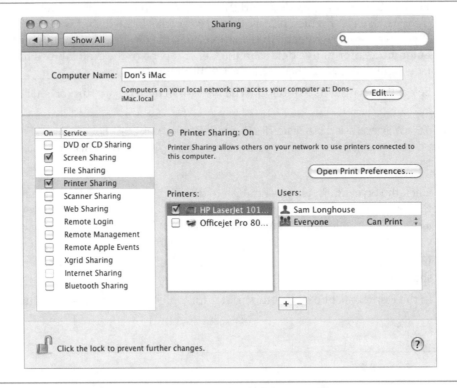

Figure 20-4. In the Sharing pane of System Preferences, choose which users may use which printer.

9. In the Users list box, build the list of users:

   ■ If you want to allow every user to print, click the Everyone entry that appears by default, and then choose Can Print from the pop-up menu next to it.

   ■ Similarly, to block everyone from printing, click the Everyone entry, and then choose No Access in the pop-up menu.

   ■ To add another user who may use the printer, click the + button below the Users list box. In the dialog box that appears, select the user, and then click the Select button. You can also add multiple users or groups of users in the same way.

NOTE   To share another printer from the Sharing pane, select the printer's check box in the Printers list box. You can then set permissions for printing on the printer.

10. When you've finished setting up printer sharing, quit System Preferences. For example, press ⌘-Q.

Connecting a Mac to a Shared Printer

To connect a Mac to a printer that another Mac is sharing, follow these steps:

1. Choose Apple | System Preferences to open the System Preferences window.

2. In the Hardware category, click the Print & Fax icon to display the Print & Fax preferences pane (see Figure 20-5).

3. Click the + button below the printers pane on the left to display the Add Printer dialog box.

4. If the Default pane (see Figure 20-6) isn't already displayed, click the Default button on the toolbar to display it.

5. In the Printer Name list box, select the printer you want to add.

6. If you want, change the default name that appears in the Name text box.

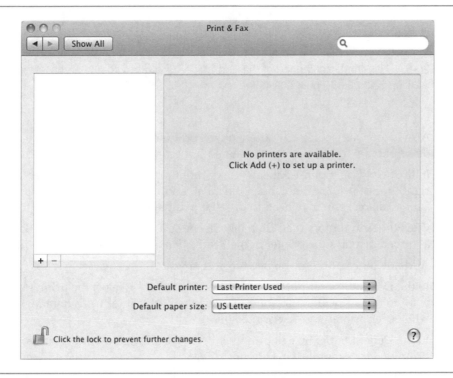

Figure 20-5. Click the + button in the Print & Fax preferences pane to start adding a shared printer to a Mac.

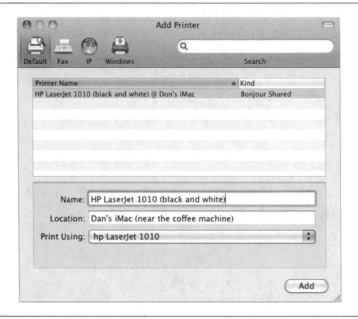

Figure 20-6.   Use the Default pane of the Add Printer dialog box to add a shared printer on another Mac on your peer-to-peer network.

7. Also if you want, edit the location in the Location text box. If you've set a clear description of the location on the shared printer, you shouldn't need to change it.

8. In the Print Using pop-up menu, make sure that Mac OS X has selected the right type of printer. If not, open the menu and choose it yourself. If the driver isn't available, you may need to install it manually.

9. Click the Add button. Mac OS X installs the software needed for the printer, and then displays the printer in the Print & Fax pane in System Preferences.

10. Add any other printers you need to add now.

11. In the Default Printer pop-up menu (see Figure 20-7). select the printer you want to use as the default. You can select the Last Printer Used item to use whichever printer you last printed on.

12. In the Default Paper Size pop-up menu, choose the default paper size to use for printing—for example, US Letter or US Legal.

13. Quit System Preferences. For example, press ⌘-Q or choose System Preferences | Quit System Preferences.

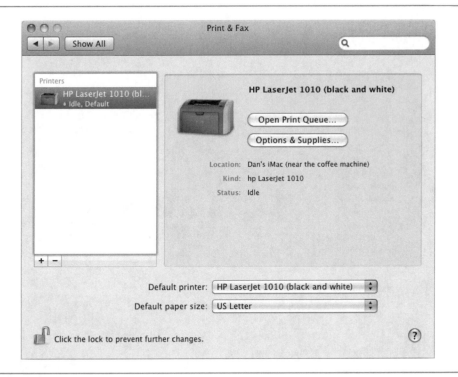

Figure 20-7.   After adding one or more printers, choose the user's default printer. You can also set the default paper size.

Sharing a Folder

The next type of item you're likely to want to share is a folder. Again, let's start by looking at how to set a Mac to share a folder; then we can move on to connecting another Mac to it.

Setting a Mac to Share a Folder

To set a Mac to share a folder, follow these steps:

1. Open System Preferences. For example, click the System Preferences icon in the dock, or choose Apple | System Preferences.

2. In the Internet & Wireless area, click the Sharing icon to display the Sharing pane.

3. In the list of services, click the File Sharing item to display the options for it (shown in Figure 20-8 with settings chosen).

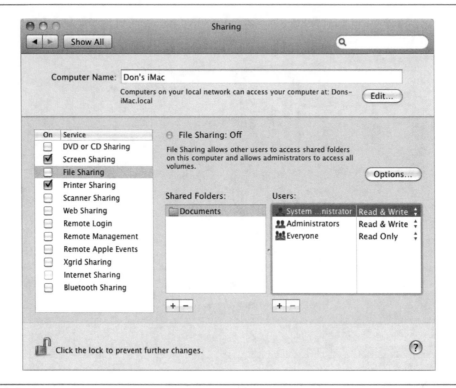

Figure 20-8. To share files, set up File Sharing in the Sharing pane in System Preferences.

 NOTE Don't select the File Sharing check box just yet—wait until you've set up the folders you want to share and the colleagues with whom you want to share them. (Yes, I'm paranoid—but they *are* out to get me. I'll prove it to you as soon as the men in white coats go away.)

4. Now choose the protocols you'll use to share the folder. Follow these steps:

   a. Click the Options button to display the dialog box shown in Figure 20-9.

   b. Select the Share Files And Folders Using AFP check box. AFP is Apple Filing Protocol, the best protocol for sharing folders among Macs.

 NOTE The dialog box for choosing file-sharing protocols lets you share folders using FTP and SMB as well as AFP. You can select as many of the check boxes as you need—but be sure to select only those you need. Use SMB if you need to share the folders with Windows PCs or UNIX or Linux boxes on your network. SMB has weaker security than AFP, but it's okay; FTP, on the other hand, doesn't use encryption, so it's terminally insecure and best avoided. (Use FTP only if you need to provide file transfer across Internet connections.)

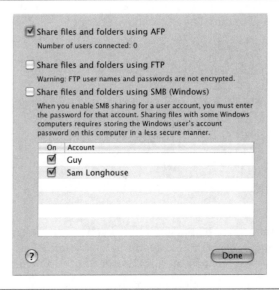

Figure 20-9. Choose your file-sharing protocol in this dialog box. Normally, you'll want to use AFP to share files with your Macs.

    c.   Ignore the list box of accounts at the bottom of the dialog box unless you're using SMB—in which case, select the check box for each account you want to allow access to the folder. You'll need to provide the password for each account.

    d.   Click the Done button to close the dialog box.

  5. Add the folder or folders to the Shared Folders list box like this:

    a.   Click the + button below the Shared Folders list box to display a dialog box.

    b.   Select the folder you want to share.

    c.   Click the Add button.

  6. Set up the users who are allowed (or denied) access to the folder like this:

    ■   If the user or group appears in the Users list box, choose the permission level in the pop-up menu: Read Only (which lets the user open files, but not save changes to them), Read & Write (which lets them open files and save changes), or No Access (three guesses).

 NOTE The fourth option on the permissions pop-up menu, Write Only (Drop Box), lets users add files to a folder without letting them see its contents. Use Write Only permission when setting up a folder in which some users can leave files for other people. This is the permission Mac OS X uses for each user's / Public / Drop Box / folder.

■ If the user or group doesn't appear, click the + button below the Users list box to display the dialog box shown here.

■ If the user or group appears in this list box, click them, and then click the Select button. You can change the category in the left column as needed, or use the search box to search for a user or group by name.

■ Otherwise, click the New Person button, and then enter the person's name and password in the New Person dialog box (shown here). Click the Create Account button to close the dialog box and create the person's account, then click the new person in the dialog box, and click the Select button.

■ After adding the user or group to the Users list box, open the permissions pop-up menu and decide how generous you're feeling.

 NOTE Each user who accesses folders that a Mac is sharing must have either a regular user account (Administrator, Standard, or Managed) or a Sharing user account on that Mac. The New Person dialog box automatically creates a Sharing user account with the details you enter. You can also create Sharing user accounts in the Accounts pane in System Preferences.

7. In the Services list box, select the File Sharing check box. The green light glows, the File Sharing readout changes to On, and sharing is a go.

Connecting a Mac to a Shared Folder

Once you've set up one or more Macs to share folders, you can connect the other Macs to the shared folders in moments:

1. Open a Finder window. For example, click the Finder icon in the dock.
2. In the sidebar, expand the Shared category if it's currently collapsed.
3. Click the Mac that's sharing the folder.
4. Click the Connect As button to display the Connect As dialog box, shown here.

5. In the Name text box, correct the user name if it's wrong. (This needs to be the user name for the Sharing user account on the other Mac, which is not necessarily the same as the account name under which the user is logged on.)
6. Type the password in the Password text box.
7. Select the Remember This Password In My Keychain check box if you want to store the password. This is normally a good idea for regular connections.
8. Click the Connect button. The Connect As dialog box closes, and Mac OS X establishes the connection.

The Mac can then work with files and folders as usual in the folder that you have connected it to.

NOTE   To disconnect from a shared folder, open a Finder window, and then click the Eject icon next to the shared folder in the sidebar. Usually, though, you'll probably want to simply leave the shared folder connected until you log out from your Mac or shut it down.

So far, so easy—but what if you want the Mac to connect to the shared folder automatically at login, so that you don't have to dredge through the Finder?
Follow these steps:

1. Connect to the shared folder as described above.
2. Open System Preferences. For example, click the System Preferences icon in the dock or choose Apple | System Preferences.

Figure 20-10.   To make your Mac automatically open a shared folder when you log in, add the folder to your Login Items list in the Accounts pane of System Preferences.

3. In the System area, click the Accounts icon to display the Accounts pane.

4. Click your account if it's not already selected.

5. Click the Login Items tab to display the Login Items pane (see Figure 20-10).

6. Drag the shared folder from your desktop (if it appears there) or from a Finder window to the These Items Will Open Automatically When You Log In list box. It appears there as a Volume (rather than an Application).

7. Quit System Preferences. For example, press ⌘-Q.

Sharing an Internet Connection

If your office has an Internet connection that connects directly to a Mac rather than to a router that can share the connection on the network, you can use the Mac's Internet Sharing feature to share the Internet connection with other computers on the network.

I'm going to sound like a broken record (do you remember records? No, not the Guinness kind—those bizarre vinyl frisbees with grooves and scratches), but we'll start once more by looking at how to set the caring, sharing Mac to share the Internet connection. Then we'll look at how the other Macs pick up the connection.

Setting a Mac to Share Its Internet Connection

To set a Mac to share its Internet connection, follow these steps:

1. Open System Preferences. For example, click the System Preferences icon in the dock or choose Apple | System Preferences.

2. In the Internet & Wireless area, click the Sharing icon to display the Sharing pane.

3. In the services list on the left, click the Internet Sharing item to display the controls for Internet sharing. Don't select the Internet Sharing check box yet.

4. In the Share Your Ethernet Connection From pop-up menu, choose the network interface that's connected to the Internet—for example, Ethernet.

5. In the To Computers Using list box, select the interface or interfaces on which you want to share the Internet connection—for example, AirPort or FireWire.

6. If you selected the AirPort check box, set up the network like this:

   a. Click the AirPort Options button to display the dialog box shown here.

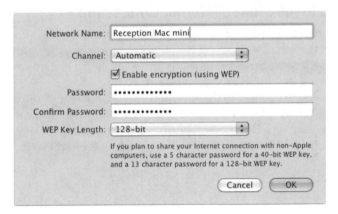

   b. Type the network name in the Network Name text box.

   c. Leave the Channel menu set to Automatic for the time being. If you find that the network seems to run slowly, try different channels to reduce interference from other wireless networks and other equipment that uses the same frequencies.

   d. Select the Enable Encryption (Using WEP) check box.

   e. Open the WEP Key Length pop-up menu, and then select 128-Bit in it.

CAUTION   Do not use 40-bit WEP. It is too weak for security.

  f. Type a 13-character password in the Password text box and the Confirm Password text box.

  g. Click the OK button to close the dialog box.

 7. In the Sharing pane, select the Internet Sharing check box. Mac OS X pops up a last-ditch objection, as shown here.

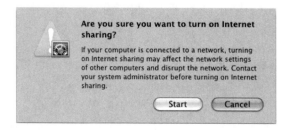

 8. Click the Start button to start the sharing.

 9. Quit System Preferences. For example, press ⌘-Q.

Connecting a Mac to the Shared Internet Connection

Once you have shared an Internet connection via Internet Sharing, all you normally need to do to get the other Macs using the shared connection is to connect them to the same network. Each Mac then automatically picks up the DHCP information for the network and starts using the shared connection.

If you are unable to connect to the Internet, open Safari (for example, click the Safari icon in the dock). When Safari bemoans the fact that your Mac isn't connected to the Internet, click the Network Diagnostics button, and then follow through the Network Diagnostics screens, which automatically detect and set the right settings to use the Internet connection.

Index

O

P

X

ML

B/10